HEIDEGGER'S *VOLK*

Cultural Memory
in
the
Present

Mieke Bal and Hent de Vries, Editors

HEIDEGGER'S
VOLK

BETWEEN
NATIONAL
SOCIALISM
AND POETRY

James Phillips

STANFORD UNIVERSITY PRESS

STANFORD, CALIFORNIA

2005

Stanford University Press
Stanford, California

Printed in the United States of America on acid-free, archival-quality paper

Library of Congress Cataloging-in-Publication Data

Phillips, James, date–
    Heidegger's *Volk* : between National Socialism and poetry / James Phillips.
      p.   cm.
    Includes bibliographical references and index.
    ISBN 0-8047-5070-X (alk. paper)—ISBN 0-8047-5071-8 (pbk. : alk. paper)
    1. Heidegger, Martin, 1889–1976.   2. National socialism.   I. Title.

B3279.H49P49 2005
193 — dc22   2005002179

Original Printing 2005

Last figure below indicates year of this printing:
14   13   12   11   10   09   08   07   06   05

Typeset by G & S Typesetters, Inc. in 11/13.5 Adobe Garamond

Dedicated with gratitude and affection to
Alexander García Düttmann and Jeff Malpas

Contents

HEIDEGGER'S *VOLK*

Introduction

Martin Heidegger's engagement with National Socialism was a philosophical engagement, even though it appeared—and more than appeared—to be an abdication of philosophy. Accosting Heidegger on a tram after his early resignation of the rectorship of Freiburg University, Wolfgang Schadewaldt asked his colleague, "Back from Syracuse?" But this question mistakes the philosophical character peculiar to Heidegger's engagement. Unlike Plato, Heidegger had not sought out the political realm as the open space for the implementation of a preconceived philosophy of the ideal state. What Heidegger desired in 1933, and what he imagined he could effect by running the university in collaboration with the new regime, was, on the contrary, the irruption of the nonideality of the political realm into philosophy. He confessed as much to Karl Löwith in Rome in 1936, explicitly identifying his concept of historicality as the basis for his engagement.[1] The political realm, in its essential historicality, was itself to philosophize under National Socialism, albeit without diverging from its anti-philosophical character as the realm of the contingent and the finite. Philosophy, as it had previously interpreted itself, was to be stood on its head. Heidegger's politics are incomprehensible and irrecoverable as an act of expansion on the part of a metaphysics of eternity, since it is in his critique of just such a metaphysics and of the timeless, abstract presence of the Platonic Idea and its avatars that an early susceptibility to a "folkish" politics can be discerned.

Arguably, for Heidegger, the year 1933 promised that overturning of the foundation of philosophy on whose necessity for the question of Being he expatiates in *Being and Time*. The subject, on which liberalism and modern metaphysics had been raised, was to give way to the people. As the liberal subject, in *truly* giving way, can but carry with itself the presence that is its own foundation, National Socialism was to offer the concrete possibility of a fundamental ontology. The regime extolled a return to the rootedness in the *Volk* (people), and in Heidegger's ears, this was taken to announce the repudiation of that abstraction from historicality in which the subject comes to itself in its autonomy and self-presence. Heidegger does not formulate the choice at issue here as a choice between autonomy and heteronomy, but rather as a choice between the alleged autonomy of the subject and the historicality in which Being is understood as other than presence. Inasmuch as it comes to itself and is thus present to itself, the autonomous subject fixes on Being only in its presence and thereby cannot think the originary Being of the time in which presence is first able to be presence. With respect to an understanding of the ecstatic character of time, the subject is constricted by the atomism of liberal thought. That Heidegger was politically reactionary is generally accepted as evident from the anti-liberalism of his engagement with National Socialism. That his notion of historicality, which he himself admitted to be the basis for his engagement, is consequently reactionary is nonetheless disputable.[2] What has to be ascertained and not assumed are the relations between historicality and nationalism and between the historicality of a people and the people of historicality. This is to ask after that which was to be conserved in Heidegger's conservatism and uncovered in his destruction of the metaphysics of presence.

If Heidegger joined the NSDAP without any prior dealings with the movement (or, for that matter, with any political movement whatsoever), the step can nevertheless not be said to have been entirely unforeseeable. There was a shared privileging of historicality that, to begin with, concealed the divergence in the understanding of historicality. Heidegger's initial responsiveness to the Hitlerian demagogy was at once naïve and calculated, because what Heidegger chose to hear in it was the long anticipated resolution of the impasse of Cartesian subjectivity. Within the anti-liberal and "folkish" pronouncements of the new regime, he was prepared to hear an echo of his own philosophical demotion of the subject in favor of historicality. The self-assertion of the German people from under the frail and allegedly imported liberalism of the Weimar Republic took on the appearance of the possibility of a disclosure of the ontological foundations of the *cogito sum* and of its certainty in self-presence. What Descartes, in the inauguration of the metaphysics of subjectity, leaves unthought, and yet nevertheless presupposes in abstracting from it, is what Heidegger discusses in *Being and Time* under the name of "world" (*Welt*). It is the existential, historical thickness of world that is flattened to the monotony of the Cartesian *res extensa* and that must first be flattened in just this way if the ahistorical and peopleless subject is to be able to assure itself of its own ontological transparency. In a space that can pass for the substratum of every object because it is always and everywhere only ever present, the subject does not encounter any challenge to its understanding of Being as presence. The year 1933 was to repoliticize the space of metaphysics by reversing its suppression of historical world.

However enthusiastically Heidegger declared his allegiance to the new regime, he was always cautious to interpret the *Volk* on parade in the streets as no more than the promise of a reversal of the suppression of historicality. Out of opposition to the flattening of the world of the people in the Cartesian foundations of liberalism, Heidegger aligned himself with National Socialism. Even beyond his disillusionment with the regime, his thinking undertook to grasp the historical thickness of the world of the German people. The "chauvinism" of the *Volk* was to be thought through to its essence. For Heidegger, this was a question of an understanding of historicality rather than eugenics. The conservatism of the regime had markedly less to do with the contestation of presence through an attention to historicality than with the preservation of breeding lines in the ahistorical manipulation of genetic material. In its abstraction from historicality, the regime amounted only to a variation on liberalism. Increasingly, for Heidegger after 1934, the singularity of the German people on which National Socialism insisted was precisely that which contested the covert liberalism of the regime. The grounds for Heidegger's engagement with National Socialism are the grounds for his disengagement: the people of the question of Being were, in the end, too political for the *Weltflucht* (flight from the world) of Nazism.

Heidegger's disillusionment with National Socialism is not a disillusionment with the notion of the *Volk*. What is the sense of "*Volk*" for Heidegger? And why should it be thought in conjunction with historicality and fundamental ontology? It is clear from the text of his "Address on 11 November in Leipzig" that in 1933 Heidegger interpreted the self-assertion of the German people under National Socialism as a precondition of the knowledge of the Being of beings. The address in question, first published in the volume *Bekenntnis der deutschen Universitäten und Hochschulen zu*

Adolf Hitler und dem nationalsozialistischen Staat (Dresden, 1933) offers the coup d'état an ontological vindication:

> We have renounced the idolatry of a rootless and impotent thinking. We behold the end of its servile philosophy. We are convinced that the luminous rigor and the befitting confidence of the inexorable and simple questioning concerning the essence of Being are returning. The originary courage either to grow or to shatter thereon in the confrontation with that which is constitutes the innermost impetus of the questioning of a folkish science.[3]

The idolatry of a rootless and impotent thinking has been replaced by the questioning of a "folkish" science. Following this account, what distinguishes a "folkish" science (*völkische Wissenschaft*) is its rootedness. Heidegger does not say that a "folkish" science is rooted in a *Volk*. Rather, he says that a "folkish" science endangers itself in its confrontation with that which is. The two assertions are not synonymous. In his declaration of loyalty to the new regime, Heidegger adopts the National Socialist term *völkische Wissenschaft* but refers thereby, not to a science that with its rootedness in a people has grown certain of its stability, but rather to a science that has become all the more vulnerable. Situating the rootedness of a "folkish" science in its originary courage either to grow *or to shatter* on the question of Being, Heidegger does not make of the "folkishness" of a "folkish" science an orienting frame of reference, a paradigm or weltanschauung. The "folkishness" of a "folkish" science calls itself and the science as a whole into question, since for Heidegger the rootedness of a "folkish" science is the originarity that is conferred upon it in its questioning concerning the originarity understood throughout his writings as Being. Heidegger does not oppose to a rootedness in the *Volk* a rootedness in the question of Being, because implicit in Heidegger's Leipzig address is a definition of the *Volk* that proceeds by reference to the question of Being. Heidegger ascribes the brittleness of a "folkish" science to its questioning concerning the essence of Being, rather than to its deficiencies according to the criteria of modern science. The rootedness of a "folkish" science is not a supplement appended to the notion of modern science that renders it more robust. It is the fragility, intolerable to modern science, whereby the latter would open itself (precisely in and by means of its inability to begin by constitutively flattening the existential, historical thickness of world) to that which it could not otherwise think. This rootedness is the obscurantism with relation to the universality of correct claims in which the more pernicious obscurantism of modern science in its relation to Being might itself be surmounted. Here the question of Being becomes the "matter" of knowledge and the guarantor of a "folkish" science in the face of its cosmopolitan simulacra.

It is in the questionableness of Being that Heidegger's exposition of "folkish" science differs from the racist doctrine of science advocated, for example, by Heidegger's Marburg colleague Erich Jaensch.[4] Having tied his notion of "folkish" science to Being rather than to the ahistorical presence in which the race knows itself as race, Heidegger is not guilty of Jaensch's inconsistency in challenging the hegemony of a science whose exactitude and universality rest on a suppression of the organic and the human, while nonetheless desiring that unimpugnable, and thus universally recognizable, distinctness of the people which is the dream and clandestine cosmopolitanism of racism. For Heidegger, the world of a people does not possess the atomistic quality that Jaensch attributes to it, by reason of which the latter is structurally bound to retain the cosmopolitan as the negated universal from which these distinct particular worlds have won an uneasy independence. If "folkish" science is the science of Being as such, it is because it seeks, rather than the derivative correctness of a rootless thinking, the Being of the world that must be known—not ontically as race, values, and character, but ontologically—if anything appearing against the background of world is to be known in its presence as well as in the abyssal foundations of its presence. The liberal conception of science, which bases its claim to scientific status on the darkness in which it remains with regard to its own rootedness, is never equal to the task of thinking Being in its worldliness. It is this worldliness of Being that favors the rooted thinking of a "folkish" science and whose appearance Heidegger wills to announce itself in the self-assertion of the national. The people of Heidegger's "folkish" science is to appear without becoming present.

Since Heidegger himself in the Leipzig address declares his allegiance to both Hitler *and* the question of Being, the prehistory of his political engagement is but sketchily reconstructed by commentaries that fasten on the lone instance of the word "*Volk*" in §74 of *Being and Time*. It is within the question of Being that Heidegger addresses the notion of *Volk* in 1927, just as it is within the question of Being that he confesses his loyalty to Hitler in 1933. To clarify the sense of "*Volk*" in *Being and Time* by its sense in National Socialism is hence reductive and of dubious worth polemically. An interpretation of the use of "*Volk*" in *Being and Time* that does not simultaneously consider the question of Being is, irrespective of its intention, even apologetic, because it isolates a suspect lexical element in Heidegger's thinking as a whole and delivers it up on its own to judgment. The step from *Volk* to Hitler is certainly one that Heidegger took, but schematized in this way, Heidegger's engagement ceases to be a scandal for philosophy, because the distance between his thinking and the intellectual squalor of the regime has been minimized. The question of the relation between nationalism and fundamental ontology is thereby settled without having first been examined.

Heidegger's nationalism is the nationalism of the rootedness of the *Volk*. It is not, however, an insurrection of the particular against the universal, if only because such an insurrection is always doomed to failure. Heidegger should not be seen to be translating Kierkegaard's anti-Hegelian individualism for the NSDAP. A *Volk* that insists on its singularity, on its condition as "this" *Volk*, is in the end, as Hegel had shown in his analysis of sense-certainty, always betrayed to the universal by its very "thisness," by the abstractness of singularity as such. A reprise of the nominalist cult of the particular does not describe Heidegger's reaction to Hegel's panlogism, since his critique of the universal pursues a different course from the beautiful soul's pathos-laden avowals of the particular's independence. Heidegger's rejection of cosmopolitanism and his engagement with a nationalistic political movement are grounded in his treatment of the universal within the question of Being. A demonstration of this can at least be attempted through a consideration, within the context of its critique of traditional ontology, of the following excerpt from the Introduction to *Being and Time*:

Being, as the basic theme of philosophy, is no class or genus of entities; yet it pertains to every entity. Its "universality" is to be sought higher up. Being and the structure of Being lie beyond every entity and every possible character which an entity may possess. *Being is the transcendens pure and simple.* And the transcendence of Dasein's Being is distinctive in that it implies the possibility and the necessity of the most radical *individuation*.[5]

Being is to be sought higher up than any class or genus because its "universality" places it beyond them. It transcends them because it is nothing else than transcendence. *"Being is the transcendens pure and simple."* In a marginal note to the *Hüttenexemplar* (the copy of *Being and Time* that Heidegger kept in his hut at Todtnauberg) Heidegger clarifies this statement: "transcendens to be sure not—despite every metaphysical echo—scholastic and Graeco-Platonic κοινόν, but rather transcendence as the ecstatic—

as temporality."[6] Being is to be sought higher up as that which transcends class and genus. For Heidegger, Being is that which transcends purely and simply, because it is time in its overreaching of the discrete "now" of Zeno's paradoxes. Being nowhere comes to rest in identity with itself and can therefore scarcely be inferred from the categories as their "principle" and law. Only if Being is grasped as the presence of beings, as the ostensible honesty with which beings give themselves up as they are to the categories (e.g., as so much and neither more nor less, as in such and such a place and not elsewhere), does Being stand in a relation to the categories that leaves the latter intact. The questionability of Being as presence, and not the independence of the particular, is what Heidegger brings up against traditional logic.

Aristotle also denies that Being is a genus, but it is by means of a different argument. In Book B of the *Metaphysics*, neither Being nor the One is admitted as the genus of what is, since the differences of each genus have to *be*, just as each difference has to be *one*.[7] Even if the scope of a genus is defined by the diversity of its subordinate species, the genus per se—as the unity and common character of its species—cannot contain this diversity within itself: otherwise, the species of a given genus would be interchangeable. Being and the One are more universal than any genus because they can be said of species not only with respect to what they share but also with respect to that by which they differ. For Aristotle, the "universality" of Being and the One thus does not at all imply a fundamental homogeneity of what is. Being and the One cannot be taken for granted as constants. Heidegger, in his 1931 lecture course *Aristoteles, Metaphysik θ 1–3*, accordingly stresses that for Aristotle, Being is still questionable in a radical sense: "All that is later thrust aside by the thesis: Being is the most self-evident of all things. (This questionability is a long way from the image that one generally has of Aristotle when one pictures his philosophy in the manner of the academic preoccupations of a medieval Scholastic or a German professor)."[8] In relation to Aristotle, Heidegger sees his task, not as the refutation of a "system," but rather as the resumption and elaboration of a questioning concerning the essence of Being. Being and the One, for Aristotle, are both said in many ways. But the multiplicity by which Being distinguishes itself from a genus does not contest the legitimacy of the notion of genus. Being is to be sought higher up than any genus, yet it is not to be sought higher up than the One, since Being is not said in a way that would not also be *one*. Aristotle does not include among the many ways of Being a way in which Being is not *one*: despite his own cautions, the multiplicity of Being will remain for the subsequent history of philosophy effectively under the sway of the understanding of Being as οὐσία, as the substance that is the propriety and decidability of the genera. Where Aristotle speaks of an analogy between the ways of Being but leaves the ground of this analogy unillumined, Heidegger names this ground the understanding of Being as presence and sets out its limitations. The Being of the differences that are always *one* is not Being as such in its transcendence and impropriety, but rather Being reduced to the substantiality of presence and thereby to the propriety that it can share with the One. The difference that *is*, but is not *one*, is the unrecognized and unrecognizable difference of transcendence from the One. *Not* All is One.[9] It is a difference that cannot be collected into any oneness without ceasing to be transcendence. Such a difference, because it does not give itself up to be known in unity, is unintelligible for Aristotle. The basis for intelligibility lies paradoxically in a blindness to the originary transcendence of time.

That even the One is transcended by Being, by the Being of the time that exceeds and encompasses the presence of the One, is no more acknowledged by later thinkers. When Kant, in his refutation of the Ontological Argument for the existence (*Dasein*) of God and within the understanding of logic laid down by Aristotle, says that existence is not a real predicate, this distinction reformulates Being's difference from a genus but still in terms of a complementarity instead of an antagonism. For Kant, existence is not a real predicate whereby the possibility or actuality of a thing could be distinguished within the concept itself, but the bare positing of a thing.[10] Kant's polemic against an aspect of medieval theology is the occasion for an exposition of Being within a theory of representation. Earlier in the *Critique of Pure Reason,* Kant humbles the understanding in its claim to totality and sets bounds on the use of its concepts through an account of the nonconceptuality of the a priori intuitions. Kant grounds the a priori intuitions in human finitude and assigns to existence an essential role in the determination of knowledge. That which is thereby shown to be irreducible to the concept is less an impetus for the question of Being than the surety of representation and the propriety of the concepts of the understanding. In the *Critique,* Kant thus devises a defense of the concepts of the understanding from their limitations regarding existence:

By whatever and by however many predicates we may think a thing—even if we completely determine it—we do not make the least addition to the thing when we further declare that this thing *is*. Otherwise, it would not be exactly the same thing that exists, but something more than we had thought in the concept; and we could not, therefore, say that the exact object of my concept exists.[11]

As the existence incorporated in a concept's set of predicates is, for Kant, not the existence of the object itself, it marks the untruth of the concept. The Kantian concept relinquishes existence as a real predicate and resigns itself to representing its object. By this modesty, it acquires something exterior to it, something nevertheless entirely tractable and tamed in advance by the a priori intuitions of time and space, and in its correspondence to this object, the concept lays claim to its truth. Furthermore, for the sake of the traditional understanding of truth as adequation, the equivocation of Being is to be "clarified" by a distinction between the copula of logic (the "is" of propositions of the kind "God is omnipotent") and the Being of existential positing (the "is" of propositions of the kind "There is a thaler in my hand"). Kant cannot rest content with rejecting the definition of Being as a predicate in favor of Being as positing. In the absence of a distinction between the logical positing of the concept of an object and the existential positing of the object itself, the concept ceases to be purely representative of its object: the concept simply *is* its object and is therefore neither true nor false in relation to it. The exteriority of Kantian existence is its intelligibility. Like Aristotle's Being, Kant's *Dasein* threatens the oneness of neither that which is to be subsumed nor that under which it is to be subsumed. Kant even surrenders Aristotle's insight into the equivocation of the many ways of Being. The equivocation between the ways of Being, which the Ontological Argument employs in its transition from the being of thinkability to the being of real existence, and as whose "ground," as the "sense" of the categorial interconnections of ontology, Heidegger will propose Dasein, is simply shut down. In existence, as the bare positing in the presence of the light of truth as adequation, the Aristotelian coextensiveness of Being with the One does not become questionable.

Through holding apart the "What it is" of a being from its "That it is," Kant wanted to place a check solely on the conceptual enthusiasm of theology, whereas Kierkegaard, in response to Hegel's sublation of the distinction, set out to interpret the extralogical character of existence as an antagonism to logic. But with Kierkegaard, the reformulation of the question of Being is stillborn, since the antagonism of existence to traditional logic is not substantiated in an account of temporality and the differentiality of Being but left to the inadequate resources of an obstinate nominalism: "Ex-

istence is always the particular; the abstract does not *exist*." [12] Kierkegaard's
nominalism, which is dictated by his attention to the Christian doctrine of
the incommensurability of the human soul, is of less importance for Heidegger than what inspired it. By neglecting the philosophy of nature,
Kierkegaard gave vent to his polemics against traditional logic entirely
within the question of what it is to be human. The human existence that,
in Kierkegaard, eludes the universal on account of its particularity becomes
the human existence (Dasein) that, in Heidegger, eludes the universal on
account of its finitude. As a result, Kierkegaard's confrontation with logic
is renewed on a more originary ground. Heidegger reformulates it as a confrontation with Plato's subordination of finitude to the Ideas in the founding of metaphysics. That by means of which a particular instantiation of a
single universal differentiates itself from its universal is set forth as the tran-
sitoriness and perishability—the existence—in which the particular is just
as much *not* present in an identity with its universal. Existence is to be understood by reference to another temporality than that in which the Ideas
stand fast in the eternity of their presence. And it is to be understood as human because, for Heidegger, it is human beings alone who, in their projects and in the determinative exposure to the truth of their outstanding
deaths, resist any description that would reduce them to what can be apprehended in presence. The human being, less as a particular than as the
Being of ecstatic temporality, is the basis for a polemic against traditional
logic.

And yet in the excerpt from the Introduction to *Being and Time* cited
above, Heidegger writes: "And the transcendence of Dasein's Being is distinctive in that it implies the possibility and the necessity of the most radical *individuation*." Is individuation here to be comprehended as a reprise
of Kierkegaard's individualism and in opposition to the *Volk* of §74? To answer tentatively, indicating the line that is to be followed: No. Inasmuch as
it is transcendence that is said to imply the most radical individuation, individuation cannot here be identified with the isolation and distinction of
one being from other beings. Heidegger attributes to transcendence a more
radical individuation than such a process of isolation and distinction. Individuation in the latter sense is an individuation on the level of properties.
The individual never completely shares its set of properties with any other,
but that which is individuated by its properties is in itself, as a raw unit of
presence, always the same. Such individuation is constrained in how much
it can differentiate the individual from the universal by the understanding

of Being as presence that the individual has in common with the universal. Heidegger's radical individuation breaks with the repeatable because it breaks with the "now" as the truth of time. Dasein all the more individuates itself the less it holds itself aloof from the existential, historical thickness of world. It is always already individuated by the corruption through which it eludes being apprehended in presence. The peculiar distinctness of the human being, which necessitates a reassessment of the theorization of temporality in order to do justice to the anticipation of death and projects' implication of the future in the present, is obscured in the logical individual abstracted from the world in which alone there can be existence. But does excluding the individual of traditional logic suffice to bring us, as Heidegger's text seems to assume, to the *Volk*? Even if the transcendence of Dasein's ecstatic temporality is overlooked in both the abstract individual and the universal of ahistorical humanity, is the *Volk* alone what remains after the exclusion?

Otto Pöggeler has objected to "the *coup de main* of an immediate introduction of the concept of *Volk*" in §74 of *Being and Time*.[13] That Heidegger seeks to downplay the abruptness by introducing the *Volk* in an apposition does not mitigate the violence of the *coup de main*. Two responses, at least, can be given. The abruptness can be held fast as an object of analysis and the transition from the question of Being to a "folkish" politics thereby rendered suspect. Such a strategy impedes the use of Heidegger's philosophical authority as an argument for fascist politics. It does, however, make it impossible to understand—in anything but an external sense—how Heidegger was able to see the mission of the *Volk* as his own. If the abruptness can be taken as a challenge to come up with alternatives to the *Volk* that could also, if not better, meet the requirements of the question of Being, it can also be taken as a violence directed against other connotations of the word "*Volk*." With this second strategy for reading Heidegger's *coup de main*, an immanent critique of one of the central concepts of National Socialism becomes practicable.

Between the individual and humanity as a whole, there are social formations besides the *Volk*. Yet Heidegger's conservatism expresses itself in an allegiance neither to the particularist interests of classes nor to the sentimentalist intimacy of the family. Heidegger's political engagement, which in the address in Leipzig, as well as in other texts, he ties to fundamental ontology, is an engagement with that which affords the chance of overcoming the metaphysics of presence. If Heidegger chooses the people—

and not just any people but the German *Volk*—it is because, in the *Volk*, temporality as such becomes a question. This is not to deny that other peoples have histories or that classes and families can be chronicled from their emergence to their disappearance. The German *Volk* is the agent of the question of the relations between Being and time, not because it is the people whose history is richest in incident, but rather because, for a specific nationalist discourse, it is the people that, through wanting to distinguish itself as much as possible from the self-evidence and positivism of the nation-states of its neighbors, long defined itself by its absence. Whether such a characterization of the essence of the *Volk* is but the hypostasis of its political backwardness is a question that seemingly does not arise for Heidegger. It is overruled by the question of Being. Heidegger's nationalism will be a nationalism of the assertion of the absence of the *Volk* that knows itself to be absent. In contrast to the class that has either already come to power or whose dialectical lot it is to realize itself as the universal class of the future, and in contrast to the family whose mythic immediacy hardly accommodates an interrogation of the understanding of Being as presence, the German *Volk* is an embarrassment for traditional ontology. It does not take its definition from its recognizability in the light of presence. Such an explanation of Heidegger's nationalism, offered here in advance of a commentary on Heidegger's various texts on the *Volk*, answers one question only to raise another. How is it that Heidegger of all thinkers could have aligned himself with a "folkish" movement that set itself the task of *eliminating* undecidability from the phenomenon of the *Volk*? Perhaps, as Heidegger wrote in his defense in December 1945, he believed that the movement could be led spiritually down other paths.[14] He misinterpreted the prevailing involvement with the notion of the *Volk* as the possibility that the movement could be directed away from a pseudoscientific elaboration and concreteness toward an attempt to grasp that absence of the *Volk* which is Dasein's difference from the present-at-hand. The people of the "folkish" uprising of 1933 will turn out to have been, not the people of the recovery of the world flattened by Descartes to the presence of *res extensa*, but rather a humanity indistinguishable from a thing.

Undoubtedly, this was to be foreseen, and Heidegger did not succeed in preventing it. He did not succeed in making *Being and Time* the bible of National Socialism. Far more clearly than his postwar critics, the prospective ideologues of the movement were able to recognize that Heidegger, lexical convergences aside, had not written a book in their spirit. The

Volk that in 1933 inquires into the essence of Being is less the electorate of the former Weimar Republic than the Dasein of the text of 1927. The Dasein of *Being and Time* has not passed from the singular to the plural, since its definition in the 1927 text as Being-in-the-world precludes any differentiation of Dasein and *Volk* on the basis of traditional grammar. As a multiplicity, as that which is not one, Dasein was already the transcendence of the Dasein of the *Volk*. *Being and Time* is a political text, albeit political in Heidegger's sense. Dominique Janicaud, who argues that *Being and Time* is abstract and hence apolitical because it addresses the possibility for any given political attitude, seemingly invokes the very understanding of possibility that Heidegger criticizes.[15] The possibilities of Dasein do not correspond to the existential neutrality of the abstract concepts of metaphysics, since it is finitude—facticity and Being-with-one-another, in short, the political realm—that grounds possibility for Heidegger.

In §74 of *Being and Time*, in a passage invariably scrutinized by commentators on his politics, Heidegger broaches the question of the people, distinguishing the *Volk* from a leveling aggregation of subjects: "But if fateful Dasein, as Being-in-the-world, exists essentially in Being-with-Others, its historizing is a co-historizing and is determinative for it as *destiny* [*Geschick*]. This is how we designate the historizing of the community, of the people. Destiny is not something that puts itself together out of individual fates, any more than Being-with-one-another can be conceived as the occurring together of several Subjects."[16] The historizing of Dasein is always a co-historizing because human beings are, for Heidegger, essentially political. Their politicality is not one attribute among others and not one that distinguishes them, as it does for Aristotle, from *other* animals. It is destiny that stands here between the notion of the *Volk* and its formulation as a species composed of individuals agreeing in certain attributes. Destiny is therefore not interchangeable with the racial "type" (*Art*). It does not unify what is separate. The *Volk* that it designates knows neither unity nor disunity, because in the transcendence of its historizing, it has always already reached beyond the isolation of individual subjects, as well as the isolation of an individual ethnic group. And yet, precisely because it reaches beyond the presence in which a people could recognize itself in its oneness, the *Volk* can just as little become the humanity that is the oneness of the peoples. For Heidegger, the *Volk* is not a point of indifference, and the "anarchic attitude" that Hans Sluga discerns in the first division of *Being and Time*, §§9–44, cannot accordingly be said to retreat with the appearance of the *Volk*.[17] The discussion of the notion of the *Volk* acknowledges the possibility and necessity of Dasein's radical individuation and, that is to say, "anarchy."

Certainly a suspension of disbelief is required before considering whether the German people is the definitive people of co-historizing, but so long as Heidegger's nationalism is taken to be utterly in agreement with the times, the task of retracing the steps from *Being and Time* to National Socialism has simply not been addressed. Everybody knows who the Germans are, but for a certain strand of German nationalism, of which Thomas Mann's *Reflections of a Nonpolitical Man* can be taken as an expression, this is something that cannot be known without overlooking the Germans' distinctness from their positivistic neighbors. Heidegger's peculiarity within this strand of nationalism will have been to raise the Germans from being one question among others to being the questionable as such. Heidegger's philosophy does not find its way to the *Volk* as to that which would be its validating law. The anxiety and alienation of *Being and Time* are not resolved by an "immersion" in the *Volk*. On the contrary, Heidegger attempts to think the utmost questionability and hence Being of Dasein by means of the *Volk*. The scandal of Heidegger's declarations of the consistency between his philosophy and his affiliation with National Socialism is that he was able to countenance an authoritarian regime for the sake of a suspected shared devotion to such an understanding of "folkishness." These declarations of consistency imply, in defiance of the liberal subject, an understanding of the most radical individuation for which the *Volk* is the "proper" domain.

Dasein's possibility and necessity of the most radical individuation rests with the *Volk*. Existing essentially as Being-with-Others, Dasein individuates itself as Dasein in the co-historizing that is the destiny of the *Volk*. This individuation is not one among others by which Dasein is differentiated. In §72 of *Being and Time*, Heidegger puts forward the thesis of the fundamental historicality of Dasein: "In analysing the historicality of Dasein we shall try to show that this entity is not 'temporal' because it 'stands in history', but that, on the contrary, it exists historically and can so exist only because it is temporal in the very basis of its Being."[18] Dasein as Dasein stands in history and, following §74, that is to say, in co-history. It always individuates itself co-historically and thus, in line with Heidegger's explication of co-historizing, as the *Volk*. Other individuations are secondary. The accretion of exclusive properties whereby the individual persons "within" the *Volk* achieve distinctness simply obscures Dasein's radical difference from beings that are present-at-hand. Heterogeneity and homogeneity at the level of properties decide nothing with regard to membership in the *Volk*. The question of which individuals belong and do not belong to the *Volk* is not a question that can be raised without an inappropriate reliance on individuation through properties. In §9, "The Theme of the Analytic of Dasein," Heidegger writes: "*The essence of Dasein lies in its existence.* Accordingly those characteristics which can be exhibited in this entity are not 'properties' present-at-hand of some entity which 'looks' so and so and is itself present-at-hand; they are in each case possible ways for it to be, and no more than that." [19] This disqualification of properties from expositions of Dasein is irreconcilable with the biologism of National Socialism. A people that is biologistically recognizable is always a people that is a class of individuals with common attributes, rather than a destiny.

In 1933, however, Heidegger allows himself to be swayed by the NSDAP's invocations of the *Volk*. Heidegger's engagement with National Socialism, which never expressed itself in an endorsement of the latter's biologism, was inseparable from the ambition to reform its thinking in accordance with what Heidegger imagined to be its historical promise. Even after the end of the war, Heidegger admitted a loyalty to this promise, denigrating everyone who was convinced of its unrealizability from the start and who thus contributed nothing to its realization.[20] National Socialism, grounding its notion of the *Volk* in biology rather than history, remained as it were a movement without a destiny, a populism without a people. The self-assertion of the German people as the self-assertion of the essential historicality of Dasein did not take place.

But if for Heidegger the *Volk* is necessarily missing from the present-at-hand, how is its self-assertion to be understood? It cannot manifest itself as a visible presence politically. A reply to the question of the nature of the self-assertion of the *Volk* can be extrapolated from Heidegger's exposition of the differential modes of Being-with-one-another. In §74 of *Being and Time*, to continue an earlier quotation, Heidegger further delineates the notion of destiny by which he defines the *Volk*: "Destiny is not something that puts itself together out of individual fates, any more than Being-with-one-another can be conceived as the occurring together of several Subjects. Our fates have already been guided in advance, in our Being with one another in the same world and in our resoluteness for definite possibilities. Only in communicating and struggling does the power of destiny become free." [21] The power of destiny that is the co-historizing of the *Volk* cannot be taken for granted, because it is conditional on communication and struggle. When there is no communication or struggle to confront Dasein with its essence in Being-with-one-another, then the power of destiny remains inhibited. The historizing of Dasein, which is to say its co-historizing and the historizing of the people, is covered over. In a note appended to this passage, Heidegger refers the reader to §26 on "The Dasein-with of Others and Everyday Being-with." There he addresses the plurality of subjects from which he distinguishes the *Volk* and derives this plurality as an interpretation from a Being-with that is constituted, not in struggle and communication, but rather in disinterest:

So far as Dasein *is* at all, it has Being-with-one-another as its kind of Being. This cannot be conceived as a summative result of the occurrence of several "subjects." Even to come across a number of "subjects" [*einer Anzahl von "Subjekten"*] becomes possible only if the Others who are concerned proximally in their Dasein-with are treated merely as "numerals" [*Nummer*]. Such a number of "subjects" gets discovered only by a definite Being-with-and-towards-one-another. This "inconsiderate" Being-with "reckons" [*rechnet*] with the Others without seriously "counting on them" [*auf sie zählt*], or without even wanting to "have anything to do" with them. [22]

Inasmuch as Dasein is Being-with-one-another, it is unable to isolate itself from others. Heidegger indicates the dubiousness of its disinterest with quotation marks. Dasein does not revoke, but conceals its concern. Appearing not to want to have anything to do with others, Dasein forswears the struggle and communication by which the power of its own destiny as Being-with-one-another becomes free. This superficial unconcern obstructs the co-historizing of the *Volk*.

The *Volk* is missing from the present-at-hand, but that is not to say that in struggling and communicating, it ceases to be missing. It is missing in another way. Dasein, according to Heidegger, cannot concern itself with others as such, and thus with the *Volk*, by fixing its attention on subjects present-at-hand:

When Others are encountered, it is not the case that one's own subject is *proximally* present-at-hand and that the rest of the subjects, which are likewise occurrents, get discriminated beforehand and then apprehended; nor are they encountered by a primary act of looking at oneself in such a way that the opposite pole of a distinction first gets ascertained. They are encountered from out of the *world*, in which concernfully circumspective Dasein dwells. Theoretically concocted "explanations" of the Being-present-at-hand of Others urge themselves upon us all too easily; but over against such explanations we must hold fast to the phenomenal facts of the case which we have pointed out, namely, that Others are encountered *environmentally*.[23]

The others, with whom in its concern Dasein is the co-historizing of the *Volk*, are not met as beings present-at-hand. They come forward out of the world of Dasein, and it is as this world that they come forward. The others can only be met in a manner appropriate to their humanity, which is to say that they can only be met as the *transcendens* encompassing the presence of the present-at-hand. The others are met as that which, strictly speaking, cannot be met, since they cannot be reduced to presence. They can only be met through meeting them as world, through thinking the "absence" that is not incidental and remediable, but essential and thus a provocation for the understanding of Being as presence.

When Dasein does not want to "have anything to do" with others, it tries to ignore this provocation. The *Volk* that is missing—albeit missing in the sense in which the world in which Dasein, nonetheless, has its Being is missing—is then even missing as missing: the *Volk*'s difference from the present-at-hand is itself absent. In the place of the *Volk*, and in a way as its reverse, *das Man* makes its appearance: "'The Others' whom one thus designates in order to cover up the fact of one's belonging to them essentially oneself, are those who proximally and for the most part *'are there'* in everyday Being-with-one-another. The 'who' is not this one, not that one, not oneself [*man selbst*], not some people [*einige*], and not the sum of them all. The 'who' is the neuter, the *'they'* [*das Man*]."[24] Insofar as Dasein denies to itself its essential existence in Being-with-one-another, it denies its own transcendence. The distance that Dasein keeps from Others in its "inconsiderate" Being-with does not individuate Dasein, but rather levels it:

This Being-with-one-another dissolves one's own Dasein completely into the kind of Being of "the Others," in such a way, indeed, that the Others, as distinguishable and explicit, vanish more and more. In this inconspicuousness and unascertainability, the real dictatorship of the "they" is unfolded. We take pleasure and enjoy ourselves as *they* [*man*] take pleasure; we read, see, and judge about literature and art as *they* see and judge; likewise we shrink back from the "great mass" as *they* shrink back.[25]

Contempt for the masses, having itself become a cliché, characterizes the modern phenomenon of the masses. Not content simply to reiterate, at the distance of a hundred years, de Tocqueville's account of the tyranny of the majority, Heidegger introduces a seemingly paradoxical twist. Here conformity is made an affair of elitist individualism, rather than of membership in the *Volk*. Denying its transcendence, Dasein stands back from the Others and thereby stands back from the question of Being. The neglect of the question of Being is the precondition of conformity, because, by not excluding from discussions of the human the logical notion of the individual (i.e., the unit of presence as the bearer of properties), it simultaneously creates the possibility of a mass bringing into line. The autonomy of the liberal subject is the beginning of its massification. For Heidegger, the individual is already fundamentally conformist because he or she is faced in the utmost isolation of individuality with the denial of the radical difference of transcendence, a denial that he or she has in common with every individual thing present-at-hand.

In this conformity, communication and struggle are drained of their vigor: "Overnight, everything that is primordial gets glossed over as something that has long been well known. Everything gained by a struggle becomes just something to be manipulated. Every secret loses its force." [26] The debasement of struggle and the vitiation of the secret are not the consequences of an encroachment of the "they" on the preserve of the individual. Struggle, as well as the possibility of the secret and the force of its potential communication, presupposes Being-with-one-another and hence, contrary to the assertion of Georg Lukács,[27] Pierre Bourdieu,[28] and many others, these passages in *Being and Time* cannot be read as elitist cultural critique. Heidegger is not retreating from the public spaces, and the opposite of the "they" is not at all the autonomous subject by which it is merely differently designated. Heidegger writes:

The Self of everyday Dasein is the *they-self,* which we distinguish from the *authentic Self*—that is, from the Self which has been taken hold of in its own way [*eigens ergriffenen*]. . . . If Dasein discovers the world in its own way [*eigens*] and brings it close, if it discloses to itself its own authentic Being, then this discovery of the "world" and this disclosure of Dasein are always accomplished as a clearing-away of concealments and obscurities, as a breaking up of the disguises with which Dasein bars its own way.[29]

This authentic self, as Heidegger explains, is not the autonomous subject: "*Authentic Being-one's-Self* does not rest upon an exceptional condition of the subject, a condition that has been detached from the 'they'; *it is rather an existentiell modification of the 'they'—of the 'they' as an essential existen-*

tiale." [30] As an essential *existentiale*, the "they" is Being-with-one-another, and the authentic Self that is its *existentiell* modification is the Dasein that understands itself as Being-with-one-another. This understanding and its abstention disclose and conceal Being-with-one-another, but do not prove anything against it in itself. The power of destiny that can or cannot become free is *existentiell* because as the co-historizing of the *Volk*, it is a matter of disclosure, namely, of the essential historicality of Dasein. The power of destiny in its unfreedom is the double absence of the *Volk*, just as this double absence is Dasein's obliviousness to its own Being. It could therefore be said that the *Volk* is not so much a being among beings as the understanding that raises the question of Being.

In 1927, the prospects for understanding were not as bleak as they would seem to the late Heidegger. Indeed, Heidegger's political enthusiasm in 1933 was inseparable from his optimism with regard to the task of understanding. The *Volk* was defined by its ontological mission. For Heidegger, the Germans in their ontic conspicuousness under National Socialism quickly proved themselves to be a people doubly in abeyance. In the lectures on Hölderlin from the mid 1930s and early 1940s, the self-assertion of the German people proclaimed by National Socialism is indefinitely deferred. Heidegger's commentary from 1943 on Hölderlin's poem "Heimkunft" denies, for instance, that the inhabitants of the National Socialist fatherland can claim to have come home to the essence of *Heimat* (native place): "this homecoming is the future of the historical being of the German people." [31] Not having yet come home to the essence of *Heimat*, the Germans cannot truly be said to be at home. They have still to assert themselves as a people. More precisely, they have to assert themselves as the people whose essence lies in the deferral of its assertion as a people present-at-hand. Heidegger does not say that the homecoming of the Germans will take place in the future, but rather that it is the future: the essence of the *Heimat* to which the German people is to come is not something that can ever be present-at-hand. In a 1934–35 lecture course on Hölderlin's poems "Germanien" and "Der Rhein," Heidegger speaks of the ignorance in which the German people persists with regard to itself as an ignorance with regard to its time:

We do not know who we are so long as we do not know our time. Our time, however, is that of the people between the peoples. Who knows this time? No one knows it in the sense that he could point it out and "date" it. Even those creative ones [*jene Schaffenden*] who dwell on the peaks of time do not know it. One thing alone they know, namely, when the time of the event of the true is *not*. Hölderlin says this at the beginning of the poem "Die Titanen":

> *It is not however*
> *The time. Still are they*
> *Unbound. The divine does not strike the indifferent.*[32]

In this passage Heidegger implies that the time of the people between the peoples is the time of the event of the true. Heidegger's people cannot know itself because it cannot know a time that is not there to be known. Its coming to itself depends on the unforeseeable event of the true, rather than on Hitler's seizure of power, and it depends on the event of the true because it is as the event of the true that this people is to know itself.

National Socialism, with its efforts to secure the distinctness of the people in the findings of a compliant biology, was unwilling to think the people in terms of temporality as such. Heidegger's 1933–34 lecture course *Vom Wesen der Wahrheit* (On the Essence of Truth) already contains a note of dissent: "There is much talk nowadays of *blood and soil* [*Blut und Boden*] as frequently invoked powers. Literati, whom one comes across even today, have already seized hold of them. Blood and soil are certainly powerful and necessary, but they are *not a sufficient* condition for the Dasein of a people."[33] In the more sarcastic language of his 1941–42 lecture course on Hölderlin's poem "Andenken," Heidegger contends that a people finding itself in skull measurements and archaeological digs is unable to find itself as a people because it confounds that which is one's own (*das Eigene*) with something present-at-hand.[34] Temporality, as Heidegger repeats again and again in *Being and Time*, is that which is one's own and the essence of Dasein. A people, as Dasein, can therefore only come to itself inasmuch as it does not come to itself, inasmuch as it knows itself as the temporality that can never be present to itself. With respect to knowing a people in its essential temporality and thus historicality, the peculiar scientism of National Socialism was, for all its taxonomical ingenuity, an evasion. National Socialism was only able to persuade itself that it grasped the singularity of the German people by paradoxically first suppressing even its difference from the present-at-hand. The ontological mission of raising a question against the understanding of Being as presence on the basis of an insight into the unique temporality of human Dasein was not allowed to become the German mission.

For Heidegger, the specificity of a people is reserved for the science of history and not for biology or the historiography that is archaeology. §76 of *Being and Time* offers the following negative definition of the science of history: "In no science are the 'universal validity' of standards and the claims to 'universality' which the 'they' and its common sense demand, *less* possible as criteria of 'truth' than in authentic historiology."[35] The "authentic historiology" of Macquarrie and Robinson's translation is to be distinguished from the science of the "they." Universality is compatible with the "they," but incompatible with the historicality by which Heidegger defines a people. And it is incompatible, not because it misses the finer "nuances" of historicality, but because it rests on an understanding of temporality that presupposes historicality and likewise cannot make sense of it. Heidegger does not recite the nominalist objection to universality, since what he criticizes is less the legitimacy of the subsumption of particulars than the discrete ahistorical now in which the particular appears in its presence and thereby appears in the repeatability proper to the universal. The specificity of a people is not a particular in its irrevocable passage to the universal, but the specificity of ecstatic time in its unrepeatability. A people apprehended in presence and analyzed into ahistorical properties is not "recognizable" as a people, because its definitive historicality has been neglected. This historicality, inasmuch as it always sets itself at odds with universality, is therefore both the reason for the plurality of peoples and the impossibility of the proof of this plurality by exact numeration: the lone people would be able to encounter its integrity only in the oneness of presence, only therefore in that in which a people could never encounter the truth of its historicality. Overreaching presence and its visibility, historicality individuates without the surety of a recognition for the differences it effects. Historicality bastardizes without cease, and yet it never results in the homogeneous. Instead, it always already fragments the peoples and prevents their recuperation into new unities. Historicality, which is less a property of a people than its world itself, is the impracticability of a demarcation of the horizons of a world. That is to say, world is only able to be world insofar as it is *not* whole and does not sever itself from the transcendence that is the historicality of a people. A people can never assert itself as *one* people among many because the world that it is can never fully present itself as something present-at-hand and hence distinct without ceasing to be world.

Heidegger's disillusionment with National Socialism was inevitable. The regime's hubris did not translate into an elevation of the *Volk*. The people that asserted itself under the regime was not the truth of Being as the historical truth of time. In place of the bastardized specificity of a people, National Socialism put forward the distinctness of a being present-at-hand. The particularism of the movement was, for all its vociferousness, at bottom too timid to break with the logic of the "type." In its scientist formulations of the specificity of the German people, National Socialism wanted a specificity that nonetheless could be universally apprehended as such. The people was to be legitimated in its distinctness because it was to reveal itself incontestably in the clarity of presence, in the abstraction from its historicality. With the abstraction from historicality, National Socialism retained the ontological basis of *les droits de l'homme*: the autonomous, ahistorical subject of liberalism is cut from the same cloth as the biologistically apprehended specimen of the Aryan race. It is thus hard to see how Goebbels, with his consistent reliance on biologism, could have proclaimed in the first months of the regime the eradication from history of the year 1789. The National Socialist revolution simply reenacted the French Revolution's disavowal of that which is a people's own. While the Jacobin motto "La force de la raison et la force du peuple, c'est la même chose" substituted for a people the "they" of the cosmopolitan voice of the liberal subject, National Socialism similarly dehistoricizes the people by a reification and dissection into properties. In both revolutions, history as such went unthought and the people failed to "appear." Heidegger's disillusionment with National Socialism cannot, therefore, be interpreted as a softening of his opposition toward liberalism, since in its universalist misapprehension of the specificity of the *Volk*, National Socialism had demonstrated the spuriousness of its own anti-liberalism.

Heidegger's people "appears" neither in 1789 nor in 1933. What appears in the two revolutions is too intent upon its own manifestness and visibility as a people to be mistaken for such. The self-assertion of a people is an affair of modesty. A people appears in its undecidable and unnamable specificity as a caesura, as . . . : its appearance is always the invisibility of the field itself of the ontic determinations of Dasein. It is the essence of a people to be absent. Heidegger, who renews the Romantic longing for the people, implicitly disputes the National Socialist readings of that longing: the people that is missing in Romanticism does not await its realization under National Socialism.[36] Heidegger's position should not, however, be interpreted as a nostalgic depoliticization of the Romantics' thinking of the

German people.[37] Heidegger defers the emergence of the *Volk* precisely in order to think its historicality and thus the political.

The apoliticality of German Romanticism in comparison with the Jacobins is itself already deceptive. The people that in the French Revolution appropriated for itself the power of legitimation formerly embodied in the person of the king did not grasp the political as the site of the historizing of a community. In its pretension to stand as arbiter, it grasped itself as the universal and confused the political with the domain of the subsumption of traditional logic. The powerlessness of the *Volk* of Romanticism should not be too quickly explained, which is to say explained away, by the negative circumstance of Germany's still larval bourgeoisie. Powerlessness does not merely distinguish the *Volk* from the people that had come to power in the French Revolution; it distinguishes it from the very logic of power in which the essence of the human goes unthought. Ernest Renan, naming Germany a land without a people, seemingly laments this absence, whereby the nation was reduced to seeking its legitimacy elsewhere, in the titles of successor to the Roman Empire and founder of the Carolingian.[38] A people as a people, however, can never be a power of legitimation, because it can never gather itself into a recognizable unity able to impose its will on and against the political realm.

Giorgio Agamben has argued that not even the people of the French Revolution was able to seize sovereignty for itself. Between *le peuple toujours malheureux* of the excluded and indigent masses and the people of an integral body politic, there is no easy transition. National Socialism announced in its very name the discord of the concept of the people in much of Western politics. Socialism, as a politics of the excluded, was to be conjoined with nationalism as a politics of sovereignty. Under Hitler, the class divisions of the German *Volk* were to be abolished, but this new inclusiveness was not so new as to formulate itself without an exclusion, an exclusion carried to the point of extermination. As the fracture in the people could not be healed by the elimination of the Jews, the mentally ill and the carriers of hereditary diseases were next in line for destruction. For Agamben, the entire populations of the so-called Third World are today the object of the murderous and futile attempt of the West to end the internecine struggle that separates the unitary People of the body politic from the inassimilable people of the biological subsistence of exploitable material, of "bare life."[39] The fracture is irremediable, since it is the originary fracture by means of which the being-outside-of-oneself of Being-with-others un-settles any pretensions to the self-identity of the human. What is required is not an extermination of one pole of the concept of the people so that the other may enjoy its status as a universal, but rather a break with the alignment of politics with the logic of the present-at-hand.

In his 1934 lecture course *Logik als die Frage nach dem Wesen der Sprache* (Logic as the Question Concerning the Essence of Language), Heidegger discusses the polysemy of the word "*Volk*" and endeavors to ascertain its inner truth in contradistinction to an inessential manifold. The truth of the *Volk* cannot be grasped as a rabble (*Pöbel*), a racial group, an electorate, or the body of workers, just as it cannot be grasped by distilling a general concept from what these various senses have in common. The *Volk* is defined by the decision: "We are *properly* ourselves only in the decision."[40] What properly constitutes the people for Heidegger is the undecidability and impropriety of the decision. The people decides and thereby throws itself into determination, and yet it is only by deciding, by casting itself into the openness of decision that it can wrest itself from the determinate and confront itself as an exception to the ontology of the present-at-hand. A people that holds itself back from decision holds itself back from undecidability. In *Homo Sacer*, Agamben notes the subtlety of the distinction between Heidegger's people of the decision and the National Socialist conception of race: where the Nazi movement formulated the *Volk* as a set of facts, Heidegger's people is defined by its facticity, by the existential thickness of the world in which facts have their place.[41] The present-at-hand is that which is decided, but it is not the decision itself. From the decisionism of the NSDAP Heidegger appears, however, to have expected a mobilization of Dasein for a necessarily political and historical understanding of its ontic ambiguity.

In his increasing disillusionment with the simple biologism of the regime, the task for Heidegger after 1934 was to lose rather than to find the Germans as present-at-hand. And it could be argued that the Romantics wanted nothing besides. Gilles Deleuze and Félix Guattari propose that the absence of a people was not the circumstance of Romanticism, but its goal: "What romanticism lacks most is a people. . . . Germany, German romanticism, had a genius for experiencing the natal territory not as deserted but as 'solitary,' regardless of population density."[42] The people of Romanticism is scattered in its essential powerlessness. This can be noted even in the approach to publication: it is, in one respect, contrary to the intention of the Romantic folksong that it attract, instead of repel, an audience, as Georg Lichtenberg was still able to perceive.[43] The hermetism of Romantic poetry is by no means a denial of the political realm. On the contrary, it is the people's all too easy self-discovery in 1789 and 1933 that constitutes a denial of the political realm, since the "..." of Being, which is the site of the historizing of Dasein and its anarchy, is buried beneath the onticality that is the measure of an integral people.

A people must beware of finding itself too easily. The *existentiell* modification of authentic Being-with-one-another that has here been heuristically identified with the *Volk* finds itself in understanding and not in its unified appearance as a being present-at-hand. The revolutions of 1789 and 1933 are thus not so much popular uprisings as inscriptions of the people in traditional logic. In both cases, the people was formulated in terms of a universal or type: in the French Revolution, it became a power of legitimation over each individual and in comparison with which, in the eyes of the Terror, each individual was, as an individual, automatically in the wrong: the individual must die so that the nominalist thesis of the reality of individuals and nonexistence of universals might be reversed. Under National Socialism, for its part, the universal constituted the common and distinct identity of the race. Heidegger's *Volk*, which as an existentiell modification is not a given, stands in need of an uprising, but not of the kind in which its universalization is substituted for an understanding of itself. Universalization falls short of the essence of the *Volk*, since what is to be understood in and as the *Volk* is, for Heidegger, the co-historizing of Being-with-one-another. This co-historizing is the temporality that eludes the presence of the discrete "now" of the universal in its repeatability, because it is the more originary temporality of the *ecstases* of human Dasein. As Being-in-the-world, Dasein always already converges with Others, and hence this convergence cannot be set apart from anarchy and made to depend upon the mediation of a universal.

If subject and *Volk* are set in opposition in Heidegger's writings, it is not an opposition of the individual and the universal, but rather of the ahistorical and the historical: a people is not the universal of numerable individuals, and authentic Dasein is itself the *Volk*. Insofar as it is grounded in an understanding of Being as presence, the mediation of the universal and the reified notion of the people it supports are of an entirely other order than the struggle and communication associated with Heidegger's notions of destiny and the *Volk*. It is only in the cessation of both struggle and communication, in the cessation of its understanding of ecstatic temporality, that Being-with is able to be seduced by its ahistorical image in the mediation of singular and universal. The conformity of a given people to a universal, and hence its homogeneity, never reaches its essence as Being-with, and never distinguishes it *as a people* among other peoples, because the plurality of peoples is less the extrinsic numerability of unities than the difference that a people carries within itself as the transcendence of its historicality and its nonuniversality. For the same reason, a people that presses its sovereignty over the political realm asserts something other than itself. The sovereignty of a people is at odds with its essential politicality since, through becoming a power of legitimation in the shape of a universal, it forgets the nonidentity proper to itself as the transcendence of Being-with-one-another in the constitution of the political. But then a people that does not seize power does not thereby automatically understand itself. It may simply be delivering power to a class, a clique, or an individual, rather than understanding itself in terms of that which in historicality is not present to be controlled. A people cannot find itself either in power or out of power, but only in that which is ontologically prior to power.

Formulated in terms of the question of the nature and role of the people during the Wars of Liberation, this entails that the Napoleonic dictatorship was not so much to be supplanted as philosophically overcome. Where the opposition of the Romantics to popular sovereignty is often seemingly involuntary and de facto, Hegel's opposition, by contrast, is de jure, and at first sight it might thus appear that Heidegger's notion of the people is closer to Hegel's than to the Romantics'. Hegel repeatedly addresses the contradictory notion of popular sovereignty, but as his analyses figure in an apologetics of sovereignty, it is solely in its dissemblance of sovereignty that the people is exhibited and thereafter passed over. In his lectures on the philosophy of history, Hegel condemns the notion of the people in the French Revolution by judging it according to the universality to which this people had itself laid claim. Criticizing the purely formal freedom propagated by the French Revolution for furnishing the popular state with no more substantial a foundation than a temporary enthusiasm, Hegel describes the people of this freedom as not so much investing the existing governmental structures as abolishing their concrete universality in favor of an abstract and thus contradictorily one-sided universal.[44] And in his very last text, "The English Reform Bill," Hegel disparages the phrase "the sovereign people" in the French opposition press for its vacuity.[45] The people, through its inability to embody the concrete universal by which Hegel defines both knowledge and the state, consigns itself to the obscurantist margins of his political thinking. The *Philosophy of Right* is hence explicitly conceived as an attempt to set forth that which is but dimly and extrinsically foreshadowed in the universalist populism of the French Revolution: the book of the Prussian state necessarily and excessively becomes the book of the truth of *le peuple*. Any question as to whether the truth of the people might not deliver itself in a refinement of the Napoleonic dialectic of the individual of *les droits de l'homme* and the universal state of the First Empire is thereby suppressed.

Hegel's assessment of the French notion of popular sovereignty is ultimately faithful to his ideal of nonpolemical criticism. However, with the people of German Romanticism, with the people that never comes to power, nothing tempers his hostility. Here it is a matter of simple rejection rather than of elaboration. In its refusal to press a claim to the universal, the people of German Romanticism sets itself wholly at odds with knowledge. J. F. Fries in the *Philosophy of Right* and E. T. A. Hoffmann in the *Aesthetics* are subjected to ridicule without compunction or concession, because the substantiality of ethical life is exchanged in their writings, not even for the enthusiasm of revolutionary *paroles*, but rather for immediate sense-perception, for magnetism and clairvoyance. Without recourse to the universal, the *Volk* dissipates. But it is precisely in this dissipation that it displays its irreducibility and specificity. Hegel, for whom everything is a hieroglyph of the concrete universal, is incapable of granting that the essence of a people could be other than Spirit.

Yet confronted with the self-assertion of the French people as the people of the universal, the German *Volk* of the Wars of Liberation could only truly maintain its specificity through its invention as the people of the unsublatably specific. At the hands of Romanticism, the abstract universals of the French Revolution were forced into a grotesque trial of strength with all that was most virulently parochial, antiquated, and petty in German culture. Romanticism was never far removed from the art of the saboteur. Into the smooth space of a Europe that revolutionary imperialism first created before sweeping across it in conquest, the Romantics injected a fatherland inaccessible beneath its garbage. Germany thereby reasserted itself in its barbaric specificity, in the idiocy by which the classical world named that which is inviolably and unenviably one's own. Ahead of the invading armies, the Romantics depopulated the countryside and the people that vanished left behind only the intractable and indigestible fragments of its superstitions. Ludwig Tieck's *Märchen* are not dissimilar in purpose to the burning of Moscow. The Nature of Romanticism is, in this respect, a scorched earth. It is only in fleeing French *civilisation* that the German people comes upon Nature, and comes upon it, fittingly stripped back to *Naturerscheinungen* (natural phenomena), as the dystopia of logical mediation. The propensity in later German nationalist circles for biologistic conceptions of the people has its roots in this political appropriation of Nature by the Romantics,[46] no matter how little the appropriation was understood in its intended disruption of the reconciliation of the individual and the universal. The Nature of German Romanticism is not the ground on which positivism later established the specificity of the people and secured it for universal recognition, but rather the abyss in which the specificity of the *Volk* is scattered as hallucinations, secrets, magical interventions, and somnambulism. In its inability to come to itself, this people is the abolition of the Enlightenment, rather than its sublation in Hegel's Absolute Spirit. The abstract universal of the autonomous subject does not give way to the Prussian state. Instead, the political stage is cleared for will-o'-the-wisps. Under Romanticism, the πόλις is to be rethought from its very beginnings.

The *Volk* is missing, and in the 1920s, in conditions at once reminiscent of and infinitely removed from the Wars of Liberation, National Socialism went looking for a people. Repudiating the possibility of democracy in the absence of a people, the movement insinuated into the political discourse of the Weimar Republic the topoi of Romanticism. As the populism of a people to come, National Socialism could deny itself any accommodation with the existing governmental structures and yet, through the citation of precedents, insist on a fundamental conservatism. In its indifference to matters of public doctrine and in its devotion to genealogy, the Nazi movement applied itself to the mass detection of forerunners. Hence, even as it declared the national revolution in 1933 and set about the provision of schooling in race doctrine (*Rassenkunde*) for the people that had come, the new regime still urged its consanguinity with incompatible previous formulations of the notion of the German *Volk*. That Heidegger could have sought admittance to the NSDAP despite his rejection of its biologism is largely inexplicable without this amorphousness of the official ideology. Although in hindsight the openness with which the regime appeared to address the question of the people was unmistakably its indiscriminate responsiveness to the shibboleth of "*Volk*", Heidegger, for the sake of what he considered to be National Socialism's promise of a revelation of the absence proper to historicality, turned a blind eye to this lack of discrimination.

But then the continuity of German nationalism was not in general subjected to criticism. Patriotic texts such as Fichte's *Addresses to the German Nation* from 1808 could thus be interpreted by zealots of the movement as an anticipation of National Socialist thinking. Max Wundt, Alfred Baeumler, and various lesser figures in the Deutsche Philosophische Gesellschaft, all paid homage to Fichte. But what was the similarity, if any, between Fichte's Germans and the racial specimens of the Nazi movement? In the seventh address, Fichte famously passes over everything positive to arrive at his definition of the German people:

All who either are themselves alive and creative and productive of new things, or who, should this not have fallen to their lot, at any rate definitely abandon the things of naught and stand on the watch for the stream of original life to lay hold of them somewhere, or who, should they not even be so far advanced as this, at least have an inkling of freedom and do not hate it or take fright at it, but on the contrary love it—all these are original men; they are, when considered as a people, an original people, *the* people simply, Germans.[47]

There is nothing of the biological in this definition. Whoever loves freedom is German. By 1808, *le peuple* of the French Revolution, which had defined itself by its love of freedom rather than by national characteristics, had shown, through its submission to the Napoleonic dictatorship, the spuriousness of its love of freedom. In contrast, the Germans, so long as they combat their oppression, are seen as the people that loves freedom and are hence *the* people. And this people, regardless of the speaker, is also always "our" people because it is the people that stands closest to us in the philosophically original freedom of humanity. Inasmuch as Fichte's *Addresses to the German Nation* were already established as canonical texts of German nationalism in Wilhelmine Germany, later nationalist movements invariably seem more indebted to their disquisitions than was, in fact, the case. The genealogical legitimacy of the nationalism of National Socialism was a moot point on which the clerks of the movement expended a frantic ingenuity. The people that asserts itself in 1933 does not, and dares not, entirely renounce its Romanticism.

Given the intellectual promiscuity of National Socialism, it is impossible, as is often noted, to set forth National Socialist thinking in anything like a comprehensive set of theses. The nationalism of the NSDAP eludes definition and has always already overtaken every critique directed at it from a nationalistic position. Heidegger's engagement and disengagement with National Socialism are complicated by this equivocation. Deviations become indistinguishable from expansions, and conformances take on the appearance of containments. Admitting, as it were, the interpenetration of his engagement and disengagement, Heidegger published in 1953 the following remarks on "the inner truth" of National Socialism: "The works that are being peddled about nowadays as the philosophy of National Socialism but have nothing whatever to do with the inner truth and greatness of this movement (namely the encounter between global technology and modern man)—have all been written by men fishing in the troubled waters of 'values' and 'totalities.'"[48] This passage from *An Introduction to Metaphysics* is almost as inscrutable as National Socialism itself. Its year of publication excludes at least one reading, namely, that Heidegger is here paying lip service to the regime. The parenthesis elucidating the "inner truth" of National Socialism is more than likely to date from a period subsequent to the 1935 summer semester in which Heidegger delivered the text in a course of lectures. Absolute certainty on this point is, however, impossible, because the page in question is missing from the otherwise intact manuscript in the Heidegger Archive at Marbach. Rainer Marten, privy to the consultations surrounding the publication of the lectures, has divulged that the parenthesis was Heidegger's concession to the editorial assistants advising him to delete the inflammatory sentence in its entirety.[49] When the parenthesis turned out not to forestall controversy, Heidegger saw fit in a letter reproduced in *Die Zeit* on September 24, 1953, to endorse an earlier reading by Christian Lewalter. On August 13, Lewalter had argued in *Die Zeit* that the sentence, allegedly judging the regime against an *inner* truth and greatness alien to its explicit pronouncements and practices, amounted to a condemnation of National Socialism. Heidegger's clarificatory intervention was too exceptional a gesture, and its circumstances too obviously crucial to the casting of his postwar reputation, for anything here to be straightforward. Thirteen years later, the interview with *Der Spiegel* on September 23, 1966, "Nur ein Gott kann uns noch retten" ("Only a God Can Save Us"), is perhaps even more tortuous. There the rectorship becomes a series of compromises with the NSDAP, and any tie between Heidegger's thinking and the regime is pushed into the background: any attempt at an exposition of this tie is taken as little more than a foray into persecution. Was Heidegger a Nazi? Was National Socialism Heideggerian? These questions do not yet really say anything, however, and it is thus imperative that those passages in which Heidegger is at least to some degree open about his engagement not be relinquished. In 1953, Heidegger is still able to defend the "inner truth" of the movement against its usurpation in the value philosophy of Bruno Bauch and the totality philosophy of Ernst Krieck. The ambiguity in the doctrine of the NSDAP that permitted conflicting presentations of its unspoken truth likewise rendered impossible its own exhaustive realization. Heidegger in 1953 stands by the "inner truth" of a movement too nebulous to have received its refutation in World War II.

Understandably unwilling to countenance the provocation of this fidelity, Silvio Vietta neglects the "inner truth" and fixes upon the "greatness" of the movement in his commentary on the text: "Nobody who has read the *Contributions to Philosophy* will be able to say that the concept of 'quantity', of the 'gigantic' and therefore of 'greatness' is being used here in a positive sense." [50] Vietta's dedication to apologetics represses Heidegger's (retrospective) insight into his engagement with National Socialism and offers—and then only implicitly, such is its reverence—the philosophical vacuity of an error of judgment.

In 1953, after having carried out a protracted, if undeniably covert polemic against National Socialism in his wartime lectures on Nietzsche and Hölderlin, Heidegger still maintains that the "inner truth" of the movement differed from what was, for him, its exoteric truth as the acceleration and intensification of technicism. Here the reality of the movement is being condemned by its promise.

What Heidegger considers the promise of National Socialism is set forth at greater length in an earlier, likewise notorious passage from *An Introduction to Metaphysics*. Expounding the opposition between German nationalism and technicism and foreseeing a people that will *as a people* avert the destruction of Europe, Heidegger writes:

This Europe, in its ruinous blindness forever on the point of cutting its own throat, lies today in a great pincers, squeezed between Russia on one side and America on the other. From a metaphysical point of view, Russia and America are the same; the same dreary technological frenzy, the same unrestricted organization of the average man. . . .

We are caught in a pincers. Situated in the center, our people incurs the severest pressure. It is the people with the most neighbours and hence the most endangered. With all this, it is the most metaphysical of peoples. We are certain of this definition, but our people will only be able to wrest a destiny from it if *within itself* it creates a resonance, a possibility of resonance for this definition, and takes a creative view of its tradition. All this implies that this people, as a historical people, must move itself and thereby the history of the West from within the center of their future "happening" into the primordial realm of the powers of Being. If the great decision regarding Europe is not to bring annihilation, that decision must be made in terms of new *spiritual* energies unfolding historically from out of the center.[51]

With its definition of "our people" as "the most metaphysical of peoples," this passage employs a trope of German cultural nationalism.[52] But Heidegger's use of this trope involves a particular understanding of "metaphysics." Is the most metaphysical people here the most nationalistic? And is nationalism to be understood as metaphysics? According to this geophilosophical excursus, America and Russia do not differentiate themselves. The specificity that would belong to them as peoples, and constitute the basis of a nationalism, is annulled in their programmatic standardization of humanity and their immersion in technicism. Owing to their positions on a periphery flimsily characterized by its distance from Central Europe, America and Russia are poor in neighbors and thus not endangered. The people that is richest in neighbors is the most endangered people and also the most metaphysical. It confronts the danger, not of effacing itself in the identity of one of its many neighbors, but rather of losing itself in the anonymity in which its neighbors have already lost themselves. The nationalism to which Heidegger could be read as exhorting the people of the center is thus less the assertion of a given people's distinct identity among the distinct identities of neighboring peoples than the assertion of the nonuniversality of a people against global anonymity. What is at issue in this nationalism is not the identification and documentation of unique properties, but instead that which in a people as such sets it apart from the uniform organization of reified humanity. Such a nationalism must ask after that which is not present-at-hand. For Heidegger, this is metaphysics (it is only in subsequent texts that metaphysics is no longer interpreted as the question of Being, but rather as the obliviousness to Being). The people of the center remains as yet the *Volk* because it is metaphysical. The *Volk* thinks the difference of Being from that which is present-at-hand and manipulable by technology, and it thinks this difference as the truth of its own historicality. The *Volk* is never anything other than spiritual because it is never other than thoughtful. In the language of *Being and Time*, the *Volk* is an *existentiell* modification. However certain Heidegger may be of the correctness of his definition (*Bestimmung*) of the Germans, it is, as a vocation (*Bestimmung*), also a definition whose time has not yet come: the *definiendum* has still to bring itself into agreement with the *definiens*. Only as the people of metaphysics will the Germans be able to fulfil their mission. Only as the people that is nothing but a "folkish" science and an understanding of the worldliness of its Being-with-one-another will they be able to transpose the West from the unchecked disposability and hence destructibility of beings under technicism into the originary realm of the powers of Being. The German mission thus reaches beyond the Germans by not reaching beyond their essence as a people. The scope of the German mission is not, however, a clandestine universalism. The Germans are to raise the promised question concerning the essence of Being less on behalf of other peoples than against the standardization by which the various peoples have fallen away from the possibility of grasping their own essential historicality.

The new spiritual energies of the center are to unfold historically. Unless Heidegger's juxtaposition of "spiritual" and "historically" is to be understood as an uncharacteristic subordination of "historicality" to "spirit," "spirit" is not here being given a sense in conformity with the metaphysics of subjectity. Derrida contends in *Of Spirit* that, with his opposition to the biologism of National Socialism, Heidegger lapses into the metaphysics of subjectity:

One cannot demarcate oneself from biologism, from naturalism, from racism in its genetic form, one cannot be *opposed* to them except by reinscribing spirit in an oppositional determination, by once again making it a unilaterality of subjectity, even if in its voluntarist form. The constraint of this program remains very strong, it reigns over the majority of discourses which, today and for a long time to come, state their opposition to racism, to totalitarianism, to nazism, to fascism, etc., and do this in the name of spirit, and even of the freedom of (the) spirit, in the name of an axiomatic—for example, that of democracy or "human rights"—which, directly or not, comes back to this metaphysics of *subjectity*.[53]

Derrida's criticism turns upon a direct association of oppositional determination with the metaphysics of subjectity. Heidegger's "spirit" stands in opposition to biologism, but that is not to say that it is determined by this opposition as a being present in its distinctness. "Spirit" is in opposition to the "matter" of American and Russian materialism, and yet it is not the spirit that comes to itself as the subject in opposition to matter, in a specious opposition to that which is present-at-hand. It does not come to itself because to do so, to be present before matter in its presence would denote precisely a mitigation of its opposition to the ontological foundations of matter in the understanding of Being as presence. Heidegger's "spirit" does not stand in an oppositional determination to the biologism of Nazi Germany or the technological frenzy of Russia and America because it is defined rather by the transcendence that precedes and ontologically encompasses all of them. The simultaneous opposition and contamination of "spirit" is to be explained by reference less to the "mistake" of a lapse into the metaphysics of subjectity than to the very nature of transcendence. Heidegger's "metaphysical" people is anything but the unambiguous concomitant of a biologistically determined race. Its metaphysicality is not a property that it would possess in the manner of physical attributes such as levels of pigmentation. Its metaphysicality is not its identifiability, but on the contrary its historicality and hence undecidability under the categories of recognition of the understanding of Being as presence.

The essence of the Germans is their mission and this mission is to be the *Volk*, to be the spirit that to the extent that it does *not* become universal is in some way to unfold outward from the center to America and Russia. In his study of the utterances of National Socialism, Jean-Pierre Faye remarks upon the etymological linkage between the Old High German word *diutisk* (of the people) and *völkisch* (folkish), calling the Germans "the people of tautology."[54] It is a tautology that Heidegger sets to work. The Germans are, paradoxically, to be the people for the West as a whole, since they alone are still capable of preserving a distance from the cosmopolitanism of the technologically undifferentiated. They preserve this distance in the questionability of metaphysics. This questionability, which is irreducible to the universal of the "they," is the element of the historicality of the *Volk*, of the struggling and the communicating of authentic Being-with-one-another. Running away from the vitiated, inauthentic communication of the universal, a people always runs toward a more authentic confrontation in the question of Being. What is thereby communicated and brought to the fore is the transcendence essential to communication and not any content whose reiterability could be mistaken for the basis of communication. It is accordingly in terms of a dialogue, in which everything rests on the "between" of the parties, that Heidegger in 1937 treats the relations between France and Germany. In the essay "Wege zur

Aussprache" ("Paths to an Open Discussion"), included in the volume *Alemannenland: Ein Buch von Volkstum und Sendung*, edited by Franz Kerber (Stuttgart, 1937), he warns against a too placid interpretation of communicating: "Authentic understanding of one another does not engender the tranquillity that at once deteriorates into a mutual indifference. On the contrary, it is in itself the unrest of the reciprocal self-questioning out of concern for the shared historical tasks."[55] Understanding between peoples neither levels nor codifies their differences. It calls the identities of the peoples into question. Heidegger's nationalism is neither pacifist nor isolationist, because a people asserts itself in its questionability against the self-evidence of that which is everywhere the same. National Socialism, which was likewise neither pacifist nor isolationist, nonetheless betrayed its own "folkish" promise by not rigorously carrying through its assertion of the people to a global confrontation with technicism.

For Heidegger, the Third Reich was ultimately too *little* of a pariah among the neighboring nations of technicism. The regime's failure to differentiate itself is manifest even in the racial policies for which its military opponents reserved their greatest vilification. The National Socialist concept of race remains subject to technicism because the beings to which it applies are exhaustively defined by properties and present themselves as material for manipulation. For the sake of certainty and the transhistorical iterability of its judgments, the *Rassenkunde* of the regime situated its field of study in the present-at-hand. Unable and unwilling to contest the thinking of modern science in anything but details, the National Socialist theoreticians of race brought to the question of the essence of a people an inapposite and paranoiac demand for certainty. The fancied self-evidence of the notion of certainty was the excuse for the open stifling of the questionability of the essence of a people as something negligently inexact. From the incontestability of a distinction grounded in "facts," anti-Semitism, for instance, was to be invested with a semblance of consistency and realism. That the biologistic efforts of the movement in *Rassenkunde* were directed precisely against the questionability of the essence of a people can be inferred from the writings of Hitler himself. For the space of a moment in *Mein Kampf*, Hitler appears to acknowledge the irrelevance of properties when he recalls an episode from his youth in Vienna:

Once, as I was strolling through the Inner City, I suddenly encountered an apparition in a black caftan and black hair locks. Is this a Jew? was my first thought.

For, to be sure, they had not looked like that in Linz. I observed the man furtively and cautiously, but the longer I stared at this foreign face, scrutinizing feature after feature, the more my first question assumed a new form:

Is this a German?[56]

It goes without saying that this incident did not become the occasion for a deepening of the questionability of the question of a people. When National Socialism comes to put the question on a scientific basis, it is simply in order to avoid it as a question. The identity of the German people is resolved into the properties of something present-at-hand and rendered certain. The question that asks "Who are the Germans?" is rephrased to read "What are the Germans?" Reification is the safeguard of the people's purity against the contamination characteristic of existentialia. The question "What are the Germans?" is National Socialism's invitation to kitsch. Alpine panoramas and Nordic sagas, granite nudes and granite temples, blonde braids and trench warfare are all swept up to be reinvented as fetishes of a people that is missing. This evidentiality of the Germans is simultaneously their bad faith, since what is adduced is never a people. National Socialism was thus incapable of disputing the etymology of "*deutsch*" that Nietzsche proposes in *Beyond Good and Evil*: the *tiusche Volk* is the *Täusche-Volk*, the people of deceit.[57] In order not to deceive, in order to bring forward *das Deutsche* in absolute clarity, National Socialism courted recognition. Letting the question of the people lapse and thus maintaining world in its oblivion, the regime solicited the attentions of its neighbors through the mendacious positivism of its conception of the Germans. The self-determination denied at Versailles was not so much made good as exaggerated to the point of parody: National Socialism was kitsch transformed into imperialism. Having staked German identity on positive attributes, the movement was, in one sense, bound from the start to a military campaign for global domination. Berlin was to become the aggressive distribution hub for "folkish" paraphernalia and everything bar the symbol and stereotype would be eradicated as an obstacle to recognition. Germany would be recognized at whatever cost. As such illusory self-determination dares ask no more of the recognizing bodies than a mere acknowledgment of its compliance to cliché, Nazi Germany could at the same time not allow itself to be recognized. Its very recognizability was, in the end, an affliction and a sign of weakness to be remedied by the annihilation of the recognizing bodies. The wars of aggression that National Socialism waged against its neighbors were, in this respect, reactive. Nazi imperialism was the hysteric regurgitation of the symbol and the stereotype, its racism its very acquiescence to the universal.

Already in 1934, Emmanuel Lévinas was in a position to expose the anti-cosmopolitanism of the new regime as a sham. In his article "Reflections on the Philosophy of Hitlerism," first published in *Esprit*, there is the following exposition and analysis:

> Any rational assimilation or mystical communion between spirits that is not based on a community of blood is suspect. And yet the new type of truth cannot renounce the formal nature of truth and cease to be universal. In vain is truth *my* truth in the strongest sense of this possessive pronoun, for it must strive towards the creation of a new world. . . .
>
> How is universality compatible with racism? The answer—to be found in the logic of what first inspires racism—involves a basic modification of the very idea of universality. *Universality must give way to the idea of expansion.*[58]

A truth that is mine alone is a contradiction. In racism, according to Lévinas, universality is modified rather than renounced, since it cannot be renounced without likewise renouncing any claim to truth. The military operations of Hitlerian Germany can accordingly be viewed as a half measure, as testimony to the apprehensiveness with which National Socialism set about breaking with the universal. Even before it declared war, the regime was in the wrong, and it was the sentence passed on its chauvinism by the universal that it sought to reverse by global conquest. Lévinas, who, in the above quotation, sees the parallel between the universality of an idea and the universalism of imperialist expansion, does not however hesitate in his subsequent anti-Romantic exoneration of the idea, "for the expansion of a force presents a structure that is completely different from the propagation of an idea."[59] Contrary to his earlier analysis, National Socialism is thus to be understood as the *unqualified* alternative to the universality of the idea it nevertheless apes. The possibility of a genuine confrontation with the universal thereby remains unexamined.

Lévinas does not go beyond a morphology of the universal. What he musters against racist imperialism is the spreading of an idea: the conscience-salving myth of the cultural benevolence of French colonialism receives a new lease on life through the comparison with Hitler's territorial ambitions. Having no idea to propagate, and thus having nothing to offer the subject peoples in an "exchange," Hitler is able to aspire to nothing more than a universality maintained by an external and inscrutable force.

Since for Lévinas the desirability of universality is never doubted, the deliberate act of offering that which cannot be accepted and rendered universal is nonsensical. By this account, the people's detritus by means of which the German Romantics sought to resist the conquering French liberalism was, in its irreconcilability with the universal, simply detritus. In this text, Lévinas displays a Hegelian disregard for the essential meagerness of a people. Isolating racism with regard to its simulation of the universality of the idea, he does not ask whether the question of the people is not similarly counterfeited in racism's community of blood. Yet, as Lévinas himself suggests, the logic of what first inspires racism is not the question of a people but expansionism. Not the singularity of a people, but rather an allegedly universal quantitative matter ("strength"), which in its unequal distribution determines the inferiority and superiority of respective peoples, is the ultimate foundation of racism.[60] Racism is already too removed from race, in the direction of the universal by which the necessarily inessential superiority of a people is judged, for its anti-cosmopolitanism to be substantial. Although it does not propagate an idea in Lévinas's sense of a cultural artifact, it does attempt to compel recognition of its own claim to instantiate the idea of the power of blood. The ferocity and clamor with which National Socialism pursued its ethnic policies should not consequently be misunderstood. Having come to signify the *ne plus ultra* of racism, the regime nonetheless did not surpass the Romantics in their dedication to the question of the people. The incompatibility of the question of the people with universality was not acknowledged.

To draw a distinction between racism and the question concerning the essence of a people does not of course establish the "innocence" of Heidegger's engagement with National Socialism. This engagement is overdetermined. Confronted with its ambiguity, and indignant at a perceived neglect of the people in *Being and Time*, Ernst Krieck interprets Heidegger's rectorial address as a cynical adaptation to the year 1933.[61] Similarly distancing Heidegger all too quickly from the regime, Jean Beaufret embarked after the war on an almost militant program of exculpation.[62] But that Heidegger would have applied for membership in the NSDAP, with a view to furthering his career, only once the party was in power seems implausible given his subsequent refusal of more prestigious chairs at the Universities of Berlin and Munich. The explanation of his refusal, "Why Do We Stay in the Provinces?" has strikingly less to do with ambition than with an inventory of the commonplaces of rustic literature. And that Heidegger's involvement with the regime was but a momentary lapse in judgment, a blind spot inassimilable to his character and work, is a decreasingly tenable interpretation: a 1929 letter by Heidegger, published in *Die Zeit* by Ulrich Sieg,[63] expresses an anti-Semitism that the inordinate controls on the Marbach archive must be suspected of wishing to conceal. For Heidegger, more was at stake in 1933 than the question concerning the essence of the people. If this question can illuminate his political engagement, it nonetheless cannot fully account for it, just as it cannot be conflated with every aspect of the Hitlerian regime: contiguity is other than identity.

The absence of this reservation leads Jürgen Habermas's presentations of Heidegger's thinking into the realm of caricature. In his defense of the universal, Habermas exploits the overdetermination of Heidegger's engagement with National Socialism. Once the question concerning the essence of a people has been associated with anti-Semitism, or with any of the enormities of the regime, the task of a meticulous refutation of Heidegger's critique of universality readily appears superfluous. In *The Philosophical Discourse of Modernity*, Habermas is keen to suggest a connection between totalitarianism and Heidegger's abandonment of Edmund Husserl's definition of truth in favor of the rootedness that he attributes in 1933 to a "folkish" science. Habermas's argument for the philosophical restoration of global intersubjectivity proceeds by innuendo. Referring to the critique of reason that Heidegger grounds in the history of Being, he writes: "It reserves the title of truth for the so-called truth occurrence, which no longer has anything to do with a validity-claim transcending space and time. The truths (emerging in the plural) of this temporalized *Ursprungsphilosophie* are in each case provincial and yet total; they are more like the commanding expressions of some sacral force fitted out with the aura of truth."[64] Habermas sets forth the truths of the Heideggerian *Ursprungsphilosophie* (philosophy of origins) as simulacra possessing no more than the "aura" of truth. The sacral force of these provincial, yet total, truths is a mere substitute for the truth defined for Habermas by its transcendence of space and time. With its mere aura of truth, the Heideggerian truth occurrence (*Wahrheitsgeschehen*) becomes a travesty of the universal. To the extent that it no longer has anything to do with a validity-claim transcending space and time, the truth occurrence has to content itself, according to Habermas, with issuing decrees. Heidegger's destruction of the correspondence theory of truth is made to arrive at the commanding expressions of ideology, rather than the clearing of beings. If Heidegger's so-called truth occurrence no longer has anything to do with a validity-claim that absolves itself from a given space and time, it is not because it is satisfied with the narrower scope of a decree. Heidegger pushes the thought of transcendence further than Habermas. For the latter, the transcendence of validity-claims is their ahistorical and atopic presence: it is transcendence as a merely extrinsic relation to that from which the validity-claims are abstracted and not transcendence as the being-outside-of-itself of the Heideggerian understanding of truth. That by which Heidegger's understanding of truth exceeds presence is, for Habermas, its deficiency, its dissipation in the dubiousness of an aura. It is as though, having been bundled under the rubric of National Socialism, whatever in Heidegger's thinking challenges the universal could ipso facto be dismissed. To put it at its bluntest: Auschwitz again becomes a means of silencing minorities, since the argument that, with an air of probity, expends itself on the nationalism of genocide slyly takes in every configuration of the social field that would contest its identification in Habermas's neo-metaphysics. The question concerning the historical essence of a people is the question of the validity of the validity-claims that transcend space and time—as such it is suspect for Habermas. What Habermas misses in Heidegger's engagement is that which is *essentially* missing: he believes he "sees" the *Volk* when all he sees is *Völkermord*.

In Nazi Germany, the people is not that which makes itself visible everywhere. On this point, Habermas is too credulous. Falling behind the Romantics, National Socialism also fell behind its own victims with respect to the modesty of the essence of a people. If this modesty was the "inner truth" of the movement, and hence the proof of its outer falsehood, the "folkish" politics by which it had characterized itself could not but have become an unbearable affront in the shape of the minorities existing under its dictatorship. Incapable of carrying through the rupture with the transnational, the regime visited genocide on the minorities from within whose powerlessness the question concerning the essence of a people still sounded. In the end, the bruited *Umbruch* of 1933, the so-called radical change that in Heidegger's view had portended for the Germans the chance of a "folkish" science, was itself the obstruction standing between them and their vocation as the "metaphysical" people. Having asserted itself, only to be diverted at once through technicism and imperialism from its essence in the question of Being, the *Volk* had become nothing but its own impossibility. Giving itself up entirely to its visibility, it surrendered the modesty in which it could have asked after the non-presence of Being. It had asserted itself as the *Volk* without becoming the understanding of temporality that for Heidegger defines the *Volk*. It is his attention to this contradiction that excuses the conspicuous alarmism with which Heidegger, in the years of Hitler's dictatorship, surveys the obliviousness to Being, since obliviousness to Being, discussed with Spinozistic equanimity in 1927, is an essential possibility of Dasein, whereas it is the impossibility of the *existentiell* modification that is the *Volk*. When Heidegger speaks of a "folkish" science in 1933, he speaks of a science that knows itself, rather than of a science that stands over against the people that it takes for its object. Not every science is "folkish," because not every science knows its own rootedness. It is the *knowledge* of this rootedness rather than its mere actuality that constitutes for Heidegger the "folkishness" of a science and the consummation of knowledge. The *Volk* knows itself as the *Volk*, and that is to say it knows itself in its world in its difference from beings present-at-hand. A "folkish" movement that, notwithstanding its "folkishness," exacerbated the obliviousness to Being could accordingly have been viewed by Heidegger only with incredulity and dismay.

And yet, at least to begin with, this was not the case. The people that was suddenly present everywhere was to be the occasion of the questioning concerning the essence of Being. Heidegger's engagement with National Socialism is clearly inextricable from his ontology. This thesis, which is familiar from innumerable polemics, remains superficial so long as it is not elaborated in an exposition of the philosophical course of this engagement. For Heidegger, in 1933, ontology was the affair of that which, in the jargon of National Socialism, was denominated *völkische Wissenschaft*. This instance of linguistic submissiveness appears scarcely resuscitable. By using the loaded word *völkisch* and not *volklich, volkhaft*, or for that matter *populär*, Heidegger marries his notion of a people's science to the infamy preordained for National Socialism in its entirety. But, it must be asked, to what extent was Heidegger simply adopting a notion already articulated by various claimants to the position of party ideologue? When Heidegger in the late 1930s and early 1940s explicitly criticizes the idea of a *völkische Wissenschaft*, it is without abandoning the conjunction of a people and understanding that he endeavored in 1933 to think within the jargon of National Socialism: *völkische Wissenschaft* is criticized as a science not of the people but of the subject masquerading as a people. For an intimation of what was at stake for Heidegger in 1933, of what was to be won and of what was lost, the conjunction of a people and the understanding of Being has to be examined in its equivocal relations to National Socialism. The *Umbruch* of the National Socialist revolution, inasmuch as it interpreted itself as the overthrow and elimination of Western liberalism at the hands of a "folkish" uprising, appeared to repeat on a larger scale the partisan response of the Romantics to the Napoleonic abstract universal. With the attempt to grasp the world of the *Volk*, the prevailing understanding of beings as present-at-hand was no longer to be merely contested but overcome in the questioning with regard to the unthought essence of Being. For this task, the *Volk* of National Socialism proved however to be too Cartesian.

The many scattered anti-Cartesian objections that Heidegger raises to the ideas of *Volk* and *völkische Wissenschaft* after his rectorship are not alien to his early thought in their argumentation. It cannot, therefore, be assumed that through these objections Heidegger disowns that which he himself had understood in 1933 by the term *völkische Wissenschaft*.[65] The objections can be plausibly read as clarifications, and even defenses, of the latter notion.

For example, in the *Contributions to Philosophy* of 1936–38, Heidegger denounces the expediency that renders a "folkish" science essentially cosmopolitan:

Only a thoroughly modern (i.e., "liberal") science can be "a folkish science" [*"eine völkische Wissenschaft"*]. Only on the basis of prioritizing procedure over the subject-matter and the accuracy of judgment over the truth of beings does modern science permit an adjustable shifting to various purposes, depending on need (implementation of extreme materialism and technicism by Bolshevism; introduction of four-year plans; usefulness for political education). In all of this, science is everywhere *the same* and becomes, precisely with these various goal-settings, basically and increasingly more uniform, that is, more "international."[66]

By placing "a folkish science" in quotation marks, Heidegger indicates that the term is not to be taken at face value. In disregard of the National Socialist antithesis of "liberal" and "folkish," a "folkish" science is here said to be, at bottom, a liberal science. Expediency for the *Volk* (expressed in the slogan "Wahr ist, was dem Volke nützt"—"True is that which serves the people") is only possible on the provision that the *Volk* has assumed the cast of the Cartesian subject and thus stands in an ontic opposition to that which is to be manipulated and exploited. By prioritizing mathematical procedure over the matter of thought and certainty over the ecstatic truth of beings, Descartes flattened the phenomenon of world to what could be wielded in the service of the needs of the moment. The "politicization" of science under National Socialism only made science still more liberal, because its subordination to the "good" of the biologistically determined *Volk* necessitated the hardening of the subjective, de-worlded, and hence cosmopolitan, starting point of modern science. In spite of its polemics against liberalism, National Socialism retained the place of the individual in science and saw to it that it was occupied by "the people." The modern identity of expediency and science, which had come under threat in the demythologization of the subject, was to be shored up by sheer weight of numbers. Through its notion of the people, National Socialism unwittingly revealed itself to be liberalism's response to its critics.[67]

When, in is 1942–43 lecture course *Parmenides*, Heidegger dismisses the antithesis of *Volk* and individual, he thereby repeats a gesture from *Being and Time* but in order to deliver the *Volk* up at once to liberalism:

> The concepts of "people" [*die Volkheit*] and "folk" [*das Völkische*] are founded on the essence of subjectivity and Ego. Only when metaphysics, i.e., the truth of beings as a whole, has been founded on subjectivity and the Ego do the concepts of "nation" and "people" obtain that metaphysical foundation from which they might possibly have historical relevance. Without Descartes, i.e., without the metaphysical foundation of subjectivity, Herder, i.e., the foundation of the concept of a people [*die Gründung der Volkheit der Völker*], cannot be thought. Whether one can retrospectively establish historiographical relations between these two is a matter of indifference, since historiographical relations are always only the façade, and for the most part the concealing façade, of historical nexuses. As long as we know with insufficient clarity the proper essence of subjectivity as the modern form of selfhood, we are prey to the error of thinking that the elimination of individualism and of the domination of the individual is ipso facto an overcoming of subjectivity.[68]

In this passage, the *Volk* is seen to rest on the subject rather than to stand in opposition to the metaphysics of the obliviousness to Being (*Seinsvergessenheit*). Is Heidegger therefore criticizing his earlier definition of *Volk*? It seems unlikely, given that in *Being and Time*, the individualism satirized in the chapter on the "they" does not make room for a *Volk* still determined by the self-identity of the modern subject. The *Volk* that apprehends itself in its certainty as a self is much more the *Volk* of National Socialism with its conviction of its oneness and distinctness. Without a comprehension of the essence of subjectivity, the transition from the subject to the *Volk*, a transition that Heidegger defends in *Being and Time* and that he believes he later greets in the National Socialist revolution, runs the risk of being frustrated in a reconfiguration of the subject. The subjectivity of the subject, and of a people, is the inability to suspect self-certainty and to question the givenness of beings, that is, both the givenness of the people-subject and that of the beings always already understood to be manipulable.

To repeat: what Heidegger holds against National Socialism is its liberalism. The exceptional character of this objection—and certainly it cannot be argued that liberalism and National Socialism are one and the same on all counts—has frequently entailed its summary dismissal.[69] In Theodor Adorno's view, for instance, Heidegger never ceased to be a Nazi. And, indeed, on the basis of Heidegger's comments concerning "the inner truth and greatness of this movement," it could be claimed that, in the context of his postwar reticence about the regime, his sole reproach against National Socialism was that it did not live up to expectations. For Heidegger, the NSDAP had turned out to be nothing but Cartesianism for the masses. The movement was too Herderian, which is to say, too Cartesian, to think the notion of the *Volk* through to the other ontology that would have been the fulfillment of its "folkish" promise. While F. M. Barnard disputes any connection between Herder and National Socialism on the grounds of the former's liberalism,[70] it is in liberalism that the Heidegger of the *Contributions to Philosophy* discerns the basis for the subordination of science to the "good" of the *Volk*. Evading an interrogation of the subjectivity of the subject, National Socialism remained dependent on Herder's own derivative formulation of the *Volkheit der Völker* and can thus be said to have been a monstrous relic of the Enlightenment. The movement did not spring from the sleep of reason but rather from the rationalism that would allow nothing to remain outside its light. At the expense of an understanding of world, it endeavored to capture the essence of a people in the clarity of presence and thereby in the ontology of the present-at-hand. Certainly a biologistic conception of humanity cannot be discovered in Herder, yet with his thesis of the individuality of peoples, he advances the notion of their unitarity and equality, and hence ultimately, albeit perversely, their commensurability. Each realizes humanity in a different and legitimate way. Herder's cosmopolitanism is always at risk of seeing beyond differences. The equality of peoples that he proposes in his essay "Von Ähnlichkeit der mittleren englischen und deutschen Dichtkunst" ("On the Similarity of Middle English and German Poetry") as a principle for historiography is more than simply contemporaneous with the equality of individuals found in the French Revolution. What the latter constitutes on the national level, Herder's principle constitutes on the global. Herder's open-mindedness toward other peoples, regardless of how incompatible it is in many respects with National Socialism, is likewise a repression of what is specific to a people and thus of a people itself. For the sake of commensurability, Herder turns aside from the historicality of a people, and thereby from the inappropriateness of the universal to this historicality.

The essence of a people is, for Herder, its "humanity." This is evident in his conception of language. In the prize essay "Ueber den Ursprung der Sprache" ("On the Origin of Language"), Herder impoverishes the phenomenon of language to an unadduced common grammar in order to emphasize its planetary unity. The *animal rationale* is the planetary, and yet worldless, animal: it enunciates its distinctness from all the endemic species through language, which is declared to be only superficially differentiated by climate, terrain, diet, and so forth. Herder thus acknowledges the differences between peoples merely so as to stage their disappearance in the ideal of humanity. Language becomes the universal under which the various peoples are subsumed. A people thereby ceases to speak as a people in its finitude and worldliness, because it always speaks away from itself and its historicality to the ahistorical generality of its humanity. In rising above its world to its humanity, a people acquires an essence that is its transhistorical recognizability and, with this reformulation in eternity, it forfeits the chance to challenge the understanding of Being as presence and thereby to think its own Being. In contrast to Herder's language of humanity, Heidegger emphasizes a language of the world of a people. In his 1934 lecture course *Logik als die Frage nach dem Wesen der Sprache*, Heidegger writes: "Language is the sway of the world-shaping and preserving center of the historical Dasein of the people."[71] A people speaks as a people by speaking within its world, and it is by this "inhumanity" that it musters the greatest opposition to the "liberalism" of the Nazi doctrine of race.

"Nazism is a humanism."[72] This sentence of Philippe Lacoue-Labarthe's faithfully condenses Heidegger's account of the movement's degeneration and disaster. For Heidegger, the master race of National Socialism (the subject that has become the measure of all things) was defeated by its own liberalism long before this defeat was revived as farce and referred to the overwhelming military, economic, and technical superiority of its opponents. The expansionism that was the occasion of this secondary defeat was the regime's grotesque reprise of the ideal of humanity and the commensurability of peoples. The master race became the planetary animal, and its confrontation with other peoples had less to do with the self-questioning of authentic understanding of one another than with the self-confirmation of its positivity. German imperialism had always deliberately set itself apart from the specious altruism of the bearers of *civilisation*. But the egotism that Wilhelmine Germany expressed in its colonialist watchword "A place in the sun," and to whose exclusive satisfaction the Third Reich consigned the conquered territories, did not distance the German people from the ideal of humanity in any fundamental sense: the people, impossible to ignore in the saturnalia of its gluttony and terror, is not the *Volk* in Heidegger's formulation, but rather the aggrandized subject of liberalism. The catastrophe of National Socialism, as it is interpreted in Heidegger's writings from the later years of the regime, was this stillbirth of the people of the question of Being. A people's self-assertion can never be comparable with the self-assertion of the worldlessness of egotism.

If Heidegger's objection to National Socialism is that it was too liberal, then it may seem that he positions himself thereby to the right of the far Right. The persuasiveness of such an appearance has led to a neglect of the similarities between Heidegger's notion of the *Volk* and, for instance, Deleuze and Guattari's notion of *le peuple à venir* and thus to the misapprehension that Heidegger's *Volk* is of no importance for anything other than a reactionary politics. Indeed, Deleuze and Guattari themselves overlook the similarities. In *Qu'est-ce que la philosophie?* (a book whose title inevitably recalls the lecture "Was ist das, die Philosophie?" that Heidegger delivered to a colloquium in Cerisy-la-Salle at which Deleuze was a participant in August 1955),[73] Deleuze and Guattari reject Heidegger's *Volk* in favor of minorities: "He got the wrong people, earth, and blood. For the race summoned forth by art or philosophy is not one that claims to be pure but rather an oppressed, bastard, lower, anarchical, nomadic, and irremediably minor race."[74] It must be asked whether Deleuze and Guattari, given their thesis in *Anti-Oedipus* concerning the fascism of the exclusive disjunction, can allow their notion of a bastard race to stand forth as clearly as this from Heidegger's people. Admitting that "it is not always easy to be Heideggerian,"[75] Deleuze and Guattari appear, however, to acknowledge the defensive character of their distinction. Heidegger's people, which in the lectures on Hölderlin is summoned forth by poetry, and which, in *Being and Time*, is defined less by purity than by the impurity of its transcendence in co-historizing, is too unsettling a precursor. And it is unsettling because, in its impurity, it could not keep itself clear even of the people of the most fanatical purity of blood. The transcendence of Heidegger's *Volk* did not come to a halt before the NSDAP. Rather than confronting the new regime with a simple negation, Heidegger set about effecting a contamination between its notion of the people and his own. In terms of an immediate resistance to National Socialism, this was to do nothing, and whatever persecution Heidegger claims he suffered after resigning the rectorship is unmentionably trivial in comparison with the measures that the regime was all too willing to take against millions of others.

Heidegger got it wrong, although Deleuze and Guattari concede that it is ultimately not a matter of getting it right or wrong: "Heidegger lost his way along the paths of the reterritorialization because they are paths without directive signs or barriers."[76] Given the arguments against a biologistic conception of humanity that can be drawn from Heidegger's own writings, his engagement is to be understood less in terms of a subscription to the model of National Socialism than as a blind spot in the interpretability of his corpus. Heidegger's greatest failure as a thinker was also his self-confessed "greatest stupidity of his life."[77] With this failure, Heidegger's thought attains, as well as falls prey to, the radical questionability that would otherwise have been denied it.

Wanting to *explain* Heidegger's engagement, rather than to *excuse* it, Deleuze and Guattari comment:

How could Heidegger's concepts not be intrinsically sullied by an abject reterritorialization? Unless all concepts include this gray zone and indiscernibility where for a moment the combatants on the ground are confused, and the thinker's tired eye mistakes one thing for the other—not only the German for a Greek but the fascist for a creator of existence and freedom.[78]

For Deleuze and Guattari, the stain of Heidegger's thinking is not so much unique as exemplary of the tiredness to which the thinker succumbs. But what is really explained by this physiological metaphor? Is an inevitability being attributed to Heidegger's engagement with the implicit reference to the inevitability of tiredness? And how does the tiredness that confuses the German and the Greek, the fascist and the creator of existence, differ from the joyful becoming that, for Deleuze and Guattari, is the transitive indeterminacy between polar identities? Interpreting Heidegger's engagement with reference to the inevitability of tiredness, Deleuze and Guattari excuse more than they explain and, by excusing, forgo an attempt to explain Heidegger's unsettling consanguinity. Heidegger's people in 1933 is a minority in Deleuze and Guattari's sense, because it does not come to itself. It is a minority because it can find itself in the presence of neither a people of a nationalistic self-assertion nor a people that "finds" itself precisely in not finding itself as a political majority. It is torn between a political and cultural nationalism. To clarify a nonpositivistic notion of the people, in explicit contradistinction to the biologistic *Rassenkunde* of the regime, can illuminate Heidegger's own notion of the people in 1933 only to the extent that it establishes the terms of its confusion, which is to say, the terms of its transcendence. Within this confusion, the minority of the Germans, both political and cultural, is prolonged. In the minority by which it overreaches the present-at-hand, the *Volk* touches uncannily on the Un-thought of metaphysics: Being is minoritarian.

Was Heidegger's political engagement less an engagement with the self-assertion of the German people in 1933 than with the self-defeating stupidity of this self-assertion? How, if at all, can the two be distinguished? Deleuze and Guattari consider the possibility that Heidegger's abdication before Hitler was still a philosophical move: "A great philosopher actually had to be reterritorialized on Nazism for the strangest commentaries to meet up, sometimes calling his philosophy into question and sometimes absolving it through such complicated and convoluted arguments that we are still in the dark."[79] Heidegger was reterritorialized on Nazism in the name, as it were, of the ambiguity and impurity of the people. That Deleuze and Guattari speak of Jews, gypsies, and blacks in their treatments of the notion of a people, whereas Heidegger speaks of the Germans, ought not to conceal that it is the status of an ontological exception that comparably inspires these treatments. The people is missing, whether it is in the works of Kafka and the Brazilian filmmaker Glauber Rocha or in the Germany of Heidegger's National Socialism. In his reflections on minoritarian cinema, Deleuze writes: "The people exist only in the condition of minority, which is why they are missing."[80] For Deleuze and Guattari, a people is always a minority because it defines itself by its inability to seize control of the state apparatus. It is too volatile to rally itself for the subjectity of the state, or even that of "the republic of letters." This ontological volatility and undecidability is not the defect of a minority, but its essence, since a minority only acquires an identity through the frustrations, failures, and deviations of its flight from the majority, either by submitting to an alien characterology or fabricating its own in servility to extant models. A people, in Deleuze and Guattari's sense, as in Heidegger's, is a rupture of the identifiable.

Heidegger's "error," and its vertiginous ambivalence, was that he sought to effect the rupture at issue here by means of the state. Drawing their definitions of the state and the people from archaeological and ethnological descriptions of the despotic formations of Asia and the nomadic tribes intermittently breaking away from them, Deleuze and Guattari shield themselves from a repetition of Heidegger's engagement. For Deleuze and Guattari, the state is fundamentally "capture" and a people is fundamentally "rupture." In 1934, when any poorly specified opposition to "the Asiatic" could have been understood as an invitation to racism, Heidegger writes of the common enemy and task of the people and the European state: "A state *is* only inasmuch as it *becomes*, as it turns into the *historical Being* of that being which is called a *people*. The true historical freedom of the peoples of Europe is after all the *precondition* for the West's coming once more *to itself* spiritually-historically and for its taking possession of its fate in the great decision of the earth against the *Asiatic*."[81] What is the Asiatic here that it composes a party in the decision of the earth? An answer that fails completely to make sense of the above quotation, but rather shows up its absurdity, is given twenty-five years later in Heidegger's critique, in "Hölderlin's Earth and Heaven," of Valéry's assessment of the future of Europe:

Immediately after the First World War (1919), Paul Valéry published a letter under the title, "The Crisis of the Spirit". In it he poses two questions:

This Europe, will it become *what it is in reality* (*en réalité*), that is, a small cape of the asiatic continent? Or will this Europe, rather, remain *as what it appears to be* (*ce qu'elle paraît*), that is, the precious part of the whole earth, the pearl of the globe, the brain of a spacious body?

Perhaps Europe has already become what it is: a mere cape, yet as such, also the brain of the entire terrestrial body, the brain that manages the technological-industrial, planetary-interstellar calculation.[82]

Valéry distinguishes from Asia a Europe that has assumed the office of planetary brain, whereas, for Heidegger in 1959, it is the assumption of this very office that recovers Europe for Asia. If Europe's position of global dominance belittles it by turning it into an appendage of the Asian continent, it is because an equation of the Asiatic and the hegemonic is implied in Heidegger's text. However problematic this equation may be, it cannot

be denied its long-standing mythic function in identifying the philosophical and political space known as Europe. Coming to itself in Greece, in
its twofold break with Eastern dogmatism and despotism, Europe has, by
definition, always already succumbed to the temptation to absolutize its
difference from Asia. Querying the absoluteness of this difference in 1959,
Heidegger effectively queries whether the *Völkerwanderung* was anything
more than an Asian colonial expedition. But, in 1934, it is a matter of securing the absoluteness of the difference. Allegedly at the service of this difference, the state is to become the historical Being of a people. Yet the state
that relinquishes its dominion over a people in order to become this people
itself does not abjure the principle of the "Asiatic," since the struggle *against*
the "Asiatic" is, in the despotism and dogmatism of its exclusive disjunction, a struggle *within* the "Asiatic" for the determination of the entities of
its control. Having to think its ownness other than by the identifiable and
controllable, Europe must reassess its critical stand on the pairing of authenticity and idiocy. Europe, if it is to be Europe, cannot risk becoming
more than a phantasm, more than a site of undecidability beyond an un-
specifiable river or mountain range. Europe as Europe cannot be defended.
But is the absurdity in which the 1959 text reveals the text of 1934 not one
of those absolutions that Deleuze and Guattari believe traverse Heidegger's
political engagement? Is it in the very absurdity of the struggle against the
"Asiatic" to which Heidegger rallies the peoples of Europe that Europe as
such unfolds its absolute difference from despotism? Everything becomes
gray in the abyss of stupidity.

Heidegger's hymns to the National Socialist state are too crass in
comparison with his thinking as a whole for these texts not to arouse the
suspicion that here the state is the object of a somber, ignominious humor.
In a speech delivered in August 1934, and thus after his resignation of the
rectorship of Freiburg University, Heidegger appears to "forget" his au-
thorship of *Being and Time*:

The essence of the National Socialist revolution consists in the fact that Adolf
Hitler has elevated that new spirit of the community to being the formative power
of a new configuration of the people. The National Socialist revolution is thus not
the superficial appropriation of the power of a state already in place by a party
grown equal to the task but rather the inner reeducation of the entire people toward the goal of wanting its own unity and oneness. Inasmuch as the people wills
its own vocation, it recognizes the new state. The rule of this state is the responsible implementation of that commanding will to which the dedicated trust of the

people empowers the leadership. The state is not a mechanical apparatus of law alongside the institutions of the economy, art, science, and religion. On the contrary, the state signifies the living configuration pervaded by alternate trust and responsibility in which and through which the people realizes its own historical Dasein.[83]

Can a people, as authentic Being-with-one-another, want, without contradiction, its own unity and oneness? What could be the ontological basis for the unity and oneness of a people? Heidegger's address makes no pretensions to an existential analytic: the people simply *wills* its own oneness. Recognition of the state follows upon this manipulated caprice of the people, and the metaphysics of subjectity in the cast of the people's oneness is perpetuated. Those relations between a people and its sovereign that Hobbes sees as a response to the violence of the state of nature are here, for Heidegger, the consequence of a bluntly posited education and will. Indeed, Heidegger's address reads like a pastiche of Hobbes. The people whose unity Hobbes in *Leviathan* sees represented in the corporeal singleness of its sovereign,[84] and whose acceptance of a sovereign defines it in *De Cive* in distinction from a multitude,[85] is shadowed by a people for whom the realities of the English Civil War have been replaced by the tabula rasa of nihilistic voluntarism. Having dispensed with the externality of circumstances, and thus with the measure that they constitute in Hobbes, Heidegger, in 1933, is able to say of Hitler: "The Führer himself and alone *is* the present and future German reality and its law."[86] This proposition with its unqualified abasement before despotism, like the critique of Valéry in 1959, declares the complete bankruptcy of the myth of Europe. Heidegger's obeisance to Hitler marks the death of philosophy because it reverses the substitution of another ground than that of authority by which Hegel, for one, and with explicit awareness of the conventionality of the definition, defines philosophy in his lectures on its history.[87] This reversal is the death of Europe. The death of philosophy—of that which in his *What Is Philosophy?* Heidegger says it is a tautology to call "Western"[88]—is nonetheless what the necessarily phantasmic character of philosophy presupposes. The Europe that dies in 1933 is the Europe that, in the substantiality of its absolute difference from Asia, never existed as other than an Asian peninsula. Foundational to the identity of that which has escaped the despotic, the myth of Europe would only itself be European if it abstained from the capture and determination proper to the "Asiatic." The struggle against the "Asiatic" thus entails a struggle against the myth of Europe, and where

Heidegger rallies the European states against the "Asiatic," and at the same time preaches unquestioning submission to Hitler, it is the myth of Europe that yields. Heidegger, accordingly, makes of the state a means to rupture the Asiatic identity of Europe.

What must, but cannot, be rescued in Heidegger's abasement before Hitler is this rupture. The intoxicated and unreserved acquiescence to dictatorship is inseparable from the suspicion of the contradictory reterritorialization of European identity and yet cannot be vindicated by it. And that it cannot be vindicated by it is because this acquiescence raises the *question* as such, as the proper-improper site of Europe's difference from dogmatism, first of all against itself. Heidegger's people is, and is not, the people of National Socialism. It is the people of National Socialism because it is the people that National Socialism courted through its promise to break with the despotism of the cosmopolitan and the universal. And it is not the people of National Socialism because the NSDAP reneged on this promise. The distance of Heidegger's *Volk* from the movement as well as its insuperable proximity to it lies in its "ideality" for the movement. The people that National Socialism courted as the self-assertion of the European essence is, in its truth as the question as such, the critical destruction of the Hitlerian dictatorship. This people always escapes despotism because as the phenomenon of world, it is never simply a determinate being for manipulation and control. Heidegger's acquiescence to National Socialism was thus an acquiescence to a despotism grounding itself in the people of its own ultimate impossibility. The ambivalence of Heidegger's engagement is the ambivalence of National Socialism itself. What for Heidegger, in 1953, has not ceased to constitute the inner truth and greatness of the movement is the latter's own impossibility, since it is the same impossibility by which the manipulation of beings in technicism is confronted with its limitations and brought to a recollection of Being.

If not National Socialism, so much as its impossibility, is what is equal to the encounter with τέχνη, then Heidegger's following remark from the interview with *Der Spiegel* is not a retraction of his clarificatory parenthesis in *An Introduction to Metaphysics*: "A decisive question for me today is: how can a political system accommodate itself to the technological age, and which political system would this be? I have no answer to this question. I am not convinced that it is democracy." [89] Democracy here is not being denied as an option alongside other political systems—as though in the past Heidegger had been convinced of the adequacy to the technical age of a given political system. Arguably, for Heidegger, National Socialism was not one political system among others. The undecidable excess of his engagement lies in its being an engagement with the political per se. Heidegger's engagement overreached National Socialism but could not leave it behind and cut itself off from it, because the essence of the Nazi movement, as that with which Heidegger felt himself in solidarity, was not an unrealized abstract ideal but rather the historical, existential thickness of world that is always happening but nonetheless neglected. The NSDAP, solely inasmuch as it was a "folkish" movement, was to reverse this neglect. It is the *Volk* in its irreducibility to reification, rather than any one political system, that is equal to the encounter with τέχνη. To the extent that a political system gives itself up to differentiation from other political systems and thereby neglects the essential indeterminacy of the people, to that extent it is unequal to this encounter. For Heidegger, liberalism and despotism, consumed with their differences from each other, are fundamentally the same in their neglect of the people. Heidegger's rejection of democracy is inextricable from his attempt to think the people as such. Democracy, which for Kant is an oxymoron,[90] is for Heidegger a debasement of the people's transcendent finitude, a debasement that reduces it to the universal by which a people exerts authority over, and in spite of, the political domain.

The Death of Hegel

When Heidegger introduces the word "*Volk*" in §74 of *Being and Time*, it is in the course of an exposition of the essential historicality of Dasein. This historicality, as he claims in the same section, has its ground in finitude: "*Authentic Being-towards-death—that is to say, the finitude of temporality—is the hidden basis of Dasein's historicality.*"[1] Here Dasein is said to be historical, not because of any participation in the events of a people's public life, but rather because of its finitude. Only once the supposedly more abstruse notion of finitude has been understood will the publicity and eventfulness of the everyday notion of history properly acquire intelligibility.

In its authentic Being-toward-death, Dasein is already historical and thus, for Heidegger at least, already the historizing of the *Volk*. Situating the ground of historicality in finitude, and mentioning the *Volk* only to define its historizing by the destiny of Dasein, Heidegger aligns the people with the question of death. The people can rise up *as the people* only in and for its finitude; it does not face its death in order to overcome it, but on the contrary to run toward it (*in den Tod vorlaufen*) and to think the temporality of this anticipation and of the Being thereby revealed as its own in its irreducibility to presence.

From *Being and Time*, Heidegger took into his engagement with National Socialism a grotesquely sophisticated receptiveness to its initially rhetorical calls for self-sacrifice. And he did not do so out of simple ingenuousness. Having brought all his perspicacity to bear on the confrontation with Hegel over the question of death, Heidegger conceived of a response to Hegel that is not a response to National Socialism. The task of an *Auseinandersetzung* (critical debate) with Hegel, announced in the final sentence of his postdoctoral dissertation,[2] in the earliest extant notes of one of his lecture courses,[3] and then addressed throughout his entire corpus, did not prevent Heidegger from ostensibly emulating his "great adversary"[4] in making his way to the state. Opening his first lecture course as rector of Freiburg University, Heidegger issues a call to arms: "We want to find ourselves within the fundamental question of philosophy and thereby within the foundational historizing of our history so that we might open up, extend, and secure the paths of our spiritually folkish destiny. This is to take place through a *historical confrontation with Hegel*."[5]

The people of the National Socialist state is to rise up against Hegel. Viewed as a motive for his political engagement, Heidegger's reaction to Hegel could not be more different from either Marx's or Nietzsche's. Without ever elaborating a philosophy of the state, Heidegger became a state thinker. But a state thinker in what sense? Referring to January 30, 1933, the date of Hitler's installation in power, Carl Schmitt writes: "On this day therefore one can say that 'Hegel died.'"[6] Yet where Schmitt merely wanted to note the politicization of the German bureaucracy, it is arguable that, for Heidegger, the National Socialist revolution signified much more than the abandonment of one facet of the *Philosophy of Right*. Hegel's "death," as the determinative negativity of the logic of Absolute Spirit, was itself to die in yielding to the state of the people of finitude.

In order to ascertain the philosophical foundations of the understanding of the state in Heidegger's engagement with National Socialism, it is necessary to review Heidegger's objection to Hegel's assimilation of death and human finitude to an ultimately still conventional logic. As a result of this assimilation, the Hegelian state remains indifferent to the essence of Dasein.

The famous passage on death from the Preface to the *Phenomenology of Spirit* reads:

The activity of dissolution is the power and work of the *Understanding*, the most astonishing and mightiest of powers, or rather the absolute power. The circle that remains self-enclosed and, like substance, holds its moments together, is an immediate relationship, one therefore which has nothing astonishing about it. But that an accident as such, detached from what circumscribes it, what is bound and is actual only in its context with others, should attain an existence of its own and a separate freedom — this is the tremendous power of the negative; it is the energy of thought, of the pure "I". Death, if that is what we want to call this non-actuality, is of all things the most dreadful, and to hold fast what is dead requires the greatest strength. Lacking strength, Beauty hates the Understanding for asking of her what she cannot do. But the life of Spirit is not the life that shrinks from death and keeps itself untouched by devastation, but rather the life that endures it and maintains itself in it. It wins its truth only when, in utter dismemberment, it finds itself. It is this power, not as something positive, which closes its eyes to the negative, as when we say of something that it is nothing or is false, and then, having done with it, turn away and pass on to something else; on the contrary, Spirit is this power only by looking the negative in the face, and tarrying with it. This tarrying with the negative is the magical power that converts it into being. This power is identical with what we earlier called the Subject, which by giving determinateness an existence in its own element supersedes abstract immediacy, i.e. the immediacy which barely is, and thus is authentic substance: that being or immediacy whose mediation is not outside of it but which is this mediation itself.[7]

Death, for Hegel, is simply another name for the negative. Hegel does not spell out why death should be simply another name for the negative; he does not press the synonymy, but rather admits, in a subordinate clause, to its arbitrariness ("if that is what we want to call this non-actuality"). And yet this arbitrariness is far from denoting a relaxation in the philosophical rigor of Hegel's text. Hegel imposes a sense on death only after death has been stripped of meaning by the very starting point of the *Phenomenology of Spirit*. Hegel's pure ego, whose experience of its own consciousness is set forth in this work, cannot die because it is nothing other than thought. In the above passage, Hegel clarifies almost at once that the purity of this ego is not the distance at which the life of the Spirit preserves itself from devastation. Death, in such a case, would retain its meaning for the pure ego in the form of a threat and a determinative opposite. Death cannot menace the ego that, as the thinkability of the thinkable, is the thought, and hence the rationality and sublation, of its own death. What in death is unthinkable is, for Hegel, merely a hypochondriac's fancy and the consequence of a refusal to *think* death. In its thinkability, death is not the extrinsic limit of thought, but rather one of its moments. It is identified with thought's own power of delimitation and hence with that which Hegel calls the Understanding. Hegel's pure ego cannot die because it is already death itself, and it is thus as already torn apart that it finds itself. The pure ego comes to itself only in and as the limits along which the positive is sundered into individual entities. According to Hegel, the pure ego is not so much finite as finitude, since it is the negation by which all other entities are contained and determined. As the finitude of what is, the Hegelian pure ego is the subject in both its ancient and modern senses. It is the subject that, as Aristotle's substance, stands outside determination and gives existence to the determinate, and it is the subject that, as thought, stands outside determination only because it is itself the power of determination. In the *Phenomenology of Spirit*, Being is already Nothing since the existence (i.e., the Kantian irreducibility of the positivity of what is to a set of determinations) that the subject bestows is the nonpositivity of the determining negation. Adhering to Spinoza's equation of determination and negation, Hegel grasps the difference of Being from beings in the very work of differentiation effected by negativity. With a provocative similarity to the thesis of *Being and Time*, the truth of Being is seen to lie in finitude.

In response to Hegel's definition of the "I" as not merely finite (limited) but as finitude (limitation) itself, Heidegger will ask whether, in this apotheosis of finitude, the genuine question of death is notwithstanding neglected. Heidegger's exposition of death is informed by the question of Being. The polemic against Hegel enunciated in this treatment is hence trivialized if it is formulated as the opposition of a realist's account of death to a logician's account. Heidegger does not restore death as a possibility of the "I" simply out of fidelity to appearances. Indeed, adequacy cannot be the criterion, because adequacy itself must first be grounded. And it is precisely such a grounding of the correspondence between an account and its object that Heidegger attempts in his analysis of the being-outside-of-itself of Dasein's Being-toward-death. The traditional understanding of truth as adequation is made an affair of the transcendence of mortal Dasein. When Heidegger reproaches Hegel's presentation of death with a lack of seriousness, he is therefore not suggesting that Hegel's death is a simulacrum: "Negativity as dismemberment and division is 'death'—*the absolute Lord*; and 'life of absolute Spirit' means nothing other than to *bear death and see it through*. (But with this 'death' it can never become serious; no κατα-στροφή possible, no fall and overthrow possible; everything offset and evened out. Everything is *already unconditionally* secured and accommodated.)"⁸ Hegel's death is never in earnest, not because it is a counterfeit of death, but because it is not a catastrophe. The seriousness of death is, for Heidegger, its character as catastrophe. But a catastrophe for whom? Hegel's death is not a catastrophe and cannot overthrow the pure ego, since it has always already been appropriated and reconciled. The pure ego is, by definition, that which cannot be overthrown. In its position of power over everything that is, the pure ego is not subordinate to any external fate. It is in no instance simply the patient of a verb. Desiring a catastrophe that is an event and not the element in which Spirit finds itself in being torn apart, Heidegger conceives of the human being as patient rather than as agent. In contrast to the permanent and thus feigned catastrophe of the death that is the self-certainty of the pure ego, Dasein is that which can suffer death as an event, and hence in its seriousness as downfall. Heidegger even makes of this possibility of suffering death the distinguishing mark of Dasein and, by the terms of the understanding of the human in Hegel's philosophy, he thereby dehumanizes Dasein.

For Hegel, it is Nature alone that can die, and it must die in order for Spirit to realize itself in death. In the *Zusatz* to §376 of his *Encyclopaedia of the Philosophical Sciences*, Hegel writes: "The goal of Nature is to destroy itself and to break through its husk of immediate, sensuous existence, to consume itself like the phoenix in order to come forth from this externality rejuvenated as spirit."[9] Death is accordingly the *event* that befalls that which is not yet Spirit. In §375, Hegel portrays death as the inevitable lot of the animal: "The universality which makes the animal, as a singular, a *finite* existence, reveals itself in it as the abstract power which terminates the internal process active within the animal, a process which is itself abstract. The disparity between its finitude and universality is its *original disease* and the inborn *germ of death*, and the removal of this disparity is itself the accomplishment of this destiny."[10] The animal thus dies because in its inadequacy to the universal it is able to die. Given that dying has always already been overtaken by the self-consciousness of Spirit in which Hegel sees the essence of the human, when a human being dies, it is therefore never as a human being: in the *Zusatz* to the preceding section, Hegel speaks of the physiological aspects of old age as a return to a simply vegetative life.[11]

In his or her adequacy to the universal, the human being is relieved of mortality, which is to say, of a susceptibility to catastrophe. Nothing can ever happen purely *to* the thinking agent, and humanity must therefore extract from itself its understanding of time. Time, for Hegel, takes its definition from Spirit. It is nothing other than Spirit's partial comprehension of itself. Insisting on death as an essential possibility of Dasein and denouncing the Hegelian assimilation of catastrophe as simply a means to have done with the question of mortality, Heidegger seeks to contest the sublation of time in the immanent movement of the concept. Heidegger's account of the human being as an entity delivered up defenseless to its own mortality is not dictated by pessimism or decadence. What is at stake for

Heidegger is neither brute "fact" nor an aesthetic, but rather a critique of metaphysics on the foundation of a more originary understanding of time. Dasein must die, so that with its very frailty it might wrest the question of Being from the narrowness and hence deficient seriousness of the logic of what is only ever present.

Heidegger's exposition of the catastrophic character of death cannot be comprehended apart from Hegel's exposition of the conceptuality, and thus ultimate stasis, of time. On the strength of this exposition, of the panlogism that has reappropriated the nonconceptuality of Kant's a priori intuitions, Hegel is able to assert that finitude is, in truth, Spirit. Heidegger will not challenge this assertion merely to reinstate time in its Kantian complementarity to the conceptual. It is Spirit itself in its self-presence that is to be interrogated, for in raising time to the concept, Hegel reduces it to presence. In the *Zusatz* to §258 of the *Encyclopaedia*, Hegel asserts:

> But in its Notion [*Begriff*], time itself is eternal; for time as such—not any particular time, nor Now—is its Notion, and this, like every Notion generally, is eternal, and therefore also absolute Presence. Eternity will not come to be, nor was it, but it *is*. The difference therefore between eternity and duration is that the latter is only a relative sublating of time, whereas eternity is infinite, i.e. not relative, duration but duration reflected into itself.[12]

For Hegel, the concept (*Begriff*) of time cannot, as a concept, be other than eternal. By conceptualizing time, Hegel does not dispute the eternity of the presence that Plato attributes to the Ideas. And yet the time in which concepts demonstrate their eternity through the subsumption of temporally divergent and finite particulars has always had to be distinct from eternity. Were the time in which concepts distinguish themselves from the transient itself the eternal and absolute present, then the distinction, and the proof of the eternity of concepts, would be impossible. In what way therefore can the concept of time amount to the truth of time?

Given his panlogism and his axiom of the ubiquity of the concept, a proof of the eternity of concepts is something with which Hegel can dispense. It is clear that what is paramount for Hegel in his exposition of time and space is the revelation of the infinity of Spirit. Space will give way to time, and time will give way to the concept that is Spirit. In §254, Hegel sets forth the nature of space in such a way that his ultimate goal is unmistakable: "The first or immediate determination of Nature is *Space*: the abstract *universality of Nature's self-externality*, self-externality's mediationless indifference. It is a wholly ideal *side-by-sideness* because it is self-externality; and it is absolutely *continuous*, because this asunderness is still quite *abstract*, and contains no specific difference within itself."[13] Nature, which is not yet Spirit, and which is thus not yet self-reflection, is that which is outside itself. At its greatest remove from Spirit, Nature is this being-outside-of-itself in its barest abstraction as the punctuality of space. And space is outside itself without thereby creating a difference within itself, since such a difference would be contrary to its abstraction from all determinations. Where Spirit, as the negativity of what is, is limitation, space is continuum. Between these parameters, Hegel means to encompass the Whole in all the wealth of its articulations. In this, his success has never really been doubted, because it is the determinate as such and alone that Hegel brings to thought. Space in its abstractness waits for nothing other than to be determined and, indeed, it cannot but be determined. Hegel's space is not so far removed from Spirit that it escapes the reach of the latter's power of determination. In its determinate indeterminacy, Hegel's space is already a continuum. That which does not stand fast, and does not appear in any determinacy, does not appear at all. Hegel's conception of the indeterminate is that which, standing fast in the light of presence, is consistent even before being determined. For Hegel, time is the truth of the continuity of space rather than the occasion for a question concerning the presence in which all beings stand fast.

In §258, Hegel interprets time as the negative unity of the being-outside-of-itself that he earlier names "space": "Time, as the negative unity of self-externality, is similarly an out-and-out abstract, ideal being. It is that being which, inasmuch as it *is*, is *not*, and inasmuch as it is *not*, *is*: it is Becoming directly *intuited*; this means that differences, which admittedly are purely *momentary*, i.e. directly self-sublating, are determined as *external*, i.e. as external to *themselves*."[14] Time is the unity, and hence fundamental homogeneity, of space. It is a negative unity because it is through the negation of the disunity of being-outside-of-itself that space attains to its unity. Time is not a negative unity in the sense that it is a disruption of unity. On the contrary, time is the negativity in which being-outside-of-itself is for itself, and it is nothing other than this negativity. Time, for Hegel, is able to be the truth of space because it is characterized equally by the punctuality in which space is a being-outside-of-itself. Time is the being-outside-of-itself in which the indifference between one point and another in space becomes the negativity by which the points are related one to the other in an albeit abstract unity.

The point, which Hegel in §254 designates a being-for-itself and the negation of space, is negated in its negativity by time. On this first step toward the absolute negativity of Spirit, Heidegger comments in *Being and Time*:

When punctuality as indifference gets transmuted, this signifies that it no longer remains lying in the "paralysed tranquillity of space". The point "gives itself airs" [*spreizt sich auf*, i.e., spreads itself apart] before all the other points. According to Hegel, this negation of the negation as punctuality is time. If this discussion has any demonstrable meaning, it can mean nothing else than that the positing-of-itself-for-itself of every point is a "now-here", "now-here", and so on.[15]

The now-sequence that Heidegger feels obliged to discover in Hegel's interpretation of time becomes the basis for a reproach:

No detailed discussion is needed to make plain that in Hegel's Interpretation of time he is moving wholly in the direction of the way time is ordinarily understood. When he characterizes time in terms of the "now", this presupposes that in its full structure the "now" remains levelled off and covered up, so that it can be intuited as something present-at-hand, though present-at-hand only "ideally".[16]

But is the negation of the punctuality of space in time overlooked in this reading? How can Heidegger attribute to Hegel the vulgar understanding of time, in which one discrete moment follows inexplicably on another, if this indifferent punctuality is precisely what Hegel negates in his account of time?

In her essay "The Dialogue Between Heidegger and Hegel," Denise Souche-Dagues takes issue with what she considers to be "the blindness of Heidegger towards the real meaning of Hegel's texts."[17] And yet, as obvious as it is that Hegel's account of time differs from the vulgar understanding that Heidegger criticizes, it is not at all clear that, in the violence of his exegesis, Heidegger has missed Hegel's real meaning. Hegel's time negates the indifferent punctuality of the vulgar understanding of time only to remain itself present-at-hand in its ideality. Thus, Souche-Dagues unwittingly argues for Heidegger's reading when she writes:

Furthermore, there is nothing like a "fall" of Spirit into time, which would mean that Spirit descends from an eternity situated out of time. Eternity is for Hegel in its immanent totalization which is its true infinity. The present (*Gegenwart*) which is responsible for presenting this absolute unification indicates clearly that time is not in truth the indefinite and formal series of here-nows, cancelling themselves in the etc., etc., of indefiniteness.[18]

Time in Hegel is eternal neither outside of time nor within time, but, on the contrary, *as* time. It is time as the totality of all periods of time, and thus as the *concept* of time, that is present for Hegel and is present because there can be no period of time outside its unity in which it would not be present. The vulgar understanding of time is thus manifest in Hegel's "elevation" of time to the concept. Time in the eternity of its concept is that which is present, and hence, although punctuality is negated in Hegel's account of temporality, the vulgar understanding of time remains determinative through the privileging of the present.

Even in its "elevation" to the concept, time constitutes a fall for the Hegelian Spirit. It is in this sense that Heidegger speaks of a fall of Spirit into time (Souche-Dagues's rejected descent from an eternity situated outside of time is simply irrelevant to Heidegger's text). Quoting Hegel himself from the concluding chapter of the *Phenomenology of Spirit*, Heidegger writes:

Because the restlessness with which *spirit* develops in bringing itself to its concept is the *negation of a negation*, it accords with spirit, as it actualizes itself, to fall "into *time*" as the immediate *negation of a negation*. For "*time* is the *concept* itself, which is *there* [*da ist*] and which represents itself to the consciousness as an empty intuition; because of this, spirit necessarily appears in time, and it appears in time as long as it does not *grasp* its pure concept—that is, as long as time is not annulled by it. Time is the pure Self—*external*, intuited, *not grasped* by the Self—the concept which is merely intuited."[19]

Time is the concept—that is, that which mediates—in its immediacy. It is therefore a contradiction. Time is Spirit that has fallen away from itself, because it is that negation of a negation that is nonetheless not reflective. It apes Spirit in its self-presence: it is the mediating negation that is external to itself as mediation. Negating the negativity of the point, time "finds" itself in the becoming that is, inasmuch as it is not, and is not, inasmuch as it is. And "finding" itself in the negativity of becoming, time already shares the infinite finitude in which Spirit is present to itself. The absolute presence of time—its negative unity over the punctuality of being-outside-of-itself—is, as the term indicates, a formulation of temporality from which transcendence has been shorn. Hegel's interpretation of time remains modeled on the discrete "now" and the vulgar understanding of time is perpetuated. To the question of the Being of time, the Hegelian answer is "presence."

The concept is able to become, for Hegel, the truth of time, because the legitimacy of unity, on which the concept relies, is not allowed to be challenged by an exposition of the essential ecstasy of time.[20] The transitions that negativity effects from one point to the other are not thought through to an interrogation of the unity of any concept of time—of that which Heidegger, in his 1924 lecture "The Concept of Time," calls meaningless.[21]

Addressing time's place between the finite and the concept, Hegel states in the Remark to §258 of the *Encyclopaedia*:

The finite is perishable and *temporal* because, unlike the Notion, it is not in its own self total negativity; true, this negativity is immanent in it as its universal essence, but the finite is not adequate to this essence: it is *one-sided*, and consequently it is related to negativity as to the power that dominates it. The Notion, however, in its freely self-existent identity as I = I, is in and for itself absolute negativity and freedom. Time, therefore, has no power over the Notion, nor is the Notion in time or temporal; on the contrary, *it* is the power over time, which is this negativity only *qua* externality.[22]

Accordingly, Spirit, for Hegel, indeed falls away from itself into time, but in the sense of a fall from the concept to the externality of "intuition" rather than from an eternity outside of time. The qualitative difference that Kant drew between the a priori intuition of time and the concept is reformulated as simply an obstacle on the path of Spirit's self-realization. Whereas, in the above passage, the finite is said to lie in the power of time because of its inadequacy to its concept, time, for its part, lies in the power of the concept because of its inadequacy to its own negativity. Having defined time by the negation of the indifferent externality of being-outside-of-itself, Hegel is able to recover time for the concept on the basis of a consanguinity: time, as the negation of the externality of punctuality, and hence as an external negation, is not yet the absolute negativity in which the pure ego is the determination of what is. Through defining time by negation and the concept by determinative negativity, Hegel brings together what Kant had held apart. The ostensible radicality of Hegel's abandonment of the definition of the concept as the universal of finite particulars is thus ultimately conservative, since it is intended to stifle the question intimated by Kant in his treatment of the extraconceptuality of time. What Kant had wrested from the sway of dogmatic metaphysics, Hegel returns. The Kantian affirmation of finitude is followed by a restoration of the concept. The Hegelian concept is installed as the power of time, and the eternal present reasserts itself over the transcendence of finitude. The Aristotelian One is secured against any suspicion of its propriety and primacy. Hegel's time stands guarantor for the foundations of traditional logic because it underwrites, through its presence, the intelligibility of whatever is. That which falls under the power of time is accordingly never able to make of its finitude an affront to the unity in which time itself is collected in its negativity in the absolute present of Spirit.

In his 1930–31 lecture course *Hegel's Phenomenology of Spirit*, Heidegger reformulates his disagreement with Hegel on the issue of finitude:

> But one may ask whether setting up a confrontation with Hegel like this is not superfluous. Was it not Hegel, in fact, who ousted finitude from philosophy in the sense that he *sublated* it or overcame it by *putting it in its proper place*? Certainly. But the question is whether the finitude that was determinant in philosophy before Hegel was the *original and effective finitude installed* in philosophy, or whether it was only an incidental finitude that philosophy was constrained to take up and transmit. The question must be asked whether *Hegel's conception of infinitude* did not arise from that *incidental* finitude, in order to reach back and absorb it.
>
> The question is whether finitude, as the innermost distress at the heart of the matter in question, determines the necessity of questioning. If not, then the confrontation with Hegel is not *in opposition to him*, in the form of a defense of the finitude which *he has surmounted*, but is concerned rather with *what* he has surmounted and the *way* in which he did so.[23]

Hegel evades the problem of finitude by grasping finitude in its *essence*, since he grasps it in that by which, as a concept, it is already infinite. He therefore surmounts that which cannot even emerge as a problem for the conceptualism, and that is to say eternalism, of metaphysics. Heidegger's preoccupation with finitude does not entail fixing upon temporality in Hegel prior to its sublation in Spirit, since the temporality in which Spirit misapprehends itself is by no means the temporality in which the self-presence of Spirit is rendered genuinely questionable. Spirit errs in time without ever straying from the path to its self-realization. It cannot truly err in time because time itself does not err for Hegel. Time's inadequacy to the self-presence of Spirit is not ascribed to the *ecstases* of originary temporality, but rather to the partiality of time's negativity with respect to the Absolute. The failure of its adequation is situated in a falling short *within* presence and not in an overreaching of presence. Hegel's time does not transcend the One. Time, for Hegel, is the unity whose deficiency is not to know itself as unity. It is a subordinate element that testifies to the unity of the self-knowledge of the Absolute even in the obstinacy of its error.

For Hegel, in his predestinarianism, every error corrects itself in advance and every distress is always already assuaged. By holding to the distress and privation (*Not*) of finitude explicitly as transcendence, Heidegger prosecutes a critique of the unitary. Here the confession of lack is not a confession of servility. On the contrary, it stems from an ambition to think Being as such and not merely Being as presence. However much Heidegger's *Not* recalls Christian disquisitions on the indigence of humanity, it cannot be said to be theological, since Heidegger is not concerned with inculcating an awareness of a dependence on God. It is dependence pure and simple that is at stake and that, in its lack of the contentment and self-containment of presence, is being opposed to traditional ontology. The neediness in Heidegger's conception of humanity is far less an affliction imposed by an external power than it is the ecstatic essence of the being that he defines by originary temporality. Heidegger thus defends a finitude that has not been surmounted by Hegel, because it was never admitted and could not be admitted without a fundamental interrogation of logic.

In the same 1930–31 lecture course on Hegel, Heidegger suggests that it is not a case of a mere revision and reform of logic:

With respect to the title "Being and Time," one could speak of an *ontochrony*. Here χρόνος stands in the place of λόγος. But were both of these only interchanged? No. On the contrary, what matters is to unfold everything anew from the ground up, by taking over the essential motive of the question of being. It is important to show—formulating it with Hegel—that it is not the concept which is "the power of time," but it is time which is the power of the concept.[24]

"Here χρόνος stands in the place of λόγος." The gathering together in the One of the λόγος, by which the entire history of the metaphysical treatment of the question of Being has been governed, is contrasted with the unrecovered being-outside-of-itself of χρόνος. Hegel's infinitude, which pretends to be a sublation of finitude, overcomes limits only to be arrested in its transgression, assuming the shape of delimitation itself. The uprising against finitude will have left the structure of the real intact. Spirit's insurrection against theology will not pass beyond its own investiture as the One that lets each and every entity be seen in its determinate unity. Is Heidegger, through identifying the λόγος in *Being and Time* with "a letting-something-be-seen,"[25] therefore proposing χρόνος as its antithesis, as a letting-nothing-be-seen? Heidegger warns against reading the substitution mechanically. The nothing that χρόνος lets be "seen" is not an entity that withholds itself from apprehension in a moment that is no longer or not yet now, that remains distinguishable in the peculiarity of its comportment and hence still subject to the One. What χρόνος lets be "seen" is the indeterminacy that is the originary dissolution of the stable identities of what is only ever apprehended in the derivative temporality of presence. Time is the "power," that is, the condition of possibility of the concept, inasmuch as it is within time and an inadequate understanding of time that the concept—the Hegelian λόγος that is self-comprehending Spirit—is able to assert itself in its presence as the Being of beings. Hegel's Spirit is the Being of beings in the Greek sense of their visibility and determinacy, which is to say their presentability.

Moreover, that the Being of beings is identified with nothingness in the *Logic* does not involve a questioning of the understanding of Being as presence, since it is nothingness in the sense of determinative negativity that is for Hegel the very ground of the presentability of what is. Distinguishing the identity of Being and nothingness in his "What Is Metaphysics?" from their identity in Hegel, Heidegger writes in the *Contributions to Philosophy*:

When the sentence from Hegel's *Logic* is quoted in "What Is Metaphysics?"—"Being and nothing are the same"—that means, and can only mean, an analogue of bringing together Being and nothing as such. However, for Hegel "Being" [*Seyn*] is exactly not only a certain first stage of what in the future is to be thought as Being [*Seyn*], but this first stage is, as the *un*-determined, *un*-mediated stage, precisely already pure negativity of objectness and of thinking (beingness and thinking).[26]

Hegel's nothingness is no more than the negation that is proper to determinacy as such. Nothingness is already a moment in whatever is, inasmuch as every being is determinate, for Hegel, in some way or another. In such an understanding of nothingness, time's difference from the visibility of the present-at-hand—its nothingness—is not thought beyond the presence in which beings are present and hence conceptualizable. The invisibility of time thereby ceases to be the occasion for a question of the primacy of the concept. Dasein, as the being that is essentially wedded to its finitude, cannot but be misunderstood by Hegel and subordinated to the concept. Plato's depreciative interpretation of finitude as μὴ ὄν remains determinative. Solely from the vantage point of the concept and the unthinkability of the unpresentable is the finitude of the being that has not overcome χρόνος to find itself in the eternity of the concept the condition of inadequacy to its own conceptual determination. From the vantage point of χρόνος, this conceptual inadequacy is, however, the "adequacy" to the more originary power of the indetermination of time.

With the exposition of the primacy of finitude, Heidegger stands the metaphysical notion of the freedom of the philosopher on its head. Freedom no longer lies in the concept and slavery no longer lies in finitude. What for an "ontochrony" accordingly turns out to be subordinate is not that which is finite but the power of limitation itself, since it is the latter that has not passed to an identity with the highest power. What has risen to become the λόγος has not become independent of time. As the power that is the unity of that which is, the λόγος falls short of the nonunity that is ecstatic temporality and remains subordinate to it. Preserving its metaphysical cast, the freedom toward which the Hegelian philosophy directs itself, and in which it is to be a sublation of finitude, is an identification with the determinacy of what is.

It is this interpenetration of positivism and infinitude that informs Hegel's political thinking. It informs the notorious sentence from the Preface to the *Philosophy of Right*: "What is rational is actual and what is actual is rational." [27] Certainly other passages in the work make it clear that Hegel is not rejecting all possible alterations to the status quo as irrational, but the sentence can notwithstanding be considered positivistic in its aligning of the determinate with the thinkable. Hegel's political positivism has nothing to do with a naïveté in the face of the "facts" and everything to do with a panlogism and the suppression of the extraconceptual. Through surmounting finitude, Hegel cannot but arrive in paradise, and yet, as he nonetheless cannot disguise from himself that he has become an official of the Prussian state, he has no choice other than to take on the role of its apologist. Hegel's *Philosophy of Right* is marked by political gullibility only to the extent that it is marked by philosophical wisdom. Canceling out the distance from the truth of what is, Hegel has made his way to the σοφία to which the philosopher merely aspired. He has become, in Alexandre Kojève's words, the Wise Man. Nothing is alien to him (i.e., to his reformulation of traditional logic). The Prussian state ineluctably assumes the aspect of the concrete universal, and the bureaucracy is revealed as the mediation between the particulars of the corporations. Where Socrates in the *Phaedo* awaits wisdom after death, Hegel is already death itself and thus already wise. The former flees the state through death; the latter becomes the state through death. The infinite and determinative negativity of Hegel's death reveals more than a mere kinship with the state's immanent organization of the social body. Whatever is not fundamentally at one with Spirit would amount to an objection against Hegel's claim to wisdom.

If Hegel's passage to the state is through in-finitude, Heidegger's is through finitude. The death that Heidegger defers and thinks as an event opens a space for a critique of the One of metaphysics, but it did not prevent his abasement before Hitler. Drawing back from the wisdom that ushered Hegel into the service of the State, Heidegger exempted himself, through the reserve and emphatic φιλία of his philosophy, from a repetition of Hegel's panegyrics. He does not extol the state whose essence is realized in logic, yet he nonetheless proceeded to a state with little interest in a conception of humanity at odds with the present-at-hand. The human being that, as an individual in the logical sense, admits of sublation in the universal of the Prussian state, will simply have been replaced by the specimen of biological material. In both cases, beings remained determined in their discreteness and identifiability by the metaphysics of presence.

Heidegger's conception of the National Socialist state cannot however simply be read off from the historiographically verifiable reality of the regime without a neglect of his condemnation of biologism. A surer indication of the basis of Heidegger's conception of the Nazi state is a passage from the 1934–35 lecture course *Hölderlins Hymnen "Germanien" und "Der Rhein"* (Hölderlin's Hymns "Germanien" and "Der Rhein"). In a reflection on the possibility of community, it juxtaposes Heidegger's own treatment of Being-toward-death with the nationalist idealization of the soldier at the front:

The camaraderie of the soldiers at the front has its foundation neither in the fact that they had to get along because others who were far away were missing nor, for that matter, in the circumstance that they met up through a shared enthusiasm. On the contrary, its foundation lies solely and at its deepest therein that before all else the proximity of death as a sacrifice placed them all in the same nothingness, so that this became the source of unconditioned co-belonging. Precisely the death that each and every human being must die on his or her own, that isolates each individual to the utmost, precisely this death and the readiness for its sacrifice are what first creates the space of community out of which camaraderie arises. Does camaraderie arise therefore from fear? No and yes. No, if like the petit bourgeois one understands by fear only the helpless trembling of a cowardly panic. Yes, if fear is comprehended as the metaphysical proximity to the unconditioned that is bestowed solely on the highest independence and readiness. If we do not force powers into our Dasein that, just as unconditionally as death in the shape of free sacrifice, bind and isolate, that is, attack at the roots of the Dasein of each individual, and stand just as deeply and utterly in a genuine knowledge, then there will not be any "camaraderie"; at best, what will come about will be an altered form of society.[28]

The authentic Being-toward-death that, in 1927, is named the concealed ground of the historicality of Dasein is identified seven years later with the experience of the trenches. Heidegger is not speaking here at firsthand, since during his brief period of military service in World War I, he was never engaged in fighting at the front. Nonetheless, he is not simply paraphrasing a passage from Ernst Jünger either, for example. Heidegger, in a gesture of continuity with *Being and Time*, concentrates on fear. As war is the juncture of circumstances in which human finitude becomes a concern through fear, Heidegger ontologically underwrites the deployment of the Wehrmacht, and *Being and Time* is thereby pulled into the German mythopoeism of the military after World War I. Heidegger's account demythologizes war by means of the very elements through which it had been demythologized. The realism of many postwar narratives, which had been received as denunciations of the experience of trench warfare, becomes simply grist for the mill of Heidegger's affirmation of fear. Fear turns into an argument for war. It becomes the task, rather than the evasion, of the soldier at the front. In §51 of *Being and Time*, Heidegger speaks accordingly of a "courage for anxiety in the face of death." [29] What Heidegger asks of the soldier is that he not steel himself in the face of death and thereby grow numb to the question of his own finitude through a leap into the infinite. For Heidegger, the enemy that the armed forces must confront in the trenches is Hegelian sublation.

Given the very different task that Heidegger sets the soldier at the front, his notion of sacrifice in the 1934–35 text sits uneasily beside the customary right-wing eulogies of the volunteers who fell at Langemarck and elsewhere. Heidegger does not so much valorize sacrifice, therefore, as valorize the readiness for such sacrifice. No doubt this is already to go too far toward accommodating a militarist politics. In the readiness for the fear of impending self-sacrifice, the soldiers at the front are to experience the transcendence and incommensurability of finitude. Through the fear it instills, war contests the fixation on the "now" in the vulgar understanding of time, bringing home to Dasein the truth of its being-outside-of-itself. Beside itself with fear, Dasein is a Being-with-others just as it is completely individuated as the unrepeatability of the uncontainable. Its free sacrifice is the event that awaits it as its own and that thus carries it beyond itself without delivering up its transcendence to an external entity. That *for which* Dasein sacrifices itself is irrelevant in comparison with the fact *that* Dasein sacrifices itself. Here in Heidegger's lectures on Hölderlin, the provocation of the National Socialist policy of rearmament is accordingly endorsed, since war is intimated to be indispensable to the fulfillment of the movement's promise to ground community. The Reich will not be the being present-at-hand that preexists Dasein's self-sacrifice and whose defense is the rationale of sacrifice. Instead, community will be that which arises in the readiness for free sacrifice. Heidegger's community of the trenches does not stand above its members in arbitration over their lives and deaths, because it is not cast in the nineteenth century's pseudoreligious conception of the state. This community is the bond of finitude itself. Death, which for Hegel tears apart and mediates everything that is, necessarily grounds a state of another order than that which arises in the individuation and binding of Heidegger's anticipation of death. Heidegger's community does not situate itself in death but rather in the shadow of death. It arises in the expectation of death.

To anticipate death, even to run ahead into death (to translate literally Heidegger's expression *in den Tod vorlaufen*), is not the same as to desire death. Heidegger's community exists in a courtship of death. Nonetheless, it can only exist if it simultaneously defers death. It can therefore be said that what both attracted and repulsed Heidegger in National Socialism was the bare physiological reality of corpses toward which the movement was hurrying. In *Being and Time*, the basis of Heidegger's future politics of a flirtation with death is clearly enunciated:

But Being towards this possibility, as Being-towards-death, is so to comport ourselves towards *death* that in this Being, and for it, death reveals itself *as a possibility*. Our terminology for such Being towards this possibility is *"anticipation" of this possibility*. But in this way of behaving does there not lurk a coming-close to the possible, and when one is close to the possible, does not its actualization emerge? In this kind of coming close, however, one does not tend towards concernfully making available something actual; but as one comes closer understandingly, the possibility of the possible just becomes "greater". *The closest closeness[,] which one may have in Being towards death as a possibility, is as far as possible from anything actual.* The more unveiledly this possibility gets understood, the more purely does the understanding penetrate into it *as the possibility of the impossibility of any existence at all.* Death, as possibility, gives Dasein nothing to be "actualized", nothing which Dasein, as actual, could itself *be.*[30]

The reality of death is, by definition, not the reality of Dasein (existence). As Heidegger writes: "The *end* of the entity *qua* Dasein is the *beginning* of the same entity *qua* something present-at-hand."[31] With death, the ontological exception that Dasein constitutes for the understanding of Being as presence is annulled. Hegel's courage in looking death in the face—in leaping into death to become one with it—lies exactly in his refusal to brook this exception to the understanding of Being as presence. It is a courage that, according to Heidegger, is much more a lack of seriousness with respect to the question of Being.

With respect to National Socialism, however, Hegel's assimilation of death renders him invulnerable to the regime's promise of catastrophe. Death always comes too late for it to have any philosophical importance for Hegel, whereas, for Heidegger, that it should cease to be impending and finally arrive is not the fulfillment of a philosophical promise but its revocation.

If Heidegger, in his confrontation with Hegel, understands death as a catastrophe rather than as the element in which Spirit thinks itself, he does not mean to construe death as an event that takes place at its given time within a sequence of "nows." Such a construction of death would merely delay the attainment to the presence of death in which Hegel establishes his thinking from the very beginning. Setting out from death, Hegel's system encompasses the whole of life, but the price of its totality is an inability to grasp the Being specific to Dasein. Hegel sees everything, but thereby misses that what characterizes Dasein is that "there is always something *still outstanding*."[32]

In §48 of *Being and Time*, Heidegger writes of the positive nature of this deficiency: "That Dasein should *be* together only when its 'not-yet' has been filled up is so far from the case that it is precisely then that Dasein is no longer. Any Dasein always exists in just such a manner that its 'not-yet' *belongs* to it."[33] The "not-yet" of Dasein is the space of its possibility. Death, as the impossibility of Dasein, cannot be viewed as the realization of this possibility:

With its death, Dasein has indeed "fulfilled its course". But in doing so, has it necessarily exhausted its specific possibilities? Rather, are not these precisely what gets taken away from Dasein? Even "unfulfilled" Dasein ends. On the other hand, so little is it the case that Dasein comes to its ripeness only with death, that Dasein may well have passed its ripeness before the end. For the most part, Dasein ends in unfulfilment, or else by having disintegrated and been used up.[34]

Death is a catastrophe that happens, so to speak, *against* Dasein. It is not assimilated to Dasein and it does not realize Dasein's possibilities. It does not make Dasein at last *one*. The "not-yet" is consumed in the moment of death simply by being torn away from Dasein. But with this moment of death, the vulgar understanding of temporality as a sequence of "nows" does not reassert itself in a containment of the transcendence of Dasein's "not-yet," since Dasein cannot be at its end, but only toward its end. Dasein is finite because it has an end, but it does not at all have this end as a check on its transcendence, since it has its end not as a possession present-at-hand but precisely as that toward which it never ceases to transcend. Death, in this sense, is itself the "not-yet" of Dasein. The catastrophic character of Heidegger's conception of death is its pure possibility. It is the event that does not take place—its "presence" is always only ever a "not-yet."

And yet death, for Heidegger, is nonetheless certain. Death is not a possibility that Dasein may or may not realize. On the one hand, unless Dasein dies, the possibility of its impending death ceases to be an *essential possibility*. The significance of finitude is overlooked once mortality, hypostasized and shorn of its futural character of the "not-yet," is interpreted as one property among others of the ahistorical essence of human beings. Death is the decision that always overtakes Dasein, securing the undecidability of its possibility of death at the very moment that it casts the actuality of the corpse present-at-hand. On the other hand, the certainty of death lies in the very nature of truth itself. That such a certainty could be derived from the overwhelming spectacle of the trenches is excluded by *Being and Time*:

We cannot compute the certainty of death by ascertaining how many cases of death we encounter. This certainty is by no means of the kind which maintains itself in the truth of the present-at-hand. When something present-at-hand has been uncovered, it is encountered most purely if we just look at the entity and let it be encountered in itself. Dasein must first have lost itself in the factual circumstances [*Sachverhalte*] (this can be one of care's own tasks and possibilities) if it is to obtain the pure objectivity—that is to say, the indifference—of apodictic evidence. If Being-certain in relation to death does not have this character, this does not mean that it is of a lower grade, but that *it does not belong at all to the graded order of the kinds of evidence we can have about the present-at-hand.*[35]

Death is not certain in the same way that one can be certain of the veracity of the proposition that the battlefield is strewn with corpses. It is of a different order of certainty, since it is the ground of the certainty of propositions relating to the present-at-hand. The "not-yet" of death constitutes the very essence of Dasein and the basis for its identification with ecstatic temporality. Heidegger accordingly speaks of the certainty of death as "indefinite."[36] Death is at once certain and indefinite because, as the "not-yet" of originary temporality, it is the ground of the certainty of the present-at-hand without being itself present-at-hand. Foreshadowing his argument in "On the Essence of Truth," Heidegger makes the certainty of a proposition—its correspondence to a state of affairs—depend upon a relation that he assigns to the transcendence of Dasein. Only within the openness of Dasein's "not-yet," within an originary nonpresence, can a proposition and a state of affairs be turned to face each other in defiance of their self-identity. To object that between the being-outside-of-itself of adequation and the being-outside-of-itself of Dasein's Being-toward-death, there is nothing more than an analogy, involves an inauthentic understanding of Dasein's end: that which can be isolated as a term in an analogy possesses the distinctness of the present-at-hand. Dasein's Being-toward-death is its Being-in-the-world and it is only with death that Dasein turns in upon itself, becoming self-identical and ceasing to be Dasein. The essence of truth is the transcendence of the mortal human being. All certainties come to rely on the indefiniteness and excess of the "not-yet" of Dasein's inevitable death:

Therefore the evidential character which belongs to the immediate givenness of Experiences, of the "I", or of consciousness, must necessarily lag behind the certainty which anticipation includes. Yet this is not because the way in which these are grasped would not be a rigorous one, but because in principle such a way of grasping them cannot hold *for true* (disclosed) something which at bottom it insists upon "having there" as true: namely, Dasein itself, which I myself *am*, and which, as a potentiality-for-Being, I can be authentically only by anticipation.[37]

Anticipating its death, Dasein anticipates itself because, in thinking that which can only be thought in its character of a "not-yet," it thinks the impossibility of its own full disclosure. As a result, it thinks its nonassimilability to the understanding of Being as presence. Running ahead into death, it runs away from the thanatography of National Socialism. In its anxiety before nothingness, it becomes an iconoclasm with respect to every presentation of death. Nourishing itself parasitically on the images of death that it destroys, Heidegger's authentic Dasein comes to an "arrangement" with the morbidity of the regime. It comes to a fragile "arrangement" with commitment to the regime, to the possibility of sacrifice conceived purely as *possibility*.

In 1933, and with little resistance, Heidegger transforms himself into an advocate of nationalistic sacrifice. On January 23, 1934, in the text "The Call to the Labor Service," he is able to write:

Those who are lame, comfortable, and effete will "go" into the Labor Service because it will perhaps jeopardize their degree and employment prospects to stay away. Those who are strong and unbroken are proud that extreme demands are being made of them: for that is the moment when they rise up to the hardest tasks, those for which there is neither pay nor praise, but only the "reward" of sacrifice and service in the area of the innermost necessities of German Being [*deutschen Seins*].[38]

What is, for Heidegger, the "reward" of sacrifice? If this "reward" lies in an understanding of the essence of Being, a willingness to sacrifice has less to do with the maintenance of the Germany of National Socialism than with fundamental ontology. The willingness to die for a fatherland present-at-hand becomes a pretext. The passage on the camaraderie of the front, from the lecture course on Hölderlin of 1934–35, indicates that community, for Heidegger, does not preexist the readiness for sacrifice, but rather arises from it. The first stage of the National Socialist revolution—the stage of the conventionality of its nationalism—is arguably to give way to a second stage in which the nation, as the pseudo-religious recipient of sacrifice, will be revealed to be a makeshift for that bond of community that is the readiness for sacrifice itself. If Heidegger's nationalism, like that of many others, was informed by the experience of the front (*Fronterlebnis*), it also bore the mark of his own meditations on finitude. The community born from the "courage for anxiety in the face of death" in the readiness for sacrifice does not shy away from its own finitude. Seeing through the eternal's pretensions to originarity, it sees through the logicist nationalism of the pseudo-religious state. Such a state is inappropriate to the being whose death is an essential possibility. Its immortality is the abstraction from history by means of which it asserts itself as the universal that rules over and mediates between its citizens. Dasein's deviation from the logic of the universal and the particular is that which, for Heidegger, constitutes the insight of the experience of the terror of trench warfare. A nationalism that grounds itself in the *Fronterlebnis* cannot but confront the metaphysics of presence. It could be said that it was in order to participate in this confrontation that Heidegger enlisted in the NSDAP. Heidegger's nationalism in 1933 was not, therefore, the "psychological solution" to the anxiety of 1927, but, on the contrary, its formulation as a philosophical-political program. For the sake of the reward of the disclosure of the originarity of finitude in sacrifice, Heidegger will commit himself to a dictatorship. But where Heidegger incorporated in his conception of nationalism the horror of the *Fronterlebnis*, the regime will reject the accounts in which this horror is depicted and have them publicly burned. However correct Marcuse may be in his thesis in *Reason and Revolution* concerning the irreconcilability of Hegel and National Socialism, for Heidegger, the dictatorship would prove to be all too Hegelian in its logicist nationalism of the repression of finitude, reneging on its promise of a continuation of the revolution.

The Hitlerian dictatorship is the state that runs ahead into death, but it is not the state that extracts from the experience of the impending catastrophe of mortality an insight into Dasein's status as an ontological exception. It is the state of control, that is, of the essential controllability of the present-at-hand. As an apparatus of state terror, it conforms itself far more conspicuously to Hegel's knowability of everything that is than to Heidegger's essential unpresentability of Dasein. The regime applies itself to the task of uncovering all secrets, cataloguing all anomalies, and tracking all movements. Aspiring to a dictatorship of absolute surveillance, it wants to be the light of knowledge in which beings are apprehended as they are in the full truth of their presence. Inasmuch as it refuses to any being an intrinsic unknowability, National Socialism overleaps the constitutive "not-yet" of Dasein and exercises its terror on a population that it cannot distinguish ontologically from the mere presence-at-hand of the dead. The regime's obsession with death amounted to a theatricalization of Hegel's understanding of death as the determinative negativity of what is, since it was a state that explicitly and concretely conceived itself as death.

This is not to suggest that Hegel was a proto-Nazi. The genealogical line is not so narrow. What is at issue in Heidegger's exposition of death is, however, an alternative to traditional ontology as it was brought to its ultimate expression by Hegel and as it underlies and unites National Socialism and all the doctrines of the state that were to stress their opposition to Hitler's dictatorship. Hegel's philosophy of the state, from out of whose sway the aspiring ideologues of the regime were unable to extricate themselves, is a philosophy that can praise the state in its identity with knowledge because it has first identified knowledge with control. Even if it is only later that Heidegger elaborates his critique of τέχνη as the reduction of knowledge to the art of the manipulation of beings, the existential analytic of *Being and Time* already raises an objection against defining knowledge by control. The essence of Dasein, and thus that which above all must be known with respect to Dasein, is the "not-yet" by which it withholds itself from an apprehension of its totality. Already dead, and hence already present-at-hand, Hegel's Spirit is not frustrated in its self-knowledge by anything outstanding to it. And knowing itself, it knows the knowability of what is, of that which, in his inaugural lecture in Berlin, Hegel says cannot help delivering itself up to be known.[39] Hegel's philosophy of the state, as the philosophy of Spirit in one of its manifestations, will necessarily place no restrictions on that which it is given to the state to know.

In the Remark to §209 of the *Philosophy of Right*, Hegel spurns cosmopolitanism for its refusal to press beyond a knowledge of the universal in its one-sidedness:

It is part of education, of thinking as the consciousness of the single in the form of universality, that the ego comes to be apprehended as a universal person in which all are identical. A man counts as a man in virtue of his manhood alone, not because he is a Jew, Catholic, Protestant, German, Italian, &c. This is an assertion which thinking ratifies and to be conscious of it is of infinite importance. It is defective only when it is crystallized, e.g. as a cosmopolitanism in opposition to the concrete life of the state.[40]

Hegel here advances his thought as the reconciliation of liberalism and nationalism. Where liberalism is criticized for the one-sidedness of its universalism, nationalism is likewise criticized for the one-sidedness of its particularism. In line with such a scheme, it could be said that, in its ambitions to become the state of total surveillance, National Socialism was checked by its exclusively racist weltanschauung: the universalism of the pure ego eluded it. With its imperialism and its adoption of strength as the universal measure of peoples, the regime found its own way to the cosmopolitan. The casting of the human as a biological sample under National Socialism is certainly a degradation with respect to Hegel's determinative negativity, yet, for Heidegger, both interpretations of the human essence are already degraded in being grounded in the ontology of the present-at-hand, rather than in an "ontochrony." In the Hegelian philosophy, as well as in the Hitlerian dictatorship, it is a logic of control that is at work.

But at once it might be contested that this is simply not a just description of Hegel. What does control have in common with the bacchanalian revel of the Absolute? Is there not a glaring disparity between the notion of certainty applied by a police state and the self-certainty of Spirit? Does not the comparison between National Socialism and Hegel indefensibly conflate the certainty of the mere understanding and the certainty of dialectical reason? And are not the frequent concessions that Heidegger makes to Hegel in their altercation simply being passed over here for the sake of the caricature of a struggle between diametrically opposed philosophies?

The reductiveness of the present reading has its rationale, however; namely, to draw attention to the foundations of a logicist politics in Hegel's treatments of finitude and time. By addressing the avowed consistency of Hegel's politics and his philosophy, it is possible to perceive the consistency of Heidegger's critique of Hegel's philosophy and his own political engagement. The tenability, for instance, of Jacques Taminiaux's thesis in his article "Finitude and the Absolute: Remarks on Hegel and Heidegger" is thereby subjected to a number of reservations.[41] Taminiaux quotes passages selected from Hegel for their affinities to certain Heideggerian texts, but whatever similarities can be rendered conspicuous between isolated propositions on truth and on nothingness, these propositions diverge in their sense when construed in connection with other statements dealing with politics. In other words, if the difference between Hegel and Heidegger is to be established, it is better sought in the discourses surrounding their respective acquiescences to the state than in the inconclusive playing off of the Infinite against finitude. That in which Hegel's Infinite distinguishes itself from Heidegger's finitude—notwithstanding their shared territory in respect of nothingness, death, and the acquiescence to the state—is the logicist conception of humanity with which it is bound up. Hegel dies, as it were, and overtakes his death in order to bring logic to politics. This could not be demonstrated more clearly than in his definition of *Volk* in the *System of Ethical Life*:

A people is not a disconnected mass, nor a mere plurality. Not the *former*: a mass as such does not establish the connection present in ethical life, i.e., the domination of all by a universal which would have reality in their eyes, be one with them, and have dominion and power over them, and, so as they proposed to be single individuals, would be identical with them in either a friendly or a hostile way; on the contrary, the mass is absolute singularity, and the concept of the mass, since they are one, is their abstraction alien to them and outside them. Also not the *latter*, not a mere plurality, for the universality in which they are one is absolute indifference. In a plurality, however, this absolute indifference is not established; on the contrary, plurality is not the absolute many, or the display of all differences; and it is only through this "allness" that indifference can display itself as real and be a universal indifference.[42]

Hegel's *Volk* is a concrete universal, neither a purely abstract unity nor a heterogeneous series of individuals. No matter how much the members of this *Volk* may differ among themselves, their identity with one another is never completely annulled. For Hegel, this identity is ethical, rather than biological. Such a qualification of the nature of the *Volk's* identity, as much as it is a necessary acknowledgement of Hegel's irreducibility to the *Rassenkunde* of the NSDAP, cannot disguise the fact that in Hegel's logicist conception, humanity remains equally under the influence of the thing-concepts (*Dingbegriffe*) of classical ontology.

Against this influence, whose interrogation Heidegger declares a continuing task in the closing pages of *Being and Time*, the earlier analyses of Being-with-one-another are explicitly conceived. Rather than in an aggregate of subjects, in, namely, the apprehension, comparison, and juxtaposition of distinct entities within the terms of the metaphysics of presence, Heidegger situates Being-with-one-another in historicality. Being-with-one-another is an affair, not of the mediation of the universal and the particular, but of the "not-yet" by which Dasein always overreaches itself. With this "not-yet," Heidegger attempts to secure the possibility of an understanding of the essence of the human without the interference of *Dingbegriffe*. In going further than Heidegger—in consuming the "not-yet" to arrive at death itself—Hegel is able to differentiate his conception of the human as the infinite negativity at one with death from the merely positive of the natural world. Yet this differentiation, for all the starkness of its opposition between the positive and the negative, is not a differentiation that delimits the scope of *Dingbegriffe*, since in the self-knowledge of its absolute negativity, Spirit is present to itself and thus perpetuates the mode of Being that classical ontology ascribed to things. The positive in Hegel thus proceeds in its dismemberment (*Zerrissenheit*) only to be re-membered in this very violence. It does not scatter to become a being-outside-of-itself without return. In this respect, Heidegger's restraint before death is a more effective step against the hegemony of *Dingbegriffe* in the understanding of the human. The threat of death, and not its reality, scatters Being in the transcendence of the "not-yet" and thereby allows for a thought of community that is not an assemblage of discrete entities under a universal. In the outstanding totality of its "not-yet," Dasein is always outside of itself and always a Being-with. It is thus always "within" the *Volk*.

Heidegger introduces the word *Volk* in §74 of *Being and Time* in order to align it with the essential Being-with-Others and Being-in-the-world of Dasein, but in doing so, he says nothing of that which could exclude Dasein from the *Volk*. Where Hegel's logicist conception of *Volk* explains both inclusion and exclusion by the scope of the ethical universal, Heidegger's transcendence cannot, by definition, come up against a limit. This absence in Heidegger's text of a criterion for distinguishing the identities of various peoples is by no means an oversight to be rectified by the supplement of the exclusive disjunctions of National Socialism's *Rassenkunde*. Heidegger's engagement in 1933 cannot be interpreted as providing the correction to his earlier "one-sidedness." The concentration on transcendence throughout his writings is simply too emphatic for it to be plausible that he should ever have straightforwardly subscribed to a containment of transcendence and a restoration of the metaphysics of presence. What is at stake in Heidegger's refusal, in 1927, to furnish a criterion for distinguishing peoples is not so much an inclusive humanism as his effort to rethink the traditional understanding of Being on the basis of the transcendence of Dasein. Without any means to limit itself, Heidegger's *Volk* does not recoil into the unity of humanity in general, because it is against unity as such that it defines itself as transcendence. Transcendence is an excess inasmuch as it presses beyond the one, and it is a restraint inasmuch as it never arrives at the other to the one it has left.

In his 1955 critique of Jünger, Heidegger will characteristically stress that it is this "in between" that more than anything else needs to be thought in the confrontation with the nihilism of metaphysics. Jünger, who wants to leap from the age of nihilism to "a new turning of Being," passes by transcendence, when, for Heidegger, it is precisely by remaining within transcendence that the nihilism of the oblivion of Being is to be brought to the sobriety of reflection. With an unmistakable Hegelian resonance, Heidegger writes:

The human being not only stands *within* the critical zone of the line. He himself—but not taken independently, and especially not through himself alone—is this zone and thus the line. In no case does the line, thought as a sign of the zone of consummate nihilism, lie before the human being in the manner of something that could be crossed. In that case, however, the possibility of a *trans lineam* and of such a crossing collapses.[43]

For Heidegger, the human being is the limit, just as for Hegel, the human understanding is the delimitation of what is. To be that which faces the limit as something external to it, irrespective of any success in "crossing the line," is trivial beside the truth of being this limit itself. Jünger is thus much further from the Un-thought of classical ontology than Hegel—he literally passes over transcendence. For this reason, the altercation with Jünger is not complicated by the exaggerations, concessions, and ambiguities of the altercation with Hegel. Given the shared privileging of the limit over that which it delimits, the question in Heidegger's confrontation with Hegel is what becomes of the limit. The political discourse that follows from its privileging is not unequivocal. There have been both revolutionary and reactionary politics of the limit. Renaming Heidegger's "transcendence," Michel Foucault, for instance, sounds uncomfortably like the author of the *Philosophy of Right* when he nonetheless speaks of the role and nature of transgression:

Its role is to measure the excessive distance that it opens at the heart of the limit and to trace the flashing line that causes the limit to arise. Transgression contains nothing negative, but affirms limited being—affirms the limitlessness into which it leaps as it opens this zone to existence for the first time. But correspondingly, this affirmation contains nothing positive: no content can bind it, since, by definition, no limit can possibly restrict it.[44]

Transgression is the limitlessness of the limit itself and, in this identity with Hegel's Spirit, it merges paradoxically and inadmissably with the state. If there is to be a difference from Hegel, and another politics than that of the Wise Man, it can only come from a transgression that transgresses itself, from a transcendence that does not cease to transcend. Thinking that which Heidegger was to term "transcendence" and Foucault, "transgression," Hegel attributes an absolute power to the delimiting activity of the understanding. But with this enthronement of Spirit, its transcendence and transgression are not unleashed, but rather curtailed. In its absolute power, Spirit transcends and transgresses whatever is, and yet it stands in need of the positive for the demonstration of its power. Spirit differs from the positive only to the extent that it amounts to the universal that glues together the entities whose definition has been inherited from classical ontology. The opportunity for an interrogation of the metaphysics of presence is thereby lost, because Spirit's distance from the positive is interpreted as its authority over—and hence responsibility for—whatever is. Power over the positive becomes nothing more than the duty to justify the positive. Crudely put, Hegel's response to the Un-thought of classical ontology is the conviction that he must justify to himself the existence of the Prussian state. As a result, Heidegger's objection to Hegel is not that he purely and simply neglected the question of Being (any number of passages can be cited from his works for their "anticipations" of Heidegger's thinking), but, on the contrary, that he did not allow his insight into the originarity of transcendence to call the positive into question. Hegel, in effect, assimilated transcendence to presence.

Yet why is it that Hegel throws the self-evidence of the present-at-hand into crisis only to rediscover the security of classical ontology in this very crisis? As far as this decision regarding the crisis of the metaphysics of presence is political, it can be traced back to Hegel's horror of the vacuity that he perceived in Romanticism. In his predilection for the substantial, Hegel is drawn to the concrete life of the state. In §257 and its Remark from the *Philosophy of Right*, Hegel writes:

The state is the actuality of the ethical Idea. It is ethical mind *qua* the substantial will manifest and revealed to itself, knowing and thinking itself, accomplishing what it knows and in so far as it knows it. The state exists immediately in custom, mediately in individual self-consciousness, knowledge, and activity, while self-consciousness in virtue of its sentiment towards the state finds in the state, as its essence and the end and product of its activity, its substantive freedom.

The *Penates* are inward gods, gods of the underworld; the mind of a nation [*Volksgeist*] (Athene for instance) is the divine, knowing and willing itself. Family piety is feeling, ethical behaviour directed by feeling; political virtue is the willing of the absolute end in terms of thought.[45]

The state is the manifestation and revelation of the ethical Idea. It is the means whereby the ethical Idea knows itself and likewise the end as which it knows itself. Through negating the actuality and substantiality of the state, the ethical Idea knows itself in its difference from the positive. And through knowing itself only by this negative relation, it simultaneously takes up this actuality and substantiality as an essential moment in its self-knowledge. Knowledge in Hegel could thus be said to betray itself even as it exhibits the greatest fidelity. Hegel's insight into the Un-thought of the understanding of Being as presence constitutes an advance in the knowledge of beings, and yet it is not a knowledge that can know itself as an advance and enrichment of knowledge without reinstating the understanding of beings that its insight had overthrown. It is perhaps in reaction to Hegel that Heidegger formulates the imperative in the *Contributions to Philosophy* to think Being by itself.

That Hegel does not think Being by itself—that he thinks it with respect to beings and hence politically with respect to the concrete life of the state—is not, of course, the grounds of the apparent National Socialist polemic. In *Mein Kampf*, it is the theorization of the state as the end of activity that Hitler rejects: "The state is a means to an end. Its end lies in the preservation and advancement of a community of physically and psychically homogeneous creatures." [46] But Hitler is not referring to the state as such. It is the existing apparatus of the purportedly racially indifferent state of liberalism that he has in view and to whose exploitation in the service of the new, racially grounded state he aspires. Hegel's thesis in regard to the state as the consummation of the self-knowledge of consciousness is neither affirmed nor denied. It is thus difficult to discern in such a statement of Hitler's an altercation with the *Philosophy of Right*, which is to say that it is difficult to discern any continuity between National Socialism's denunciations of the Weimar Republic and Heidegger's commentaries on Hegel. Were it not for the fact of Heidegger's engagement and the importance of his confrontation with Hegel, there would be little incentive to try to find in the regime any encouragement of an anti-Hegelian politics.

What is it, then, in the NSDAP that could have drawn Heidegger to it? More cautious than many of Heidegger's critics, Ernst Cassirer suggests, in *The Myth of the State*, that Heidegger's relationship to National Socialism has more to do with a lack of resistance than any obvious attraction and convergence: "a theory that sees in the Geworfenheit of man one of his principal characters [has] given up all hopes of an active share in the construction and reconstruction of man's cultural life." [47] Cassirer notes in the thrownness of Dasein the abjectness of resignation, but he misses its own specific, ontological task. Was Heidegger's engagement with National Socialism fundamentally an engagement with the abjectness of such an engagement, with its affront to the self-collectedness of the liberal subject? Insofar as the regime's spurious anti-statism furnishes nothing for an altercation with Hegel, it is a matter of looking elsewhere for any polemical inspirations that may lie behind Heidegger's engagement.

In 1933, the repellent submissiveness to Hitler that Heidegger enunciates in propositions that appear at variance with Heidegger's earlier thinking does not leave untouched the question of his relation to Hegel. There is in these texts a slavishness that outstrips anything in Hegel, as though Heidegger wanted to arrest the dialectic of Master and Slave. In the *Phenomenology of Spirit*, Hegel's slave proceeds too quickly from the fear of death to self-certainty:

> For this consciousness has been fearful, not of this or that particular thing or just at odd moments, but its whole being has been seized with dread; for it has experienced the fear of death, the absolute Lord. In that experience it has been quite unmanned, has trembled in every fibre of its being, and everything solid and stable has been shaken to its foundations. But this pure universal movement, the absolute melting-away of everything stable, is the simple, essential nature of self-consciousness, absolute negativity, *pure being-for-self*, which consequently is *implicit* in this consciousness. This moment of pure being-for-self is also *explicit* for the bondsman, for in the lord it exists for him as his *object*. Furthermore, his consciousness is not this dissolution of everything stable merely in principle; in his service he *actually* brings this about. Through his service he rids himself of his attachment to natural existence in every single detail; and gets rid of it by working on it.[48]

The Hegelian bondsman (*Knecht*) or slave does not rid himself of his fear of death by work. Work is rather the actuality of the fear of death and the dissolution of everything stable. It is thus no longer the lasting monument that cheats mortality. Hegel breaks with the tradition that considers the fear of death something to be surmounted. Heidegger's writings from the 1920s and 1930s are closer to Hegel's text, for example, than to the ataraxy of the Stoics, Boethius's *Consolation of Philosophy*, and Montaigne's essay "That to Philosophize Is to Learn to Die."[49] But the resemblance should not be overestimated. The "fear" of Hegel's slave receives its definition from the metaphysical understanding of knowledge: "Without the discipline of service and obedience, fear remains at the formal stage, and does not extend to the known real world of existence. Without the formative activity, fear remains inward and mute, and consciousness does not become explicitly *for itself*."[50]

Fear, for Hegel, is most truly fear when it is realized, that is, rendered concrete in the work. It is not fear as such that is surmounted, only its formalism and mute inwardness. By contrast, in Heidegger's account of fear in §40 of *Being and Time*, this formalism and mute inwardness will be set forth as the very essence of fear—its "realization" in the experience that the thingly is precisely that which is missing. Hegel's fear becomes objective because, within the understanding of Being in which it occurs, the decision has already been made for the present-at-hand. Not even the nothingness of fear is allowed to withstand the pull of the actual, since that which is fully known is that which is known in its concreteness. If the fear of death is here embraced as the starting point of philosophy, whereas prior to Hegel, philosophy was considered to begin from its repression, it is because finitude no longer arises as an issue. The absolute, and thus nonimpending, negativity of self-consciousness is the sole experience of this fear. Hegel's slave is incapable of an abasement that would involve even his self-certainty. He works for the master only to the extent that he works against him and fashions with the product the reality of his independence.

In the collection of notes "Overcoming Metaphysics," Heidegger is blunt in his appraisal of work: "The still hidden truth of Being is withheld from metaphysical humanity. The laboring animal is left to the giddy whirl of its products so that it may tear itself to pieces and annihilate itself in empty nothingness." [51] Without a relation to the truth of Being, Dasein is no more than a laboring animal. The work by which the Hegelian slave raises himself to the element of thinking is that by which humanity, according to Heidegger, is tumbled toward its ruin. But is this note from the years 1936–46 to be interpreted as a self-criticism? Is it simply a retraction of the 1934 text "The Call to the Labor Service" with its differentiation between the animal and the spirituality of work? Can the earlier text be taken at face value? If Heidegger's engagement truly constituted an adoption of the Hegelian position on work, then a Marxist party would seem a much more obvious choice than the NSDAP. The Nationalsozialistische Deutsche Arbeiterpartei is, however, a party of the workers who do not work in Hegel's sense. They work without ever finding in work their independence from the decrees of the Lord, and their fear of death is correspondingly never "realized" in the concreteness of the product. The Nazi worker is the slave who has been left behind by the dialectics of the history of Spirit. The charge cannot be dismissed out of hand that, in his engagement with the NSDAP, Heidegger seeks to become, as it were, the mouthpiece of the lumpenproletariat. That which, from a Marxist-Hegelian point of view, is repulsive in National Socialism—namely, the aborted emergence of class consciousness through work—is not what, in itself, attracts Heidegger to the movement. This aborting of class consciousness is, nonetheless, the corollary of the challenge raised to the metaphysics of presence by the being-outside-of-itself of fear.

Heidegger's political engagement was directly grounded in his confrontation with Hegel. If this seems implausible, then it should be remembered what Heidegger explicitly stated with regard to communism after the war in a letter to Marcuse: "Concerning 1933: I expected from National Socialism a spiritual renewal of life in its entirety, a reconciliation of social antagonisms and a deliverance of Western Dasein from the dangers of communism."[52] And that communism was, in Heidegger's eyes, by no means an illegitimate descendent of Hegel is clear from the "Letter on 'Humanism.'" Beneath its superficial generosity,[53] the more famous text is a restatement of the belligerent position expressed simultaneously in the letter to Marcuse and formulated with respect to the Hegelian principle of "work" in "Overcoming Metaphysics." The merit of Marx is not distinct from the dangers of communism, since his merit is to provide the philosophical exposition of that fundamental, metaphysical danger of which communism is but one, albeit overwhelming, manifestation. This danger is the danger of τέχνη, namely, the danger that according to the contentious parenthesis from *An Introduction to Metaphysics* cited earlier, it is the "inner truth and greatness" of National Socialism to encounter. Marx's status in the "Letter on 'Humanism'" is thus similar to Jünger's in "On the Question of Being," in that Marx brings a problem to light without understanding it *as a problem*:

What Marx recognized in an essential and significant sense, though derived from Hegel, as the estrangement of the human being has its roots in the homelessness of modern human beings. This homelessness is specifically evoked from the destiny of being in the form of metaphysics, and through metaphysics is simultaneously entrenched and covered up as such. Because Marx by experiencing estrangement attains an essential dimension of history, the Marxist view of history is superior to that of other historical accounts.[54]

Marx is here praised for placing the experience of estrangement at the center of his account of history, just as "On the Question of Being" compliments Jünger for his focus on the phenomenon of nihilism. Although Marx's critique of the expropriation of labor under capitalism, and the reduction of humanity to manipulable material, rests on the notion of estrangement, he does not, in Heidegger's judgment, recognize the roots of estrangement themselves in homelessness. Marx correctly grasps estrangement as the essence of the history of metaphysics, but he does not grasp that this essence is an evasion with respect to the question of Being.

Continuing to speak of Marxism and its Hegelian legitimacy, Heidegger aligns communism with τέχνη, and thereby indicates what he sees as the essential danger of communism:

The modern metaphysical essence of labor is anticipated in Hegel's *Phenomenology of Spirit* as the self-establishing process of unconditioned production, which is the objectification of the actual through the human being, experienced as subjectivity. The essence of materialism is concealed in the essence of technology, about which much has been written but little has been thought. Technology is in its essence a destiny within the history of being and of the truth of being, a truth that lies in oblivion. For technology does not go back to the τέχνη of the Greeks in name only but derives historically and essentially from τέχνη as a mode of ἀληθεύειν, a mode, that is, of rendering beings manifest. As a form of truth technology is grounded in the history of metaphysics, which is itself a distinctive and up to now the only surveyable phase of the history of being. No matter which of the various positions one chooses to adopt toward the doctrines of communism and to their foundation, from the point of view of the history of being it is certain that an elemental experience of what is world-historical speaks out in it. Whoever takes "communism" only as a "party" or a "Weltanschauung" is thinking too shallowly.[55]

Communism is inadequately described as a party or a weltanschauung because in communism there takes place a primordial experience of beings in their objectification through labor. Unless it is believed that Heidegger's preference for the NSDAP over Marxism can be fully explained by the attitudes prevalent among the provincial petite bourgeoisie of the 1930s, then such statements with regard to the philosophical significance of communism have to be taken seriously as a confession of what Heidegger thought was at stake in his political engagement. As much as communism is an insight into the essential estrangement of the human being, it is also a danger, because its insight does not reach far enough into the ground of estrangement. Derived from Hegel's understanding of labor, Marx's insight remains metaphysical. The homelessness of modern human beings is not experienced as such, since it is experienced as the expropriation of labor rather than as a falling away from the equation of the human essence with originary temporality. Whereas both Marx and Heidegger criticize the reification of humanity, Marx, unlike Heidegger, does not argue that any logicist conception of humanity amounts to a reification. Marx's response to estrangement is thus inspired by a definition of the human essence that is still governed, according to Heidegger, by the *Dingbegriffe* of classical ontology.

That to which Marx objects in capitalism, and in Hegel's theory of the State, is that the logicist conception of humanity has not yet come to its full flowering. Marx thus condemns Hegel in his *Critique of Hegel's "Philosophy of Right"* for deviating from his logic in order to accommodate the political constitution of his day: "It is not a question of developing the determinate idea of the political constitution, but of giving the political constitution a relation to the abstract Idea, of classifying it as a member of its (the Idea's) life history. This is an obvious mystification."[56]

Hegel's mystification of the positive is, for Marx, an obfuscation of his own recognition of the absolute negativity of the human being. Hegel's philosophy becomes the expression of the inconsistency of capitalism and its "hypocritical, bourgeois cosmopolitanism."[57] Having emerged into history through the dissolution of the positive in the slave's fear, the universality of human Spirit still lacks the immanent determinative power that Hegel himself attributes to it. Under capitalism, it remains the extrinsic universality of *homo oeconomicus*, that is, the universal of quantifiable labor that regulates trade and allows the disparities in the living conditions of concrete human beings to persist unchecked. It is accordingly against the *speciousness* of bourgeois cosmopolitanism that Marx expostulates, reserving for a genuine cosmopolitanism the deliverance of humanity from its reification. The reduction of workers to the commodity of their labor is to be reversed by a substantive dissolution of the particularity of the positive in the element of the universality of self-consciousness. In Hegel, this dissolution was merely "ideological." Hegel, for Marx, is too little a logician, since his philosophy retains much that is irrational and obscurantist. The task that Marx sets himself in his own confrontation with Hegel is a perfection of the universalism of the latter's thought, rather than its ontological destruction. The estrangement of modern human beings is to be countered in communism by a recovery into the universality of the human essence (*Gattungswesen*).

But such a recovery will decide nothing with regard to Heidegger's notion of homelessness, because even in its universality, the human essence continues to be thought inauthentically. Communism cannot effect a deliverance of humanity from the sway of reification, since the equality of a genuine cosmopolitanism is grounded in the understanding of Being as presence. Without the apprehensibility of the distinctness of beings in presence, there is no foundation for the claim of their equality. Under communism, Dasein will have been disentangled from its identifications with the commodity only to be still thought as a being present-at-hand in the iterable distinctness of its logicist essence.

But is the "Letter on 'Humanism'" really, at bottom, a criticism of Marx? To overlook the antagonism of its position involves any commentary on Heidegger in a number of difficulties. The remark on the dangers of communism in the contemporaneous letter to Marcuse cannot be reconciled with any endorsement of Marx, just as Heidegger's enlistment in a political party vociferously opposed to Marxism must itself be considered to indicate, at least, a mistrust of the latter's tenets. But if Heidegger wanted to distance himself from National Socialism after the war, could he have found a better means than an appeal to the resurgent Marxism of the French intelligentsia? And yet, inasmuch as this appeal would consist in a textually unfounded identification of Marx's account of estrangement and Heidegger's account of homelessness, it is hard to envisage how Heidegger, as a historian of philosophy, could have so forgotten himself. To dwell here on the unacceptability of the identification may illuminate a negative reason for Heidegger's political engagement, namely, his rejection of Marxism. This can be done by addressing a reading of the two thinkers that does not notice the fundamental difference between their conceptions of alienation and that confounds the universalism of the one with the other's suspicion of the well-foundedness of the ontic.

Kostas Axelos, in *Einführung in ein künftiges Denken: Über Marx und Heidegger* (Introduction to a Future Thinking: On Marx and Heidegger), seemingly takes for granted Lucien Goldmann's thesis that *Being and Time* ends with an exhortation to elaborate and deepen Lukács's (and not, more plausibly, Husserl's) [58] theory of reified consciousness. [59] Drawing attention to a distinction in the young Marx with the purpose of "radicalizing" Marx and bringing him closer to his own equally peculiar understanding of Heidegger, Axelos writes:

He speaks of the "presupposition" of socialism-communism and even writes on a badly ripped and scarcely legible page of the Paris manuscript: "If we still characterize communism itself—because as negation of the negation, as the appropriation of the human essence that mediates itself with itself through negation of private property, accordingly not yet as the *true* [Marx's emphasis] position that begins from itself but, on the contrary, from private property" (p. 264), then that must mean that estrangement is not actually sublated. [60]

But is it the object per se that Marx wants to overthrow or simply the institution of private property? Is any object whatsoever an obstacle to genuine cosmopolitanism? Or merely reified humanity in its particularity? For Axelos, in 1966, the quoted passage from the *Economic-Philosophical Man-*

uscripts is, extraordinarily, a reservation on Marx's part with respect to communism, as though Marx considered an absolute recovery of the human essence—the *true* negation of that negation which is the externality of, among other things, private property—to be the highest political good.

In his 1967 preface to *History and Class Consciousness*, Lukács confesses that it was precisely under the impact of reading in 1930 this text by Marx that he repudiated his earlier blanket opposition to objectification:

> In the process of reading the Marx manuscript all the idealist prejudices of *History and Class Consciousness* were swept to one side. It is undoubtedly true that I could have found ideas similar to those which now had such an overwhelming effect on me in the works of Marx that I had read previously. But the fact is that this did not happen, evidently because I read Marx in the light of my own Hegelian interpretation.[61]

Axelos, who translated Lukács's *History and Class Consciousness* into French, is perhaps under the sway of the Hegelian Marxism of Lukács's text in interpreting the *Economic-Philosophical Manuscripts*. He takes the *true* sublation of externality to be desirable. A *true* sublation of externality, as Lukács later argues, could only be desirable from "a failure to subject the Hegelian heritage to a thoroughgoing materialist reinterpretation."[62] The consequence of such a sublation would be the very impossibility of materialism:

> But as, according to Hegel, the object, the thing exists only as an alienation from self-consciousness, to take it back into the subject would mean the end of objective reality and thus of any reality at all. *History and Class Consciousness* follows Hegel in that it too equates alienation with objectification [*Vergegenständlichung*] (to use the term employed by Marx in the *Economic-Philosophical Manuscripts*). This fundamental and crude error has certainly contributed greatly to the success enjoyed by *History and Class Consciousness*.[63]

The "crude error" of *History and Class Consciousness* is that the object was to be taken back into the subject without remainder: the destruction and preservation of Hegel's *Aufhebung* (sublation) is reduced to destruction. That which in Hegel is ideological, namely, the reappropriation of the human essence that nonetheless leaves existing conditions intact, is also what constitutes the realism of his philosophy. Lukács acknowledges his own earlier lack of realism when he compares the identical subject-object in Hegel with the messianic proletariat of *History and Class Consciousness*:

> Of course, in Hegel it arises in a purely logical and philosophical form when the highest stage of absolute spirit is attained in philosophy by abolishing alienation

and by the return of self-consciousness to itself, thus realising the identical subject-object. In *History and Class Consciousness*, however, this process is socio-historical and it culminates when the proletariat reaches this stage in its class consciousness, thus becoming the identical subject-object of history. This does indeed appear to "stand Hegel on his feet"; it appears as if the logico-metaphysical construction of the *Phenomenology of Mind* had found its authentic realisation in the existence and the consciousness of the proletariat. . . . But is the identical subject-object here anything more in truth than a purely metaphysical construct?[64]

In 1967, Lukács answers in the negative. He has made his peace with objectification, "for objectification is indeed a phenomenon that cannot be eliminated from human life in society."[65] When Axelos attributes to the young Marx the political ambition of a complete reappropriation of objective reality, it is thus in defiance of what Lukács will have come to view as the essence of Marxist materialism. And by virtue of his sociohistorical recasting of Hegel, Axelos is likewise in defiance of Heidegger. The solution that Axelos proffers to estrangement is the reappropriation of objective reality, whereas for Heidegger the oneness of such a delivered humanity would still denote an estrangement from the ecstases of originary temporality.

Heidegger does not attempt to overcome estrangement in the wisdom that is at one with all that is, namely, in Lukács's words, to "out-Hegel Hegel."[66] Instead, Heidegger attempts, one might say, to "out-die" Hegel. Heidegger's critique of Hegel is, accordingly, informed by a stricter adherence, not so much to universalism, as to the ontological possibilities of mortality. Hegel's philosophy is a philosophy of death that is at once a philosophy of eternity. It begins at a point beyond death and, inasmuch as it is born in the ruin of sensuous immediacy, it faces from the outset the universal and its absolute present. For Hegel, the Whole is the True, because he begins at the point at which everything is unconcealed. That which is essentially concealed, and still announced itself for the Greeks in the genuine contest between ἀλήθεια and forgetfulness, simply does not exist in his philosophy. Hegel is unable to think the catastrophic character of Dasein's "not-yet." Being is already resolved into the totality of the mediation between the universal and the particular, between the subject and the object. It is at least in part Heidegger's understanding of death that renders him insusceptible to a politics that defines itself by the goal of genuine cosmopolitanism or the totality of subject and object. Heidegger's rejection of the universalism of Marxism cannot be wholly ascribed to provincialist prejudices but must be appraised also in the context of his interrogation of the appropriateness of the universal to Dasein. In the essential "not-yet" of its Being-towards-death, Dasein never ceases to die and thus never ceases to defer the moment in which it would be sundered from the ontological undecidability of sensuous immediacy and handed over definitively to the absolute present of the universal. What is handed over in death is not Dasein but a being present-at-hand. By its elevation to the universal, humanity is tricked, as it were, into accepting the authority of the *Dingbegriffe* of classical ontology. The realization of the universal class in early Marx is, for Althusser, a "religious" concept of the proletariat,[67] and, indeed, there is something numinous in a substantive cosmopolitanism. Without a stake in empirical reality, the proletariat is at once transcendental and hence logically the truth and rule of what is, as though its poverty were best interpreted in the language of Christian and Kantian asceticism. But more than simply for its religious analogy, the universal class is to be criticized for obscuring Dasein's status as an exception to the ontology of the present-at-hand. The humanity that has come to itself in its universality is no longer the being-outside-of-itself that transcends the metaphysics of presence. Where estrangement, for Marx, lies in reified humanity's being outside of its own universalist essence, for Heidegger the estrangement of reification lies, in contrast, in humanity's being outside of its essential being-outside-of-itself. And because being-outside-of-itself is originary for Heidegger, estrangement can never be reappropriated. Fallenness (*Verfallenheit*), as Heidegger stresses again and again in *Being and Time*, is not a condition to be rectified or deplored. It is, however, a condition to be understood—and understood despite the metaphysical determination of understanding—in its foundations in the essential being-outside-of-itself of Dasein. In its lostness in the "they," in its fallenness and inauthenticity, Dasein is still essentially and conspicuously a being-outside-of-itself, even as it takes itself for something present-at-hand. Marx's critique of alienation notes the being-outside-of-itself of reified humanity, but inasmuch as Marx interprets it as a condition to be made good in the regulated transcendence of the universal, Marx's critique remains true to its Hegelian roots in its relation to the Un-thought of classical ontology. In communism, everything is pulled back to the center of the absolute present of the death of Spirit.

Heidegger wanted to give direction to the Nazi opposition to Marx. As he makes clear in the 1933–34 lecture course *Vom Wesen der Wahrheit* (On the Essence of Truth), he wanted to deepen the opposition to Marx to the point of a contestation with metaphysics as a whole:

Up until today the entire spiritual Dasein of the West has been determined by this doctrine of Ideas. The concept of God has its source in the Idea, and natural science is also oriented toward it. Christian and rationalist thought converge in Hegel. Hegel is also the basis for intellectual and ideological currents, for Marxism above all. If there were no doctrine of Ideas, there would be no Marxism. Thus we shall be able to finish Marxism off for good only if the doctrine of Ideas and its two-thousand-year history is first confronted.[68]

In the Platonic doctrine of Ideas, the visibility and presence of the εἶδος rises to preeminence at the cost of an obliviousness to invisibility and transcendence.

It is accordingly not easy to discover what could have attracted Heidegger in the emphatic visibility of the NSDAP's biologism. Heidegger was receptive to the *possibility* of the movement's hostility to Marxism. It goes without saying that this hostility did not develop in the direction of a questioning concerning the truth of Being. National Socialism broke with the consciousness of Hegel's pure ego and the class consciousness of the Marxist proletariat, but it did not escape the sway of the metaphysics of presence. In the *Contributions to Philosophy*, Heidegger censures a notion of the *Volk* that still admits the model of the "I": "*It is only on the basis of Da-sein that the essence of the people can be grasped* and that means at the same time knowing that the people can never be goal and purpose and that such an opinion is only a 'folkish' [*völkisch*] extension of the "liberal" thought of the 'I' and of the economic idea of the preservation of 'life.'"[69] Situated in Dasein's Being-there in a world, the essence of the *Volk* is situated in that which is lost to view with the abstraction of the "I." The people can never be made a goal or a purpose in, for instance, the propaganda of a "folkish" state, because the abstraction presupposed for the setting of any goal or purpose never comes up with anything that could properly be called the *Volk*. Defined by the historicality, that is, the transcendence of Dasein, the *Volk* is too indefinite to fulfil the role of a purpose. It transcends itself and thus lacks the stability to constitute a measure. The ontic instability of the *Volk* is not a shortcoming, but rather a necessary consequence of its originarity. The *Volk* cannot be modeled on the "I," because it precedes it in the very same sense that the transcendence of Dasein precedes the presence and self-identity of the subject. Nothing needs to be added to Dasein in order to arrive at the *Volk*.

Heidegger's path to the *Volk* is not distinct from his excavation of Dasein from the concealed foundations of modern metaphysics. The subject gives way to the Dasein of the *Volk*. Without distorting matters too much, it could therefore be contended that Heidegger's people can be traced back to Husserl's demotion of the epistemological subject of Neo-Kantianism, since it is in his critique of psychologism and anthropomorphism that Husserl opened Heidegger's eyes to the primacy of intentionality and what he was to call and rethink as "transcendence." With the early theory of the categorial intuitions, Husserl short-circuits the transcendental subject in the *Logical Investigations*. He raises the possibility of no longer conceiving knowledge as the commerce between the individual intuitions of the phenomenal world and the categories that have their seat in the stability and unity of the subject of modern metaphysics. The Hegelian sublation of finitude in Spirit becomes questionable. Hegel's pure ego is to be displaced from its position of authority over what is, and being-outside-of-itself is not automatically to fall under the rule of the One in being known. The self-presence of death ceases to be as desirable as its anticipation and deferral. For Heidegger, his political engagement will have been determined in part by this courtship of death.

Ontological Opportunism

Everywhere he goes, José Ortega y Gasset encounters the masses. Suddenly, and without anyone knowing why, the hotels, famous doctors' waiting rooms, theaters, railways, and seaside resorts have become over-crowded. And yet, as Ortega y Gasset notes in his account of European demagogy, the population has not increased: "Approximately the same number of people existed fifteen years ago."[1] For Ortega y Gasset in 1930, the masses do not define themselves in terms of a quantitative result, just as for Heidegger in 1927, a people is not the sum of many subjects. The congestion with which the masses have enveloped the public places is not a consequence of a numerical excess, since, for Ortega y Gasset, it is as the quality of numerical excess per se that the masses appear at all. Endemic to public places, they necessarily resist the analysis and decomposition into isolated individuals by which their numerability could be assured. They are a number that cannot be counted. In their character of a pure "too much," the masses push themselves forward as perverse suitors for the Kantian sub-lime. At every turn, Ortega y Gasset witnesses the collapse of the spectacle of the individual under the monolithic quantity of homogeneous human-ity. For Ortega y Gasset, lacking Heidegger's suspicion of the antithesis be-tween the individual and the "they," and thus lacking any insight into the appeal of his individualism for a fascist readership, the uprising of the masses is nothing but the failure of individuation. It is thus a population at a loss what to do with itself that overruns the public places. Heidegger's political engagement was an attempt to assume the leadership of this up-rising, as was National Socialism itself.

For Heidegger in 1933, the masses were not to be urged to retreat from the public places. On the contrary, the uprising of the masses, once it had been led beyond a satisfaction with the externality of "folkish" accoutrements, was expected to become the *Volk* of the question of Being. This transformation of the masses was to coincide with a transformation of the German university. From his position as rector of Freiburg University, Heidegger wanted to bring the university into line with the ontological mission of the German *Volk*. This did not entail imposing a framework on faculties that had previously been autonomous. In Heidegger's judgment, the apparent autonomy of the faculties was nothing other than their homogenization in the liberal conception of science. The faculties were autonomous merely in the sense that they no longer contested one another in the understanding of knowledge: the pretense of autonomy rested on an implicit consensus and apathy regarding the definition of knowledge. The "crisis" of the specialization of the sciences was a consequence of the fundamental aimlessness of this homogenization. It is the question of the aim of the sciences, and of the *Volk*, that Heidegger raises in the address "The Self-Assertion of the German University."

In his essay "But Suppose We Were to Take the Rectorial Address Seriously . . . Gérard Granel's *De l'université*," Christopher Fynsk accordingly writes:

Heidegger posed the . . . question to the German university: were the sciences to *be*? He . . . posed it from the basis of the . . . conception of the university's founding function, asserting that if the sciences were to assume their possibility, they would have to recapture their essence in a renewal of the Greek concept of τέχνη (what Heidegger named ". . . the innermost center of the entire *Dasein* as a people in its state," "the power that hones and embraces *Dasein* in its entirety"). Finally, he asked this question with [a] revolutionary design. For he argued that only by recovering their originary "revolutionary" essence would the sciences be able to serve—in the sense of guiding and impelling—the National Socialist revolution.[2]

The sciences were to guide and impel the National Socialist revolution by renewing the Greek concept of knowledge (τέχνη). Fynsk, who does not take the rectorial address seriously enough, omits asking after the aim of a renewal of τέχνη. That which was to be known in this renewal, and could be known only by the *Volk*, was Dasein itself. To the mobilized population of Hitler's Germany, the truth of Dasein, and thus the fundamental truth of all the sciences, was to reveal itself. And that is to say, Dasein was to reveal the impossibility of its revelation in the light of the understanding of Being as presence.

"The Self-Assertion of the German University" is addressed to a popular uprising, but it is concerned with concealment. What interests Heidegger in the sudden publicness of the masses is, not a nostalgia for the privacy of Ortega y Gasset's individual, but rather the concealment that is the essence of the German *Volk*. In "The Self-Assertion of the German University," Heidegger arguably aspires to involve the "folkish" uprising in his own confrontation with the metaphysics of presence. Incited in their nationalism and drilled in the definition of the nonpositivity of the German *Volk*, the masses were to be led to a collision with what is.

In hindsight, it is easy to see that Heidegger expected too much from the masses. The cynicism of hindsight, which rests on the positivism with which it views the past as completely determinate, is incapable of appreciating the task that Heidegger set both himself and the "folkish" uprising. For hindsight, Heidegger will always have come too late to direct the uprising down another path. And once the philosophical ambition of the rectorial address has been overlooked, Heidegger's political engagement loses any distance from National Socialism.

In the name of the *Volk* of the question of Being, in the name of the Germans' long-standing metaphysical mission, Heidegger appealed to the masses of a nationalist uprising. If Heidegger's appeal was to have a chance of success, the masses had to be nationalistic. The masses had to be open to an appeal to their nationalism, and inasmuch as an appeal needed to be made, the masses had to differ as yet from the *Volk* of the question of Being. Heidegger did not confuse the masses of National Socialism with the *Volk* of the question of Being, but he failed to bring about a transformation of the masses.

The people Heidegger addresses in 1933 does not conspicuously differ from the populations public by default in which the various fascist movements took root. The possibility of the *Volk* of the question of Being is overshadowed but not excluded by the reality of a racist mobilization. Indeed, for Heidegger, this reality was not yet assured. It could still be asked who these masses were that had no means of resisting the public spaces of National Socialism.

When Heidegger stepped forward as rector of Freiburg University to preach the fulfillment of the promise of ancient Greece with respect to the understanding of Being, it was wittingly among the grandiose and yet likewise shabby stage scenery of *Blut und Boden*. Everywhere the *Hakenkreuz* declared the break with Christianity and, implicitly, the return of a proto-Germanic and hence supposedly non-nihilistic, preontological understanding of Being (the Sanskrit word *svastika* derives from the words *su* [good] and *asti* [being]).[3] The scandal of Heidegger's rectorial address is that the juxtaposition of ontology and demagogy is without irony.

What could Heidegger have seen in the people of fascism? That the people was to be *seen* constituted an imperative of the fascist movements. The nation is a result rather than the starting point of fascism. It has to be produced. In his speech "The Tasks of the German Theater," delivered on May 8, 1933, in the Hotel Kaiserhof in Berlin, Goebbels notoriously pressed the movement's claim to creativity: "I am even of the opinion that politics is the highest art there is, since the sculptor shapes only the stone, the dead stone, and the poet only the word, which in itself is dead. But the states-man shapes the masses, gives them statute and structure, breathes in form and life so that a people arises from them."[4]

A people is the work of art for which the masses are the material and fascism the artist. For Goebbels, as for Heidegger, a people cannot be taken for granted. Yet, for Goebbels, a people that is missing is not Being-with-one-another in its inauthenticity, but dead, unindividuated matter. The people that is brought to life through the artistry of politicians is not es-sentially at odds with reification. To the extent that it comes to itself only inasmuch as it furnishes proof of the will to power of the politician as cre-ator, the people does not come to itself at all, remaining an object over against an absolute subjectivity. Hence the fascist aestheticization of poli-tics acquires a more sinister meaning than the diremption of public dis-course from the workings of government. In fascism, the masses cannot even be duped, because outside the fiction of the politician-aesthete, in which alone they become animate, they lack the means to be gullible. Here politics as the highest art—as that through which, according to Demokri-tos (fr. 157), human beings come to praiseworthy successes—is reduced to taking its cue from Shaw's *Pygmalion*.

On May 27, 1933, less than three weeks after Goebbels's speech in Berlin, Heidegger delivered his inaugural address as the newly elected rec-tor of Freiburg University. The stance taken in this address toward Na-tional Socialism and the "glory" and "greatness of this decampment [*Auf-bruch*]" is by no means unambiguous, and not least because after the war, Heidegger insisted on a recognition of the defiance in its title, "The Self-Assertion of the German University." This defiance is better understood, however, in terms of Heidegger's ontological opportunism. Grounds for such an interpretation can be drawn from the address itself, and even from

Heidegger's own apologetics. Heidegger was always too convinced of the philosophical superiority of his motivations to hide completely what was at stake.

In the text "The Rectorate 1933/34: Facts and Thoughts," Heidegger writes that a rector who had joined the NSDAP—but, unlike himself, not out of "defiance"—would have chosen another title than "Die Selbstbehauptung der deutschen Universität." But in pressing the case for his opposition to the new regime, Heidegger makes a slip:

> One could excuse oneself from reflection and hold onto the seemingly obvious thought that, shortly after National Socialism seized power, a newly elected rector gives an address on the university, an address which "represents" National Socialism [*welche Rede "den" Nationalsozialismus "vertritt"*]—that is to say, proclaims the idea of "political science," which, crudely understood, says "True is what is good for the people." From this one concludes, and rightly so, that this betrays the essence of the German university in its very core and actively contributes to its destruction; for this reason, the title should be "The Self-Decapitation of the German University" ["Die Selbstenthauptung der deutschen Universität"].⁵

What jars with the exculpatory reasoning in this passage is the use of scare quotes in the original German around the definite article before "National Socialism." It is as though Heidegger in 1945 only wishes to distance himself from the National Socialism of convention. To another and "private" National Socialism, such as that with which Otto Wacker, the Baden minister of art, education, and justice, charged him after hearing the address,⁶ he seemingly retains his loyalty. "The Self-Assertion of the German University" is thus a title that restricts its defiance to "the" NSDAP. Even in 1945, Heidegger's "private" National Socialism did not cast aside its obvious mask in order to present itself unequivocally as an expression of opposition to the regime. No doubt the motif of a "private" National Socialism was Heidegger's compromise between exculpation and plausibility. Heidegger's National Socialism must be said to have always been private. *Being and Time* had not been repudiated by 1933, and its emphatic distinction of Dasein from the present-at-hand is inconsistent with the conception of humanity as manipulable material formulated in Goebbels's speech to his audience in the Kaiserhof Hotel and later put into practice in breeding programs and extermination camps. This "private" National Socialism of Heidegger's composes a gray zone of servility and resistance. In "The Self-Assertion of the German University," Aeschylus, Nietzsche, Clausewitz, and Plato are referred to by name, but not Hitler, and yet this appearance of a rebuff is contradicted by the assiduity with which Heidegger as rector oversaw the *Gleichschaltung* (bringing into line) of Freiburg University. Heidegger, who boasts in his interview with *Der Spiegel* in 1966 that no other rectorial address of the period dared as much in its title,[7] nonetheless telegramed Hitler on May 20, 1933, to ask for a "postponement of the planned reception of the executive committee of German universities until the moment when the direction of the university association [*Hochschulverband*] has been brought about in the sense of the *Gleichschaltung* that precisely here is especially necessary."[8] It would be easy and, within a certain context, justified to dismiss as merely verbal the defiance that in a frantic postwar apologetics Heidegger uncovers in the title of his address. To do so, however, entails forgoing any convincing reconstruction (which is not the same as a defense) of the terms on which Heidegger could align himself with a movement whose understanding of humanity was irreconcilable with his own. What is involved in a convincing reconstruction is more than the continuity and coherence of a biography. The irreconcilability with National Socialism of the understanding of humanity set forth repeatedly in Heidegger's writings is, for its own sake, what must be defended in the face of ad hominem arguments.

The defiance of "The Self-Assertion of the German University," insofar as it is the text itself that is in question and not just its free-floating title, lies in an excess, rather than in an opposition. Heidegger does not set himself against the movement but seeks to follow it through to the point of exhaustion where it must give way to something else. In this sense, Heidegger is comparable to the Stalinist critics of the 1920s and 1930s who all but welcomed fascism as the catastrophic preamble to socialism. That Heidegger situates the merit of the mobilization of the German people in its chance of failure is evident from the extraordinary interpretation that he offers in the address of a verse by Aeschylus:

Among the Greeks there circulated an old report that Prometheus had been the first philosopher. It is this Prometheus into whose mouth Aeschylus puts an adage that expresses the essence of knowledge:

τέχνη δ' ἀνάγκης ἀσθενεστέρα μακρῷ

"But knowledge is far less powerful than necessity." That means: all knowledge of things remains beforehand at the mercy of overpowering fate and fails before it.

It is precisely for that reason that knowledge must develop its highest defiance, for which alone the entire might of the concealedness of what is will first rise up, in order really to fail. Thus what is reveals itself in its unfathomable inalterability and confers its truth on knowledge. This adage about the creative impotence of knowledge is a saying of the Greeks, in whom we all too easily see the model for knowledge that, taking its stand purely on itself and thereby forgetting itself, counts among us as the "theoretical" attitude.[9]

It is noteworthy how little attention has been given to this passage in the secondary literature. William McNeill, one of the few commentators to discuss it, nonetheless elides the exhortation to failure.[10] Failure is, for Heidegger, not simply a method that knowledge has at its disposal in uncovering what is. Knowledge must fail in earnest, and hence in its every method, so that what is will reveal itself in its truth. Prior to its failure, knowledge is not strictly knowledge, but rather an unwitting collusion with the concealedness (*Verborgenheit*) of beings.

But why in the first months of the National Socialist regime did Heidegger expound this failure as the mission of the German university? Curiously, Heidegger declared in 1966 that he would be willing to repeat the rectorial address, and with a still greater vehemence than before.[11] The untimeliness with which he no doubt wanted this confession to imbue the text—an untimeliness that he believed would likewise have marked the text's repetition in the BRD—is, in the circumstances of Heidegger's engagement, the untimeliness less of the apolitical than of the opportunistic. In the name of the failure of knowledge, Heidegger was prepared to disregard the long and public list of Nazi acts of brutality under the Weimar Republic and assume the office of rector after the Social Democrat Wilhelm von Möllendorff had been dismissed by the new regime as unsuitable. Even if other motivations can be adduced for Heidegger's engagement, in his most significant text as rector, it is on knowledge defined by failure that he fixes his attention in the altered conditions. Heidegger's "private" National Socialism is the National Socialism of the openly exhorted failure of knowledge. Bewitched by his own definition of the movement and assured of its superiority, Heidegger is not cynical in his opportunism. He is not even able to see his engagement as opportunistic. For Heidegger, the failure of knowledge, by virtue of its status as the limit toward which knowledge must strive in order to be what it is, cannot be anything other than the truth of knowledge and, ipso facto, of a political movement, whether in 1933 or 1966. The excess of "The Self-Assertion of the German University," and its equivocal defiance, is the excess by which it reaches beyond everything that lies unconcealed before knowledge in order to founder on

the concealedness of necessity. In reaching beyond whatever lies unconcealed, "The Self-Assertion of the German University" reaches beyond an
empirical National Socialism to the meta–National Socialism that is the
historical truth of the movement. It is this meta–National Socialism that
will be known when necessity itself is known and knowledge is truly
knowledge of what is.

Heidegger's politics is a politics of concealedness. The conception of
politics underlying Heidegger's engagement in 1933 is inseparable from the
preeminence of failure before concealedness in his account of knowledge.
If Heidegger, in his address, exhorts the university to genuine failure, it is
because only in genuine failure does knowledge exchange the presumption
of its "theoretical" attitude for the truth of its ground in beings. As the visibility of what is, θεωρία comes to grief on the fate that is both essential
and essentially concealed. With the proposition of the superior power of
fate, Heidegger participates in the National Socialist demotion of the concepts of pure science and academic freedom.[12] But Heidegger's understanding of fate should not be identified with the common National Socialist understanding of fate and the accompanying supremacy of the
"political." The regime's complacent efforts to render the political visible
suffice to indicate a distinction. The regime did not seek to founder on the
invisibility of the political; instead, it sought to pass off the pervasiveness
of its paraphernalia as the politicization of the society (*Gesellschaft*) of liberalism. The NSDAP was too positivistic in its understanding of fate. In
the rectorial address, Aeschylus becomes the mouthpiece of Heidegger's
own repeated criticism of the ontological presuppositions of the positivism
of modern science. Grounded in classical ontology's inability to think Being as other than that which is present and visible to the gaze of θεωρία,
modern science does not see that Dasein cannot be seen.

Genuine failure, as it were, politicizes knowledge, since it tears knowledge from the abstractness in which, forgetting its Being and thus forgetting itself, it believes it stands purely on itself. The event, and not the act,
of genuine failure is the worlding of the world always tacitly presupposed
by knowledge. It is essentially that which cannot be made and thus inter-
rupts the hegemony of technicism (*Machenschaft*). In its genuine failure,
knowledge encounters its limits as its own questionability and not simply
as proofs of the Hegelian autonomy of Spirit. What it encounters is its own
constitutive unknowable. As the historicality that is arrested and dehistori-
cized when a being becomes visible in its presence and is known, fate can-

not itself become visible. It cannot do so because it cannot reveal itself to knowledge, so long as knowledge, in a disavowal of failure, keeps within the limits of presence. Fate is the concealedness of the world that is the site of all political occurrences. It is the possibility of knowledge (objective genitive) and the impossibility of knowledge (subjective genitive). In order really to fail, knowledge must develop the highest defiance of the necessity (*Notwendigkeit*) of its failure. It must fail utterly and, that is to say, without guile. Following through its ambitions on the infinite, it must seek to encompass world even as knowledge of world is never a knowledge encompassing world, but rather a knowledge encompassed by world. In the "Letter on 'Humanism,'" Heidegger writes: "As long as philosophy merely busies itself with continually obstructing the possibility of admittance into the matter for thinking, i.e., into the truth of being, it stands safely beyond any danger of shattering against the hardness of that matter. Thus to 'philosophize' about being shattered is separated by a chasm from a thinking that is shattered."[13]

Knowledge that merely counterfeits failure—that mistakes its willful abdication of the concept for an immediate intuition of what is, for example—retains the limitations of the "theoretical" attitude. In the conviction of the authority of its caprices, it secretly still believes it stands on itself. Such knowledge plays its voluntaristic irrationalism off against the rationalism of Descartes and his successors, but it thereby only varies the *Seinsvergessenheit* (obliviousness to Being) of the metaphysics of subjectity. Such knowledge is illusory because it cannot think the transcendence that is its own ground. Unable to think the worldliness of its Being, it is excluded from the truth of its essential politicality.

Heidegger's political engagement can therefore be said to have been an engagement *for* the political, namely, for that which will come solely at the consummation and defeat of the knowledge of the metaphysics of subjectity. Heidegger's National Socialism was governed by the ancient saying of the Greeks on the impotence of knowledge and the future realization of the truth of this saying. In "The Self-Assertion of the German University," the actuality of the movement resolves into the *possibility* of an authentic politics. And it is as the task of the German people that Heidegger puts forward this possibility:

But neither will anyone ask us whether we will it or do not will it when the spiritual strength of the West fails and the West starts to come apart at the seams, when this moribund pseudocivilization collapses into itself, pulling all forces into con-fusion and allowing them to suffocate in madness.

Whether such a thing occurs or does not occur, this depends solely on whether we as a historical-spiritual *Volk* will ourselves, still and again, or whether we will ourselves no longer. Each individual *has a part* in deciding this, even if, and precisely if, he seeks to evade this decision.

But it is our will that our *Volk* fulfill its historical mission.[14]

The historical task and possibility of the Germans is that they will them-selves, not as individuals within the metaphysics of subjectity, but as a people. According to the above quotation, only the German people's will to self-assertion stands in the way of the collapse of the West. But here the will is to be differentiated from the voluntarism and vulgar Nietzscheanism propagated within the NSDAP. Precisely because Heidegger never dis-owned the rectorial address, the polemic against the will to power in his lectures from the late 1930s and early 1940s cannot be interpreted as self-criticism. Heidegger's Prometheus is not the Prometheus of Goethe or Shelley. The German people's will to self-assertion is not its will to take on the role of the politician-aesthete among the masses of the globe. It is not its will to absolute subjectivity but its will to the genuine failure of knowl-edge, and thus to the failure of will and its forgetfulness of world. Dasein's Being-in-the-world is to be recovered from oblivion.

That the self-assertion of a historical-spiritual people is better under-stood in terms of failure, than in terms of success, is the import of an ear-lier passage from the rectorial address: "This *Volk* is playing an active role in shaping its fate by placing its history into the openness of the overpow-ering might of all the world-shaping forces of human existence and by struggling ever anew to secure its spiritual world. Thus exposed to the ex-treme questionableness of its own existence, this *Volk* has the will to be a spiritual *Volk*."[15]

Understandably, the *Volk* cannot win its spiritual world from a *supe-rior* power. Through its defeat at the hands of the superior power, the *Volk* wrests its world from its own forgetfulness. The spiritual world that is se-cured is secured not *against* the utmost questionability of a people's own Dasein, but, on the contrary, *as* this very questionability in the openness of the superior power of fate. The seeming paradox of Heidegger's rectorial address is that the German people comes to itself in its ruinous collision with fate. It comes to itself and knows itself as other than a being present-at-hand in coming to its ground in the unknowability of world.

At times during the rectorate, the struggle to secure the spiritual world of the *Volk* seems indistinguishable from the regime's own struggle. Heidegger, like Hitler, calls the German people to struggle.[16] This struggle does not involve contests between like-minded opponents such as those that characterized the Greek ἀγών. The struggle is against the enemy. But who is the enemy? In the 1933–34 lecture course *Vom Wesen der Wahrheit* (On the Essence of Truth), with its exposition of Heraclitus, Heidegger asserts, again like Hitler, that the real enemy lies in wait within the people:

An enemy is whoever poses an essential threat to the Dasein of the people and its members. The enemy does not have to be external, and the external enemy is not even always the more dangerous. And it can accordingly seem that there is no enemy. It is then a fundamental requirement that the enemy be found, brought to light, or even created so that this stand against the enemy may take place and Dasein not become torpid.

The enemy can have established himself in the innermost root of the Dasein of a people, opposing himself to the latter's essence and working against it. The struggle is all the more fierce, severe, and arduous because only to the smallest degree does it consist in an exchange of blows; it is often far more difficult and time-consuming to detect the enemy as such, to flush him out, to refuse to be fooled by him, to hold oneself in readiness for attack, to maintain and intensify a constant state of alert, and to begin the long-term assault with the goal of complete extermination.[17]

Is this a slab of anti-Semitic rhetoric? How much credit can be given to the image of a post-Nazi Heidegger when he was able for decades to tolerate the persistence of such a passage in his unpublished writings? That Heidegger never expunged it cannot be "excused" by a commitment to the historical integrity of the edition of his works. The incident with the missing page of *An Introduction to Metaphysics* (see p. 30 above) indicates the limits of his commitment in the face of a general outcry. Heidegger's confidence in the inoffensiveness of his private National Socialism was never easily disturbed, and it is not itself proof that between his description of an internal, treacherous enemy of the people and Nazi vilifications of German Jewry, no bond should be discerned. Consistently rejecting the biologistic foundations of Nazi racism, Heidegger is nonetheless recklessly able to accommodate the regime's culture of hatred within the language of his own thought. The invisibility of the assimilated Jew becomes an issue for Heidegger *as invisibility*. The struggle is to be a struggle against the invisibility of the enemy. The most dangerous enemy is the one that is invisible, because with this enemy not even the clearing of beings in the light of presence is shared. Not to struggle against this enemy, not to grasp the struggle as a struggle of life and death is to relinquish the chance of questioning the ontological foundations of the understanding of Being as presence. To be sure, Heidegger does not name the Jews as the enemy, and indeed the enemy cannot be named at its most dangerous—and hence at its ontologically most essential—because of its invisibility. This reservation has to be put forward should Heidegger be charged with anti-Semitism in this passage. It is neither very much nor nothing. Likewise, Heidegger advocates extermination of the enemy *as a goal* because it is through extermination as a goal, and not as a realization, that the ontological power of struggle comes to the fore: "beings are only in their constancy and presence when they are governed and protected by struggle as their ruler." [18] Victory in the struggle would be disastrous for the question of Being, but victory is only possible against an inessential enemy, an enemy that can be disentangled from invisibility and destroyed as something present-at-hand. Hence, for Heidegger, the struggle against German Jewry to which the SA and the SS were committed was an inessential struggle beside the struggle of the university against concealment itself. Heidegger, who goes along with the Nazi cult of death, also goes along with its fear of enemies. Even if he pulls away before arriving at the destination of suicide and genocide, he still goes further than the task of a redefinition of knowledge requires. For the sake of mobilizing the people against classical ontology and the metaphysics of subjectity, Heidegger concedes too much.

As the university's will to knowledge is the means to the collision with fate, it is the university and the university's struggle against invisibility that is the proper means to the eruption of the political from under the metaphysics of subjectity. It is the university that founds a people. In favor of such a definition, Heidegger in his rectorial address does not hesitate in rejecting the "negative" notion of academic freedom proper to an autonomous institution within the liberal state. Instead, in a sentence at once imperious and subservient, he contends: "The will to the essence of the German university is the will to science as the will to the historical spiritual mission of the German *Volk* as a *Volk* that knows itself in its state." [19] The prospects of the National Socialist revolution are thereby tied up with the prospects of Heidegger's own rectorship. Already, in the 1928–29 lecture course *Einleitung in die Philosophie* (Introduction to Philosophy), Heidegger speaks of the *Führerschaft* of the university and of its role in guiding the destiny of the people.[20] The political self-assertion of the German people does not merely coincide with the self-assertion of knowledge, since the political, in the broadest sense as the site of the clearing of beings, is the truth toward which knowledge aspires.

In 1933, Heidegger did not want a "private" National Socialism. He did not want to come across merely as an opportunist and a fellow traveler. Born in the same year as Hitler, Heidegger even alters his moustache in his aggressive design to become Hitler's doppelgänger. Under the cover of the euphoria of his commitment and the peculiarly dogmatic haziness of the official doctrine, Heidegger endeavored to foist his "private" National Socialism on the new Germany as its thought. The ontological revolution of *Being and Time* was to be taken up as the work of the *Volk. Vom Wesen der Wahrheit* attests to this ambition:

The decision in the sense of the abandonment of something that had been self-evident for the Greeks is that which had carried and determined Platonic philosophizing. In *The Sophist*, Plato goes so far as to say that he must become the murderer of his own father (Parmenides) by abandoning the proposition that something either is or is not. Plato thereby reveals the depths into which this decision reaches down. By means of this decision, the world is seen in a fundamentally different way.

Today, we ourselves have been standing not just for a year but rather for a number of years in a *still greater decision* of philosophy, which in grandeur, scope, and depth far exceeds the former decision. In my book *Being and Time*, it is given expression. A transformation from the ground up.

What is at stake is whether the understanding of *Being* is transformed from the ground up. It will be a transformation that will first of all provide the *project* for the spiritual history of our people. This cannot be proven; on the contrary, it is a *belief* that must be borne out by history.[21]

As far as Heidegger is concerned, the Nazi seizure of power one year before was less important than the publication of *Being and Time*. His faith in the ontological future of the German people was, needless to say, abashed. When the attempt to lead the leadership foundered and the regime collapsed in obloquy and murder, Heidegger quickly redrew the boundaries of his "private" National Socialism.

In a letter from December 15, 1945, to the chairman of the university committee investigating political activities under the Nazis, Heidegger urges against taking his dealings with the regime, such as the telegram to Hitler, at face value: "When the word *Gleichschaltung* is used in the telegram, I intended it in the sense in which I also understood the name 'National Socialism.' It was never my intention to deliver the university up to the doctrine of the party, but quite the reverse, to try from *within* National Socialism and in relation to it to initiate a spiritual transformation."[22] Accordingly, in the language of Heidegger's unintentionally private National Socialism, the *Gleichschaltung* of Freiburg University is not the bringing of the university into line with the regime, but rather the bringing of the regime into line with the university under Heidegger's leadership.

Whether a *Gleichschaltung* of any kind was needed is not a doubt that Heidegger could have entertained, given the conception of the political underlying his "private" National Socialism. Wanting the concealedness of fate to reveal itself, Heidegger wanted the German *Volk* to reveal itself. The *Volk* was to be the consequence of *Gleichschaltung*, rather than that which was to be brought into line. All efforts were to be directed toward the ontological mission of the German people, since it is on a fulfillment of this mission that the knowledge of the truth of beings depends. Heidegger's vision in the rectorial address is of the university with which the state has been brought into line and mobilized for the highest of all tasks. The concealment of fate is to be defied, so that the truth of the historicality of Dasein might be understood in its originary character. In other words, and in the language of the regime, the truth of the *Volk* is to be placed above the truth of the abstract subject.

Heidegger concurred with Nazi policy on the desirability of a politicization of the sciences, but he differed in his understanding of "politicization." In "Only a God Can Save Us," Heidegger says of the National Socialist position on science: "Science as such, its sense and value, is assessed with reference to its practical usefulness for the people. The counterposition to *this* politicizing of science is specially expressed in the rectoral address."[23] Heidegger wanted to politicize the sciences through an interrogation of their foundation in the world of a people, where the regime wanted to subordinate the sciences to the maintenance and amplification of its police and military apparatus. The choice for Heidegger was not between the autonomy of the faculties and the *Gleichschaltung* of totalitarianism, but rather between a *Gleichschaltung* in the question of the historicality of Being and a *Gleichschaltung* in a racist organization of control.

With regard to Heidegger's veritable totalitarianism of the university, the rectorial address is timelier in 1933 than it would have been in 1966. But if the totalitarianism of the Hitlerian dictatorship sought the liquidation of the abstract subject by ultimatum, and on this account was unable to break with the metaphysics of subjectity, Heidegger, in 1933, advances an utterly singular strategy of epistemological exhaustion. His "private" National Socialism was to be the National Socialism at least capable of attempting to carry out its program of politicization, since it remained considerably more faithful than the movement itself to its distinction between the abstract subject of liberalism and the political. As the foundations of the subject are, for Heidegger, philosophical, it is only by a painstaking philosophical confrontation with these foundations that the subject can be overcome and the political inaugurated. If Heidegger intimates to Hitler in his telegram that he is going too fast, he thereby voices nothing but his appraisal of the Nazi movement as a whole.

What is frequently overlooked in "The Self-Assertion of the German University" is this sobriety. The afflatus of Heidegger's "private" National Socialism blows very coolly on the triumphalist reckoning that the revolution had already taken place. Having implied that the revolution against liberalism and the metaphysics of subjectity rests with the failure of knowledge, Heidegger cautions: "If, however, the Greeks needed three centuries just to put the *question* of what knowledge is on the proper footing and on the secure path, then *we* certainly cannot think that the elucidation and unfolding of the essence of the German university can occur in the present or coming semester."[24]

The German university, which is to demand more of itself than simply the *question* of what knowledge is, needs time. Through dispensing with the development of knowledge's highest defiance, a revolution by fiat amounts solely to a variation of the terms laid down in the metaphysics of subjectity. The National Socialism of Hitler (if such a locution can be permitted for the moment) was unequal to the task of overcoming the subject, since the domain of the subject must first be accurately delimited before it can be overcome.

For Heidegger, the revolution has first and foremost to be an enquiry into the foundations of knowledge and the ontological presuppositions of the epistemological subject. Translated as "knowledge," the τέχνη of Aeschylus's verse thus signifies something quite different in 1933 from the manipulative ingenuity of advanced industrial societies by which Heidegger would later understand technicism. In "The Self-Assertion of the German University," τέχνη is characterized by its defiance of the superior power of fate, rather than by any obliviousness to fate. Τέχνη does not aspire to the mastery of material, but to the impossible illumination of its own blind necessity, to the unconcealedness of what is essentially concealed in its difference from the present-at-hand. For Heidegger in 1933, τέχνη is to jump over its own shadow, to borrow more than an image from *What Is a Thing?*[25] The necessity that is the unacknowledged ground of the theoretical attitude is, in unavailing defiance of this definition, to become the object of the theoretical attitude. Heidegger accordingly repeats speculative idealism's project of absolute knowledge precisely in order to come up to its failure. He endeavors to seize hold of the finitude of knowledge, where Hegel jumped away from it into the metaphysical sun of the dialectic. Heidegger's "private" National Socialism, in one respect and in contrast to the *Blut und Boden* mysticism of the regime, wants to be more Hegelian than Hegel, since it wants to think rigorously the finitude of world that Hegel ultimately evaded through its conceptualization. And if it wants to be more Hegelian than Hegel, it is nonetheless so as to have done with Hegel. Heidegger's long-standing desire to outdo Hegel in sobriety complements his deriding of the subaltern antics of irrationalism. Both can be derived from his assessment of the scope of metaphysics and the corresponding magnitude of the especially philosophical task of its destruction. As it is formulated in Heidegger's "private" National Socialism, the revolution is the self-assertion of sobriety within metaphysics.

Sobriety, rather than the intoxication of blood, is Heidegger's response to the metaphysics of subjectity. The idea of a "folkish" science (*völkische Wissenschaft*) that, under National Socialism, circulated as the repressed truth of the cosmopolitan notion of science lacked sobriety and stringent enquiry into the foundations of knowledge. It could scarcely hope to pass off its irrationalism—by which it fell short even of the cosmopolitanism of the concept, and thus avoided a confrontation with the concept—as the understanding of world before which the concept falls short. In such a "folkish" science, knowledge does not so much fail as hold itself aloof. It cannot "really," which is to say "openly," fail, because it dares not call its own determinacy into question. Knowledge is accepted as knowledge only inasmuch as it is an expression of the positivistically determined German *Volk*.[26] The German *Volk* has become the truth of the cosmopolitan notion of science, but only in the sense that it has arbitrarily replaced it.

The embarrassment in which the various Aryan sciences ignominiously expired does not find its unambiguous apology before the fact in

Heidegger's rectorial address. In one respect, the failure of these sciences has little in common with Heidegger's understanding of failure. The object of defiance in "The Self-Assertion of the German University" is not the global community of scientists but necessity; not the liberal notion of science but its Un-thought. When Heidegger uses the term "folkish science" in 1933, it is not to denote a contraction in the range of the liberal notion of science, as though a science were "folkish," that is, German, only to the extent that it forfeited its claims to validity outside an identifiable people. Such a relativistic doctrine of science is alien both to Heidegger and to National Socialism in general.

A "folkish" science, inasmuch as it more than pretends to seek to be the truth of the liberal notion of science, must make itself a party to the latter at the scene of its determination through the forgetting of world. And as it is through the concept that the liberal notion of science forgets world, recoiling from its rootedness into the ahistorical repeatability in presence with which it equates knowledge, it is only by holding to the concept, and specifically to the violence of its retreat, that a science might still confront its world and become the truth of its own "folkishness." A "folkish" science, therefore, dares not renounce the concept. One year after the rectorial address, in the lecture course *Logik als die Frage nach dem Wesen der Sprache* (Logic as the Question Concerning the Essence of Language), Heidegger declares: "What is at stake is the overcoming of the definition of the concept as a husk. Consistent with this is not the deposing of the concept, but rather the higher necessity of conceptual questioning."[27] For Heidegger, the romantic objection to the lifelessness of the concept is itself objectionable. Deposing the concept in favor of an immediate intuition of what is does not solve the problem presented by the concept's lifelessness. The absolute and voluntaristic subjectivity that convinces itself of its ability to issue binding decrees on the concept perpetuates the abstraction from world for which the concept is reproached. Wherever the concept is said to have been deposed, the forgetfulness of world rather lords it all the more peremptorily in the absence of proper criticism. A truly "folkish" science does not begin with the *Volk* in the manner of a perspective or as the guarantor of its immediate intuitions. Instead, only at the very end does it come to its people as the world that reveals itself in its concealedness in the genuine failure of knowledge.

What a "folkish" science awaits from the concept is the birth of the *Volk* that would be thought's own. This people would be the world as it has always eluded thought and preceded it as its ground. Understood in its irreducibility to the metaphysics of subjectivity, the people of a truly "folkish" science is not identifiable by physical properties or cultural practices, but is rather the world as the broadest dimension of the political. Such a people is the transcendence of Being-with-one-another and can thus never fully reveal itself in the presence of knowledge. Knowledge in its metaphysical determination has always proceeded from an ignorance of the people. The loyalty of Heidegger's "folkish" science to the concept is necessarily a tactical loyalty, since what this science sets out to know with the concept is that which is not conceptualizable because it is not knowable within the limits of presence. A "folkish" science must fail in its conceptualization of the *Volk*. It awaits from its failure an unrecognizable people. Heidegger's "folkish" science is the science of the absurdity of German racism, because it is the science of the reserve of the world of the *Volk*, of that which is never present-at-hand. As such, it has the most to gain from the failure of racist nationalism and from the rebuff to the latter's claims on the world of the *Volk*. Spying its chance in a nation that mistakes its integration in a people-subject for the uprising of world, Heidegger's "folkish" science cynically incites this nationalism to grasp fate itself in order that it might fail all the more thoughtfully. A "folkish" science, in Heidegger's definition, is essentially opportunistic. It always seeks to outwit nationalism, but in the end it is perhaps too clever: on account of its philosophical sophistication, it is taken for the truth of what it attempts to exploit. Contributing to the *Gleichschaltung* of the German nation under Hitler, Heidegger sees beyond the unification of the masses in a people-subject to the collision of this people-subject with necessity. Heidegger's extreme, yet nonetheless tactical, nationalism merges with an anti-nationalism. But it was Heidegger, the one sober participant at the saturnalia of German nationalism, who would be asked for an explanation after the war.

Given the meta–National Socialism of "The Self-Assertion of the German University," it would be inexact and therefore misleading to ascribe Heidegger's resignation of the rectorship in April 1934 to his disillusionment with the regime as such.[28] In and for itself, the regime was not the object of his engagement. Strictly speaking, Heidegger's disillusionment was with the regime's amenability to his leadership. That which was never expected to turn out well had within a year proved itself intractable to an unfolding of the philosophical possibilities of its inevitable failure: Hitler was no more Heidegger's puppet than he had been Papen's. In his letter of December 15, 1945, defending to the university what he could of his rectorate, Heidegger scrambles to muster a still broader appearance of naïveté:

Already in 1933–34, I stood in the same opposition to the National Socialist weltanschauung teachings. I was, however, then of the belief that the movement could be led spiritually down other paths and considered this attempt compatible with the social and general political tendencies of the movement. I believed that, after assuming responsibility for the entire people in 1933, Hitler would rise above the party and its doctrine, and that everything would come together on the basis of a renewal and rallying to a responsibility for the West. This belief was an error: I recognized it as such from the events of June 30, 1934.[29]

On what grounds could Heidegger have believed that Hitler was destined to undergo a change of heart after seizing power in January 1933? Such credulity verges on the implausible. That many other adherents of the regime expressed a similar credulity does not render Heidegger's statement any more plausible: it simply indicates the conventionality of the defense. And if, by his reference to June 30, 1934, Heidegger is implying that his engagement was an innocent dream from which he was awakened only by the bloodbath of the Night of the Long Knives, then the SA itself would have had to have been known in its time as something other than organized thuggery. In his postwar apologetics, Heidegger frequently overreaches himself. As much as its distance from the regime must not be overlooked, Heidegger's meta–National Socialism cannot be converted into a position of resistance.

After 1934, Heidegger is considerably more wary of nationalism's prospects of failure. The failure that is quickly seen to lie beyond the grasp of National Socialism now becomes the affair of poetry. In this respect, Heidegger's commentary from 1939 on Hölderlin's poem "Wie wenn am Feiertage . . ." reads as an epilogue to "The Self-Assertion of the German University" and as a repudiation of its opportunism. The defiance to which the university and the state as a whole are admonished in the rectorial address is, in the later text, the duty of the poet. Aligning "the Open" of Hölderlin with that which he terms "world,"[30] Heidegger arguably retains the same understanding of the concealedness of the superior power:

The open mediates the connections between all actual things. These latter are constituted only because of such mediation, and are therefore mediated. What is mediated in that way only is by virtue of mediatedness. Thus, mediatedness must be present in all. The open itself, however, though it first gives the region for all belonging-to and -with each other, does not arise from any mediation. The open itself is the immediate. Nothing mediated, be it a god or a man, is ever capable of directly attaining the immediate.[31]

The Open mediates and, by virtue of its mediating, is that which itself cannot be mediated. Through its immediacy, the Open humbles gods and human beings in their ambition to mediate it. In the face of the impossibility of mediation, the poets nonetheless cannot resign themselves: "The poets must leave to the immediate its immediacy, and yet also take upon themselves its mediation as the unique."[32] And if the poets are able to mediate the immediate, the success of this defiance of their limitations does not fall to their credit: "When the grasping and offering of their hands is permeated by a 'pure heart,' these poets are capable of the task that has been entrusted to them. . . . The 'pure heart' is not meant here in a 'moralistic' sense. This phrase means one kind of relation, and one manner of correspondence to 'all-present' nature."[33]

The "pure heart" is not a property of the poets. It names their relation of correspondence to "omnipresent" Nature. In this commentary on Hölderlin, where the impossible mediation of the immediate is said to begin at the point of the poets' reconciliation with the Open (or omnipresent Nature), the defiance that is to fail before fate in the rectorial address is still discernible. The discord of the earlier taxonomy, however, is missing. In place of the violent rupture between the theoretical attitude and necessity, there is not even so much as a transition from the poet to omnipresent Nature, since it is only within the latter that the poet, for Heidegger, truly is a poet. This tranquillity in the 1939 text does not follow from any intervening peace with the subject, because the poet has nothing in common with the theoretical attitude's abstraction from world. Heidegger's tranquillity is more calculating than resigned. In 1933, on the basis of his antisubjectivism and its accompanying Manichaeism, Heidegger is able to make concessions to a voluntaristic political movement with an opportunist's eye to its other side.[34] Yet the beyond to which he aspires remains —by the logic of reversal he would later expound in his lectures on Nietzsche—determined by the metaphysics of subjectity. With time, Heidegger's wariness of nationalism's prospects of failure gives way to a wariness of failure's prospects. Whereas the early Heidegger seemingly wishes to push everything to its point of crisis, the late Heidegger will no longer be prepared to break even a jug.[35] By the end of the 1930s, the invocations of power (*Macht*), violence (*Gewalt*), and mastery (*Herrschaft*) that mark

An Introduction to Metaphysics, for instance, recede in favor of meditations on releasement (*Gelassenheit*) and that which is free from power (*das Macht-lose*).

Heidegger's disengagement with the regime has to be thought through as a disengagement with his own meta–National Socialism. As National Socialism itself was not the object of his engagement, it often seems that Heidegger is closer to the movement after 1934 than he ever was during his rectorship. A virulent suspicion of the ontic, for instance, renders the early Heidegger proof against kitsch. With the interrogation of this suspicion's entanglement in the metaphysics of subjectity, there emerges in later texts a susceptibility to the charms of *Bodenständigkeit* (indigenousness) painfully redolent of the idylls of Nazi literature.

In dissolving the agonistic taxonomy of his rectorial address, Heidegger dissolves precisely that which, in 1937, Clemens August Hoberg, who subsequently established himself in the police apparatus as an expert on the "Jewish question," finds incompatible with National Socialism. At the start of his polemic against Heidegger, Hoberg declares that his objections arise "not from a philosophical system, but rather from the simple, straightforward attitude of a young German";[36] in short, that it is his intention to play *misère* in this game of cards. Reducing the passage on failure in the rectorial address to a personal admission of the author,[37] Hoberg proceeds to situate National Socialism in that same relaxation of the exclusive disjunction toward which Heidegger likewise directs his thinking after 1934. For Hoberg, National Socialism is not itself a crisis: "The decisive difference between Heidegger and us consists in the fact that, in everyday life, we create and make ourselves felt, rather than lose ourselves in mere bustle. So long as we are active in the work assigned to us, Heideggerian dread cannot possibly rise up in us and compel everything to appear for us in its nullity."[38]

The work stands between self-absorbed bustle and the Nothing, and thus against the volatility of their alternation. What might further determine the work is, for Hoberg's purposes, superfluous information. For Hoberg, the National Socialist revolution resolves the Heideggerian "dilemma" of triviality and dread. By assigning work, Hitler showed himself to be the answer to the Manichaeism of the early Heidegger. On the basis of Hoberg's polemic, it could be contended that National Socialism comes to the jargon of authenticity, and its bathos of unquestioning obedience, before Heidegger and in opposition to him. Having earlier sought to outwit the movement, Heidegger renounces the dualism of his meta–National Socialism only to find himself ostensibly recuperated.

In 1933, Heidegger joined the NSDAP out of a philosophically motivated shame, and his inaugural address as rector turns upon the hope of a failure of the theoretical subject. As an obstacle to the truth of that which is, this subject is consumed with shame of itself and works toward the fulfillment by which it is not entrenched but overcome. Through the absoluteness with which he distinguishes knowledge and necessity in 1933, Heidegger seeks from necessity a revolution in which the subject might be swept aside but thereby also retain its externality. The anti-liberalism that expresses itself in shame over the subject is still too liberal. It continues to forget world as the clearing of beings, because it does not make it as far as the world in which the subject also has its Being for itself.

In this respect, "The Self-Assertion of the German University" belongs, alongside Ernst Jünger's 1930 treatise *The Worker*, to a class of texts composed between the two world wars that remains under the sway of liberalism in the manner of its opposition to it. As much as he stresses the irrelevance of the subject for the gestalt of the worker, Jünger only arouses the suspicion that this declaration of irrelevance is the half-hearted disguise of an absolute subjectivity. In passing from the individual human being to the gestalt of the worker, Jünger does not overcome the subject. Instead, he discovers that configuration of the subject in which its abstraction and autonomy could escape the commonly perceived debunking of the liberal subject. The myth of the subject, which a lone individual cannot maintain in the face of the reality of technical civilization, is to find its defense in the unified masses. Jünger's worker is the subject that can work and still maintain its abstraction as a subject. Rather than working on account of any subordination to circumstances, it works because it lies in its declaimed transcendental definition as the worker to work. In comparison with the rectorial address, the sleight of hand in Jünger's "overcoming" of the subject is risibly clumsy.

Defining itself by its opposition to liberalism, "The Self-Assertion of the German University" renounces the possibility of developing an anti-liberalism that would not at once be dialectically reappropriated. It wants to think the superior power of necessity through the failure of the theoretical attitude and thus wants to think necessity in its absence from the knowledge yielding itself to the theoretical attitude. Necessity, which had been forgotten by the autonomous subject of liberalism, is to take its revenge without ceasing to be forgotten. Instead of remembering its world, the subject shatters on the emergence of its world that is for it properly a nonemergence. The subject comes to grief on the severity with which world withholds itself from that which is present (*das Anwesende*). On the one hand, world, as that which, for Heidegger, is not present because it is the presencing (*Anwesung*) of that which is present, cannot be sufficiently distinguished from that which is present. Its distinctness, on the other hand, cannot be made distinct, since as the presencing of beings in the light of knowledge, world is the possibility and domain of distinctions. In 1933, Heidegger's choice within this dilemma—and the crux of his inverted liberalism—is to insist on the distinctness and to think the presencing of world by itself as absence. "The Self-Assertion of the German University" concentrates on the forgetfulness in the forgetfulness of Being and thus concentrates on the philosophical tradition's relation to Being, rather than, as it were, on Being itself. That which is forgotten by the subject is to be remembered *as forgotten*, and thereby remembered in a distinctness alien, so to speak, to Being as such. The theoretical subject, in its shame, is not so much to heed the voice of conscience, as it is analyzed in §§54–60 of *Being and Time*, as to provoke its wrath. The subject is not called back to the authenticity of its Being-in-the-world and thus to the transcendence by which Dasein undecidably differentiates itself from that which is present. Instead, the subject suffers defeat for the sake of the problematic clarity of the ontological difference.

Heidegger's anti-subjectivism in 1933 was intended to contest classical ontology's understanding of Being as presence. This contestation, in the very radicality with which it ventured to think absence and to seize hold of it in its distinctness, solidified into simply the complement of the *Seinsvergessenheit* of classical ontology. As such, it was an "error"—one, however, that can be recognized but not rectified. The error can only be committed differently: in later Heidegger, it appears in the serenity before classical ontology that, by comparison, refrains *ab ovo* from a contestation. If, in 1966, Heidegger declares that he would repeat the rectorial address with a still greater vehemence, it is perhaps more with a regard to the necessity of thinking through its error than out of a protectiveness for any of its discernible truths. It is the inevitability of the error of not thinking Being as such that is, for later Heidegger, thought's innermost provocation.

In 1933, Heidegger's error in relation to classical ontology is that he endeavors to overcome it by a reversal. Heidegger's concomitant error in relation to National Socialism is that he chooses—without, however, any unavoidability—not to foresee how the movement would quash a contestation of classical ontology. National Socialism failed, but its failure was not the failure of knowledge exhorted in the rectorial address. From the overtaxing of the regime's paranoiac classifications and monitoring of the social field, Heidegger was to await in vain the presencing of that which is present, the revelation of the Being of beings in its precedence to governmental control. Even in its failure, National Socialism refused to allow the question of Being to become the overt and pervasive question of Germany. It ensured that Dasein would either quickly find itself in its everydayness in the task of the reconstruction of an occupied Germany or not find itself, in death. World was not permitted to light up in the failure of the regime, since the question of the state, of its relation to its world, was not revived in response to the collapse of the National Socialist dictatorship, but settled in advance by the occupying powers. A Germany outside the control of a state, and thus outside the understanding of Being as presence fundamental to control, was not something to which either the Nazis or the Allies aspired. In a sense, the dictatorship was a failure of failure and, on that account, it was perhaps the exemplary system of control. Having in 1933 wagered on the worlding of the world in the regime's failure, Heidegger after the war can only rue his opportunistic hopes for an exposure of the ontological foundations of control.

Heidegger's engagement with National Socialism rests on a misprojection. In Hitler's seizure of power, he insanely managed to see the chance of a fundamental redefinition of the political. The ontology presupposed in the classical understanding of the πόλις was to be contested by the simultaneous emergence and nonemergence of the Being of the German *Volk*. Heidegger wants to stand the πόλις on its head and to ground the new Germany in concealedness. To the Greek πόλις of the full visibility of the glorious deed, of the deliverance from anonymity and the establishment in the lasting fame of presence, Heidegger opposes the πόλις that, by its failure rigorously to defend its claim to self-groundedness, lies open to Being in its essential withdrawal. Heidegger's πόλις is the πόλις that knows its own essential unknowability. It is the πόλις whose self-knowledge reaches the point of the failure of knowledge. Implicit in the rectorial address, and therefore unobtrusive in its absurdity, is the conception of a National Socialism that would reach beyond the controllability of beings (their recognizability in presence as the bearers of such and such properties, and thus their trackability) to their truth in the transcendence of Being. The πόλις of the recollection of Being is the πόλις of concealment rather than of control. It is without glory but not privatively. In *An Introduction to Metaphysics*, Heidegger sets forth the relations between the Greek notion of fame and the understanding of Being as presence:

> To glorify, to attribute regard to, and disclose regard means in Greek: to place in the light and thus endow with permanence, being. For the Greeks glory was not something additional which one might or might not obtain; it was the mode of the highest being. For moderns glory has long been nothing more than celebrity and as such a highly dubious affair, an acquisition tossed about and distributed by the newspapers and the radio—almost the opposite of being.[39]

Heidegger does not disparage the celebrity of radio and newsprint simply out of nostalgia for the Greek notion of glory. Greek glory is here suggested only to be preferable.[40] Heidegger dismisses celebrity as almost the opposite of Being: the understanding of Being as presence is inherited without being appropriated, let alone contested in a questioning concerning the essence of Being. If Heidegger, in 1933, evokes a tragic conception of the πόλις as a whole and an accordingly anonymous catastrophe before necessity, it is because the question of Being can only be raised anew by calling glory itself into question. For Heidegger, the aim of the *Gleichschaltung* (falling into line) under Hitler was not to bring about the unity of the public realm and its reformation as the site of the full visibility of the glorious deed. Instead, its aim was the mobilization of the masses for the knowledge of the concealment at the heart of unconcealment, of the inglorious essence of glory. Heidegger's πόλις is to ask more of itself than glory, because it is to ask after that which is never merely present. Raising the question of Being, this other πόλις endeavors to think Dasein in its uncontrollability. Control is to be overcome for the sake, not of a pacifist utopia, but of the violence of time tearing identity away from itself in presence. The Being of Dasein, which for Heidegger is temporality, is no longer to go unthought. In glory's understanding of Being as presence, the debasement of Dasein has its inconspicuous, and thus insidious, beginnings. Appealing to their love of glory, classical ontology was able to estrange the Greeks from their other great love—falsehood.[41] The powers of untruth, which still convulsed the πόλις, retreat before the increasing verifiability of beings. From the glorious deed of the Greek πόλις, a genealogical line can be traced down to the breeding programs dear to National Socialism. Heidegger, in the rectorial address, thus covertly goads Hitler to failure so that Dasein might be recovered for its world from the derivative certainty of self-groundedness. Within the new regime's prospects of failure, Heidegger believes he makes out, if there alone, an understanding of the transcendence of Dasein at variance with the espoused biologism. Out of an attention to failure, the praiseworthy deed, in which Aristotle situates the *causa finalis* for the institution of the πόλις,[42] comes under a suspicion that is likewise the most arrant gullibility with respect to the truth of the failure in store for Nazi Germany.

As much as National Socialism failed, it did not thereby usher in the era of Dasein's authenticity. The understanding of Being as presence, in which the glorious deed enjoyed its recognizability, and recognizability deployed itself as state control, did not yield to an understanding of the transcendence of Dasein. Dasein was delivered up to death and the administrative measures of the occupying powers, since the regime refused to be survived by its failure. Not unlike Heidegger, but out of Byronic hypochondria rather than opportunism, it ultimately viewed its failure as its work and achievement. Once the regime could no longer appropriate its own failures, it strove instead to assimilate itself to the catastrophe that was befalling it. National Socialism would make this disaster its own by contributing to it. As it had created everything, everything would have to accompany it in its destruction. The Fatherland that the regime had invented as a sponge for surplus labor was not to remain behind. In the name of national defense, the NSDAP had preached rearmament and courted military disaster for the purpose of an immediate economic remedy. In the event, the regime was not prepared to defend its ad hoc Fatherland by a surrender on conditions.

National Socialism was state suicide. It is by this aspect that Gilles Deleuze and Félix Guattari, following Paul Virilio, distinguish it from Stalinism: "Unlike the totalitarian State, which does its utmost to seal all possible lines of flight, fascism is constructed on an intense line of flight, which it transforms into a line of pure destruction and abolition. It is curious that from the very beginning the Nazis announced to Germany what they were bringing: at once wedding bells and death, including their own death, and the death of the Germans."[43]

The Nazi regime knew how to turn away from the understanding of Being as presence, but only by carrying all beings with it into a black hole. From the insight into its own unviability as an enduring state, it grasped that if it were to prove its control over life and death, it had to do so as quickly as possible through destruction. National Socialism cannot be said to have been an anti-state simply because it was suicidal. It was rather a grotesque parody of a state—a state running fast. The war would thus not have been over the question of the state as such, but over its tempo, as Deleuze and Guattari suggest: "Conversely, if capitalism came to consider the fascist experience as catastrophic, if it preferred to ally itself with Stalinist totalitarianism, which from its point of view was much more sensible and manageable, it was because the segmentarity and centralization of the latter was more classical and less fluid."[44]

If dissolution was finally perceived by capitalism as the real danger, it was not because it announced the reemergence of the stateless and borderless Germany of literary myth. No Romantic *Volk* of poets and thinkers was about to raise the question of Being against the very possibility of control.

In *The Life of the Mind*, Hannah Arendt recalls that Heidegger was not alone in his appraisal of the situation:

The changed mood reflected Germany's defeat, the "point zero" (as Ernst Jünger called it) that for a few years seemed to promise a new beginning. In Heidegger's version: "Do we stand in the very twilight of the most monstrous transformation our planet has ever undergone . . . ? [Or] do we gaze into the evening of a night which heralds another dawn? . . . *Are* we the latecomers . . . at the same time precursors of the dawn of an altogether different age, which has already left our contemporary historiological representations of history behind?" It was the same mood that Jaspers expressed at a famous symposium in Geneva in the same year: "We live as though we stood knocking at gates that are still closed. . . . What happens today will perhaps one day found and establish a world." This mood of hope disappeared quickly in the rapidity of German economic and political recovery from "point zero"; confronted with the reality of Adenauer's Germany, neither Heidegger nor Jaspers ever expounded systematically what must very soon have appeared to them as a complete misreading of the new era.[45]

National Socialism did not go quietly, needless to say. Neither the Hitlerian dictatorship nor the occupying powers were prepared for the state to retreat to a minimal threshold of control, let alone to yield to the transcendence of Being-with-one-another.

That Heidegger, in 1933, could have harbored any expectations of a survival from the failure of the Western state is perhaps in the end less a sign of his naïveté than of his desperation. It may have been that, with none of the confidence that follows from a scrupulous assessment of existing conditions, Heidegger joined the NSDAP on the off-chance that the course of the movement might be directed toward the failure in which Dasein would be recovered for its world. Inasmuch as the NSDAP was a German nationalist movement, its course, in Heidegger's eyes, was already set for the failure of knowledge in the encounter with the truth of the *Volk*. It was a matter of maintaining its course. However unfathomable Heidegger's engagement was with regard to the divide between his conception of humanity and the regime's, it was not arbitrary. Heidegger mistook the fragility of National Socialism for the weak point in the hegemony of reification, and he chose its insanity over the insanity of doing nothing. No doubt the choice was for Heidegger, in his cruder sympathies, a little too easy. The object of his choice, moreover, did not simply perpetuate the nihilism of the reification of humanity, but dedicated itself to its aggravation.

Heidegger's intimations of a πόλις of Being in the rectorial address are exposed to misinterpretation through contiguous passages. "The Self-Assertion of the German University" does not always abstain from employing the motifs of the NSDAP. But neither does it restrict itself to bare citation. Unlike other, less heterodox texts from his term as rector, Heidegger did not disown the address. He did not disown it, just as he did not disown his "private" National Socialism. The rectorial address is, for Heidegger, the point of continuity between his writings before and after 1933. As such, it is the most overt expression of that "private" National Socialism which arguably is to be discerned elsewhere in his work. This "private" National Socialism is the politics of the failure of knowledge, of the truth that confers itself as both the punishment and reward of the defiance of concealedness. In his engagement with the Nazi regime, Heidegger did not interrupt the thinking on the essence of truth that runs through his writings of the 1930s. What Heidegger all too cursorily sets out in the commentary on Aeschylus in the rectorial address can thus be read in conjunction with his more expansive treatments. Indeed, it must be read in this manner if the radicality of his other understanding of the political is to be ascertained.

In speaking of a defiance of concealedness in the rectorial address, Heidegger is not referring to knowledge's quantitative progression into the unknown. Concealedness is not to retreat before knowledge but is itself to become the matter of knowledge. Concealedness is to reveal itself *as concealedness* and thereby confer on knowledge the truth of beings. In his 1931–32 lecture course *Zu Platons Höhlengleichnis und Theätet* (Plato's

Parable of the Cave and Theaetetus), Heidegger contends that the Greek definition of truth rests on an evasion of the task of a knowledge of concealedness:

The signification of Being in the sense of presence is the reason that ἀλήθεια (unconcealment) is ground down to mere presence-at-hand (not gone), and concealment correspondingly to mere being-gone. This means however: the classical understanding of Being prevents the already dawning foundational experience of the *concealment* of beings from being able, *at* its origin, to unfold itself in its proper depth.[46]

Concealedness, according to this early reflection on the dilemma of any exposition of the ontological difference, is neither present nor absent. For classical ontology, concealedness is, by contrast, the condition of that which is not present. Whatever does not stand determinate in the light of knowledge is, for classical ontology, nonetheless able, inasmuch as it is, to stand in the light of knowledge—the obstacles to a being's unconcealedness are ultimately extrinsic to what it is in itself. Concealedness thus does not become the occasion of a questioning of the understanding of Being as presence, because it is subordinated to presence and defined negatively by it as absence. Never permitted to confront knowledge with that which essentially cannot stand in its light, with that which is absent even as it is present, concealedness does not reveal itself as concealedness to classical ontology.

Classical ontology does not ask after the secret of concealedness, which for Heidegger is the being that he names "Dasein." It shies away from a meditation on its uncanniness such as that which Heidegger reads in Greek tragedy. In his lectures on Hölderlin's hymn "Der Ister," Heidegger addresses the chorus from Antigone in order to confront the ontological exception that is the human being: "Uncanniness does not first arise as a consequence of humankind; rather, humankind emerges from uncanniness and remains within it—looms out of it and stirs within it. The uncanny itself is what looms forth in the essence of human beings and is that which stirs in all stirring and arousal: that which presences and at the same time absences."[47]

The uncanniness of Dasein is its undecidability with respect to the understanding of Being as presence. As the *ecstases* of originary temporality, Dasein essentially conceals itself from the presence in which knowledge stands fixed. Dasein conceals itself from the knowledge that only comes to itself by falling away from a knowledge of the temporality from which its

presence is derived. Knowledge can thus only fail in its defiance of the superior power of concealedness and, in its failure, it must open up presence
to the truth of Dasein. Only in that failure of knowledge which is likewise a failure of presence will an authentic understanding of humanity
arise. Within such an understanding, the transcendence of Being-with-
one-another at the basis of the πόλις would no longer be reduced to the
controllable identity of the subjects of a state. The autonomy of the subject, the abstraction by which it won to the independence that was likewise
and still more its controllability, is exchanged for the anarchy of time.

In the failure of the German university, the state itself is to fail.
Through committing itself to the mission of the German university, the
state commits itself to a knowledge of that which cannot be known and
that notwithstanding, as the foundation of knowledge, is that which
knowledge must above all seek to know. In the rectorial address, the desirability of this failure is assumed, rather than proved. Why the truth of what
is should resist being known, and why it should confer itself on the knowledge that fails is set forth in "On the Essence of Truth." The latter text, according to Otto Pöggeler, was in its first version much closer to the language of the rectorial address: "The discussion in the 1930 lecture was . . .
about Dasein's standing up against the concealment of beings as a whole,
about a stand which shatters on the power of concealment." [48] The published version from 1943, in which the later Heidegger's notion of releasement is already evident, appears alien to the tragic conception of the rectorial address. But even in this version, the less occasional and more
expansive "On the Essence of Truth" lends itself to attempts to interpret
the 1933 text. Failure in "The Self-Assertion of the German University," as
a failure with relation to knowledge, is error in "On the Essence of Truth."

How can error, then, be desirable? The belief in its undesirability, as
Heidegger writes in the 1933–34 lecture course *Vom Wesen der Wahrheit*,
and as Hegel had argued before him, is itself the error: "We have no logic
of *error*, no real elucidation of its essence because we always take error *negatively*. This is the fundamental error that dominates the entire history of
the concept of truth." [49] Knowledge is to fail but not in the way that failure
is understood and contained in theodicies. In saying that there has never
been a logic of error, Heidegger asserts that even in theodicies, error is
taken negatively. The explanation and exoneration of error in the Hegelian
theodicy, for instance, is a negation of the inexplicability and inexcusabil-
ity specific to error. Heidegger's proposed logic of error would not explain

away error by subordinating it to truth as unconcealment. Error is to be elucidated by being acknowledged in its questionability. The exhortation to failure in the rectorial address has to be set out in terms of the task of a "logic" of error. The objection to National Socialism is that it erred too little. After 1933, Heidegger cannot simply put the error of his own engagement behind him.

In its reliance on the argument of the earlier lecture "On the Essence of Truth," "The Self-Assertion of the German University" resolves into the same fundamental thesis regarding freedom. The apparent arbitrariness of Heidegger's adoption of the word "freedom" for an enquiry into the essence of truth is belied by the exposition of Dasein in which it occurs. The lecture "On the Essence of Truth," properly speaking, does not adopt the meaning of the word "freedom," but rather defines it with an originarity from which the freedom of the autonomous subject at once derives and deviates. The freedom of the latter, as the freedom of a subject determined by an abstraction from its world by fiat, presupposes an understanding of Being in which beings have been established in their distinctness. Heidegger's enquiry into the essence of truth is an enquiry into the claim to originarity of this understanding of Being. In the conventional definition of truth as adequation, the distinctness of beings ensures the plurality in which the referentiality of both true and false judgments is deployed, as well as the unequivocality in which true judgments consist. But the referentiality itself of adequation goes unexplained in an understanding of beings in which each being is held apart in the fullness of its presence.

Discussing adequation in the example of a statement and a coin, Heidegger stresses the convergence alongside the divergence:

How can what is completely dissimilar, the statement, correspond to the coin? It would have to become the coin and in this way relinquish itself entirely. The statement never succeeds in doing that. The moment it did, it would no longer be able as a statement to be in accordance with the thing. In the correspondence the statement must remain—indeed even first become—what it is. In what does its essence, so thoroughly different from every thing, consist? How is the statement able to correspond to something else, the thing, precisely by persisting in its own essence?[50]

The statement, according to Heidegger, is adequate to its object only inasmuch as it remains in its distinctness and does not converge with it. Yet by remaining in its distinctness, it is unable to converge with its object and state its truth.

This convergence is not the matter of the distinctness of beings, but rather of that which Heidegger calls the Open:

> As thus placed, what stands opposed must traverse an open field of opposedness [*Entgegen*] and nevertheless must maintain its stand as a thing and show itself as something withstanding [*ein Ständiges*]. This appearing of the thing in traversing a field of opposedness takes place within an open region, the openness of which is not first created by the presenting but rather is only entered into and taken over as a domain of relatedness. The relation of the presentative statement to the thing is the accomplishment of that *bearing* [*Verhältnis*] that originarily and always comes to prevail as a comportment [*Verhalten*].[51]

The adequation of a statement to an object is a relation consummated in neither the statement nor the object. Truth has to be sought elsewhere, namely, in the comportment that brings about the relation because it alone is free to do so: "The openness of comportment as the inner condition of the possibility of correctness is grounded in freedom. *The essence of truth, as the correctness of a statement, is freedom.*"[52] The essence of truth, as the condition of possibility of reference, is the ontological freedom that transgresses the distinctness of beings.

Heidegger immediately cautions against interpreting this proposition as ascribing the essence of truth to human caprice. Certainly, the human being is introduced in the discussion with the notion of comportment, but the human being is to be first defined by the notion of comportment in the essence of truth: "Consideration of the essential connection between truth and freedom leads us to pursue the question of the human essence in a regard that assures us an experience of a concealed essential ground of the human being (of Dasein), and in such a manner that the experience transposes us in advance into the originarily essential domain of truth."[53]

It is with a notion of freedom obtained through a meditation on truth that Heidegger comes to the question of the human in the sense, as he clarifies in a parenthesis, of Dasein. Heidegger's ontological notion of freedom is not simply imposed as a further attribute on the human; rather, it brings to the fore the ontological freedom that is proper to Dasein itself in its transcendence. Emphasizing that the human being is to be understood as Dasein, Heidegger is emphasizing in this passage that which has traditionally been considered as other than an attribute, namely, existence. The human being is to be understood in its relation to originary temporality, that is, to the finitude of its existence, rather than in terms of the attributes by which it is apprehended as a being present-at-hand. For Heidegger, only the human being exists and is Dasein, because only the human being—in his or her projects and Being-toward-death—has a definitive relation to temporality as such, and not simply to the present.

The enquiry into the essence of truth turns to the human being as a being that exists and must exist because the understanding of truth as adequation remains inexplicable on the basis of beings that are present-at-hand and whose identity is defined without recourse to the temporality that reaches beyond the discrete "now." The actuality of adequation is accordingly a proof of existence, of mortality and of the freedom of existence. It is a proof of a being that is able to hold together two distinct beings and overcome even the greatest separation in the moments of their apprehension. The synthesis in adequation, which is the achievement of memory and projection, cannot be ascribed to a faculty of a being present-at-hand without at once relinquishing any insight into the role of ecstatic temporality in the traditional understanding of truth. Dasein is the freedom of time itself. Freedom, as it is disclosed in the essence of truth, is not the familiar freedom of the subject. It is not a property that accrues to the subject in the abstraction from its world and that, given the questionable feasibility of this abstraction, must always remain a tenuous possession. The freedom of the essence of truth is the truth of the vitiated freedom with which the subject raises only a feeble protest against its reification. This other, originary freedom does not belong to a humanity whose definition already does not essentially distinguish it from an object. Freedom, according to Heidegger, is transcendence: "The human being does not 'possess' freedom as a property. At best, the converse holds: freedom, ek-sistent, disclosive Da-sein, possesses the human being—so originarily that only *it* secures for humanity that distinctive relatedness to beings as a whole as such which first founds all history. Only the ek-sistent human being is historical." [54]

Freedom is not a property of the human being. As existence, as "existence" grasped etymologically in its standing outside of itself, freedom belongs to a different understanding of Being than that according to which beings stand within themselves and deliver themselves up to a recognition of their properties. For classical ontology, the presence of beings is their unconcealment and thus their truth. But the properties of that which is unconcealed can, for Heidegger, never constitute the truth of Dasein. Dasein *is* freedom. It is the freedom of originary temporality as it makes sense of the now-sequence by which the conventional understanding of time issues in aporias. For Heidegger, the freedom of humanity is not its "elevation" above history into the presence that is simply the neglect of originary temporality. Instead, humanity is freedom precisely to the extent that it is historical. The historicality of humanity, and thus its freedom, is its rootedness in the world of a people. By adhering to this rootedness, and not by repudiating it, Dasein escapes the identifiability consequent on an abstraction from its world and the reduction to a being present-at-hand. A people is Dasein's power of indetermination and the basis of its title to the essence of truth. The freedom that as the truth of adequation transgresses the distinctness of the statement and its object is the historicality of Dasein.

Only inasmuch as Dasein is historical, only inasmuch as it is always being carried beyond the presence that can never be its own but is rather the presence of the things in its world, is adequation between a statement and an object possible. Adequation takes place in the openness of Dasein, in the openness that is its Being-with. But this openness, which is the essence of truth, of unconcealment (ἀλήθεια), is not itself unconcealed, since it always transcends the presence in which it could be apprehended in its openness. After isolating the attunement of beings in adequation from these beings themselves, Heidegger thus suggests that the essence of Dasein is concealment:

Letting beings be, which is an attuning, a bringing into accord, prevails throughout and anticipates all the open comportment that flourishes in it. Human comportment is brought into definite accord throughout by the openedness of beings as a whole. However, from the point of view of everyday calculations and preoccupations this "as a whole" appears to be incalculable and incomprehensible. It cannot be understood on the basis of the beings opened up in any given case, whether they belong to nature or to history. Although it ceaselessly brings everything into definite accord, still it remains indefinite, indeterminable; it then coincides for the most part with what is most fleeting and most unconsidered. However, what brings into accord is not nothing, but rather a concealing of beings as a whole. Precisely because letting-be always lets beings be in a particular comportment that relates to them and thus discloses them, it conceals beings as a whole. Letting-be is intrinsically at the same time a concealing. In the ek-sistent freedom of Da-sein a concealing of beings as a whole comes to pass [*ereignet sich*]. Here there *is* concealment.[55]

In the freedom of Dasein there is concealment. This freedom is the essence of ἀλήθεια, but it is also that which refuses to be unconcealed. As such, freedom is the originary un-truth of ἀλήθεια. It is the error that is inextricably both the failure and fulfillment of knowledge. In the concealment of

Dasein, the revelation of beings as a whole occurs and thus does not occur. The revelation of beings as a whole reveals itself as concealment. Truth, understood in its essence, merges with the darkness of error. If to know the truth of a given being presupposes a knowledge of the essence of truth, beings can only be known in the presence of truth by first being known in the failure to apprehend Dasein. It is as the world intangible to everyday reckoning, and not as subjective caprice, that Dasein is the truth—and essential error—of beings. Dasein's freedom is that which never fell within the scope of classical ontology, because it constituted the Un-thought of its understanding of Being as presence. Metaphysics did not set itself the task of failing before a knowledge of time. The enduring dissatisfaction of metaphysics with the definition of truth as *adaequatio rei et intellectus* (already disputed, as it were in advance, by Plato in the *Theaetetus*) never passed beyond dissatisfaction. An inquiry into the essence of truth—in which an understanding of humanity irreducible to reification could have gained ground—was not undertaken.

In 1933, Heidegger believed the opportunity had arisen for a confrontation with the truth of Dasein. "The Self-Assertion of the German University" is testimony to that conviction. How could National Socialism—and not merely in retrospect—have encouraged such a conviction? The 1933–34 lecture course *Vom Wesen der Wahrheit* says of Hitler:

When today the Führer repeatedly speaks of reeducation in conformity with the National Socialist worldview, this does not mean teaching a few slogans. On the contrary, it means bringing about a *complete change*, a *world schema* on the basis of which he educates the people as a whole. National Socialism is not one doctrine among others, but rather the change from the ground up of the German and, as we believe, also the European world.

This beginning of a great history of a people, as we see it with the Greeks, extends to all dimensions of human activity. With it things step into openness and truth. But in the same moment human beings also step into *untruth*. The latter begins only then.[56]

Hitler is the promise of an encounter with untruth. What criteria could have determined the philosophical success of the encounter without at once proving, through the certainty of the judgment, that an encounter with the abyssality of error had not taken place? Even if the question is unavoidable, even if the philosophical project of 1933 appears unfeasible (in the sense that it could never be carried to the point of a clear result), it does not excuse reading the rectorial address simply for what it says in the jargon of the regime. Beyond what it all too clearly says in "the worst of rhetorics,"[57] "The Self-Assertion of the German University" speaks of a defiance of concealment that in all likelihood has no counterpart outside Heidegger's own writings. The interpretation of the verse by Aeschylus is Heideggerian rather than National Socialist. But Heidegger's refusal to keep his philosophical utterances separate from his utterances as a proselyte of the NSDAP means that he himself was persuaded of the convergence between his thinking and the regime. Inasmuch as what is at issue is a convergence and not an identity, the relations between jargon and philosophy in the rectorial address are not without a noticeable friction. This friction was seized upon by Heidegger after the war and exaggeratedly depicted as antagonism. The trade-offs and the insane stratagems that unify the text, and that rendered possible its attempt at a redefinition of National Socialism, were thereby pushed to the rear.

Under Heidegger's leadership, the German university was to assert itself in accordance with its essence as the will to knowledge. It was to assert itself as a defiance of concealment, rather than as a defiance of Hitler. National Socialism was to be incited to participate in the failure that is reserved for the defiance of concealment. In the rectorial address, the only enemy of National Socialism is invisibility. Even after 1933, in his criticisms of the regime's nihilism, Heidegger does not admit any other opponent. Whatever stands in the presence of the light of knowledge stands already in the forgetfulness of the concealment of Being, and as it shares this with National Socialism, it is never able to mount an opposition on the basis of an alternative. Heidegger's "private" National Socialism in his rectorial address is the substitution of the regime's fundamental alternative for the regime itself: the essence of National Socialism ceases to be an apparatus of control resting on classical ontology and becomes the chance of an encounter with the concealment from which control definitively retreats.

This substitution in the rectorial address explains the laudatory tone in which Heidegger greets the new era and for which he has been both justly and unjustly reproached. The justice and the injustice of the reproach involve, not Heidegger's person, but the question of a response to the enduring reality of fascism. To wish to hear nothing in the rectorial address of the other National Socialism that is the other of National Socialism is to wish to hear nothing of the ambiguity that is arguably the element of a fundamental confrontation with fascism. The rectorial address offers concealment by way of an alternative to National Socialism and, in a sense, thereby offers nothing by way of an alternative. What it rallies against National Socialism is the power of the false. An alternative to the regime that stood against it in the clarity of an exclusive disjunction would have mitigated its opposition through its very distinctness. The principle of the control of beings, of which National Socialism was the exemplary implementation, would not have been contested.

Heidegger's "private" National Socialism is the alternative to National Socialism that is at the same time the essence of its truth. It is the thought of the originary concealment of beings on which the regime rested and on which it could not, in its certainty concerning the controllability of beings, acknowledge itself to rest. Heidegger's "private" National Socialism is not so much the theory of the fascist revolution of 1933 as the thought of the πόλις that is always already founded in concealment before it is brought to light and established in its identity within presence. This other πόλις is "other" only inasmuch as it is the πόλις that is never other, since, in the transcendence by which it is a Being-with, it never fully reveals itself as one πόλις set apart from another. It is the πόλις that is the community of the erring of transcendence. According to the lecture course *Hölderlins Hymnen "Germanien" und "Der Rhein,"* the πόλις is comparable in its originarity to poetry and thought. With the comparison to poetry, Heidegger's πόλις is distinguished from Plato's conception. It is distinguished for the sake of that ambiguity (i.e., the concealment, not the polysemy) of the poetic word which led Plato to banish poets from the πόλις that is to be founded in presence. Heidegger's πόλις is the inconspicuous πόλις that precedes foundation in presence, because it is the πόλις of the transcendence that is the originary concealment of Dasein. In its failure, knowledge is to open itself up to this other πόλις. It is to open itself up to the authentic Being-with-one-another by which Heidegger understands the German *Volk*.

"The Self-Assertion of the German University" is a "folkish" text. Its "folkishness" does not confine itself to a few terminological concessions made to the regime but rather reaches into the heart of Heidegger's thinking. In 1933, Heidegger attempts to lead the masses of National Socialism to the confrontation with classical ontology from which the *Volk* might have been born. The opportunism of Heidegger's engagement marks even the peroration of the rectorial address. Heidegger concludes:

We can only fully understand the glory and greatness of this decampment, however, if we carry within ourselves that deep and broad thoughtfulness upon which the ancient wisdom of the Greeks drew in uttering the words:

> τὰ ... μεγάλα πάντα ἐπισφαλῆ
> "*All that is great stands in the storm . . .*"
> (Plato, *Republic*, 497d, 9)[58]

Heidegger's translation of Plato's text is infamously inaccurate. But the storm that in the jargon of National Socialism substitutes for what Friedrich Schleiermacher had translated as "thought-provoking" (*bedenklich*) is likewise the storm of a total mobilization for the task of provoking thought to its failure before fate. The philosopher is no longer to shelter against a wall from the storm of dust and hail with which Plato compares the lawlessness and impiety of political life (496d), since the great has its element in the storm as much as it is threatened by it. Everything great is at risk (to give yet another, and more conventional, interpretation of the line quoted from Plato), and for Heidegger in 1933, it is the decision implicit in risk that seemingly constitutes greatness.

3

The Feast

Heidegger's resignation of the rectorship of Freiburg University in 1934 cannot be understood as a simple withdrawal from politics. The question of the essence of the German people, which Heidegger raises repeatedly in the months of his open engagement with National Socialism, does not surrender its sudden prominence in his writings with the transfer of office. Instead, this question becomes the site of a confrontation with the regime and its understanding of the political, because it becomes entwined for Heidegger with the question of the essence of poetry. The alleged apoliticality of the latter—"this most innocent of occupations"[1]—assumes a critical force.

It lies, however, in the nature of this confrontation to risk being overlooked. In Heidegger's lectures on Hölderlin, poetry is not presented in rivalry with National Socialism. It is not shown to contend with National Socialism for power. What poetry disputes, according to Heidegger, is not so much the regime's possession of power as the very definition of the political underlying disputes over the possession of power. Refusing to dispute the possession of power, poetry refuses the commensurability with National Socialism that a common object would guarantee. And through this refusal, it rebuffs the claim of the universal to arbitrate over politics. Poetry challenges National Socialism by not challenging it. It cannot contend with it for *possession* of the German people, because only within a deracinated politics does a people cease to be the political itself—the openness of the πόλις and the clearing of beings—and become an *object* of struggle. The more originary politics of poetry, and its auspiciousness for the question of the essence of the *Volk*, consists in its irreducibility to the *Dingbegriffe* (logical categories) of classical ontology. Poetry is itself the political: Heidegger's texts in the 1930s and early 1940s think through this identity in distinction from a politics of the present-at-hand.

That Heidegger's question concerning the essence of poetry, as it is formulated in numerous lectures in the years following the resignation of the rectorship, is a question *against* National Socialism appears to be Heidegger's own estimation in the interview conducted with *Der Spiegel* in September 1966, where he says: "After I stepped down as rector I limited myself to teaching. In the summer semester of 1934 I lectured on 'Logic.' In the following semester I gave the first Hölderlin lecture. In 1936, I began the Nietzsche lectures. Anyone with ears to hear heard in these lectures a confrontation with National Socialism." [2]

Out of impatience with the delay in his "rehabilitation," Heidegger pronounces the confrontation in his lectures unmistakable. This declared unmistakability, nonetheless, can scarcely be brought into agreement with the conventional sense of "confrontation." What is unmistakable after the lecture course *Logik als die Frage nach dem Wesen der Sprache* is that Heidegger elaborates its treatment of both language and the *Volk* into a critical destruction of aesthetics. It is in the meditations on art—without any clear precedent in the texts composed before the resignation of the rectorship—that Heidegger's disaffection with National Socialism is to be discerned. For Heidegger, with the question of art, the question of the German essence is raised.

The confrontation in the lectures on Hölderlin and the confrontation in the lectures on Nietzsche, however closely related in their focus on art, are by no means reducible to the one stratagem. Although Hölderlin did not escape appropriation by the regime (in 1943, the one-hundredth anniversary of his death was the occasion of a visit by Hitler to his grave and the founding of the Hölderlin Gesellschaft under Goebbels's patronage), Heidegger never asserted that there was ultimately a consistency between Hölderlin and National Socialism. But, as Heidegger wrote to the new rector of Freiburg University on November 4, 1945, with Nietzsche it was another matter:

Beginning in 1936 I embarked on a series of courses and lectures on Nietzsche, which lasted until 1945 and which represented in even clearer fashion a declaration of spiritual resistance. In truth, it is unjust to assimilate Nietzsche to National Socialism, an assimilation which—apart from what is essential—ignores his hostility to anti-Semitism and his positive attitude with respect to Russia. But on a higher plane, the debate with Nietzsche's metaphysics is a debate with *nihilism* as it manifests itself with increased clarity under the political form of fascism.[3]

Whether even on a higher plane the assimilation of Nietzsche to National Socialism is justified has become a familiar question through the commentaries of Deleuze, Derrida, Klossowski, and others. For Heidegger, the higher plane on which Nietzsche reveals his affinity with National Socialism, his essential truth as a thinker, is the doctrine of the will to power. The interrogation of the preconditions of this reading, such as its reliance on the magnum opus manufactured by Elisabeth Förster-Nietzsche, its deficient suspicion of the admissibility of the National Socialist appropriations and its systematization of a corpus that owes more to the feuilleton than to scholasticism, has not of itself diminished the force of Heidegger's critique of National Socialism. In certain respects, Nietzsche functions largely as an expedient cipher in this critique.

"Nietzsche" becomes the proper name of nihilism just as "Hölderlin" becomes, as is explicit in the title of the 1936 lecture in Rome, the proper name of poetry. As such, Heidegger views them in the lecture course *Hölderlins Hymne "Andenken"* (Hölderlin's Hymn "Andenken") as poles in the question of the essence of the people: "'Nietzsche and Hölderlin'—an abyss separates the two. In abyssally different ways, both of them determine the nearest and the most distant future of the Germans and of the West."[4] The abyss that divides Hölderlin and Nietzsche is the abyss that divides poetry and National Socialism. And it is in this abyss, rather than on a common ground, that the confrontation takes place. If Heidegger claims that his lectures on Hölderlin amount to a confrontation with the regime, it is because he exhibits Hölderlin as the poet who promises another Germany than that of National Socialism, the more originary Germany portrayed by Hölderlin as the priestess at the feast of the peoples. This other Germany is not present-at-hand. As the question concerning the essence of poetry involves, for Heidegger, a destruction of the understanding of Being as presence, it is a question that involves the ontological mission of the German *Volk*. Raising the question of the Un-thought of nihilism, the lectures on Hölderlin inform the critique offered in the lectures on Nietzsche. Heidegger's resignation of the rectorship is not an abdication before the political as such. In his subsequent lectures, he undertakes a critique of the politics of the present-at-hand and its constitutive inability to question the will to power and, hence, to think the Un-thought of nihilism. To attempt a repetition of Heidegger's thinking on the essence of poetry is thus to seek to understand the nature, and positive inspiration, of his disavowal of National Socialism.

For Heidegger, his confrontation with nihilism in the 1930s and early 1940s was a confrontation with National Socialism. Yet, inasmuch as he was permitted to lecture until the end of the war and at the height of the terror, the confrontation must be said to have been ambiguous. National Socialism itself was expressly a confrontation with nihilism in the guise of liberal democracy. In his 1936 lecture course on Schelling, Heidegger still subscribes to this view, praising Hitler and Mussolini for introducing countermovements to nihilism.[5] The nihilism that Heidegger, in the reigning atmosphere of denunciation, disputed in Hölderlin's name came to encompass National Socialism because it encompassed a general conception of the political. Although the regime is criticized, it is never on account of its particularity as one political formation among many. Heidegger's confrontation with National Socialism is likewise ambiguous because Heidegger retained the Nazi topoi of German renewal and the lament over nihilism. Everything thus depends on the way these topoi are used.

In order to establish poetry's irreducibility to nihilism and thus the people's irreducibility to National Socialism, it must be asked in what Heidegger's conception of nihilism consists. How does it differ, if at all, from the National Socialist caricature of liberal democracies? In his 1942 lecture course *Hölderlin's Hymn "The Ister,"* Heidegger subscribes to this caricature of the declared enemies of Germany:

We know today that the Anglo-Saxon world of Americanism has resolved to annihilate Europe, that is, the homeland [*Heimat*], and that means: the commencement of the Western world. Whatever has the character of commencement is indestructible. America's entry into this planetary war is not its entry into history; rather, it is already the ultimate American act of American ahistoricality and self-devastation. For this act is the renunciation of commencement, and a decision in favor of that which is without commencement. The concealed spirit of the commencement in the West will not even have the look of contempt for this trial of self-devastation without commencement, but will await its stellar hour from out of the releasement and tranquillity that belong to the commencement.[6]

It is difficult to see a confrontation with National Socialism in such a passage. Indeed, Heidegger's "spiritual resistance" never formulated itself, in either his lectures or even his posthumously published private notes, in terms of a solidarity with the enemies of the regime. Heidegger suggests that the entry of Roosevelt's America into the war does not pose a threat to the Europe of National Socialist imperialism. Nihilism, which the movement never failed to attribute to Anglo-Saxon America, is manifest in the latter's self-devastation just as the originarity of Europe ensures its invulnerability. Heidegger's thesis is that victory lies with the originary, and hence danger arises not from an opponent's military and industrial superiority but from an inability to remain within the origin. Such reasoning appears little more than propaganda. But is the origin the Germany of National Socialism? Heidegger's confrontation with the regime enacts itself as the drawing of a distinction between the two.

In the 1941–42 lecture course *Hölderlins Hymne "Andenken,"* Heidegger is explicit on the character of the origin and the danger it faces: "The sporadic abandonment of the German essence to Americanism already reaches the disastrous point at which Germans are ashamed that their people was once called 'the people of poets and thinkers.'"[7] The essence and originarity of the German people is to be the people of poets and thinkers. And that this should be their essence and originarity is not because they are, ineluctably, a people of poets and thinkers, but rather because they will be essential and originary only as such a people. In 1941–42, the Germans are surrendering their essence and hence the essential. Germany itself threatens the people of poets and thinkers. It is in fidelity to the essential that the *Volk* attests to its originarity and thus to its invulnerability. By breaking with the definition of the German people as the people of poets and thinkers, by mobilizing the population as workers and soldiers, and hence by emulating that which Jünger in *The Worker* considers Anglo-Saxon America's preeminent achievement, National Socialism relinquishes its only possibility of withstanding invasion. National Socialism mistakes what is to be defended and surrenders the very moment it begins preparations for war.

For Heidegger, invulnerability rests with the maintenance of the essence of a people and not with the survival of the biologically determined entities of which it is seemingly composed. Nihilism, rather than death, is the seemingly fateless danger that lies in wait for a people and its historical, that is, mortal, essence. As the people of poets and thinkers, Germany is made perfect in military and industrial weakness. In *Hölderlins Hymnen "Germanien" und "Der Rhein,"* Heidegger accordingly favors Hölderlin's image of Germany as a maiden lost in reverie and hidden in the forest over the Niederwald monument's bloodthirsty figure with a giant sword.[8] On the assumption that its distance from the perceived practices of Anglo-Saxon America preserves the *Volk* because it preserves its essence, Heidegger regards the motorization of the armed forces with the hostility toward technology characteristic of his works of this period. In a note from the incompletely delivered lecture course *Nietzsche: Europäischer Nihilismus* (Nietzsche: European Nihilism), he writes: "Within the horizon of bourgeois culture and 'intellectualism' one might, for example, view the complete, that is, fundamental 'motorization' of the military from the ground up as a manifestation simply of untrammelled 'technicism' and 'materialism.' It is in truth a metaphysical act that in its range certainly surpasses, for instance, the abolition of 'philosophy.'"[9] The devastation that Heidegger fears is a withdrawal of the essence of the *Volk*. This devastation by which nihilism announces itself can occur as much through military success as through military defeat.

In 1943, while lecturing on Heraclitus, Heidegger refers to the devastation of the cities on the Rhine and the Ruhr but proclaims that the real disaster lies elsewhere. Everything pales before the calamity of nihilism:

> Let us, however, posit the moment when the possibility of saying and understanding "is" is withdrawn from human beings. Let us attempt to think through, even if only for a few minutes, what would then become of humanity. No catastrophe that could break over the planet can be compared with this most inconspicuous of all events in which the relation to "is" is suddenly taken from humanity. But this catastrophe has already taken place; it is simply that no one has yet noticed it in its essence. Historical humanity has gone so far as to forget "is" and "Being," renouncing all thought of that which is named in this word. Indifference toward "Being" lays siege to the planet. Humanity allows the flood of the forgetfulness of Being to wash over it. In truth, however, there is no longer even a diving within this flood, since for that to be the case, the forgetfulness of Being would still need to be experienced. This forgetfulness of Being is itself already forgotten, which, of course, conforms with the essence of forgetfulness, drawing down into itself like a whirlpool everything that enters its vicinity.[10]

Another name for this obliviousness of Being is given in *An Introduction to Metaphysics*: "To forget Being and cultivate only beings—that is nihilism. Nihilism thus understood is the *ground* of the nihilism which Nietzsche exposed in the first book of *The Will to Power*."[11] Nihilism, by which the essence of the *Volk* is surrendered, shows itself in the inauthentic captivation with beings. In losing sight of Being for that which is and which as such inhabits the repeatability of the now, classical ontology was itself nihilistic—its legacy places itself between the *Volk* and its essential mission of the question of Being. Classical ontology is the ground of the nihilism that Nietzsche analyses in various contemporary manifestations without ever grasping it in itself. Heidegger believes he thus comes to Nietzsche's assistance by furnishing both a single foundation for nihilism and the possibility of thinking its Un-thought.

A note from 1887 included in *The Will to Power* confesses:

Nihilism. It is *ambiguous*:

  A. Nihilism as a sign of increased power of the spirit: as *active* nihilism.

  B. Nihilism as decline and recession of the power of the spirit: as *passive* nihilism.[12]

Taking the term "nihilism" from Turgenev, Nietzsche extends its range but, in doing so, renders the term ambiguous—Nietzsche does not grasp that which Heidegger will name the essence of nihilism. For both Heidegger and Nietzsche, and in contrast to many National Socialist pronouncements, nihilism is everywhere. For Heidegger, however, it is everywhere precisely because it names the temporally derivative structure of the repeatable: "nihilism" is the fundamental meaning of "everywhere." In itself, the ubiquity of nihilism betrays the irreducibility of Being to presence. The people of poets and thinkers that disappears within nihilism is the people of Being and, that is to say, of the alignment of the definitions of poetry and thought with the question of Being.

Heidegger's analysis of the planetary catastrophe of nihilism in the passage from the lecture course on Heraclitus quoted above does not, therefore, need to be understood as a retraction of his defiant remarks a year earlier. The indestructibility that he attributes to the originary in 1942 is not the spurious indestructibility of the untried, since the intervening military offensives of Anglo-Saxon America have no bearing upon the hidden spirit of the originary. The originary is indestructible because, as the Un-thought of a ubiquitous nihilism, it cannot be found and hence cannot be destroyed. That the originary withholds itself is, in 1942, grounds for disregarding the escalation of hostilities, whereas, in 1943, it is itself the catastrophe. The one proposition does not contradict the other, and it is from within their coherence that Heidegger asserts: "The planet is in flames. The essence of humanity is out of joint. Only from the Germans, assuming that they find and defend what it is that is German, can the world-historical sobriety [*Besinnung*] come."[13] That which is German (*das*

Deutsche) is hidden from the Germans themselves and in its secrecy it consigns the planet to ruin. National Socialism is, properly speaking, a consequence, rather than a cause of the ruin of the age, which is alternately called the forgetfulness of Being and the withholding of what it is that is German.

In the same lecture course, Heidegger explains that the sobriety that is to come from the Germans will only come from them in their as yet unattained specificity as the people of Being:

Irrespective of the substance and manner in which the external fate of the West may be articulated, the greatest and proper test of the Germans still lies ahead, that test in which, at the hands of the ignorant, they are perhaps to be tested unwillingly as to whether they, the Germans, are in harmony with the truth of Being, whether they are strong enough—over and above a readiness to die—to save the originary in its inconspicuous brilliance against the small-mindedness of the modern world.

The danger in which the "holy heart of the peoples" of the West stands is not that of a decline; it is rather the danger that, in confusion ourselves, we will capitulate to the will of modernity and be driven along with it.[14]

Hölderlin's "holy heart of the peoples" faces a test in which it is to prove itself properly German through the defense of the originary. The National Socialist topos of German renewal is cited here without simply being replicated. The originarity of the German people, by which they stand in a contestation with modernity, is not, for Heidegger, the rustic gloss of a program of industrialization, but rather the priority of Being as it presses on them its claim as the Un-thought of modern technicism. Heidegger advocates a willingness to die in the defense of this Un-thought in a war necessarily other than the one being waged by the regime. A Germany defined as this Un-thought and nonetheless defended by the means of modern technicism is a Germany left undefended before nihilism. The campaign against nihilism by which his writings recall National Socialism is likewise what distinguishes Heidegger from the regime.

In "Overcoming Metaphysics," a collection of notes from this period, Heidegger refuses the world war, on account of the nihilism of its parties, any fundamental oppositionality or crisis. He thus suggests that the confrontation will not take place between National Socialism and the alliance of its military opponents, but between power and that which is forgotten in power: "The struggle between those who are in power and those who want to come to power: on every side there is the struggle for power. Everywhere power itself is what is determinative. Through this struggle for power, the being of power is posited in the essence of its unconditional dominance by both sides. [. . .] This struggle is [. . .] in its essence undecidable." [15]

In *What Is Called Thinking?* Heidegger will reiterate that the war has decided nothing. [16] The decision must come from elsewhere. As the war has not issued from a conflict, there is no dispute that could be resolved in order to arrive at a peace. The difference between war and peace, according to a further note from "Overcoming Metaphysics," is inessential to the nihilism of the manipulation of beings:

> There are effects everywhere, and nowhere is there a worlding of the world and yet, although forgotten, there is still Being. Beyond war and peace, there is a mere erring of the consumption of beings in the plan's self-guaranteeing in terms of the vacuum of the abandonment of Being. Changed into their deformation of essence, "war" and "peace" are taken up into erring, and disappear into the mere course of the escalating manufacture of what can be manufactured, because they have become unrecognizable with regard to any distinction. The question of when there will be peace cannot be answered not because the duration of war is unfathomable, but rather because the question already asks about something which no longer exists, since war is no longer anything which could terminate in peace. War has become a distortion of the consumption of beings which is continued in peace. [17]

As the originary, and thus as that which is inconspicuous within the manufacture and consumption of beings, Germany is not at stake in such a war, just as it falls to none of the parties in such a peace. It is this other Germany that must be defended and yet, as this other Germany, it cannot be defended, at least not in the sense of safeguarding the integrity of geographical borders. As the Un-thought of modern technicism, Heidegger's Germany is not a being among beings, which might thus be preserved rather than exploited. Its defense involves the defense of the people within Being. In order to defend this other Germany, the people must first find themselves within Being. The Germans must defend themselves by becoming the people of poets and thinkers that they never were except in literary journalism. Needless to say, it is not a matter of producing verses and treatises in place of armaments. The people of poets and thinkers is the people that defines itself otherwise than through production. It is the people that does not produce, because it does not tear beings away from nothingness and place them in the light of presence and the possibility of their manipulation. In Heidegger's confrontation with National Socialism, poetry and thought are attributed an irreducibility to the nihilism of production.

For Heidegger, the Germans will only survive the war as well as its peace if they become the people of Hölderlin. In the 1934–35 lecture course *Hölderlins Hymnen "Germanien" und "Der Rhein,"* Heidegger calls Hölderlin the "founder of German Being."[18] As it is Hölderlin who grounds the people of the Un-thought of nihilism, it is in the commentaries on Hölderlin that Heidegger attempts to think the confrontation between art and National Socialism. What is brought to the fore in this confrontation is the originary Germany forgotten by Nietzsche, National Socialism, and its military opponents.

Poetry, for Heidegger, does not exhaust itself within nihilism. Such a claim as yet says too little. Its resemblance to certain formulations of Nietzsche's on art's relation to nihilism should not be overestimated. A passage that Heidegger himself quotes from Nietzsche's literary remains (and, again, it is solely the Nietzsche of Heidegger's polemic who is at issue) imputes a distance between art and nihilism. But significantly, it is as the power of enervation, and not as the obliviousness of Being, that Nietzsche here understands nihilism: "Very early in my life I took the question of the relation of *art* to *truth* seriously: even now I stand in holy dread in the face of this discordance. My first book was devoted to it. *The Birth of Tragedy* believes in art on the background of another belief—that it *is not possible to live with truth*, that the 'will to truth' is already a symptom of degeneration."[19]

The decadence of the "will to truth" is its opposition to "life". Heidegger quotes this passage in a reading of Nietzsche's exposition of Platonism as nihilism. Summarizing this exposition, Heidegger writes:

The major debility of the basic force of Dasein consists in the calumniation and denigration of the fundamental orienting force of "life" itself. Such defamation of creative life, however, has its grounds in the fact that things are posited *above* life which make negation of it desirable. The desirable, the ideal, is the supersensuous, interpreted as genuine being [*das eigentlich Seiende*]. This interpretation of being is accomplished in the Platonic philosophy. The theory of Ideas founds the ideal, and that means the definitive preeminence of the supersensuous, in determining and dominating the sensuous.[20]

To overcome nihilism is here, for Nietzsche, to overturn Platonism. Heidegger continues:

Overturning Platonism means, first, shattering the preeminence of the supersensuous as the ideal. Beings, being what they are, may not be despised on the basis of what should and ought to be. But at the same time, in opposition to the philosophy of the ideal and to the installation of what ought to be and of the "should," the inversion sanctions the investigation and determination of that which is—it summons the question "What is being itself?" If the "should" is the supersensuous, then being itself, that which is, conceived as liberated from the "should," can only be the sensuous. But with that the essence of the sensuous is not given; its definition is given up. In contrast, the realm of true being, of the true, and thereby the essence of truth, is demarcated; as before, however, already in Platonism, the true is to be attained on the path of knowledge.[21]

With respect to the question of Being, Nietzsche's inverted Platonism is as reductive as the metaphysics it overturns, since both ground themselves in the conviction that the truth of beings is a matter to be expounded in theories of knowledge. As a result, truth remains, with Nietzsche, that which must be isolated from its doubles. Nietzsche's affirmation of the sensuous, of what he terms "life" and "art," constitutes simply a further variant of the nihilism of the obliviousness of Being. It is an affirmation that is fundamentally a negation, and not simply because the sensuous that is affirmed defines itself as the negative of the supersensuous. The negation is the continued exclusion of Being as such through forgetfulness. Nietzsche retains the antithesis of the sensuous and the supersensuous and thereby retains the ontology of the Platonic doctrine of Ideas. The confrontation with the reductive ontology of nihilism cannot, for Heidegger, take place through the sensuousness of the work of art. It is not by a single aspect that the work of art presents this confrontation; it is not even by its entirety, since this entirety—as the distinct assemblage of qualities—falls within the understanding of truth as adequation. The work of art, which for Heidegger is essentially poetry, enacts a confrontation with nihilism because it restores truth as adequation to its other origin in the concealment and unconcealment of Being.

Yet why should this be the privilege of the work of art? To what extent does Heidegger thereby replicate the nihilistic one-sidedness of Platonism and its Nietzschean inversion? These objections are addressed in Heidegger's most explicit response to the task of defining the work of art. In "The Origin of the Work of Art," composed in the period of the lectures on Nietzsche and Hölderlin, Heidegger writes: "The work as work sets up a world. The work holds open the open region of the world."[22] The privilege of the work of art thus disappears into the world it establishes. That the work of art is never simply "itself" for Heidegger can be read in his commentary, in "The Origin of the Work of Art," on an inexactly specified painting by van Gogh: "Van Gogh's painting is the disclosure of what the equipment, the pair of peasant shoes, *is* in truth. This being emerges into the unconcealment of its Being. The Greeks called the unconcealment of beings ἀλήθεια."[23] Van Gogh's painting discloses what the pair of peasant shoes truly is. This is not to disclose the peasant shoes in conformity with the understanding of truth dominant in the natural sciences. What emerges into unconcealment in the painting is not the comprehensive set of properties of a being present-at-hand, but rather the Being of the peasant shoes. What is thus unconcealed in van Gogh's painting is the very questionability of unconcealment. Van Gogh's painting reveals the limits of revelation. Through depicting an object, it remains within the conventional understanding of representation and yet it likewise depicts the unrepresentable. In being depicted, the peasant shoes step beyond their ontic self-evidence into the truth of their Being and the existence (Da-sein) of their truth. The painting, Heidegger continues, restores to the shoes their world: "But above all, the work did not, as it might seem at first, serve merely for a better visualizing of what a piece of equipment is. Rather, the equipmentality of equipment first expressly comes to the fore through the work and only in the work."[24] The true object of depiction in the work of art is the object's otherwise overlooked equipmentality. In van Gogh's painting, equipmentality is the peasant's world of the open fields in which the use of the shoes is sustained. That the disclosure of equipmentality is not being identified in "The Origin of the Work of Art" with an insight into the optimal use of a piece of equipment is clear from Heidegger's own expansive description:

From the dark opening of the worn insides of the shoes the toilsome tread of the worker stares forth. In the stiffly rugged heaviness of the shoes there is the accumulated tenacity of her slow trudge through the far-spreading and ever-uniform furrows of the field swept by a raw wind. On the leather lie the dampness and richness of the soil. Under the soles slides the loneliness of the field-path as evening falls. In the shoes vibrates the silent call of the earth, its quiet gift of the ripening grain and its unexplained self-refusal in the fallow desolation of the wintry field. This equipment is pervaded by uncomplaining worry as to the certainty of bread, the wordless joy of having once more withstood want, the trembling before the impending childbed and shivering at the surrounding menace of death.[25]

For Heidegger, van Gogh's painting discloses the peasant woman's Being-in-the-world. That which defines the peasant shoes as equipment, namely, that which is their equipmentality, is the phenomenon of world in all its fullness. In van Gogh's painting of a pair of peasant shoes, a world "appears."

But why should a pair of peasant's shoes become so voluble through being depicted in the work of art? In what way is the equipmentality that, according to "The Origin of the Work of Art," comes to light *only* in the work of art different from the equipmentality disclosed, according to *Being and Time*, in the broken, inappropriate, or missing tool? Perhaps the exclusiveness of the emergence of equipmentality claimed for the work of art in the later text is not to be interpreted as a revision of the treatment in the earlier text. Perhaps the work of art is nothing other than a broken, inappropriate or missing tool and can be nothing other if it is to be the means of a confrontation with technicism. The *Volk* of the Un-thought of nihilism and the immersion in the manipulation of beings would therefore more clearly be the people of the poets.

In *Being and Time*, art does not feature as a matter for exposition. In what way is the argument of "The Origin of the Work of Art" prefigured, if at all, in Heidegger's earlier examination of the disclosure of the equipmentality (*Zeugsein*) of the equipment (*Zeug*)? In §15 of *Being and Time*, Heidegger writes of the character of readiness-to-hand that is proper to the tool: "The peculiarity of what is proximally ready-to-hand is that, in its readiness-to-hand, it must, as it were, withdraw [*zurückzuziehen*] in order to be ready-to-hand quite authentically." [26] That which is ready-to-hand, and can thus be used as a tool (*Zeug*), is only ready-to-hand by means of the withdrawal whereby, as Heidegger explains, the context of its readiness-to-hand effaces itself. Without this context, a tool ceases to be a tool, and yet this context must also withdraw if the tool is to be a tool: "Taken strictly, there 'is' no such thing as *an* equipment. To the Being of any equipment there always belongs a totality of equipment, in which it can be this equipment that it is. Equipment is essentially 'something in-order-to . . .' [*etwas um-zu* . . .]." [27] In presenting itself immediately for use, a tool cannot present the mediation of the equipmental totality whereby it is what it is as something ready-to-hand. The totality of equipment is not the sum of interrelated tools, but rather the context, in the fullest sense, of the use of a given piece of equipment. Absorbed in the use of a tool, Dasein overlooks its context and ignores the open-endedness of its in-order-to. So long as it is employed, the tool keeps the world in which it is employed secret. Alongside its individual function as a given piece of equipment, equipment—as equipment that is employed—has the function of ward-ing off threats to Dasein's immersion in the realm of that which Heidegger in *Being and Time* describes as the everyday:

> To the everydayness of Being-in-the-world there belong certain modes of concern. These permit the entities with which we concern ourselves to be encountered in such a way that the worldly character of what is within-the-world comes to the fore. When we concern ourselves with something, the entities which are most closely ready-to-hand may be met as something unusable, not properly adapted for the use we have decided upon. The tool turns out to be damaged, or the material unsuitable. In each of these cases *equipment* is here, ready-to-hand. We discover its unusability, however, not by looking at it and establishing its properties, but rather by the circumspection of the dealings in which we use it. When its unusability is thus discovered, equipment becomes conspicuous. This *conspicuousness* presents the ready-to-hand equipment as in a certain un-readiness-to-hand.[28]

Here the inappropriate or damaged tool, like the unwearable peasant shoes of van Gogh's painting in "The Origin of the Work of Art," discloses its world.

But is world in *Being and Time* to be understood differently from world in "The Origin of the Work of Art"? Certainly the style in which they are described is different, but the prose of the earlier text does not imply that it is a prosaic world that is at issue. If Heidegger in 1927 had meant by "world" only the systematic interrelations of a production process, then *Being and Time* would be a work of simple pragmatism rather than of fundamental ontology. Reflecting on the misinterpretations of his work, Heidegger writes in 1941:

> For Heidegger, the world consists only of cooking pots, pitchforks, and lampshades. He has no relationship to "higher culture," not to speak of "Nature," because none of that is to be found in *Being and Time*.
>
> The actual basis for this misinterpretation does not lie however in the sheer superficiality of the "reading," but rather in the fact that one takes it for granted that the author can be ascribed a desire to put forward a "system of the world," while something nonetheless quite different is being asked.[29]

The conspicuousness of equipment in the text of 1927 is not the clarity with which it presents itself to the skilled eye of a time-and-motion expert. This conspicuousness has to be understood more radically, as a rupture in the very understanding of Being. Where readiness-to-hand "presents" itself, it is the transcendence of Dasein's constitutive engagement with the world that is at issue. The commentators who are unable to find Nature in

Being and Time have arguably placed limits in advance on Dasein's transcendence and can thus make nothing in §15 of the readiness-to-hand of poetic Nature: "If its kind of Being as ready-to-hand is disregarded, this 'Nature' itself can be discovered and defined simply in its pure presence-at-hand. But when this happens, the Nature which 'stirs and strives', which assails us and enthralls us as a landscape, remains hidden." [30] As this excerpt suggests, the world of *Being and Time* is not narrower than the world disclosed by the work of art.

The claim in "The Origin of the Work of Art" that it is *only* in the work that the equipmentality of equipment—its readiness-to-hand—first comes to the fore does not contest the radicality of the ontological rupture in *Being and Time*. The work of art does not exclude broken, inappropriate, or missing equipment, and neither is it simply interchangeable with such equipment. Instead, it is its truth. The work of art sets up the world that broken, inappropriate, or missing equipment merely discloses. The disclosures of broken, inappropriate, or missing equipment are thus dependent on the work of art. Such a claim is, of course, no less peculiar than the claim that the work of art is nothing other than a broken, inappropriate, or missing tool. But with the assertion of the priority of the work of art, Heidegger endeavors to overcome the incidentality and fortuitousness of the disclosures of broken, inappropriate, or missing equipment. The work of art becomes the truth of these disclosures inasmuch as it is *essentially* that which the tool is only *accidentally*, namely, the occasion for the question of Being. The work of art is, as it were, the tool that is at once broken, inappropriate, and missing in its very essence.

In van Gogh's painting, the equipment of the peasant woman's shoes is missing, and it is a loss that can never be made good and can never be overlooked. Readiness-to-hand does not withdraw behind the ready-to-hand. The missing tool—and it is its absence that the work of art presents through the nonpresentation of depiction—never reveals merely itself. In *Being and Time*, Heidegger writes:

Similarly, when something ready-to-hand is found missing, though its everyday presence [*Zugegensein*] has been so obvious that we have never taken any notice of it, this makes a *break* in those referential contexts which circumspection discovers. Our circumspection comes up against emptiness, and now sees for the first time *what* the missing article was ready-to-hand *with*, and *what* it was ready-to-hand *for*. The environment announces itself afresh.[31]

The absence of the object of depiction is never a simple defect of the work of art, because it exposes the object's transcendence (its in-order-to . . .). Van Gogh's painting does not show a pair of peasant's shoes, so much as the environment (*Umwelt*) in which they are worn. The shoes present themselves to circumspection (*Umsicht*), insofar as the painting does not present a tool for use. The work of art frustrates the call for a tool in offering only its image, and yet by this frustration, it gives more than the tool itself: it gives the world from which technicism sustains itself in forgetfulness.

In conformity with his critical destruction in the 1930s of the nihilism of the traditional understanding of truth, Heidegger is emphatic in "The Origin of the Work of Art" that the truth of the work of art is not to be measured by the accuracy of the image of its object. More is at stake:

> Agreement with what *is* has long been taken to be the essence of truth. But then, is it our opinion that this painting by van Gogh depicts a pair of peasant shoes somewhere at hand, and is a work of art because it does so successfully? Is it our opinion that the painting draws a likeness from something actual and transposes it into a product of artistic—production? By no means.[32]

In painting the peasant shoes, van Gogh paints *more* than their mere image—and the measure of the work of art is thus not the measure of its representational accuracy. The above extract does not banish the notion of representation from discussions of art.[33] Heidegger's rejection of the view that the truth of art lies in its adequation to an extant object does not amount to an appeal against the sentence that Plato lays upon mimesis in *The Republic*. In order to follow Heidegger's confrontation with both Platonism and its Nietzschean offshoot, the common underestimation and superficial rebuttals of Plato's thinking of mimesis must first be dismissed.

In Book X of *The Republic*, Plato contends that mimesis is not the preserve of the artist but also characterizes the product of the manual worker in its distance from the Idea and thus from truth:

> And what of the maker of the bed? Were you not saying that he too makes, not the idea which according to our view is the real object denoted by the word bed, but only a particular bed?
>
> Yes, I did.
>
> Then if he does not make a real object he cannot make what *is*, but only some semblance of existence; and if anyone were to say that the work of the maker of the bed, or of any other workman, has real existence, he could hardly be supposed to be speaking the truth.

Not, at least, he replied, in the view of those who make a business of these discussions.

No wonder, then, that his work too is an indistinct expression of truth.[34]

As truth does not lie with the extant object, truth for Plato cannot be ascribed to the work of art on the basis of its adequation to an extant object. Heidegger writes therefore in *Nietzsche*:

The distance from Being and its pure visibility is definitive for the definition of the essence of the μιμητής. What is decisive for the Greek-Platonic concept of μίμησις or imitation is not reproduction or portraiture, not the fact that the painter provides us with the same thing once again; what is decisive is that this is precisely what he cannot do, that he is even less capable than the craftsman of duplicating the same thing. It is therefore wrongheaded to apply to μίμησις notions of "naturalistic" or "primitivistic" copying and reproducing. Imitation is subordinate pro-duction.[35]

It is not its distance from the extant object but its distance from Being determined as presence in the Idea that is decisive for Plato's thinking on the work of art. With differing inspirations, both Plato and Heidegger consider art as a relic of a nonmetaphysical understanding of Being.[36] Heidegger, for whom the possibility of a confrontation with the nihilism of Platonism rests with this distance from metaphysics, thus proposes mimesis as the definition of art. In what is other than an impartial citation of Plato, he asserts: "But μίμησις is the essence of all art."[37]

It is worth noting that this sentence does not express a blindness to nonrepresentative art, since the disavowal of an adequation with an extant object that such art practices does not affect its subordination to its ἰδέα. The ἰδέα of a nonrepresentative work of art, as of any work of art, is its appearance, its εἶδος. It is thus not because mimesis is the essence of all art that Heidegger later queries, in *The Principle of Reason*, with its analysis of an age of the total manipulation of material, whether abstract art is indeed art: "That in such an age art becomes objectless testifies to its historical appropriateness, and this above all when nonrepresentational [*gegenstandlose*] art conceives of its own productions as no longer being able to be works, rather as being something for which the suitable word is lacking."[38] Such nonrepresentational art still appears and is thus, for Platonism, still subordinate to its ἰδέα.[39] Yet it endeavors to suppress the possibility of the question that mimesis offers to the understanding of Being as presence.[40] Such art seeks to erase its distance from its ἰδέα.

In "Plato's Doctrine of Truth," a reading of Plato almost as frequently contested as his reading of Nietzsche,[41] Heidegger clarifies the meaning of appearance in Platonism: "Plato does not regard this 'visible form' as a mere 'aspect.' For him the 'visible form' has in addition something of a 'stepping forth' whereby a thing 'presents' itself. Standing in its 'visible form' the being itself shows itself."[42] That which is presents itself in its appearance as it is, and it is the ἰδέα that presents itself:

> The "idea" does not first let something else (behind it) "shine in its appearance" [*erscheinen*]; it itself is what shines, it is concerned only with the shining of itself. The ἰδέα is that which can shine [*das Scheinsame*]. The essence of the idea consists in its ability to shine and be seen [*Schein- und Sichtsamkeit*]. This is what brings about presencing, specifically the coming to presence of what a being is in any given instance.[43]

Every work of art appears as its presence but also fails to appear as its presence. It falls short of its own ἰδέα and therefore cannot be said to be true even to itself. And that it fails to appear as its presence is because it does not emerge into the constancy of knowledge.

Already in the 1924–45 lecture course *Plato's Sophist*, Heidegger expatiates on the relation between presence and knowledge: "And the pure letting the world be encountered is a making present. As *such*, it is only temporally that it can express *itself* in the appropriate speaking about the world: the Being of the world is presence."[44] Knowledge in Platonism is explicitly defined as encounter. Mimesis is the frustration of the encounter. The work of art, for Plato, is obscure because it does not fully give itself up to be known. It cannot do so, because its perishability is its essential possibility of absence. The work of art deceives, but the substitution of a depiction for an extant object is incidental to the deception of mimesis. The work of art offers itself but never ceases to offer itself because its offer is never accepted, its subordination to the ἰδέα is never revoked in consummation. The act of offering, as its distance from presence, deprives it of Being and, that is to say, of appearance. In one respect, the essence of the work of art is, for Plato, the threat of invisibility. The work of art, contrary to Nietzsche's complementary readings of art and Platonism, refuses itself to the senses—it withdraws from the gaze of knowledge.

The truth of metaphysics has to be won in the face of this secretiveness, as Heidegger writes: "Everything depends on the ὀρθότης, the correctness of the gaze. Through this correctness, seeing or knowing becomes something correct so that in the end it looks directly at the highest idea and fixes itself in this 'direct alignment.' In so directing itself, apprehending conforms itself to what is to be seen: the 'visible form' of the being." [45] The gaze has always, as it were, to look beyond the work of art in order to behold the truth that the work of art itself is, because appearance grants its immediacy solely to presence. That which is not present deludes. Truth, as that which is, retracts in Platonism into the opposite of nonbeing. Rediscovering the alternative to presence in the work of art, Platonism defines the work of art by the indigence that can but compel the work of art to seek adequation with that which is present. The representation of an extant object becomes the sum of the truth of the work of art.

This contraction of truth into presence is, for Heidegger, the ground of nihilism that Nietzsche himself failed to recognize and thus failed to challenge in his overturning of Platonism. Nietzsche adheres fundamentally to the understanding of Being that arises with the contraction of truth:

Nietzsche's determination of truth as the incorrectness of thinking is in agreement with the traditional essence of truth as the correctness of assertion (λόγος). Nietzsche's concept of truth displays the last glimmer of the most extreme consequence of the change of truth from the unhiddenness of beings to the correctness of the gaze. The change itself is brought about in the determination of the Being of beings (in Greek: the being present of what is present) as ἰδέα. [46]

By following Plato in defining truth within an antithesis with the false, Nietzsche does not see beyond the corresponding contraction of Being. For Heidegger, Nietzsche is "the most unrestrained Platonist in the history of Western metaphysics," [47] because his opposition to Plato never develops into a confrontation on the basis of an alternative. Nietzsche's maintenance of truth in an antithesis prevents him from raising a question against the determination of Being as presence and against the nihilistic conception of art dependent on this determination. Nietzsche, according to Heidegger, abolishes the distance that falsehood opens between the work of art and the Platonic determination of Being. In so doing, he ostensibly affirms art when it is precisely art's failure within Platonism that carries the possibility of thinking through nihilism. Nietzsche's conception of art as the true remains nihilistic, in Heidegger's sense, because it is, so to speak, too affirmative. The will to power hinders Nietzsche from grasping failure as such. Everything becomes a manifestation of will to power. Even the false is absorbed into the presence of its appearance. Heidegger's response to Plato, by contrast, does not involve disputing the definition of art as the failure of presence. Heidegger wishes to grasp this failure as failure, since it is an understanding of this failure that puts into question the entire metaphysics of presence from Plato to Nietzsche.

To this end, Heidegger repeats the judgments of metaphysics on the failure of art.[48] The afterword to "The Origin of the Work of Art" acquiesces to Hegel's judgment on the supersession of art in order to keep in view art's distance from metaphysics. The passage is worth quoting at length, and not merely on account of its implicit critique of Nietzsche's affirmation of art:

In the most comprehensive reflection on the essence of art that the West possesses —comprehensive because it stems from metaphysics—namely, Hegel's *Lectures on Aesthetics*, the following propositions occur:

> Art no longer counts for us as the highest manner in which truth obtains existence for itself.
>
> One may well hope that art will continue to advance and perfect itself, but its form has ceased to be the highest need of spirit.
>
> In all these relationships, art is, and remains for us, on the side of its highest vocation, something past.

The judgment that Hegel passes in these statements cannot be evaded by pointing out that since Hegel's lectures on aesthetics were given for the last time during the winter of 1828–29 at the University of Berlin, we have seen the rise of many new artworks and new art movements. Hegel never meant to deny this possibility. But the question remains: Is art still an essential and necessary way in which that truth happens which is decisive for our historical existence, or is art no longer of this character? If, however, it is such no longer, then there remains the question as to why this is so. The truth of Hegel's judgment has not yet been decided; for behind this verdict there stands Western thought since the Greeks. Such thought corresponds to a truth of beings that has already happened. Decision upon the judgment will be made, if at all, from and about this truth of beings. Until then the judgment remains in force. But for that very reason, the question is necessary as to whether the truth that the judgment declares is final and conclusive, and what follows if it is.[49]

Hegel's judgment remains binding in spite of Nietzsche. Hegel's judgment that art has ceased to be the highest form in which truth attains existence does not incite Heidegger to restore art to its alleged earlier dignity, since the sentence expresses a thoroughly metaphysical reading of art's irreducibility to metaphysics. As it is only with metaphysics, and its contraction of Being to presence, that truth begins to attain existence in higher and lower forms, neither art nor anything else is able to yield preeminence to metaphysics. Art is thus not so much superseded by metaphysics as obscured in its other understanding of truth. The constitutive absence of a highest form, rather than its historical loss, defines this other understanding, which within metaphysics can only be recalled as failure.

This "failure" has to be grasped as what it is in itself—and not merely as an incidental negation of the highest form—if the truth of Being is not to be overlooked in the preoccupation with presence. The "failure" of art is Being's failure to be merely present. To grasp the "failure" of presence as the essence of art is to grasp art as indeterminate. It is to grasp art as the questionability of the apprehension of beings in the light of presence. Through distinguishing itself from the originary understanding of Being, the highest form of truth establishes that from which it distinguishes itself as the distinct entity known as "art." Metaphysics hence reifies even that from which it distanced itself for the sake of the reification of beings as a whole in the light of presence. It is the distinctness of the entity known in metaphysics as "art" that risks interposing itself and reformulating Heidegger's question here concerning the essence of truth as the property of a superseded form in which truth attains existence. Once art becomes a being among beings, the question of Being loses its urgency, because the originary understanding of truth has become regional. Heidegger's thinking on art seeks to answer to the essence of truth by grasping failure in its originarity as a contestation of the determination of Being as presence. For Heidegger, what is at stake in the *Auseinandersetzung* is a disclosure of the modesty of Being in contrast to the triumphalism of the will to power.

Art's distance from nihilism is its failure before presence. It falters in the reproduction of its ἰδέα and through its faltering it shows more than its ἰδέα: it "shows" the world that the ἰδέα otherwise conceals. With the example of the van Gogh painting in "The Origin of the Work of Art," Heidegger is not proposing that the work of art is necessarily the depiction of a tool, but rather that any object of depiction, as ἰδέα, is restored in the work of art to the world suppressed in its presence. Heidegger's example recalls the exposition of equipmentality in *Being and Time*, but in the later text there has been a shift from the accidental to the essential. The work of art sets up the world that the broken, inappropriate, or missing tool discloses in deviations from their use. That the work of art sets up a world is not because it is a distinct entity, falling within the purview of metaphysics, but rather because it is the understanding of the Being of the phenomenon of world. Quarantined in the metaphysically determined entity known as "art," this other understanding still announces itself in its transcendence. Art's failure before presence recovers beings for Being, and in this uncontained failure, it is the originary failure of Being. The failure is ecstatic and transcends presence. Failing before presence, art is never itself, never a distinct identity, and thus the privilege of truth with which Heidegger endows the work of art is never an exclusive privilege in a further variation of the hierarchical thinking of Platonism. In short, it is not as any given extant and identifiable work of art, but rather as the failure of presence that the work of art restores adequation to the Open of the essence of truth.

And yet the work of art is a *work*. It is present and yields itself to sensuous appreciation. It brings beings to a stand and allows them to appear. This, however, is not a shortcoming in the work of art with respect to its opposition to the understanding of Being as presence. The work of art is a work in the Marxist sense, as well as a failure of work, a breakdown in the processes of externalization and reification. And it must be such, occupying the zone of undecidability between the two, in order for presence to fail: the nonwork, pure and simple, does not contest the understanding of Being as presence because its determinate absence maintains the presence of the recognizable. Krzysztof Ziarek, in *The Historicity of Experience: Modernity, the Avant-Garde, and the Event*, clarifies the transformed essence of work in Heidegger's writings on art:

Art ceases to be a work in an organic sense, a unified object accessible to and judged by the aesthetic gaze. Transferring the emphasis from the work as an object that is produced or created to work in the sense of the working of art, of setting into work that takes place in art, opens the door to the idea that art works by unworking its own articulations. . . . The work crosses into the unwork; the line between working and unworking becomes increasingly fine, like the corresponding play between concealment and unconcealment.[50]

Ziarek's exposition of the work of art in Heidegger uncovers, beyond the similarity to Blanchot's *désœuvrement*, a Kantian resonance. The work of art works and unworks, reveals and conceals and thus announces itself as an heir to the presentation of the unpresentable in the "Analytic of the Sublime." As a warning against the dogmatism that unmoors Ideas from their grounding in the phenomenal world and drifts off into an incorrigible conceptual enthusiasm, the Kantian Idea must present itself in the world of the senses even as it cannot present itself there. Heidegger, who is even more suspicious of the empirical–transcendental divide, writes of the presentation in the work of art of that which can never be present. The work of art is the work of undecidability. It is the decision between the empirical and the transcendental rather than their Hegelian reconciliation, as it is in the undecidability of this decision that ontology acquires its "proper" space. The work of art is the thing that fails in its thingliness, just as it fails to be other than a thing. Does the work of art, in its dual nature, thereby reformulate the aporias that confronted the Fathers of the Church? From the sixth century, Christian art is seen to respond, by means of a strictly paradoxical fidelity to the prohibition of images, to the dilemma of either the heresy of pantheism or the heresy of the Gnostic conception of the *deus absconditus*. The work of art, for Heidegger, makes this impossibility an affair of ontology.

That which in its distance from the ἰδέα is understood within Platonism as failure cannot, however, in its ecstasy be derived from presence. For Platonism, the distance from the Idea becomes a frustrated movement toward the Idea. The μιμητής is unable to create, because mimesis is, by definition, the inability to overcome the distance from presence. The works of the μιμητής remain shadowy and insubstantial (μὴ ὄν). They do not enunciate a clean break with nothingness and hence waver in undecidability between presence and nothingness. It is the inability of the μιμητής that Heidegger retains and formulates as the originarity of art. The work of art does not create because world *as world* cannot be severed from nothingness in order to be created. World fails; it is the suppression of this failure that constitutes the essence of creation as the ascendancy of presence over nothingness.

In *The Symposium*, Diotima's definition of poetry and all the crafts mistakes the derivative for the originary and offers a speciously anti-Platonic appraisal: "By its original meaning poetry means simply creation, and creation, as you know, can take very various forms. Any action which is the cause of a thing emerging from non-existence might be called poetry, and all the processes in all the crafts are kinds of poetry, and all those who are engaged in them poets."[51] The opportunity to interrogate presence is forgone. Here "poetry" is exhibited as the essence of handicraft because, more than the names of the other arts, it signifies creation. In "The Origin of the Work of Art," Heidegger retains this precedence of poetry, but for other reasons: "*All art*, as the letting happen of the advent of the truth of beings, is as such, *in essence, poetry*."[52] It is its relation to the truth of beings, and not its creativity, that establishes poetry, in Heidegger's view, as the essence of art. As the historical name of that from which metaphysics had to disentangle itself in order to come to itself in presence, "poetry" is, for Heidegger, the name of a nonmetaphysical understanding of truth. It is in this sense that Heidegger is able to speak of poetry as the essence of art in a text whose chief examples are a van Gogh painting and a Greek temple. And that "poetry" is not to be interpreted in the sense of creation is also the admonition in a note from *Metaphysik und Nihilismus* (Metaphysics and Nihilism) from 1940–41: "*Poetry*—no longer as art; with the end of metaphysics the end of 'art'—τέχνη."[53] As poetry (*Dichtung*) is neither ποίησις nor τέχνη, as it neither creates nor produces, its status as the essence of the arts must have another, more originary foundation.

For Heidegger, it is because "poetry" is "language" that it constitutes the *internal* condition of possibility of the other arts. In "The Origin of the Work of Art," he asserts of language: "It not only puts forth in words and statements what is overtly or covertly intended to be communicated; language alone brings beings as beings into the open for the first time."[54] "Poetry" is the essence of the arts, and "language" is that which *alone* brings beings as beings into the open. The work of art, inasmuch as it is language, reveals beings as such and thus reveals them in their Being. Revealing them not merely in the presence of their apprehensibility, it reveals them in their truth. The essence of all art is poetry, because poetry, in its turn, is defined, for Heidegger, by language's foundation of world. In comparison with its foundation of world, all other characteristics of language are inessential. Insofar as it founds a world, the work of art is language.

Language founds because it fails to create. If the work of art functions—and thus does not function—as a broken, inappropriate, or missing tool, is language itself a tool of this kind? Heidegger in "Hölderlin and the Essence of Poetry" denies, however, that language is a tool at all: "Language is not merely a tool which man possesses alongside many others; rather, language first grants the possibility of standing in the midst of the openness of beings."[55] As the precondition of every tool, language cannot be a tool among others that the human being possesses. It is, nevertheless, of the concealed essence of language that Heidegger writes, as a remark from the "Letter on 'Humanism'" emphasizes: "Language still denies us its essence: that it is the house of the truth of Being. Instead, language surrenders itself to our mere willing and trafficking as an instrument of domination over beings."[56] Language itself becomes a tool to be restored to its world through the work of art. In "Hölderlin and the Essence of Poetry," it is the work of art that is rather the precondition of language: "Poetry is a founding: a naming of being and of the essence of all things—not just any saying, but that whereby everything first steps into the open, which we then discuss and talk about in everyday language. Hence poetry never takes language as a material at its disposal; rather, poetry itself first makes language possible. Poetry is the primal language of a historical people."[57] What is essential to the work of art, to language, and to poetry is the foundation of world. But that the foundation of world is essential does not mean that it is an invariant of the positivistic entities known as the work of art, language, and poetry. The foundation of world is the highest task, and it is by means of the execution of this task that the work of art, language, and poetry prove themselves to be essential to whatever is. Poetry as poetry, which is to say, in its essence as the foundation of world, precedes language understood as a material at its disposal. Poetry is language's condition of possibility and as such it sustains, regardless of whether it is acknowledged or not, not only every discourse, but also every activity. Poetry itself is the clearing of beings.

Heidegger's turn to poetry after the resignation of the rectorship was not a turn away from any given being. As the turn to poetry was an engagement with the essential, it cannot be equated with a renunciation of the political. Poetry is itself the truth of the πόλις. The decision that delimits the domain of the political as one domain among others presupposes the grounding of beings in poetry. Every essence becomes poetic with the establishment of the originarity of poetry's understanding of Being. In addressing the question of the essence of poetry, Heidegger addresses the question of the essence of the political. But why should poetry be a privileged point of access to the essence of the political? It is because, in the context of National Socialism, the essence of the political had withdrawn from politics. In his confrontation with Nietzsche and the Hitlerian dictatorship, Heidegger has recourse to a notion of poetry as the Un-thought of the will to power. Poetry becomes that which hesitates and it thereby founds world in the openness that nihilism suppresses in its drive to the absolute presence of beings. Judged by the criteria of metaphysical nihilism, poetry is a failure. Only when language fails, that is, only when it is *more* than the unambiguous transmission of items of information, does it disclose its essence and show itself to be poetry. That language is essentially not a tool in the mobilization of the masses is the suspicion initiated through its being "broken" as a tool in poetry. The disclosure of the essence depends on an abuse of mere serviceability, since use in general, for early and middle Heidegger, is opposed to a revelation of essence. The essential is the unmanageable. A tool displays its essence—the world within which it is employed and "explained"—when it is broken, missing, or inappropriate, and thus its use always presupposes a neglect of the task of understanding its essence. It is, in a sense, always a broken, missing, or inappropriate tool that is *unwittingly* being used. To the extent that the work of art has been traditionally defined by being at odds with unmanageability, by the fashioning of its material, by its creating and bringing forth, it is less a work of art, for Heidegger, than a figure of the secondary realm of τέχνη: only the inessential knows perfection. Where National Socialism evaded the foundational failure composing, in the shape of poetry, the essence of the political and the ground of a historical people, it promulgated the nihilism of the obliviousness of Being under the cover of its achievements. Technicism can never be the essence of a people; the essence of a people is always to be a people of the "failure" of world to reduce itself to presence.

It is on account of the priority of failure over technicism that the ultimate foundation of a people is poetry. In *Hölderlins Hymnen "Germanien" und "Der Rhein,"* Heidegger writes:

Poetization is foundation, it is a realizing [*erwirkend*] grounding of the enduring. The poet is the one who grounds Being. That which, in the everyday, we name the real [*das Wirkliche*], is, at bottom, unreal. Because the sign of the gods is, as it were, built by a poet into the foundation walls of a people's language (perhaps without the people's suspecting this at first), Being is founded in the historical Dasein of the people, and in this Being a directive and a dependence are laid and left behind.[58]

Poetry composes the historical ground of a people, inasmuch as it is that which is not reducible to the ahistoricality of presence. Its distance from presence—and it is distant from presence only inasmuch as it always overreaches presence—is its distance from the unreal. That which we are accustomed to call real is ultimately unreal, because its transparency and familiarity is the consequence of its abstraction from world. Technicism, realizing itself in the obliviousness of world, does nothing but produce its own realization, and yet all the proofs it *creates* of its reality are, for that very reason, insufficient. It merely proves its remoteness from Being and hence, for Heidegger, its "unreality."

In the 1941 lecture course *Basic Concepts*, Heidegger traces back to Nietzsche the retreat of the originary poetic foundation of the people in favor of the mobilization of the worker and the soldier and the hegemony of τέχνη:

> In the interim, it has been decided that *"the worker"* and *"the soldier"* completely determine the face of the actual, all political systems in the narrow sense notwithstanding. These names are not meant here as names for a social class or profession. They indicate, in a unique fusion, the type of humanity taken as measure by the present world-convulsion for its fulfillment, giving direction and foundation to one's relation to beings. The names "worker" and "soldier" are thus metaphysical titles and name that form of the human fulfillment of the Being of beings now become manifest, which Nietzsche presciently grasped as the *"will to power."* [59]

The "worker" and the "soldier" are distinguished by their engagement in reality, but Heidegger queries whether such experience can satisfy its claims to essentiality:

> But do "workers" and "soldiers", in virtue of this experience, also know the Being of beings? No. Yet perhaps they no longer need to know it. Perhaps the Being of beings has never been experienced by those who directly shape, produce, and represent beings. Perhaps Being was always brought to knowledge merely "by the way," like something apparently "superfluous." [60]

Inasmuch as they are absorbed solely in that which is, the "worker" and the "soldier" disavow Being and hence the ground, that is, the "reality," of their engagement. Being lies elsewhere. A people, if it is to ground itself, must ground itself within Being, and for Heidegger, it is within the failure of production that is poetry that Being offers itself as ground.

Here Heidegger's critique of metaphysics is the elaboration of a topos of German conservatism. That the essence of the people rests with the Unthought of τέχνη is a contention not at all alien to the strain of German nationalism that sought to make a virtue of the country's economic backwardness, and even of its defeat in war.[61] Expounding the contingency of momentary underdevelopment as spiritual resistance to industrialization, this nationalism prided itself on the absence of any achievements outside the very constricted sphere it defined as culture. Modernization, insofar as it challenged the preponderance of this sphere and involved leveling differences between Germany and its Western neighbors, was demonized as an assault on the national character. Economic development was cultural regression and an aping of the foreign. Even though Heidegger is perhaps the most eloquent and profound advocate of this version of German nationalism, its tone and principles are to be heard in Thomas Mann's *Reflections of a Nonpolitical Man*, Hofmannsthal's address "Literatur als geistiger

Raum der Nation" (Literature as the Spiritual Space of the Nation), and—notwithstanding its corrective cynicism—Adorno's brief text "On the Question: What Is German?" What is peculiar to Heidegger's critique of industrialization is that he does not hypostasize the nation's backwardness as its essence but rather defines its essence in relation to a future other than modernization. That Germany has not yet realized itself is an assessment that Heidegger shares with the exponents of industrialisation.[62] But, for Heidegger, Germany is to realize itself in the future as such, that is, in the future as *ecstasis* rather than as a present whose time is yet to come. Germany awaits itself, and it must await itself if it is to maintain a distance from presence and the nihilism of τέχνη.

In "Abendgespräch in einem Kriegsgefangenenlager in Rußland zwischen einem Jüngeren und einem Älteren" (Evening Conversation in a Russian Camp Between a Younger and an Older Prisoner of War) [1945]), Heidegger accordingly draws together the notions of the people, poetry and waiting:

> THE ELDER: My supposition is that the poetic character of your thinking lies rather in its nature as a waiting and that basically your thinking already was a waiting even before it was raised for you today into clear knowledge.
>
> THE YOUNGER: Perhaps the poets and thinkers of a people are nothing other than those who are waiting in the noblest sense, through whose presence [*deren Gegenwart*, whose wait toward] toward the coming the word is reached into the answer of the human essence and thus brought to language.
>
> THE ELDER: Then indeed the people of poets and thinkers would be in a unique sense the waiting people.[63]

The *Volk* waits because it is poetic, and it waits in relation to the essence of the human. It is, however, *essentially* backward with regard to its own essence. As it is always awaiting itself, it is unable to submit itself in its presence to the manipulation of τέχνη and thus preserves the human in its essential distance from reification. Heidegger suggests that the inviolability of this people lies in its absence:

> THE YOUNGER: The people that is waiting would necessarily be for others even quite useless, because that which always simply waits and forever awaits the coming yields nothing tangible that could be of use for progress and the upswing of the performance curve or for the expeditious course of business.[64]

This people is not so much waiting *for* something as waiting *away from* something. It is a people that waits precisely in order not to be the people whose essence is present-at-hand. Heidegger's *Volk* is the people of mimesis and of the treason of the "false priest" Hölderlin.[65] It waits in order not to produce. It waits against presence in order not to emulate its neighbors' obliviousness to the undecidability of Being in the prosecution of the extant. A people that does not wait—that Being abandons to presence—is a people without a future and without a past. For Heidegger, industrialization is not a plan for the future of a people, but rather a means for abolishing the future in favor of the nihilism of that which is solely present. Being is lost to view behind material, which remains fundamentally the same whether it is accumulated in "peace" or devastated in "war."

To lose sight of Being is arguably for Heidegger also to lose sight of the political. The reification of everything that is in the understanding of Being as presence secures the undisputed reign of the logic of universals and the neglect of the political realm's incompatibility with such a logic. Once the political has been demarcated as the field of the struggle for recognition as the universal, the essential specificity of the *Volk* becomes apolitical. The resulting apoliticality of the specificity of the *Volk* denotes, not simply a neglect of the question of the essence of the *Volk*, but also an impoverishment of the concept of the political itself. A politics of the universal is political only in spite of itself, since the universality toward which it strives constitutes the extirpation of the political: the openness of the πόλις is to be replaced by the constrictedness of the οἶκος, in which the universal exercises its paternalism unchallenged.[66] The *Volk* composing the public realm, and in its essential specificity forever opening a distance from the universal, is the Un-thought of the struggle for power. The openness of the people is likewise its furtiveness, because the definitive politicality of its historical specificity renders it invisible within the prevailing nihilistic struggle for power.

Of the uncanny guardians of the openness of the political—the poets and thinkers, priests and rulers who are the true founders of the State—Heidegger writes in *An Introduction to Metaphysics*: "Preeminent in the historical place, they become at the same time ἄπολις, without city and place, lonely, strange [*Un-heimliche*], and alien, without exit amid the entirety of beings, at the same time without statute and limit, without structure and order, because they themselves *as* creators must first create all this."[67] Occurring in a commentary on *Antigone*, this passage defines the creator of the πόλις rather than reflects on the amoralism of the tyrant. The creators of the πόλις in Heidegger's sense stand outside the πόλις as the field of the struggle for power. Their creativity is negative: they found the πόλις, but they found it in the openness of that which has not yet been created, that is, fully determined and rendered positive. The "apoliticality" of these creators is the condition of possibility for the statutes and limits, structures and orders under which the openness of the political nonetheless disappears from view. They are ἄπολις, without city and place, but for that very reason they are not at the mercy of the homelessness of the universal. The πόλις first grounds itself in their refusal of the struggle for power just as the universal grounds itself in the disavowal of the πόλις. The strangeness of the creators—their *Un-heimlichkeit*—is the corollary of their originarity and unrecognizability within the universalist light of presence.

Heidegger's commentaries on Hölderlin in the 1930s and early 1940s address the uncanniness of the originary. In these texts, Heidegger's nationalism, as an attention to the uncanniness of the originary, is at odds with the nationalism expressed, for instance, in Max Kommerell's commentary on Hölderlin. Kommerell in the late 1920s writes of the notion of the people in Hölderlin: "The doctrine that a century finds intolerable is the doctrine of which it stands in the greatest need. In ours, Hölderlin's occupies this position: when a people is truly a people, its war is a holy war. Just as the individual through beauty or great deeds enters upon its higher reality, so does a people through war; indeed, it requires an opponent in order to glorify itself." [68] Hölderlin here becomes the poet of a Hitleresque nationalism. Whereas for Heidegger Hölderlin's poetry promises the nationalism of the Un-thought of nihilism, for Kommerell it promises military expansion and the struggle for recognition. Irrespective of his affection and esteem for Kommerell, Heidegger is consistent in his antagonism toward the illusoriness of such "politicizations" of the work of art.

In the collection of notes published under the title *Besinnung*, Heidegger asserts that the work of art is as alien to the National Socialist realm of the struggle for recognition as it had been earlier to the interiority of bourgeois criticism: "It remains essentially withdrawn as much from the "public" as from "private" play, belonging solely to the persistence in the decline (*Untergang*) that alone can become a history in keeping with the essential, and that leaves in its wake a clearing of Being." [69] The work of art commits itself to neither internal migration nor public spectacle. It is withdrawn from the choice between the individual in its Cartesian isolation and the universal of the deracinated masses. Persisting in its decline and thus its finitude, the work of art eludes the abstraction from historicality by which the autonomous subject and the "they" are determined. The essential decline of the work of art is the originarity of its other understanding of Being. It declines in transcending its presence and, through its decline, it retires from the struggle for recognition. The work of art never gives itself up to be apprehended in the light of presence. It is originarity that renders it too frail for the struggle, because power, as Heidegger continues, is the property of the derivative:

Only now in the history of humanity does the obliviousness of Being come to its position of total power. But what if this abandonment of beings by Being were the beginning of an originary history in which Being [*Sein*] is Being [*Seyn*], so that the actual in its ever greater actuality would be ever more hopelessly cast out from Being, from Being [*Seyn*] as refusal, to which no power and no supremacy could be equal because they must necessarily and always mistake the essence of the *utterly* power-less. The powerless can never be deprived of power. This, however, is not attributed to it as a deficiency. On the contrary, it is merely a consequence—and one not even necessary and fitting—of its *nobility*.[70]

For Heidegger, in contradistinction to the medieval metaphysics of *actus* and the modern metaphysics of the will-to-power, Being is power-less. It is not so much without power as before power. The originary is always misjudged in its powerlessness because it has not the "strength" to reduce itself to presence. Hölderlin, who speaks of tragedy as a revelation of the originary in its weakness,[71] speaks likewise of the revelatory caesura of tragedy:[72] the originary shows itself in letting "nothing" appear in the midst of the present-at-hand. By the criteria of technicism, the originary is deficient because beings have not yet come to the presence on which their manipulability rests. Hölderlin, as the poet of weakness, is, for Heidegger, the poet of the impossibility of National Socialism. He is the poet of the Un-thought of the movement's nihilism, the poet of the properly political, of, namely, the unamenability of Being-with-one-another to the categories of power and making. In the 1931–32 lecture course *Zu Platons Höhlengleichnis und Theätet*, Hölderlin is not even included in a list of great poets.[73] Although Heidegger had been familiar with Hölderlin's texts since 1908,[74] it is only after 1933 that the poet of modesty becomes the essential poet.

In this regard, Heidegger's reading of Hölderlin displays less of an affinity with Kommerell than with Benjamin's early text "Two Poems by

Friedrich Hölderlin," with its discussion of a passivity central to the hymns.[75] Moreover, a complementarity could be said to exist between Benjamin's and Heidegger's readings: for the one, passivity alone is able to serve as a point of mediation and occupy the center, because, for the other, weakness is the essence of the originary. Inasmuch as the center is reserved for the weak, a nationalism unavailable to National Socialism is to be heard in the concluding strophe of Hölderlin's hymn "Germanien" with its interpretation of the geographical centrality of central Europe:

> Yet at the centre of Time
> In peace with hallowed,
> With virginal Earth lives Aether
> And gladly, for remembrance, they
> The never-needy dwell
> Hospitably amid the never-needy,
> Amid your holidays,
> Germania, where you are priestess and
> Defenceless proffer all round
> Advice to the kings and the peoples.[76]

The paranoia and megalomania of National Socialism are missing from Hölderlin's patriotism. Germany occupies the center neither as the common object of the rapacity of her neighbors nor as the seat of a military empire. Instead, defenselessly Germany gives counsel to the kings and the peoples assembled around her in the feast.

Germany is the priestess among the nations and must remain such for their sake as much as for her own. For Heidegger, the essence of the German people is not to be one people among others, but rather to be the people of the essential. The eschatological pretensions of National Socialism concerning the German people are shadowed in Heidegger's writings by the elaboration of the mission of the German people in the history of Being. The German essence is to be found in the task of "priestess" among the nations. Through bringing themselves into conformity with their essence, the *Volk* serves the other peoples as their "priests."

The sobriety that will come over the world from out of a discovery and defense of that which is German will not be the sobriety of unlimited rational communication. It will be the sobriety of an insight into *das Eigene*, into the transcendence proper to Dasein as it is secured in the mimesis and technicist incompetence of the holy heart of the peoples. The world-mission of the Germans is to "instantiate" transcendence, and hence the unrepeatable and nonglobal, in a confrontation with the globalism of τέχνη. This mission of a staging of the unpresentable is necessarily impracticable, but it is in the attempt and its failure that Heidegger situates the *Auseinandersetzung* with technicism.

In his commentary on Hölderlin's hymn "Germanien," Heidegger develops his notion of the priest as the tender of the Un-thought of τέχνη:

Just as at the beginning of the flight of the gods, it is the priest who is first affected (it goes without saying that it is not ministers of the established churches who are in question), likewise for a new advent of the gods, a priest or a priestess must again be the first affected, awaiting, hidden and unknown, the messengers of the gods, so that temple, image, and custom might lovingly follow them. If that does not occur, then regardless of aircraft, radio, and conquest of the stratosphere, the peoples will tumble irretrievably toward their end. If matters are to turn out differently, then the gods-lessness [*Götterlosigkeit*] of historical Dasein in its entirety must first be experienced, that is, Dasein must be open to such experience and if it is not, it must be made so, precisely by those who truly endure the flight of the gods. They are the ones who *doubt*, the legend of that which has been dawns and darkens [*dämmert*] about their heads, and they are those of which not one of them knows what is happening to them, while the self-certain and robust know-alls always know what happens to them, because they punctiliously take care that nothing at all can happen to them.[77]

The sobriety that will come from the German people is the questioning of the priest. The priest introduces hesitation into the self-assurance of technicism, but not in order to temper this self-assurance, to see it vindicated in a more encompassing success. The doubt of the priest restores τέχνη to its essence in the originarity of doubt. This involves less the abolition of the tool than its fracture, since the doubt of the priest is not a call to return to an ethnologically fantastic toolless society but, rather, the anticipation of the recovery from the reductive ontology of τέχνη into its essence as world.[78]

Germany is the priestess among the nations only so long as she is the "incompetent" among the nations. Her hesitation before τέχνη is the feast day on which the nations assemble around her. In the lecture course *Hölderlins Hymne "Andenken,"* echoing the remarks to the College of Sociology that Roger Caillois had made only a few years earlier concerning the feast, Heidegger reviews the conventionally negative definitions of the holiday: "Celebrating the feast [*feiern*] means in the first place: not working. It can thus come about that the feast days stand in exclusive relation to workdays, that they are an interruption in the time of work and a change in the routine of labor, and ultimately a pause introduced solely for the benefit of work."[79] The cessation of labor is however an inessential definition of the holiday: "Now the cessation of work is no longer essence and ground of the celebration of the feast. On the contrary, it is already a consequence of that catching of oneself which seemingly brings human beings back only to their egos, but which in truth transposes them out into that region to which their essence clings. Wonder begins or else terror."[80] The feast day is recuperative, not because it allows human beings to replenish the stores of energy expended in labor, but because it exposes Dasein to its essential possibilities of wonder and terror in the face of the worlding of the world. Like the work of art, the feast day is the essence of that which the broken, missing, or inappropriate tool is only accidentally. Alluding to the sun in Plato's parable of the cave, Heidegger writes: "At the time of the festival and on feast days, the proper [*das Eigene*], the ground itself of history, comes purely to appearance; but that which appears is there not an object for observation, that which appears [*das Erscheinende*] is a shining [*ein Scheinen*] in the sense in which we say: the sun shines."[81] The sun that shines on the feast day is the Un-thought of τέχνη. World in its originary weakness illuminates Dasein and every tool discovers itself as *essentially* broken, missing, or inappropriate. No longer ready-to-hand, the tool reveals its essence in the temple. The temple is the work of art that raises itself on the feast day in its distance from labor's immersion in presence. In this distance from presence lies its title to mimesis and thus to the name of art. The feast day, with its focus on the temple, is the recollection of the unsettling origin of the everyday: "Celebrating the feast is a becoming free from the usual through a becoming free for the unusual."[82] This becoming free for the unusual is the beginning of wonder or terror. The feast day is never entirely distinguishable from misfortune, from the uncanniness of the originary rupture in which the world of a people worlds.

Heidegger's definitions of the work of art and the feast day are both directed toward the Un-thought of τέχνη. The work of art and the feast day are a failure of the self-certainty of τέχνη and it is within this failure that a people becomes the people of poets and thinkers. The Greeks, who made a show of despising the βάναυσοι, nonetheless did not go far enough in criticizing τέχνη, because in their love of glory, they shunned the anonymity and concealment of failure. The *Volk* of poets and thinkers is not a revival of the Greek πόλις so much as a revival of the missed opportunity of the Greeks to raise the question of Being. This *Volk* is the people of the fundamental failure of presence.

Incompetence is the essence of art's "revelation." This proposition, implicit in Heidegger, is explicit in Kafka. Josephine in the tale "Josephine the Singer, or the Mouse Folk" cannot sing, yet it is precisely her failure as an artist—the discrepancy between her claims and her achievement—that reveals her people to themselves and binds them to her. Kafka writes of the nature of her performances:

And indeed this is all expressed not in full round tones but softly, in whispers, confidentially, sometimes a little hoarsely. Of course it is a kind of piping. Why not? Piping is our people's daily speech, only many a one pipes his whole life long and does not know it, where here piping is set free from the fetters of daily life and it sets us free too for a little while.[83]

Josephine's voice rediscovers the world in which the piping of the mice has its place. It does so, not because it *is* more than a piping, but because it *claims* to be more. It is an instrument that is inappropriate to its task, and in this distance from its concept, in its abject subordination to its ἰδέα, Josephine's piping is, in Plato's sense, art. Josephine is able to impose on not a single one of the listeners gathered around her. She is even encouraged in the extravagant claims of her art, regardless of the danger to which she at times exposes her people:

Josephine exerts herself, a mere nothing in voice, a mere nothing in execution, she asserts herself and gets across to us; it does us good to think of that. A really trained singer, if ever such a one should be found among us, we could certainly not endure at such a time and we should unanimously turn away from the senselessness of any such performance. May Josephine be spared from perceiving that the mere fact of our listening to her is proof that she is no singer.[84]

Josephine is considered an artist among the mice only so long as she fails to sing. The failure is the essence of her art. For Plato and Kafka, the artist is the one who fails the most conspicuously.

Certainly, National Socialism failed to substantiate its claims, but inasmuch as its failure came through its defeat at the hands of other powers, its distance from its Idea did not become the occasion of the question of the Un-thought of metaphysics. Instead, this failure became the (still prevailing) argument for the claims of its Western conquerors: liberal democracy proceeded to consummate its relations with its own Idea. To be the *Volk* of poets and thinkers is to be the people that fails—as clearly as possible—of itself. Germany, as the land of poets and thinkers, is the land of industrial backwardness. Its poetry and its thought are not to be registered in any accumulation of volumes in the world's libraries, but rather in its failure to execute the actions by which the economies of other nations are sustained. It fails and thereby tears open the distance between the essential possibilities of Dasein and the degradation of the realized self-presence of things. Heidegger and Kafka are both of the conviction that if failure is to be grasped *as such*, it can be neither contemptuously dismissed nor blunderingly affirmed.

It is between these two misinterpretations of failure that Heidegger's commentary on Hölderlin's understanding of Germany in *Hölderlins Hymnen "Germanien" und "Der Rhein"* must be read:

> The poet does not mean that Germany of those poets and thinkers as the rest of the world imagines and wishes them: the simple dreamers and innocents who then at decisive moments are easily persuaded and made into fools for everyone else; rather he means that poetizing and thinking that plunges into the abysses of Being, not content with the shallow waters of a universal world-reason, that poetizing and thinking that in the work brings the being new and primordially to appearance and to a stand.[85]

Germany is the land of poets and thinkers because it is the land that can only ever dream of what it might be. Heidegger is not arguing against the discrepancy so much as against the inability of nihilism to grasp and maintain the discrepancy. Nihilism mistakes for the validation of τέχνη the failure of poetry and thinking that precisely as failure is to contest the hegemony of τέχνη. This ambiguity is a consequence of the undecidable ontological status of failure. It is in this ambiguity that Heidegger's nationalism exhibits its irreducibility to National Socialism and likewise forgoes an open confrontation. It limits itself to failing before the will to power.

4

Toward the Uncanny Homeland

In a manuscript from 1796, Hegel discusses the mythologies then acceptable to the tastes of the German reading public and concludes with the question: "Is Judaea, then, the Teutons' Fatherland?"[1] For National Socialism, such a question was strictly unutterable. But that the question could never have been enunciated does not mean that it went unanswered. Finding itself incapable of establishing the living national mythology upon whose absence Hegel reflects, National Socialism declared that the Germans indeed possessed a Fatherland that lay elsewhere, and that the name of this *unheimliche Heimat* (unhomelike home) was Greece.

At the very time when the Greece that had been degraded into the paradise of anti-Semites announced itself in the sullen clumsiness of Speer's architecture, in the callisthenics of an embryonic Wehrmacht, and in a bookish and expedient paganism, Heidegger was lecturing on the necessity for the German people of a *confrontation* with classical Greece. The simultaneity is not fortuitous. Heidegger's texts of the late 1930s and early 1940s are distinguished by a heightened tone of opposition toward the legacy of Greek thought: Greece, without ever being confounded with its National Socialist travesties, is set forth as that which must be overcome. Since the imperialism and spectacle by which National Socialism recreated for itself a distinctly Roman antiquity were, according to Heidegger, nothing but a consequence of an increasingly pernicious complacency regarding Greek thought, it is in an interrogation and destruction of the latter that "the other beginning" (*der andere Anfang*) might be anticipated and the forgetfulness of Being retrieved. In itself, a return to Greece would not be a solution to nihilism. Greece is to be made to give way to its Un-thought.

For Heidegger, the name of this Un-thought is Being. Asking after that which was not revealed in Greece, Heidegger does not ask simply after that which was revealed elsewhere. That which has been revealed elsewhere is still too Greek by virtue of its having been revealed at all. To bring to the confrontation with classical Greece a positive content with a different genealogy is to conceive the confrontation within the terms of the Greek privileging of the visible. Such a confrontation is decided in advance in favor of Greece. And as the confrontation with Greece implies a confrontation with the neoclassicism of the NSDAP, no one should be surprised that Heidegger did not oppose a warmed-over liberal humanism to the movement's warmed-over paganism. What Heidegger ranges against the legacy of Greece is the concealed as such. In place of the visibility of beings in ἀλήθεια, Heidegger invokes the prohibition of images.

By asking after the non-Greek, Heidegger calls the whole of the West into question, and yet he does so with a question by which the West has likewise come to define itself. The question, as it has been raised against metaphysics by Luther and Kierkegaard as the definitive question concerning the essence of Christianity, is the question of the other, namely, Judaic origin of the West. Denying this other origin and endeavoring to demonstrate its independence from Judaea, National Socialism slavishly courted a resemblance to Greece. Anti-Semitism can be suspected not only in the movement's neoclassicism but also, beyond its aesthetics, in the general, obsessive cultivation of the visible.

The dilemma of National Socialism was that the German people could assert themselves in their originarity as a people of the West solely as either Greek or Jewish. National Socialism did not invent this dilemma: it is prefigured in the eighteenth century in that bifurcation of the national literature into Weimar classicism and Christian romanticism on which Hegel, among others, comments. At stake in the contest between the visibility of Greece and the invisibility of Judaea is the definition of the German *Volk*. The *Volk* is the people of the constitutive impossibility of the West. That which is specific to this people, that which it can receive as a possession neither from the Greeks nor from the Jews, is the contradiction itself between the visible and the invisible itself. To attend to its specificity, this people has to grasp, without mitigation, the unity of this discord. The *Volk* finds itself in the confrontation with Greece, not as the Other of Greece, but as the confrontation itself. If it is "at home" in the definitively non-Greek, it is in order, however, to enact the confrontation with Greece that is proper to it. The *Volk* must become Jewish in order to become itself. In defiance of National Socialism, it must counterbalance the fixation on the visible by plunging into the invisible: it has to think through to its essence the unnameability of Judaea.[2]

In the 1933–34 lecture course *Vom Wesen der Wahrheit*, Heidegger refuses to return to Greece simply to take up where it left off:

It means: learning to comprehend that this great beginning of our Dasein stands thrown ahead and in advance of us as that with which we have to catch up—not, however, in order to bring to completion a Greek world [*ein Griechentum*] but, on the contrary, in order to draw out the fundamental possibilities of the proto-Germanic ethnic essence [*die Grundmöglichkeiten des urgermanischen Stammes-wesens*] and bring them to power.[3]

Heidegger here uses the sinister vocabulary of *Rassenkunde*, but what he understands by "the fundamental possibilities of the proto-Germanic ethnic essence" does not lend itself to a biologistic racism: the essence of the *Volk* is not Greek enough to find itself in classical ontology and thus in the basis for such a racism.

As little as it understood Greece, National Socialism was still too Greek to be German. That the movement failed to be German had less to do with its neoclassical aesthetics and anti-Christian rhetoric than with its ensnarement in the categories of classical ontology. National Socialism was too Greek to grasp the irreducibility of the world of the *Volk* to metaphysics. The movement's trumpeted rootedness in a self-evident homeland does not differentiate it from Greece, since this rootedness was not seen to be incompatible with the extendable space of *Lebensraum*. The quantifiable and culturally indifferent territory of the National Socialist *Heimat* remained modeled on the homogeneous space of classical geometry. Heidegger's question in the late 1930s and early 1940s concerning "the other beginning" does not issue, as might have been expected from its precedents, in a moral or religious critique of National Socialism. Instead, it gives rise to an immanent critique of National Socialism's abortive nationalism, since it is with "the other beginning" and the overcoming of metaphysics that the homeland can at last be thought. The otherness of "the other beginning" is the chance it provides, in the context of the prevailing homelessness of nihilism, of thinking the homeland as such.

Is Judaea to become the fatherland of the Germans? Heidegger does not speak of a confrontation with the Jewish people, but inasmuch as he speaks of a confrontation with the Greeks, he aspires to the radical differentiation of the German people that would render a confrontation practicable. The Germans are to become *other* than Greeks, when within the his-

tory of the West it has always been the Jews who have counted as the definitive non-Greeks. Heidegger's Germans resemble the Jews, not only in their
character of being different from the Greeks, but also in the way that they
are different. Through defining the *Volk* by its resistance to the positivism
of its neighbors, Heidegger brings the essence of the Germans into contact
with the people of the prohibition of images. And yet Heidegger does not
acknowledge the contact. He does not admit that his conception of the
Volk has a model, but then the possibility of an *Auseinandersetzung* with
Greece requires a disavowal of the Platonic logic of the subordination to
the Idea. Once the *Volk* has a model, once it models itself on Judaea, positivism and the Greek privileging of the visible and the present reassert
themselves.

Certainly, it cannot be said that Heidegger's spiritual-historical conception of the *Volk* would have gained anything by the extermination of
the Jews. To have erased the Jewish model *physically* would not have liberated the *Volk* from its last trace of positivism, since the definition of
the *Volk* would then have been dependent, implicitly if not explicitly, on
the *fact* of Auschwitz. What remains in question is whether Heidegger's
silence on the Jews positions them alongside the many other peoples who,
viewed within the history of Being, are seemingly expendable or whether
that silence functions as a disavowal of the Jews' excessive proximity to his
conception of the *Volk*. In *Heidegger et "les juifs,"* his response to the controversy provoked by Victor Farías's *Heidegger et le nazisme*, Jean-François
Lyotard ascribes to Europe as a whole a constitutive disavowal of the
"jews," of which Auschwitz would be the absolute manifestation. Lyotard
recognizes that he himself, as a European, cannot escape this disavowal,
and that he must admit this continually, in the use of scare quotes. But the
senses in which Lyotard speaks of disavowal are inconsistent. Auschwitz
will always have come too late for its disavowal of the "jews" not to be superfluous, since it can mount only a grotesquely ontic reenactment of the
West's initial scene, substituting European Jewry for the unnameable ". . ."
of primal repression's constitutive disavowal: the "jews", in Lyotard's account, become (once again) scapegoats. When Lyotard writes that "*Ver-
nichtung*, the Nazi name for annihilation, is not so different from fore-
closure, *Verleugnung*,"[4] he overlooks the incompatibility of the respective
"objects" of extermination and primal repression. The hubris of National
Socialism, and the error in which Lyotard fails to catch it out, was that it
sought to achieve a transformation of the ontological ground of the West

by an eradication of the ontic traces of a people and culture. National Socialism underestimated the proximity of Judaea. It believed that the Being of the West was not always already contaminated and that the work of purification—because it need concern itself only with the domain of beings present-at-hand—was therefore feasible. Properly speaking, the regime did not disavow Judaea. Instead, it insisted on its reification, on its maintenance as a stable object within the field of perception in defiance of the prohibition of images by which Judaea has marked the West.

Disavowal is not incidental to the Judaea that has created the West and that the West has created for itself, since Judaea exists as the exception to the present-at-hand. It is ungraspable precisely because it is too close to be grasped. Christianity's comparable irreducibility to metaphysics harbors itself outside the limits of the ontic as the interiority of the soul. The existential analytic of Dasein in *Being and Time* constitutes a critique of the subjectivization and delimitation of this exception to the ontic, but it will stop short of abandoning the proximality attributed to it in Judeo-Christian thought. That which is ownmost, for Judeo-Christian thought and for Heidegger, is that which is not assimilable to the thingly. The exception to the hegemony of the ontic carries with it, in its Judeo-Christian definition, the chance of understanding the nearness of the homeland. Heidegger's nationalism depends for its viability on Judaea. An exposition of Heidegger's Semitism cannot mitigate the odiousness of his occasional anti-Semitic utterances. At best it can announce the nature and problematic provenance of the question that Heidegger sought to address in his meditations on the *Volk* and on the Fatherland.

Under the cover of the qualified Hellenism he shares with Hölderlin, Heidegger writes of the Fatherland in terms more suggestive of the Jewish Diaspora than of the National Socialist uprising.[5] In the 1941–42 course on Hölderlin's poem "Andenken," there appears the following: "That which is most our own [*das Eigenste*], the Fatherland, is the highest, but it stands for that reason under the heaviest prohibition. Thus only at the end will it be found, after protracted searching, after many sacrifices and severe exertions. . . . The national [*das Vaterländische*] is found only if the highest is sought. Seeking the highest means keeping quiet about it."[6]

The Fatherland, as the highest, stands under the heaviest prohibition. For Heidegger, it is prohibited to find the Fatherland too easily. The Fatherland is the highest because it is what is most proper to us, and as what is most proper to us, it can never be found in the way that something merely present-at-hand is found. It will be found, if at all, as *missing* from the realm of the thingly. In the realm of the thingly, the Fatherland is found as that for which we must seek—for Heidegger in the 1937–38 lecture course *Grundfragen der Philosophie*, the goal of the Germans is the search itself.[7]

Inasmuch as Heidegger's Fatherland lies outside the scope of classical ontology, it recalls the missing homeland of Franz Rosenzweig's *The Star of Redemption*:

> To the eternal people, home never is home in the sense of land, as it is to the peoples of the world who plough the land and live and thrive on it, until they have all but forgotten that being a people means something besides being rooted in a land. . . . In the most profound sense possible, this people has a land of its own only in that it has a land it yearns for—a holy land. And so even when it has a home, this people, in recurrent contrast to all other peoples on earth, is not allowed full possession of that home. It is only "a stranger and a sojourner."[8]

The land of this people never fully surrenders itself to possession. It is to be found as yearning and not as property, as οὐσία. At the end of World War I, Rosenzweig writes from within the millenary absence of a Jewish state, whereas Heidegger, two decades later, employs the same topos of the missing homeland at the zenith of German imperialism. How is the similarity to be understood? As an instance of the expropriation of Jewish *Eigentum* (property) under Hitler or as sabotage of the objectives of the Wannsee Conference by means of a *Verjudung* (Judaization) of the essence of the Fatherland?

Both, in a secondary sense, are at issue. And that both might be at issue is because Heidegger, following Hölderlin, believes that the Germans are compelled to seek out a way to differentiate themselves from the Greeks. Hölderlin's texts and Heidegger's commentaries can be read for what they say regarding the necessary and promised non-Hellenism of the German people. Only once this task of differentiation has been outlined will it be possible to query to what degree both Hölderlin and Heidegger admit of rediscovery within the literature of the Jewish Diaspora. Of course, such an admittedly strained interpretation simply inverts Alfred Rosenberg's fatuous image of Hölderlin as a proto-Nazi.[9] What is properly at stake is a treatment of the essence of the national overlooked by the Greeks and never even suspected by National Socialism.

Heidegger's reiterated objection to National Socialism was that it was insufficiently national. The so-called politicization of every sphere under the regime did not hesitate to style itself as Greek and to assume that the essence of the political was exhaustively understood in classical Greece. In the 1942 lecture course *Hölderlin's Hymn "The Ister,"* Heidegger criticizes the classical scholarship of the period for conflating the Greeks and the NSDAP: "Today—if one still reads such books at all—one can scarcely read a treatise or book on the Greeks without everywhere being assured that here, with the Greeks, 'everything' is 'politically' determined. In the majority of 'research results,' the Greeks appear as the pure National Socialists." [10] For Heidegger, these works are unjust both to the Greeks and to the National Socialists. The specific task of a German nationalist uprising is overlooked and Greece is misrepresented as the model or precursor of the Nazi mobilization. It is simply assumed in these works that the political determination of everything that is draws the Greeks and the National Socialists together.

The failure to understand the political, notwithstanding its compulsive invocation, that Heidegger observes in his contemporaries is a deficiency that he then proceeds to attribute, albeit to a lesser degree, to the Greeks themselves. The authentic understanding of the essence of the political depends on a revelation of the essence of the πόλις:

Who says that the Greeks, because they "lived" in the πόλις, were also in the clear as to the essence of the πόλις? Perhaps the name πόλις is precisely the word for that realm that constantly became questionable anew, remained worthy of question, made necessary and indeed needed certain decisions whose truth on each occasion displaced the Greeks into the realm of the groundless or the inaccessible. If *we* therefore ask: What is the πόλις of the Greeks? then we must not presuppose that the Greeks must have known this, as though all we had to do were to enquire among them. [11]

The πόλις resists historiographical reconstruction from the utterances of the ancient Greeks; it resists it because the πόλις is the precondition of these utterances. Heidegger further writes of the πόλις: "It is neither merely state, nor merely city, rather in the first instance it is properly 'the stead' [*die Statt*]: the site [*die Stätte*] of the abode of human history that belongs to humans in the midst of beings." [12] For Heidegger, the πόλις thus has to be understood more fundamentally as the clearing of Being: "The pre-political essence of the πόλις, that essence that first makes possible everything political in the original and in the derivative sense, lies in its being the open site of that fitting destining [*Schickung*] from out of which all human relations towards beings—and that always means in the first instance the relations of beings as such to humans—are determined." [13] Again, in the 1942–43 lecture course *Parmenides*, Heidegger speaks of the πόλις in this way: "The πόλις is the essence of the place [*Ort*], or, as we say, it is the settlement [*Ort-schaft*] of the historical dwelling of Greek humanity. Because the πόλις lets the totality of beings come in this or that way into the unconcealedness of its condition, the πόλις is therefore essentially related to the Being of beings. Between πόλις and 'Being' there is a primordial relation." [14] This interpretation of the πόλις as the clearing of Being follows from and illuminates a fragment by Hölderlin that Heidegger quotes:

> *do you think*
> *It will proceed*
> *Along the course of old? Namely, they wanted to found*
> *A realm of art. But thereby*
> *The national [das Vaterländische] was neglected*
> *By them and pitifully*
> *Greece, the fairest of all, was destroyed.*
> *Now presumably matters*
> *Stand otherwise.* [15]

For Hölderlin, the Greeks neglected the national. This appears a perverse claim because the Greeks, in their attachment to the graves of their ancestors and in their refusal of anything above their respective cities, are usually said to have possessed the preeminent sense of place and of *Heimat*. But this preeminence of the Greeks is relative to other Western peoples and not absolute. For Heidegger, that which the Greeks neglected, namely, the essence of the πόλις as the site of their historical Dasein, they could not but have neglected without a contestation of classical ontology. In the 1934–35 lecture course *Hölderlins Hymnen "Germanien" und "Der Rhein,"* the conjunction receives its sharpest form: "*The 'Fatherland' is Being* [das Seyn] *itself.*" [16] The imperative that informs Heidegger's destruction of the ontological tradition is the task of addressing the national. So long as the hegemony of the ontic remains unchallenged and Being unthought, even the most vehemently proclaimed patriotic renewal will amount to a dereliction of the Fatherland. In the history of Being, National Socialism figures as cosmopolitan.

As the Fatherland is explicitly associated with the central question in Heidegger's thinking, it cannot be interpreted as a nonphilosophical residue in an otherwise stringent corpus. [17] However aphoristically Heidegger speaks of the Fatherland, he does so within the context of his elaboration of the question of Being, rather than in the form of asides. Having been identified with Being (*das Seyn*), and thus with the Un-thought of the Greeks and the hegemony of the ontic, the word "Fatherland" is differentiated from the jargon of the regime. The degree of difference is easily underestimated given the cursory nature of Heidegger's presentation, and it is thus not redundant to set out this difference at greater length. It has first to be asked on what grounds Heidegger identifies the Fatherland with Being. Between the discourses of nationalism and metaphysics, there is no obvious transition. The Fatherland is what it is only as Being, because whatever the originarity to which the Fatherland lays claim, it claims it as the originarity of Being. The Fatherland of conventional nationalism, which marks itself off straightforwardly from other countries as the country of origin, has to dispute with Being for the title to the originary. In this dispute, conventional nationalism finds its claims rebuffed.

Why this should be so and why the Fatherland has in the end to be understood as Being is the import of Heidegger's treatment of Being-in-the-world in *Being and Time*. Already in the 1927 text, the origin of Dasein is shown to lie elsewhere than among beings. As Being-in-the-world, Dasein cannot have its origin—in the sense of its ground—in any being present-at-hand. In the distinctness of a geographically determinate Fatherland, Dasein would be unable to recognize the ground of its own status as an exception to the ontology of the distinct. It has to turn instead to the world in which the distinct first appears and that thus precedes the Fatherland of conventional nationalism. Where National Socialism neglected the ontic indeterminability of world in favor of a Fatherland with border controls and commissions for cartographers, it subscribed to classical ontology and the apprehensibility of what is. The Fatherland, in the thingliness whereby it was recognizable, was also discovered to be manipulable and to lend itself to expansion. For the purpose of thinking that which is most our own, National Socialism had at its disposal only relics of the thing-concepts of classical ontology. Heidegger, in contrast, conceives that which is most our own as the Un-thought of τέχνη and hence of that planetary domination under which the "inner truth" of National Socialism was forgotten. The *inner* truth of the movement was the truth constituted by the ownmost (*das Eigenste*). Since neither among the Greeks nor among the later peoples sustained by their legacy was the originary ever grasped in its essence, it cannot justifiably be interpreted as the preserve of reactionaries. The originary, in the incomprehensibility with which it haunts τέχνη, is less the reassuring habitat of backward Luddites than the still indiscernible site of the disclosedness of beings.

If, for Heidegger in 1934–35, the Fatherland is Being itself, it is because the Fatherland is the world of the *Volk*. The world in which the German people carries out its mission of thinking the question of Being is itself the clearing of Being. The conspicuous untimeliness of Heidegger's dictum in *Hölderlins Hymnen "Germanien" und "Der Rhein"* is not explained away by equating Being with the world of the *Volk*, since the use Heidegger makes elsewhere of "world" and "*Volk*" is itself untimely with relation to the nationalist discourse of the Nazi regime. Even though Heidegger never speaks of the Fatherland in *Being and Time*, the basis for his definition of the Fatherland in 1934–35 can be ascertained in the earlier text with its discussions of the ontological status of world and the worldliness of the Being-with-one-another of the *Volk*. Only as Being—that is, only as the untimely Un-thought of the age of metaphysics—is the Fatherland truly the world of the *Volk* and not, for instance, an intraworldly (*innerweltlich*) object of exchange in the territorial struggles of Social Darwinism. As the world of the *Volk*, the Fatherland is that which is at once closest and least tangible. Its proximity cannot be grasped as the proximity of an object present-at-hand, since as the clearing of beings in which an object first appears, it is closer than any object. It is the condition of possibility for the closeness of an object. The proximity of the Fatherland has to be grasped differently from the proximity of one object to another. It is in the way this difference is worked out, and in the question that thus arises concerning the scope of thing-concepts , that the fervor of Heidegger's nationalism reveals itself as inimical to the Nazi regime and its metaphysical foundations.

The proximity of the Fatherland is its originarity. For conventional nationalism, this originarity is unambiguously manifest in one's country of origin. But does one's country of origin truly stand on itself in distinction from that which is derivative and not originary? For Heidegger, the Fatherland does not lie at any given moment at a greater or lesser distance in space from the *Volk*, since what is at issue is not a fixed point on the globe from and toward which one might move at will. The Fatherland is originary, not in the sense that it constitutes the backdrop of an act of parturition, but rather in the sense that its proximity is insuperable. In its originarity, the Fatherland is that which is essentially nearest. The Fatherland is the origin and thus whatever can be shown to be derivative is, ipso facto, not the Fatherland. Heidegger's idiosyncratic nationalism is, accordingly, already in evidence in his destruction of the philosophical tradition. Once the tradition has been destroyed, once the ground of all previous philosophy has been laid bare, the originary, which is to say the Fatherland in Heidegger's sense, will have been secured. Nationalism, inasmuch as it takes the notion of originarity seriously, cannot evade the task of philosophical genealogy and must exclude the derivative from its definition of the Fatherland.

In this respect, Kant's cosmopolitanism is a more rigorous nationalism than the territorial bigotry of the Nazis because it is more originary: the measurable *Lebensraum* of the latter presupposes the homogeneous space in which the Kantian subject asserts its rights as a citizen of the world. If Heidegger rejects this most philosophical of cosmopolitanisms, in turn, as derivative, it is without disputing its philosophical superiority over the sundry aborted nationalisms postdating the *Critique of Pure Reason*. For Heidegger, the insuperable proximity of the Fatherland is not spatial because the Fatherland is nearer than space itself, let alone any object contained within space, and it is nearer because, as Being (*Seyn*), it is ontologically prior.

Heidegger's nationalism, and its pertinence to his thought as a whole, lies in an attempt to think the nearness of the nearest. As the nearest, the Fatherland is necessarily Being in its originarity. Advancing such a definition, Heidegger is by no means ransacking the vocabulary of philosophy simply in order to furnish the *Heimat* of National Socialism with an ontological gloss. On the contrary, Heidegger thereby concisely states his opposition to the nationalism of the regime. Inasmuch as the *Heimat* of National Socialism—in its ready convertibility into *Lebensraum*—was the quantifiable territory of an organism and not Being, that which is essentially nearest to the *Volk*, and hence that which is the *Volk* itself, became a quantum. The reification of Dasein propagated in the biologism of the regime thereby had its counterpart in an understanding of the Fatherland as an object in space. Whatever the quantitative aggrandizement of the Fatherland through military expansion, its initial debasement to an object within space, and thus to that which is doubly derivative, was not redressed. The Fatherland of imperialist discourse, inasmuch as it is more a geometrical figure than a *Heimat*, is inseparable from the theorization of space established by the Greeks: both rest upon classical ontology's neglect of the essence of the πόλις. This is why an opposition to imperialism that simply falls back upon the cosmopolitanism of the spatially indifferent is always inadequate. Where Heidegger criticizes homogeneous space in the name of the many ways of Being, he does so, not in order to ground philosophically the otherwise rhetorical immediacy of a fetishized fatherland, but rather in order to interrogate in homogeneous space the ontological presuppositions of a reified Fatherland. Since what identifies a *Heimat* is not a spatial immediacy but the nearness by which it is one's own, this nearness must be the matter of an existential analytic before it is, if at all, the matter of geometry.

The question of Being, as that which is existentially nearest, is the question of the *Heimat* of Dasein. Being-at-home, by which a *Heimat* is recognized as such, is thus, for Heidegger, an orientation within the question of Being. In this sense, orientation is not an orientation among objects but an orientation within the non-thingly. Heidegger's *Heimat* is "recognizable" as such by that which is not recognizable in it, by that which is uncanny. Orientation becomes an orientation by that which stands too close to be an object, and then not because it is the subject itself, since it is still closer than the subject. Any orientation that is a finding of oneself as a subject among and over against objects is thus, properly speaking, a disorientation, because the exception to the understanding of Being as presence, the exception that is nearest to Dasein and by which Dasein has first of all to orientate itself, is forgotten. Orientation within the Fatherland of Being is, conversely, a disorientation with regard to the objectivity of the objects in one's vicinity. Orientation within a Fatherland that has been reified and subordinated to geometry proceeds by a mensuration between objects: it is less a being-at-home in what is closest to Dasein than an inclusion of Dasein in an inventory of the present-at-hand.

But, then, orientation within the homogeneous space that is the cosmopolitan subject's native element is also a forgetting of Dasein's Being, because homogeneity in general is inconceivable without a suppression of transcendence. Heidegger already formulates this objection to the originarity of homogeneous space in the covert treatment of the notion of the Fatherland that is the existential analytic. To see how much of Heidegger's nationalism was in place by the late 1920s, and how little he received from the hands of the Nazis, the existential analytic can therefore be reread for what it says on orientation and that which is nearest to Dasein. Heidegger criticizes there the cosmopolitanism of homogeneous space but without offering a premature defense of the parochialism of the Nazi regime. Criticizing this cosmopolitanism in the course of his exposition of the phenomenon of orientation, Heidegger does not have recourse to the "realism" on which National Socialism prided itself and on which the practicality of orientation is conventionally believed to rely. On the contrary, Heidegger's criticism follows from a completely novel definition of orientation. Orientation within the question of Being replaces orientation within the "reality" of objects and the homogeneous space into which this "reality" must, as Kant had argued, collapse.

Heidegger's reading of Kant's text "What Is Orientation in Thinking?" can easily give the impression of obtuseness, because it does not share Kant's definition of orientation and cannot, accordingly, be seen to improve on it. For Heidegger, Dasein as Being-in-the-world is always already oriented, and orientation, as it is set forth by Kant in his friendly critique of Moses Mendelssohn's metaphysics, is but one mode of Dasein's Being-in-the-world. To explain orientation with reference to the subject is to risk all understanding of the worldly constitution of Dasein. In *Being and Time*, Heidegger repeats his objections from *History of the Concept of Time* to the meaningfulness of Kant's reconstruction of orientation from the difference between the left and right sides of the body:

Left and right are not something "subjective" for which the subject has a feeling; they are directions of one's directedness into a world that is ready-to-hand already. "By the mere feeling of a difference between my two sides" I could never find my way about in a world. The subject with a "mere feeling" of this difference is a construct posited in disregard of the state that is truly constitutive for any subject—namely, that whenever Dasein has such a "mere feeling", it is in a world already *and must be* in it to be able to orient itself at all. This becomes plain from the example with which Kant tries to clarify the phenomenon of orientation.

Suppose I step into a room which is familiar to me but dark, and which has been rearranged [*umgeräumt*] during my absence so that everything which used to be at my right is now at my left. If I am to orient myself the "mere feeling of the difference" between my two sides will be of no help at all as long as I fail to apprehend some definite object "whose position", as Kant remarks casually, "I have in mind". But what does this signify except that whenever this happens I necessarily orient myself both *in* and *from* my being already alongside a world which is "familiar"? The equipment-context of a world must have been presented to Dasein. That I am already in a world is no less constitutive for the possibility of orientation than is the feeling for right and left. While this state of Dasein's Being is an obvious one, we are not thereby justified in suppressing the ontologically constitutive role which it plays. Even Kant does not suppress it, any more than any other Interpretation of Dasein. Yet the fact that this is a state of which we con-

stantly make use does not exempt us from providing a suitable ontological explication, but rather demands one. The psychological Interpretation according to
which the "I" has something "in the memory" ["*im Gedächtnis*"] is at bottom a way
of alluding to the existentially constitutive state of Being-in-the-world. Since Kant
fails to see this structure, he also fails to recognize all the interconnections which
the Constitution of any possible orientation implies. Directedness with regard to
right and left is based upon the essential directionality of Dasein in general, and
this directionality in turn is essentially co-determined by Being-in-the-world.
Even Kant, of course, has not taken orientation as a theme for Interpretation. He
merely wants to show that every orientation requires a "subjective principle". Here
"subjective" is meant to signify that this principle is *a priori*. Nevertheless, the *a
priori* character of directedness with regard to right and left is based upon the "subjective" *a priori* of Being-in-the-world, which has nothing to do with any determinate character restricted beforehand to a worldless subject.[18]

This passage needs to be read carefully. The difference between left and
right, inasmuch as it is a nonconceptual difference, too quickly becomes
for Kant a matter of mere feeling. But that which Kant names a "feeling"
cannot be reduced to the subject without contradiction. A worldless, hence
bodyless, subject is not able to feel a difference between left and right that
in the circumstances simply does not exist. With its feeling for the difference between its two sides, the Kantian subject does not, strictly speaking,
make sense of its world, since it is rather world that in advance makes sense
for the Kantian subject of the difference between its two sides. Insensitive
to its own Being-in-the-world, the Kantian subject discovers what has already been uncovered yet discovers it by nonetheless mistaking its nature.
In other words, it successfully orientates itself within its world, not by
grasping world as such, but rather by piecing together its feeling for the difference between its two sides and an object whose position it remembers.
What the Kantian subject discovers in the moment of its reorientation is
that which was already "there" for it, albeit without the familiarity of the
everyday. Orientation, in Kant's account, ceases explicitly to be an existential mode of Dasein and becomes an epistemological problem for the
subject.

   Heidegger and Kant thus differ in the sense they give to finding oneself in the world. For the former, what is involved is an understanding of
the world in which one finds oneself even as one is disoriented within it,
whereas, for the latter, one finds oneself in the world at the moment one
overcomes the disorientation by which one is, so to speak, outside the
world. Presupposing its orientation as Being-in-the-world and yet turning

aside from it as a question, the Kantian subject in its momentary and superficial disorientation searches among phenomena for the point of familiarity by which it could assure itself of the continuity of its "world" and feel
orientated. In Kant's example, the point of familiarity is the object in the
darkened room whose position he remembers and from which he is then
able to reassemble the context of his everyday activity. For Heidegger, what
is important is less the reestablished context of everyday activity than the
world in which Kant first remembers an object's position and whose ontological explication he notwithstanding omits. Hoping to pass off the skele-
tal marriage of proprioception and a remembered object as the richness of
the phenomenon of orientation, Kant swiftly passes over their common
ground in Being-in-the-world to the successful orientation within the un-
worlding of world in everyday activity.

If Heidegger stresses the subjectivity in Kant's account of orientation,
it is not in order to suggest that orientation, for Kant, is solely the affair of
the feeling for the difference between the two sides of one's body. The casualness with which Heidegger hears Kant introduce the object whose position he recalls is, for Heidegger, the casualness with which one might
speak, not so much of a superfluity, as of something self-evident. It is this
appearance of self-evidence and its uninterrogated ontological presuppositions that Heidegger seeks to address and that he can only address by
abandoning the conventional definition of orientation as a familiarizing of
oneself with one's environment. Being-in-the-world, as the possibility of
orientation and hence as the site of the distinction between the familiar
and the unfamiliar, can never be the point of familiarity by which the subject orientates itself and recovers itself for the immersion in everyday activity. For the sake of an understanding of its primary orientation as Being-
in-the-world, Dasein has therefore to resist the seductions of the familiar
and the comfort of feeling itself oriented within the context of its everyday
activity.

This resistance, in turn, cannot without contradiction become a vol-
untary activity. It cannot become the enduring task that develops into the
point of familiarity by which Dasein orientates itself within as well as
against its world. Dasein must lose itself even in its disorientation, since
only then can it hope to find itself in world as such. In the definitive example of orientation, the sun—on the basis of whose familiarity one is
able to align the horizon with the points of the compass and continue
on one's way—does not "illuminate" Being-in-the-world, but rather con-

tributes to its obfuscation under the reassertion of everyday activity. By fixing his attention on the world that is tacitly presupposed in Kant's account of orientation, Heidegger does not, as it were, fill out a lacuna in Kant's account, because this account is adequate to its definition of secondary, i.e. everyday orientation *only so long as* Being-in-the-world is not thematized.

Heidegger's reading of "What Is Orientation in Thinking?" does not succeed as an immanent critique of Kant. Heidegger freely admits that Kant had set himself a quite different task: Kant's interest in treating orientation was to show that every orientation by the familiar involved a subjective principle. In several respects, Kant's brief essay of 1786 constitutes a digest of the earlier *Critique of Pure Reason*. By means of his opening description of orientation in a darkened room, Kant arrives at the subjective principle that is none other than the a priori intuition of space, and from this reprise of "The Transcendental Aesthetic," he then proceeds to a comparable discipline of theology. Orientation is, for Kant, the occasion to demonstrate, once again, the complementarity of intuition and concept and thereby to reprove the exclusive conceptualism of dogmatic metaphysics. Given the task that he had set himself, Kant has to extract from the phenomenon of orientation, not world as such, but that which is at once nonconceptual and a priori. Already in his precritical writings, Kant had adduced the difference between the two sides of one's body as an example of a nonconceptual difference. And in the feeling of this difference, on account of the role it plays in every orientation, Kant willingly notes the a priori and thereafter turns to his critique of Mendelssohn.

As it is not his aim in "What Is Orientation in Thinking?" to confound empiricism, let alone nationalism, Kant makes very little of exposing a transcendental moment in orientation. On his way to his encounter with dogmatic metaphysics, Kant thus calls into question with what right any phenomenon could be taken for that which is most familiar. Whenever it orients itself, whenever it feels that it is "at home," the Kantian subject has recourse to the feeling of the difference between left and right. This a priori feeling is more familiar than any of the various objects that must combine with it in the process of orientation. The Kantian subject is thus more "at home" in the a priori than it is among any given phenomena. Its well-known cosmopolitanism is the consequence of this demotion of the familiarity of phenomena. What is decisive for the Kantian subject's being-at-home is the application of the subjective principle, rather than the *spatial* immediacy of a *Heimat*. For Kant, the object whose position he remembers in the darkened room is not superfluous to orientation, but its familiarity is certainly subordinate to the familiarity of the difference between the two sides of his body.

Heidegger does not protest this subordination. In his reading of "What Is Orientation in Thinking?" Heidegger does not rescue the object in the darkened room. He does not seek to reverse the demotion of its familiarity and to enter an empiricist's claim for the originarity of phenomena. What Heidegger protests is the disregard of the world that first renders familiar both the object and the subjective principle of the difference between left and right.[19] It is Being-in-the-world that is, for Heidegger, the true a priori of orientation, just as it is Being-in-the-world that is experienced by Dasein, however, as disorientation when it is torn from its immersion in the everyday.

The true a priori, as that which is ontologically closest to Dasein, is the true *Heimat*. It is neither the feeling for the difference between right and left nor an object whose position one remembers: it is the ground of these individual components by which Kant reconstructs the phenomenon of orientation. Being-in-the-world can never become familiar. It is also, one might say, the strangeness at the heart of what is taken to be familiar. When one's surroundings are experienced as unsettling and alien, this is for Heidegger not a merely subjective disturbance in the apprehension of things as they are. What a thing is said to be in its everyday acceptation, how an object can appear familiar within a darkened room, presupposes the suppression of the undecidability of Being-in-the-world. Heidegger's account of orientation effectively concludes with the statement that orientation, in Kant's sense, is impossible: the more meticulously one studies one's surroundings and endeavors to grasp them philosophically as they are so as thereby to become oriented, the more one is overwhelmed by the uncanniness of Being-in-the-world.

Kant's account of orientation thus undergoes in Heidegger's reading a suggestively oriental, that is to say Jewish, destruction. The stability of the points of reference by which Kant orients himself is undermined in Heidegger by the intrusion of that which refuses to stabilize. In its resistance to reification and to its incorporation in a frame of reference, Being-in-the-world stands under the prohibition of images. Kant orients himself in spite of Judaea. With a northerner's perception of the sun's position at noon, Kant writes:

To *orientate* oneself, in the proper sense of the word, means to use a given direction—and we divide the horizon into four of these—in order to find the others, and in particular that of *sunrise*. If I see the sun in the sky and know that it is now midday, I know how to find south, west, north, and east. For this purpose, however, I must necessarily be able to feel a difference within my own *subject*, namely that between my right and left hands.[20]

Kant supplements the constancy of the Orient as the fixed point of orientation with the constancy of the subject. For Heidegger, however, it is not a matter of finding what is constant, since making sense of the subject, which in Kant's exposition makes sense of the sun, is the inconstancy of the transcendence "proper" to Being-in-the-world. In his destruction of the traditional account of orientation, Heidegger does not come upon the fixed point whose stability is grounded in classical ontology's understanding of Being as presence. Heidegger's Orient does not turn out to be Greek.

For Heidegger, orientation is a being-at-home in Being-in-the-world. As Dasein is essentially Being-in-the-world, Dasein is always at home. But Dasein misunderstands the character of its *Heimat*. In confusing its *Heimat* with a given intraworldly being or a subjective principle, Dasein convinces itself that is "at home" in what is at a remove from its Being. It is only in Being as such that Dasein can be at home and it is at home to the extent that it is disconcerted. Dasein is always at home because it is always in some manner disconcerted. When Dasein errs in believing that it is at home in a familiar environment, it nonetheless finds itself at home in the bewilderment of its error.

By comparison, Descartes arguably retains the conventional definition of the security of *Heimat* when he grounds modern metaphysics on the terra firma that is subjectivity. In his lectures on the history of philosophy, Hegel discusses the transition from the philosophy of the Middle Ages to the philosophy that, with Descartes, knows itself as self-consciousness and is at home:

Philosophy in its own proper soil separates itself entirely from the philosophizing theology, in accordance with its principle, and places it on quite another side. Here, we may say, we are at home, and like the mariner after a long voyage in a tempestuous sea, we may now hail the sight of land; with Descartes the culture of modern times, the thought of modern philosophy, really begins to appear, after a long and tedious journey on the way which has led so far.[21]

Here the considerable differences between the Cartesian *res cogitans* and Hegel's Spirit are not brought into play, so that the identity with respect to the self-certainty of thought might be all the more conspicuous. The Cartesian doubt that questions everything except the certainty of itself as doubt is that alienation from the thingly by which the subject is forced to—or more precisely, created by—the acknowledgement that, henceforth, it is only with itself that it can feel at home. With the guarantee of this self-certainty of alienation, a knowledge of what is can again be attempted. But by retaining the conventional definition of the security of *Heimat* in the foundation of his metaphysics, Descartes conceals from himself the questionability of requiring certainty from a starting point. He begins from what is familiar and certain and employs its familiarity and certainty as the stable measure of beings.

Kant, who inherits from Descartes the conviction of the desirability of certain foundations, is too ready to find a use for the constancy of the transcendental subject. The certainty with which the transcendental subject can be held to repeat its "I think" alongside every judgment and thereby provide the foundation for possible syntheses is not itself originary. The repetition and constancy of the transcendental subject's "I think" is only conceivable within the discrete "nows" of derivative temporality. The certainty of the transcendental subject, as the immutability of that which can be taken for granted, is its reification into that which is always only ever present-at-hand. Kant's cosmopolitanism is a being-at-home everywhere, because it finds itself everywhere in the very possibility of judgment. It encounters itself in whatever is, since the encounter always involves the "I think" of original apperception. But in being only ever present-at-hand, the cosmopolitan subject is shut out from the originary as such and is properly homeless. The true *Heimat*, judged by the originarity of originary temporality, cannot be present-at-hand.

Strictly speaking, Heidegger does not reassert in the phenomenon of orientation the object that Kant pushes to the background in concentrating on the subject. Heidegger dwells on the object whose position Kant remembers not for its own sake but for the sake of its foundation in Being-in-the-world. Heidegger pulls the object back to the foreground in discussions of orientation in order to interrupt the process by which the Kantian subject finds itself at home in subjectivity, rather than—more originarily—in Being-in-the-world. He recalls Kant's dependence on the object in orientation and disputes the plausibility of the subject's absolute withdrawal into itself. With the reassertion of the object in orientation, Heidegger recovers Being-in-the-world from its suppression in the founding of the metaphysics of subjectity.

Contending that the subjectivity of the subject precedes any relation to an object and underplaying Dasein's Being-in-the-world, Kant makes the a priori intuition of space the native element of the subject. In the "Transcendental Aesthetic," Kant argues of space:

Space is nothing but the form of all appearances of outer sense. It is the subjective condition of sensibility, under which alone outer intuition is possible for us. Since, then, the receptivity of the subject, its capacity to be affected by objects, must necessarily precede all intuitions of these objects, it can readily be understood how the form of all appearances can be given prior to all actual perceptions, and so exist in the mind *a priori*, and how, as a pure intuition, in which all objects must be determined, it can contain, prior to all experience, principles which determine the relations of these objects.[22]

Receptivity, which always remains receptivity in the face of the variety of the empirical intuitions received, becomes for Kant the independent form in which these intuitions are received. On the basis of the constancy of its reception, the subject is situated in the ideality of the pure a priori intuition here named space. That Kant does not ask whether a receptivity in abstraction from every reception is meaningful is of course explained, albeit not justified, by his desire to salvage the integrity of geometrical space from what he understands to be Hume's critique. As the form of all possible appearances, space is present in all objects and its homogeneity lies in the definitional invulnerability with which it continues to be affectivity through every instance of affection. It is the abstract form of appearances, but this abstractness cannot be converted into homogeneity without reinstating space as a concept, namely, as the genus common to all appearances.

What is at stake in Heidegger's reading of "What Is Orientation in Thinking?" is not a restoration of the heterogeneity of the space of pre-Kantian empiricism. The "heterogeneity" of Being-in-the-world, which Heidegger sets against homogeneous space, is not a set of sundry objects but rather the transcendence by which Dasein steps beyond its containment in self-presence.

It is in this sense that Heidegger's remark on geometrical space in *History of the Concept of Time* needs to be understood: "What is homogeneous is the pure space of metrics, of geometry. For these have destroyed the peculiar structure of aroundness only in order to arrive at the possibility of the discoverability of homogeneous space."[23] The peculiar structure of aroundness is misapprehended if it is resolved into the objects in one's vicinity. Aroundness, for Heidegger, precedes the discovery of homogeneous space and it cannot therefore be grasped in a cobbling together of homogeneous space and objects that are only *incidentally* defined by their proximity. Unless the proximity of the objects is understood as what is essential—and that is to understand objects no longer in terms of the topological indifference of the objectivity of the object and thus no longer, strictly, as "objects"—then the presence in which the objectivity and potential reproduction of the object stands and in which space is discovered as homogeneous remains determinative. The structure of aroundness is the sitedness of each respective Dasein in the transcendence to and of its world. Destroying this structure first establishes the objectivity and "realism" of the object. The finitude of the peculiar structure of aroundness is thus not *overcome* in order to arrive at the possibility of the discoverability of homogeneous space, since it is in a *retreat* from this structure that homogeneous space first opens itself up. The infinity of this space is the consequence of its retraction into the uniformity of presence. The peculiar structure of aroundness is always beyond the reach of the subject and, given the originarity of this structure, the subject cannot be held ever to be at home. It is only that which exceeds the subject, not numerically but ontologically, that can ever be at home. Only Dasein, in its transcendence of the presence by which the subject is defined, finds itself in the originarity of aroundness. Aroundness precedes the pure space of metrics because the latter presupposes the difference between left and right, a difference that is inconceivable for a disembodied subject in homogeneous space but not for Dasein amid the ontic articulations of its world. The directedness of the three lines of the purportedly ahistorical definition of a triangle, for example, only makes sense because Dasein first makes sense of the difference between left and right in the historical and corporeal thickness of its world. This historical thickness, as what comes first, is the true *Heimat* and the Being-with-one-another of the *Volk*.

It is a people, as authentic Being-with-one-another and not as an aggregate of territorially minded subjects, that dwells in a *Heimat* and, as Being-in-the-world, even is this *Heimat*. When Kant raises his famous question "What is man?" in the introduction to his lectures on logic, and does so explicitly within the cosmopolitan concept of philosophy, it is without any consideration for the question of the historicality of a people.[24]

This question is in fact closed to Kant because in the consistency with which he expounded the understanding of Being as presence, he could not hesitate between the abstract individual subject and the rediscovery of this subject everywhere: it is therefore not without a tacit reference to Kant's transcendental subject that Heidegger in *Being and Time* analyses the way of Being of the "they."

In the *Contributions to Philosophy*, Heidegger summarizes his objection to Kantian space:

What one otherwise and up to now has thought about space and time, which belong back into this origin of truth, is—as Aristotle for the first time worked out in the *Physics*—already a consequence of the previously established essence of beings as οὐσία and of truth as correctness and of all that which follows from that as "categories." When Kant calls space and time "intuitions," that is within this history only a weak attempt to rescue what is ownmost to space and time. But Kant had no access to the *essential sway* of space and time. In any case the orientation to "I" and "consciousness" and re-presentation mislays all the ins and outs.[25]

Here Heidegger disowns his earlier thesis in *Kant and the Problem of Metaphysics* regarding the grounding in originary temporality of the "I" of Kant's transcendental apperception. Kant's attempt to rescue what is ownmost to space and time through their theorization as a priori intuitions founders on subjectivity. Having set forth a distinction between intuition —as the domain of nonconceptual differences such as that between left and right—and concept, Kant does not carry this distinction to the point of a rupture with classical ontology. The repetition by which the subject is convinced of both the formal independence of its receptivity and the purity of space does not ultimately differ from the repetition in which the concept manifests its authority over a plurality of appearances. In the "Transcendental Aesthetic" in the second edition of the *Critique of Pure Reason*, Kant writes:

Space is represented as an infinite *given* magnitude. Now every concept must be thought as a representation which is contained in an infinite number of different possible representations (as their common character), and which therefore contains these *under* itself; but no concept, as such, can be thought as containing an infinite number of representations *within* itself. It is in this latter way, however, that space is thought; for all the parts of space coexist *ad infinitum*. Consequently, the original representation of space is an *a priori* intuition, not a concept.[26]

The difference between concept and intuition is confined to the way in which they contain representations. Where a concept admits an infinite number of representations, the infinity does not so much lie in the concept itself as in that by which the individual representations differ from their common character, that is, from their concept. With space, the differences between its representations can themselves be spatial. In the scope of both intuition and concept, the previously established essence of beings as οὐσία grounds the possibility of repetition and of the infinite number of representations. Kant does not sever space from the concept by severing it from the foundations of the concept's ahistoricality in the intelligibility of Aristotelian substance. Indeed, Kant makes the critical philosophy a new bastion of the doctrine of the substantiality of space: in the "Anticipations of Perception," Kant prides himself on providing a transcendental proof of the uniformity, which is to say, for Kant, the intelligibility of space where earlier attempts at an empirical proof had failed.[27] The substantiality of space as an a priori intuition is the substantiality of the transcendental ego, namely, of that of which "The Paralogisms of Pure Reason" is a critique in the Kantian sense rather than a refutation (the transcendental ego is the intelligibility of what is, even if it is not itself intelligible). With the substantiality of a space that is everywhere fundamentally the same, the *Heimlichkeit* and originary undecidability of Being-in-the-world has, however, little to do. Betraying the promise of the distinction between concept and intuition, Kant expels the unrepeatable from a priori space: within the publicness of Kant's cosmopolitan space, Dasein lacks the means to do anything but keep the whereabouts of its singular *Heimat* to itself.

Does the fact that Heidegger criticizes the cosmopolitanism of homogeneous space suffice to make him an advocate of the National Socialist *Heimat*? Heidegger's notion of Being-in-the-world is clearly not the theoretical justification of the smugness and xenophobia of the sanctioned but politically unrepresentative cultural products of the regime. The Fatherland that remains recognizably the same is already an abandonment of the existential thickness of world for the objectivity of positivism. A patriotic literature that does not allow its upsurge of feeling to derail the epistemological categories by which the *Heimat* is apprehended as a stable and distinct entity is not a literature of the originarity of the world of a people. Emotive descriptions of a landscape within the national borders bring together feeling and the object, but the union remains external: abstracted from Being-in-the-world, feeling and the object rub up against each other without calling their abstraction into question. The facticity of mood (*Stimmung*) is reduced to being an ornament of the Fatherland, when it is rather a central phenomenon of the originarity of Dasein's Being-in-the-world.

Politically more important, Hitler's *Lebensraum* is also incompatible with Heidegger's notion of *Heimat*. Indeed, alongside the muddled reading of Darwinian theories on which the notion of *Lebensraum* rests, there can be discerned in Hitler's conception a cosmopolitan indifference to place.[28] Hitler's biologistically conceived *Volk* faces the task of conquering for itself a territory from whose resources it will then be able to sustain itself: the exigencies of the struggle for survival do not permit any sentimental predilection for one's native soil. In the notion of *Lebensraum*, space remains thought within the understanding of Being as presence, because territory takes on the stability and thingliness of that which is recognized in presence. With its plans for the exploitation of resources and its absolute subjectivity, the biologistically conceived *Volk* bears an unmistakable resemblance to the entrepreneur of high capitalism. Under the guise of the animal, Nazi Germany thus remained in the thrall of the model of nineteenth-century England, and the spirit of emulation for which it reproached the *Gründerjahre* of the Hohenzollern Reich went unchecked. On the first anniversary of Hitler's installation in power, Heidegger criticized this biologism as it was put forward in an earlier address by the cultural functionary Erwin Guido Kolbenheyer:

Kolbenheyer does not see, he cannot and does not want to see:
1. that the biology in question from 1900 rests on the basic starting point of Darwinism and that this Darwinian doctrine of life is not something absolute, that it is not even *biological*. On the contrary, it is historically *spiritually* determined by the liberal view of humanity and human society as it prevailed in English positivism in the nineteenth century.[29]

One might say that for Heidegger, the biologistically conceived *Volk* of National Socialism would have had to seek its *Heimat*, if anywhere in the positivity of nation states, in Manchester. Yet National Socialism was imperialistic not because it sought a *Heimat*, but rather because, in its subjectivity, it had no proper comprehension of *Heimat*. In the abstractness with which it stood over against its environment, it had already come to the possibility of an expandable and domitable territory that is the inspiration of imperialism.

If Heidegger, in his 1934–35 lecture course on Hölderlin, speaks of the Fatherland as Being itself, it is, therefore, in order to initiate a discourse that, despite every appearance, had not yet begun. Heidegger's nationalism, as an interrogation of the originary, understands *das Deutsche* through the question of Being. That which is German is not self-evident. For Heidegger, the otherness of the other foundational reception of Being that is *das Deutsche* is only to be fully revealed through the encounter with the Greeks. In this, he heeds Hölderlin's exhortation to such an encounter. But although Heidegger follows Hölderlin, he interprets him in an elaboration, rather than a rejection of his own earlier thinking. Intimations of a discourse on *Heimat* and *das Deutsche* can be discovered in Heidegger's writings before his engagement with Hölderlin. To address these notions with reference to Hölderlin is, however, to address them with reference to the Judeo-Christian legacy that Heidegger, as a philosopher, believed he had to disown and silence. In Hölderlin, this legacy, which has nothing to do with the continuity of a tradition, stands more clearly, if still polemically, out in the open.

Repeatedly in his commentaries on Hölderlin, Heidegger devotes his attentions to Hölderlin's letter to Casimir Ulrich Böhlendorff of December 4, 1801. It is here, in the course of offering Böhlendorff a response to his drama, *Fernando oder die Kunstweihe*, that, in Heidegger's exegesis, Hölderlin sets forth the question of what it is to be German. The passage reads:

We learn nothing with more difficulty than to freely use the national. And, I believe that it is precisely the clarity of the presentation that is so natural to us as is for the Greeks the fire from heaven. For exactly that reason they will have to be surpassed in beautiful passion—which you have also preserved for yourself—rather than in that Homeric presence of mind and talent for presentation.

It sounds paradoxical. Yet I argue it once again and leave it for your examination and use: in the progress of education the truly national will become the ever less attractive. Hence the Greeks are less master of the sacred pathos, because to them it was inborn, whereas they excel in their talent for presentation, beginning with Homer, because this exceptional man was sufficiently sensitive to conquer the Western *Junonian sobriety* for his Apollonian empire and thus to veritably appropriate what is foreign.

With us it is the reverse. Hence it is also so dangerous to deduce the rules of art for oneself exclusively from Greek excellence. I have labored long over this and know by now that, with the exception of what must be the highest for the Greeks and for us—namely, the living relationship and destiny—we must not share anything identical with them.

Yet what is familiar must be learned as well as what is alien. This is why the

Greeks are so indispensable for us. It is only that we will not follow them in our own, national [spirit] since, as I said, the *free* use of *what is one's own* is the most difficult.[30]

It is worthy of note that nowhere in this passage does Hölderlin use the word "German" (*deutsch*). For Heidegger, it is, however, understood that "the national" (*das Nationelle*) of which Hölderlin writes is the nationality of the German. Thus the lecture course *Hölderlin's Hymn "The Ister"* reprises the letter to Böhlendorff in the following manner:

What the Germans lack, what must therefore first come to be encountered by them as that which is foreign to them, is the "fire from the heavens." It is this that the Germans must learn to experience so as to be struck by the fire and thereby to be impelled toward the correct appropriation of their own gift for presentation. Otherwise the Germans will remain exposed to the danger and the weakness of suppressing every fire on account of the rashness of their capabilities, and of pursuing for its own sake the ability to grasp and to delimit, and even of taking their delimiting and instituting to be the fire itself. It is therefore the pure self-experiencing of his own poetizing when Hölderlin says of the Germans, as distinct from the Greeks: "whereas the main tendency in the manners of representation in our time (i.e. the time of the Germans) is the ability to hit on something, to have destiny [*Geschik*], since the lack of fate [*das Schiksaallose*], the δύσμορον, is our weakness."[31]

Rather than securing the interpretation, Heidegger's parenthesis "(i.e. the time of the Germans)" betrays its peremptoriness. How is it straightforward that the time that Hölderlin names as "our time" in its difference from the time of the Greeks in the "Remarks on 'Antigone'" is "the time of the Germans"? By what authority can Heidegger assert that Hölderlin's use of the first person plural here limits itself to an evocation of the community of the Germans? Yet, conceivably, Heidegger's parenthesis is neither an elucidation nor a stopgap whereby a presupposed rift between Hölderlin's text and a general comprehensibility is sealed. The expression, "the time of the Germans" is, if anything, more obscure than Hölderlin's "our time." It is Hölderlin who elucidates rather that which Heidegger intends by "the time of the Germans." And indeed, according to Heidegger, this is how it should be. In the lecture course *Hölderlins Hymnen "Germanien" und "Der Rhein*," Heidegger writes of Hölderlin:

He is the poet of the Germans. But Klopstock and Herder, Goethe and Schiller, Novalis and Kleist, Eichendorff and Mörike, Stefan George and Rilke are German

poets as well, belonging likewise to the Germans. Yet we do not mean it in that
sense. "Poet of the Germans" not as subjective genitive, but rather as objective genitive: the poet who first poetizes the Germans. But have not the others also, and in
their way, said and sung the German essence? To be sure,—and yet Hölderlin is
in the superlative sense the poet, that is, founder of German Being, because he has
projected the latter the furthest, namely, cast it out and ahead into the furthest
future.[32]

The sense of Hölderlin's "our time" is consequently not so much to be elucidated as enforced: for Heidegger, his employment of the first person plural decides the German essence. When Hölderlin, in the letter to Böhlendorff, speaks of the West and Heidegger hears only the Germans, there is
thus a double aggression. It is not merely that all the peoples of the West
have been subsumed under the rubric "German"—the Germans themselves, in their historical and geographical contingency, have disappeared
before the arrival of this other Germany: *we, the non-Greeks . . .*

Clearly the precise nature of the negation in this formula is not to be
grasped in a bare allusion to dialectics. It is not enough to say that the
Greeks and the Germans stand in a negative relation to each other. The
identity of the Germans does not remain as a residuum once the stable, self-
referring identity of the Greeks has been subtracted, because the Greeks, in
the sobriety of their gift for depiction, are to all appearances the most Western and thus the most German of peoples. The essence of the West is to
be encountered, if it is to be encountered at all, in the alien—Hölderlin
would say, oriental—territory of Greek art. In what sense, then, can the
Germans be more German than the Greeks, when every appearance suggests that it is the Greeks who are the Germans? Given that Hölderlin
writes that what is one's own must be learnt just as much as that which is
strange, the two principles by which Hölderlin defines Western and Greek
art—namely, clarity of depiction and holy pathos—do not differentiate
the Greek and Western peoples. The differentiation becomes, rather, a future task: "I . . . know by now that, with the exception of what must be the
highest for the Greeks and for us—namely, the living relationship and
destiny—we must not share anything with them." Hölderlin's first person plural, and hence Heidegger's "Germans," are the people who are not
permitted to be Greek—we, the Germans, must not share anything with
them. What alone distinguishes the Germans is the imperative under
which they stand.

In the essay "The Perspective from which We Have to Look at Antiquity," Hölderlin explicitly presents this imperative as the necessity of an
insurrection against antiquity:

We dream of education, piety, p.p. and have none whatsoever; it is appropriated—
we dream of originality and autonomy; we believe to be saying all kinds of new
things and, still, all this is reaction, as it were, a mild revenge against the slavery
with which we have behaved toward antiquity. There seems to be indeed hardly
any other choice than to be oppressed by what has been appropriated and by what
is positive, or, with violent effort, to oppose as a living force everything learnt,
given, positive. What seems most problematic here is that antiquity appears altogether opposed to our primordial drive which is bent on forming the unformed,
to perfect the primordial-natural so that man, who is born for art, will naturally
take to what is raw, uneducated, childlike rather than to a formed material where
there has already been pre-formed [what] one wishes to form.[33]

The despotism of Greece is not to be eluded through the choice of the material to be fashioned into a work of art because the very fashioning of material is Greek. Under such conditions, the human being who is born for
art prefers the crude and shapeless, which in the absence of any articulation
and formation never emerges as such into the light of day. The artist who
is not Greek creates nothing. Such an artist, without ceasing to be an artist, lives under a prohibition of images and can thus never be at home in
the ontic.

Once Greece has been defined, however summarily with respect to
the art of other cultures, as the essence of the positive, a confrontation with
Greece and Greece alone becomes indispensable, if the task of a radical differentiation is to be adequately formulated. Greece, as the essence of the
positive, becomes the origin of every manifest culture: in November 1802,
in the second of his two extant letters to Böhlendorff, Hölderlin can thus
speak of his journey through the south of France as an encounter with
Greece.[34] Heidegger similarly absolutizes Greece. As the site of the determination of the essence of the planetary culture of the West, Greece is recalled by everything that is. It is the first beginning, which must be exhaustively thought through to its Un-thought merely in *anticipation* of the
other beginning. The scope of Greece, as the scope of classical ontology, is
not to be underestimated.

In one of the first studies dedicated to Hölderlin, let alone to his relations to antiquity, Wilhelm Michel perceives an "occidental turn" (*abendländische Wendung*) in the late poetry and interprets it as an ultimately

unavailing defense against the heavenly fire of the Greeks.[35] But what is the West toward which Hölderlin is said to have turned? The earlier poetry is not lacking in Swabian place-names, just as the later is not lacking in Greek ones—that which Hölderlin opposes to the Greeks is not a matter of cartography.[36] The imperative voiced in the letter to Böhlendorff, as Hölderlin's recent realization of the limits imposed on his labors in the sphere of Greek art, does not and cannot issue in a poetics for the establishment of a specifically Western poetry. The imperative is left to sound by itself. The negation that announces itself at first as a failing and as a deficiency (the inability to equal the Greeks) is to be reclaimed as an affirmative divergence in another art, a non-art. Hölderlin, as the founder of German Being, founds a people in this poverty and necessity.

For Heidegger, it is this very poverty and necessity that constitute the affirmative divergence of Hölderlin's poetry:

Hölderlin puts into poetry the very essence of poetry—but not in the sense of a timelessly valid concept. This essence of poetry belongs to a definite time. But not in such a way that it merely conforms to that time as some time already existing. Rather, by providing anew the essence of poetry, Hölderlin first determines a new time. It is the time of the gods that have fled *and* of the god who is coming. It is the *time of need* because it stands in a double lack and a double not: in the no-longer of the gods who have fled and in the not-yet of the god who is coming.[37]

Hölderlin's art is the negation of art and, in the age of "a double not" and its crisis, it is the essence of poetry. Hölderlin's art is the art of the gods who have fled and of the god that is coming because it is the most mimetic, the most rigorously deferring. It is too poor in "reality" to be nihilistic. As the art that is the furthest removed from "reality," it is the closest to the non-nihilistic essence of a nihilistic age. It is the art of the inconspicuous.

Listing in his commentary on the hymn "Der Rhein" three reasons for choosing Hölderlin as his subject, Heidegger contends that this art has to be known in its inconspicuousness:

1. Hölderlin is the poet of the poet and of poetry. 2. In accordance with that, Hölderlin is the poet of the Germans. 3. Because Hölderlin is this concealed and difficult thing [*dieses Verborgene und Schwere*], poet of the poet as poet of the Germans, he has not yet become the power in the history of our people. Because he has not yet become this, he has to become it. To contribute to this is "politics" in the highest and authentic sense, so much so that whoever achieves something here has no need to talk about the "political."[38]

Inasmuch as they neglect a confrontation with the concealment and difficulty of Hölderlin, the Germans are oblivious of their essence and, that is
to say, of the political character of their essence. Strictly speaking, therefore, the Germans as Germans do not yet exist and their Fatherland cannot yet be thought. The impropriety that Hölderlin intimates to Böhlendorff as the possession specific to the West remains to be grasped as such
and thus truly possessed. This impropriety is the caesura of the decision between art and non-art, between Greece and Judaea.

The counterfeit witticism on the emptiness and hence indecisiveness
of Heidegger's thinking of decision that circulated among the auditors of
his lectures in the late 1920s ("I am resolved, but to what I don't know")
belittles Heidegger's attempt to grasp the impropriety of the caesura. For
Heidegger, it is in the impropriety of resoluteness that Dasein properly
gathers itself into its distance from the reification holding sway in the
thought of humanity since the inauguration of classical ontology. The
people that comes to be within the decision would not be Greek, and not
because of any extant and thus decidable and mutually exclusive attributes.

Even before the explicit concern with Hölderlin's poetry, Heidegger,
in the 1934 lecture course *Logik als die Frage nach dem Wesen der Sprache*,
approaches the question of what it is to be German by way of the existential of resoluteness. What defines the *Volk* is the decision under which it
stands and by which it is directed into the happening of the future. The
Volk is not a fact but the openness of the temporal in which the cast of the
factual is decided. Having rejected as unduly metaphysical all expositions
of the essence of a people based on notions of the body, the soul and the
spirit, Heidegger declares that the question "Who are we?" and its answer
"We are the people" remain incomprehensible unless the nature of decision is first clarified.[39] But who constitutes the "we" in this passage? The
"people" composed of Heidegger and the racially monitored student body
of 1934? To be sure, in this lecture course, Heidegger's fascination with
the new regime frequently appears undisguised. At one point, he suggests
that a museum is the fitting resting place for the airplane that had recently
conveyed Hitler to his meeting in Venice with Mussolini.[40] The suspicion
cannot therefore be dismissed that Heidegger is promoting a National Socialist conception of the *Volk*. And yet it would likewise be suspect to assert that nothing besides a National Socialist conception of the people is at
work in these lectures. Heidegger, who in 1934 discourses on the people of
the decision and commends service in the SA, retains, in the later lectures

on Hölderlin, the same definition of the people and yet employs it polemically against the existing populism. It is as though National Socialism had
revealed itself as a feeble makeshift for Hölderlin.

The essence of Heidegger's *Volk* is its decision. The *Volk* cannot take
itself for granted but must rally itself for the decision under which it stands
and learn that which is its own. That a given people should be confronted
with its essence as with something alien is a paradox from which Hölderlin does not shrink and upon which he insists in the first letter to Böhlendorff. It is the same paradox that Freud in 1919 and Heidegger in 1927 will
discuss as "the uncanny." Since the passage in question in *Being and Time*
reads implicitly as a critique of the Freudian position it nonetheless in several aspects resembles, it is perhaps worthwhile to place Freud's text openly
beside Heidegger's. Doing so will also enable us to give closer attention
to Heidegger's notion of the ownmost (*das Eigene*). That which is ownmost
to Dasein, that which is its essence as an exception to classical ontology, is
that which it is the mission of the *Volk* to understand.

Meticulously determining the domain of "the uncanny" (*das Un-
heimliche*), Freud begins his text of that title:

The German word "*unheimlich*" is obviously the opposite of "*heimlich*" [homely],
"*heimisch*" [native]—the opposite of what is familiar; and we are tempted to con-
clude that what is "uncanny" is frightening precisely because it is *not* known and
familiar. Naturally not everything that is new and unfamiliar is frightening, however; the relation is not capable of inversion. We can only say that what is novel
can easily become frightening and uncanny; some new things are frightening but
not by any means all. Something has to be added to what is novel and unfamiliar
in order to make it uncanny.[41]

Having urged that what is not the one is not necessarily the other, Freud
then queries whether the opposites themselves are exclusive. After quoting
Jacob and Wilhelm Grimm on the connotations of *heimlich* as that which
is disguised and perilous, private and hence mysterious, he continues:
"Thus *heimlich* is a word the meaning of which develops in the direction
of ambivalence, until it finally coincides with its opposite, *unheimlich*. *Unheimlich* is in some way or other a sub-species of *heimlich*."[42] Freud thereupon allows a usage of the word "uncanny" to illuminate this relation:

It often happens that neurotic men declare that they feel there is something uncanny about the female genital organs. This *unheimlich* place, however, is the en-
trance to the former *Heim* [home] of all human beings, to the place where each
one of us lived once upon a time and in the beginning. . . . In this case too, then,

the *unheimlich* is what was once *heimisch*, familiar; the prefix "*un*" [un] is the token of repression.[43]

The origin has become something alien as a consequence of repression.

§40 of *Being and Time* will speak similarly of the uncanny as the origin that has become alien and disquieting, but there the agent of repression is not so much Oedipus as classical ontology. In the exposition of *Angst* (Macquarrie and Robinson's "anxiety"), Heidegger describes the uncanny: "Anxiety pulls Dasein back from its falling-away emergence in the 'world'. Everyday familiarity collapses. Dasein is isolated, but isolated *as* Being-in-the world. Being-in enters into the existential 'mode' of the '*not-at-home*'. Nothing else is meant by our talk about 'uncanniness'."[44] The world from which anxiety withdraws Dasein, and for which Heidegger employs ironizing quotation marks, is the worldliness of chatter and curiosity. Dasein is thrown back upon itself in the uncanny and, in being thrown back upon itself, it is bereft of its familiarity with its environment. And yet it is world, now without quotation marks, that suddenly emerges from under the instrumentalization by which Dasein falls away from itself in falling toward the cosmopolitan realm of its inauthenticity. The world that emerges is Dasein's Being-in-the-world even as Dasein suffers on account of its intense strangeness: "*That in the face of which one has anxiety* [das Wovor der Angst] *is Being-in-the-world as such*."[45] Dasein abruptly finds itself both within the world and not at home. Heidegger stresses: "*From an existential-ontological point of view, the 'not-at-home' must be conceived as the more primordial phenomenon*."[46] In the being-outside-of-itself of anxiety, Dasein experiences the truth of its originary transcendence.

Elaborating on this more originary phenomenon as it manifests itself in anxiety, Heidegger writes: "That in the face of which one is anxious is completely indefinite. Not only does this indefiniteness leave factically undecided which entity within-the-world is threatening us, but it also tells us that entities within-the-world are not 'relevant' at all. Nothing which is ready-to-hand or present-at-hand within the world functions as that in the face of which anxiety is anxious."[47] Through anxiety the hegemony of the ontic is challenged. Something else, something that exists besides reification and that is thus "nothing," makes itself felt.

Like Freud, Heidegger permits himself an elucidatory example: "Anxiety can arise in the most innocuous Situations. Nor does it have any need for darkness, in which it is commonly easier for one to feel uncanny. In the dark there is emphatically 'nothing' to see, though the very world itself is *still* 'there', and 'there' *more obtrusively.*"[48] The night is not nothing, but in the dark Dasein no longer sees itself surrounded by the objects of its everyday existence. It becomes disoriented, and so long as it sets about orientating itself, it is still disoriented. Orientation, as the experience of the uncanniness of Being-in-the-world, becomes an issue for Dasein. Although it otherwise neglects the uncanniness of Being-in-the-world, in its dread before nothingness, Dasein is unable to reorient itself in its everyday environment by disorienting itself in its understanding of its own Being. Strictly speaking, Dasein never reorients itself in the everyday—its reorientation in the everyday is not the culmination of the process of orientation as the understanding of Dasein's Being-in-the-world but rather its abandonment. Orientation as such, because it brings into play the undecidability of Dasein's Being-in-the-world, is always a disorientation. Dasein is no longer and not yet at home in the everyday, and it cannot make itself at home. No longer confronted with beings, Dasein finds itself in the uncanny before the Nothing. It exists authentically in orientation and the uncanniness that it encounters in its vicinity is its own Being-in-the-world. In anxiety, Dasein experiences the origin that is the alienation of Being from the "world."

The proper homeland of Dasein is its disorientation in the ontic and not any object to which its genesis could be attributed. *Heimat*, which is defined by originarity, acquires, with Heidegger's exposition of the "not-at-home" as the more primordial phenomenon, a sense at odds with its conventional signification. Heidegger's *Heimat* is proximal to the extent that it is uncanny. It is uncannily familiar, but not because it recalls something that momentarily cannot be specified. What is at once familiar and unsettling in the "not-at-home" is Dasein's own Being. Heidegger does not follow Freud in providing an ontic answer to anxiety. The homeland of Dasein's originarity pushes itself to the fore in anxiety by its proximity to the being that Dasein itself is: it is that which is nearest in an essential sense. This nearness, in its metaphysical unthinkability, is nowhere: "That which threatens cannot bring itself close from a definite direction within what is close by; it is already 'there' [*da*], and yet nowhere; it is so close that it is oppressive and stifles one's breath, and yet it is nowhere."[49] In anxiety the *Da* itself of Dasein slips out of reach. Anxiety comes not from anything that is close by, but from the insuperable nearness of the *Da* as it suddenly shatters the faith in the manipulability of what it otherwise allows to appear present-at-hand. The *Da* of Dasein is in anxiety nowhere because it disrupts the familiar contexts in relation to which it could be recognizably somewhere in particular.

In "The Origin of the Work of Art," in an apothegm reminiscent of Heraclitus, Heidegger again addresses the uncanny nature of the proximal: "The familiar is ultimately not familiar [*geheuer*]; it is monstrous [*un-geheuer*]."[50] The becoming-monstrous of the familiar is its becoming-world. The homeland is always, and by definition, monstrous. As an essential possibility of the everyday, *Heimat* is not threatened but threatening. It is not an object whose threat is incidental to its essence; it is the threatening itself as it bears down upon Dasein before it is obscured by being explained with reference to a given ontic cause. *Angst* before the nothingness of Being is the mode of dwelling in the fatherland.[51] Can it be said then that for Heidegger, in some sense, it was the victims of the National Socialist terror still living uncertainly within the Fatherland who were its "proper" inhabitants? Here the legitimacy of a claim to the title of inhabitant of the Fatherland demands of the claimant an inability to make of the title a prerogative. To dwell truly in the Fatherland is to dwell in the consternation of the undecidability of Being. In dread the originarity that is definitive of any notion of *Heimat* is experienced in its most radical cast as the being-beside-oneself of ecstatic Being.

Heidegger differs from Freud through a complicity with the uncanny. He refuses any explanation of the phenomenon whereby the rupture it effects in the everyday's character of self-evidence might be made good through its reification. For Heidegger, the uncanny does not admit of resolution into an object. That Freud's maternal body has been removed from the scene leads Luce Irigaray to criticize Heidegger for perpetuating repression, "the reduction to nothing of that whence, matter-flesh, he proceeds."[52] But in what manner could repression *not* be perpetuated? Certainly, Heidegger's theorization of *Angst*, to the extent that it interprets it as a mode of authentic Dasein, prizes the return of the repressed in its unavowable shape as ". . ." and thus maintains repression. And yet, in naming this ". . ." as the maternal body, Irigaray has recourse to an object, and hence to the recognizability instituted by metaphysics, in order to repress the challenge to the hegemony of the ontic that Heidegger seeks to hear in the silence of the uncanny.[53]

Although Heidegger's text is later than Freud's, it says less, because it wishes to think the uncanny as such. A decipherment of the uncanny, a treatment that solves its "riddle" clarifies only by obscuring the essence of the phenomenon. As the uncanny ceases to be uncanny once it has been

explained and the explanation accepted, Freud's explanation of the uncanny is entailed by a curative practice dedicating itself to the preservation
of Dasein in its reification: Dasein is to be safeguarded in its domesticity
among beings. Heidegger does not propose an "explanation" of the uncanny. In naming the Fatherland as Being and in discussing anxiety as the
experience of the originarity of Being-in-the-world, he does not place the
Fatherland in simple rivalry with Freud's maternal body. The Fatherland
that is defined as Being, and thus by inference as Nothing, cannot be encountered within metaphysics as an object. Its repression cannot be over-
turned as it cannot stand in the light of presence as a distinct entity. The
Fatherland is too near to acquire substance and, for that reason, it can neither be defended nor extended.

In his commentary on Hölderlin's poem "Heimkunft," anticipating
the meditations on nearness from the 1949 lectures in Bremen, Heidegger
thus writes:

The nearness that now prevails lets what is near be near, and yet at the same time
lets it remain what is sought, and thus not near. We usually understand nearness as the smallest possible measurement of the distance between two places.
Now, on the contrary, the essence of nearness appears to be that it brings near that
which is near, yet keeping it at a distance. This nearness to the origin is a mystery
[*Geheimnis*].[54]

Nearness to the origin is essentially a secret (*Geheimnis*) because there cannot come a time in which it is divulged. The secretiveness of this nearness
derives from the reserve with which the origin stands toward the light
of presence. The origin that is not a secret, that exhibits itself in the public spectacle of a nationalistic uprising is never originary in Heidegger's
sense. What is originary in the National Socialist *Heimat* is neither the *Blut
und Boden* of the Aryan "type" nor the *Lebensraum* of German monopoly
capitalism—what is originary in this *Heimat* is the dread experienced by
the victims of this nationalistic uprising. The Fatherland was the secret
(*Geheimnis*) that the victims of National Socialism could not but keep to
themselves.

It is thus with an idiosyncratic patriotism that Heidegger in *Being and
Time* is on the alert for uprisings of the uncanny: "This uncanniness pursues Dasein constantly, and is a threat to its everyday lostness in the 'they',
though not explicitly."[55] Dasein is shadowed by the experience of its own
originarity, of the *Heimat* that is its Being-in-the-world. Uncanniness constantly threatens to recover Dasein from the worldless cosmopolitanism of

the "they." When anxiety overtakes Dasein, it disorients it, disrupting the impoverished frame of reference by which Dasein orients itself in the way of Being of the "they." In the grip of anxiety, Dasein is no longer and not yet able to differentiate between its left and right sides and is thus unable to orient itself in the flattened world of Kantian cosmopolitanism. In anxiety, world recovers its existential thickness, disturbing even the stability of the environment by means of which Heidegger is able to advance directedness within a world as the truth of the Kantian ability to differentiate left and right. Dasein is thrown back on itself *as* transcendence. And orienting itself in the more primordial phenomenon of the "not-at-home," Dasein does *not* come to itself as the pure ego of Hegelian negativity.[56] It does not get the better of fear and compose its ontological apology for the metaphysics of subjectity. Dasein remains a being-outside-of-itself in the essential "not-at-home" of its *Heimat.* The home of Dasein eludes it as a stable possession and must elude it in order to remain the Nothing. Dasein is born from nothingness in the sense that any other derivation would amount to its reification, just as it lives in nothingness as the uncanniness of its orientation in Being-in-the-world.

World, revealing itself in the Nothing, does *not* reveal itself. Even in the overwhelming experience of the uncanny, it continues to be a secret (*Geheimnis*). Dasein is able to say neither where it comes from nor where it is without reifying the Nothing. The home of Dasein is a secret because it is too private (*heimlich*) to ecstatic temporality for it to assume the cast of a repeatable entity. To put it differently, it is the untransmittable that, for Heidegger, constitutes the *Heimat* of Dasein, since transmission is the substance of the "they," of the everyone that is everywhere. The strangeness of the *Heimat* is the impenetrable idiocy of time.

Heidegger's provincialism, notwithstanding its conventionality and occasional kitschiness, never lies far removed from the question of an understanding of originary temporality. *Heimat*, for Heidegger, is defined by the unrepeatability of the originary. The following passage on dialect from "Language and Homeland" thus needs to be read for its polemic against the understanding of language as the vehicle for the transmission of information:

The essence of language has its roots in dialect. If dialect is the mother's language, the homeliness of the home, the homeland has its roots in it as well. Dialect is not only the mother's language but, at the same time and still more so, the mother of language. Yet at the present hour, as we heed what has just been said, I refer to the world-historical hour of our age, the inherited and traditional relations between language, mother tongue, dialect, and homeland are already out of joint. Humanity appears to be losing the language fatefully allotted to it in each age, becoming in this sense speechless, although never in human memory has the globe been so uninterruptedly encircled by chatter. Humanity appears to be becoming homeless, so that the pronouncement holds good that Nietzsche in 1884 delivered to the future in a poem with the title "Ohne Heimat":

> *The ravens shriek*
> *And in whirring flight head toward the city:*
> *—soon it will snow,*
> *Woe to him who does not have a homeland.*[57]

Dialect, and with it language as a whole, retreats before universal exchange and its necessary deracination from the world founded by language. The superiority of a dialect is that it does not erase its world, that it knows how to keep secrets. A dialect is, as it were, a secret to the highest degree because it can never be divulged: it has no other content apart from its secretiveness. A dialect says the incomprehensibility of world. For Heidegger, a universal language is anathema: "Language in the singular does not exist. To put this more cautiously: language in the sense of a universally comprehensible and uniquely binding world-language does not *yet* exist, even though there are many indications that it is readying itself for a dominance that only to a small degree rests on human planning and intrigues."[58]

What a dialect has to say is less important than the manner in which it says it, *in which it does not say it*. The content of an utterance in dialect is its point of weakness regarding a universally comprehensible language, since it is the content that admits of transmission and that is consequently the promise of a global language. The dialect in its secrecy stands opposed to reification and in place of an extralingual object, it harbors *Heimat* as the originary idiocy of Dasein. Dialect is dialect only if it is uncanny, if, by failing to transmit something intact into another dialect, discourse, or language, it thereby communicates the Nothing. In this failure that is, properly speaking, its merit, dialect discloses itself as originary: it is the language of originary temporality. The essential provincialism of Dasein rests on its utmost exposure to nothingness. In not reaching beyond its world, dialect reaches beyond the limits of classical ontology.

That there might be something other than simple bigotry in Heidegger's provincialism is never conceded by Theodor Adorno, who in his essay devoted to Hölderlin, "Parataxis," writes: "Hardly anywhere did Höl-

derlin prove his posthumous champion more wrong than in his relationship to what is foreign. Hölderlin's relationship to it is a constant irritation
for Heidegger. For Heidegger, the love of a foreign woman requires an
apology. She is 'the one who at the same time makes us think about our native land.'"[59] Heidegger's provincialism here becomes a disavowal of the
exotic. But is such an interpretation the only one possible? Does the exotic
suggest that which is native merely as its opposite? In order to accuse Heidegger of a misinterpretation of the letter to Böhlendorff, Adorno passes
over the interplay between the exotic and the national, between what is assigned (*Aufgegebenes*) and what is consigned (*Mitgegebenes*) in Hölderlin's
and Heidegger's texts and arrives at the conclusion: "The exiled Hölderlin,
who said in the same letter to Böhlendorff that he wished himself away in
Tahiti, is made into a trustworthy German living abroad."[60]

On the basis of the published archival material, it can be argued that
Heidegger's nationalism is not as straightforward as Adorno pretends. In
his 1944 lecture notes *Einleitung in die Philosophie: Dichten und Denken*
(Introduction to Philosophy: Poetry and Thinking), Heidegger again comments upon Nietzsche's poem "Ohne Heimat" (or, as it is given in the critical edition, "Abschied") *and* its counterpart, "Antwort." The second poem,
clarifying the first, reads:

> *God have mercy!*
> *He thinks I was longing*
> *For German warmth,*
> *For the stifling joys of German domesticity!*
>
> *My friend, that which here*
> *Hampers me and holds me back is your understanding,*
> *Compassion for you!*
> *Compassion for German wrong-headedness!*[61]

For neither Nietzsche nor Heidegger is the homeland an object of conventional nostalgia. As Heidegger writes in his commentary—and as Hölderlin writes to Böhlendorff—it is something that must be won: "In the complementary poems 'Ohne Heimat' and 'Antwort,' there speaks this doubly
directed compassion that suffers back and forth between the incapacity of
the former homeland and the heights of the future homeland."[62] The incapacity of Bismarck's and of Hitler's Germany follows from its homelessness. This helplessness is belied neither by military victories nor by in-
creases in production, because such "successes" reveal themselves precisely
as a flight from nothingness to the realm of reification and calculation. Fly-

ing from nothingness, imperialism flies from the question of world, from the question of Being-in-the-world that can be raised only in a challenge to the hegemony of the ontic and that alone contests homelessness.

Hölderlin's poetry, by contrast, stands fast within the uncanniness that he expounds as the tragic caesura. In a letter to Erhart Kästner, Heidegger writes: "What does Hölderlin's poetry say? Its word is: the Holy. It speaks of the flight of the gods. It says that the fled gods spare us. Until we are capable and of a mind to dwell in their vicinity. This place is that which is unique to the homeland." [63] What characterizes the homeland is the nearness of the gods. The absence of the gods is equivalent to the absence of the homeland. The gods who have fled before onto-theology have borne the homeland with them as the nothingness that is the Un-thought of metaphysics: what metaphysics cannot think constitutes the specificity of the homeland. It is the homeland as such that metaphysics cannot think in its rush toward the universal, in its pursuit of the reification that is the precondition of exchange.

Standing in the caesura between the "no-longer" and the "not-yet" of the gods, Hölderlin says the homeland that is missing. He does not think so much the challenge to the hegemony of the ontic as the absence of this challenge. On account of the absence of this challenge, it cannot be said that we have any understanding as yet either of nothingness or of *Heimat*. Hölderlin, more than any other poet, is the founder of German Being because he experiences, more than any other, the national as a question *against* rather than *of* metaphysics. Hölderlin founds German Being as a question that is nonetheless still unheard. That is to say, he founds the *possibility* of a people that would be, in the true sense, the German *Volk*.

Insofar as Hölderlin can found only the possibility of a people, it can be said that, in one respect, there has never been a people. A fragment preserved in the Homburg folio notebook, and quoted earlier, suggests that the Greeks were not for themselves a people:

> *do you think*
> *It will proceed*
> *Along the course of old? Namely they wanted to found*
> *A realm of art. But thereby*
> *The national was neglected*
> *By them and pitifully*
> *Greece, the fairest of all, was destroyed.*
> *Now presumably matters*
> *Stand otherwise.*

In wanting to found a realm of art, the Greeks neglected, not the nation, but the national and thereby initiated their decline. Hölderlin's choice of the substantive *das Vaterländische* (here translated as "the national") works against any interpretation that here the Greeks are being reproached with impracticality. Certainly, "the national" is distinguished from the realm of art, yet "the national" cannot be taken to refer to the defenses of a country, to the maintenance of its economy and public order. These matters are to varying degrees of concern in every nation and, in themselves, do not make the nation national. In their neglect of the national, the Greeks neglected that which was specific to them. It is by means of this neglect that they fell into decline. It was the beautiful that they put in place of the national. As a result and contrary to traditional accounts, Greek decline is not subsequent to the age of outstanding achievements in Greek art: the Greeks created works of art precisely in falling away from themselves as a people.[64] The inauthenticity of Greece is its beauty, and it is this beauty, rather than any foreign invasion, that signals and consummates its decline. As the most beautiful, Greece sentenced itself to decline because it neglected the specificity and privacy of world in its unpresentability for the sake of the universality and presence of art. The world of the Greeks disappears in its surrender to the recognizability of the public sphere. Greece manifested itself as the realm of art and thereby fell away from the Nothing of its world. That which was specific to the Greeks, and thus necessarily private, could not be made present in the work of art without becoming an item of exchange in the traffic of peoples. Art reveals too much — it tears too much from the native earth.[65] Having transformed themselves into the people of art, the Greeks no longer possessed a homeland and, in complicity with their unacknowledged diaspora, they even forgot what it was not to be homeless.

Hölderlin is not the only artist of his age who brings to the *querelle des anciens et des modernes*, a suspicion of art itself. In the *Aesthetics*, Hegel, from the vantage point of his thinking, has to denounce the nonproductive artist of Romanticism: "For what is supreme and most excellent is not, as may be supposed, the inexpressible — for if so the poet would be still far deeper than his work discloses. On the contrary, his works are the best part and the truth of the artist; what he is [in his works], that he *is*; but what remains buried in his heart, that *is* he not."[66] For Hegel, production is existence. Greece exists in having produced itself. For Hölderlin, a people that does not wish to produce, that does not want to be recognized, which is to say, that does want to be recognized as Greek, is the people that finds itself, as it were, in not existing. Not neglecting its specificity, not destroying itself through art, this people is an invisible people, a people that *is* as missing—an uncanny people.

Hölderlin, in the letter to Böhlendorff, does not speak of national arts. Art, for Hölderlin, is essentially anational. The distinct gifts of the Greeks and the Hesperians do not hinder them from approaching a common art; instead, these gifts establish the differing tasks by whose execution the goal is to be attained. Art draws the peoples together. Hölderlin's essay "On the Operations of the Poetic Spirit" rejects one-sided definitions of the work of art "in favor of the coordination of those operations as not merely primordial simplicity of the heart and of life where man feels himself uninhibitedly as in a restricted infinity, nor merely attained simplicity of the spirit where that very sensation which is purified to a pure [and] formal mood receives the entire infinity of life, (and is ideal), but which is instead spirit reanimated by the infinite life, not chance, not ideal, but is accomplished work and creation."[67]

One of the most deeply classical aspects of Hölderlin's poetry is this emphasis on reconciliation. The bridal feasts shared by gods and humans at the center of many of the hymns depict, at the very least, the celebration of that peace among the nations which is promised by art.

And yet, in the "Remarks on 'Oedipus,'" the bridal feast becomes the monstrous violence at the heart of tragedy.[68] Here reconciliation loses its innocence but remains art's dominant imperative. Hölderlin, notwithstanding his increasing sense of the magnitude of the task of reconciliation, is unable to conceive of an art that does not aspire to reconciliation, and he thus figures within eighteenth-century aesthetics as its impossibility. The notion of the beautiful that in Kant's *Critique of Judgment* aligns itself in part with a universal accord of the respective judgments and that in Schiller's "On the Aesthetic Education of Man" is defined by the reconciliation of sense and intellect receives an extraordinary reformulation in Hölderlin's *Hyperion*. There the ἕν διαφέρον ἑαυτῷ ("The One differing in itself") of Heraclitus is interpreted in terms of beauty, since the beautiful has become the community of beings as a whole.[69] It is not that Hölderlin (and with him the eighteenth century) does not question whether art's concern is with the beautiful. He does, but it is for the sake of the beautiful that art first assumes its importance.

Greece, as the most beautiful, cannot but neglect the national since, as the most beautiful, it is the site of reconciliation and thus also the most cosmopolitan. Hölderlin writes in the fragment from the Homburg folio notebook quoted earlier:

> *Now presumably matters*
> *Stand otherwise.*

The Greek neglect of the national is no longer fitting. Something other than art is required, because the unity effected in the beautiful had been revealed as pernicious. Greece, the most beautiful, fell into ruin. That which is now required as other than art is required on the grounds of that which in it is not beautiful. This negative quality is not ugliness, but the irreconcilable, since the beauty of a work of art is its harmoniousness. And this harmoniousness, as the decline of Greece demonstrates, was never more than ostensible. Art reconciled only by suppressing the intractable and the failure of its reconciliation was the failure of Greece.

Hölderlin confesses to Böhlendorff that the study of Greek art has instilled in him a desire for self-assertion: "I have labored long over this and know by now that, with the exception of what must be the highest for the Greeks and for us—namely, the living relationship and destiny—we must not share anything identical with them." "We" must differ from the Greeks, so that the living mediation and destiny, shared with them as the highest, might not lack that resistance from which the vitality of mediation and destiny issues. The difference, as Hölderlin's letter to Böhlendorff makes clear, is not to be found in the realm of art where the inhabitants of Greece and of Hesperia converge, if by separate paths. Hölderlin is not able to say where the difference would lie and it is this inability that maintains the force of the imperative. The visible failure of Greek art is precisely its visibility, the ease with which it occupies the public sphere and abandons the secrecy of the intimate and the originary: the imperative to differ from the Greeks is the call of the uncanny.

Hölderlin asks of himself the impossible. Witnessing the fall of Greece through art, he nonetheless does not renounce poetry. What Hölderlin asks of himself is a differentiation from the Greeks that does not depart from their realm. Poetry is to retain the concreteness of the reified and yet it is to heed the uncanny of the national. The beauty of such a poetry is to lie in its reconciliation: it would, in effect, be the poetry of the ontological difference, reconciling beings and Being without suppression. Being, which announces itself in the uncanny as the "nothingness" of world, would here be heard even in the reification by which it has otherwise concealed itself. Such a poetry, in which the work of art's question against metaphysics would no longer be misinterpreted, is as it were commanded by the age:

> *Now presumably matters*
> *Stand otherwise.*

The national, as the originarity that is forgotten in reification, no longer allows itself to be neglected, although why that should be so is not apparent from these verses.

If there is a neglect that Hölderlin admits and endeavors to rectify in his later poetry, it is a neglect of Christianity. Certainly, a poet will seem more national in a Christian country if his poetry addresses Christian themes, but nationality and Christianity are to be thought in a more demanding sense in Hölderlin's poetry. In the lecture course on the poem "Andenken," Heidegger suggests that the nationality and Christianity of the later poetry receive their sense only in the elaboration of the question of Greece: "The new relationship to Greece is not a turning away, but rather a more essential turning toward Greece and a pressing for a more originary confrontation, without of course seeking in Greece the origin and ground of the proper [*Grund des Eigenen*]." [70] It is in the quest for this origin and ground of the proper that nationality and Christianity open up in their abyssal character as the Un-thought of Greece. This search for the origin is, for Hölderlin, a poetic search.

Hölderlin's own experience is that he cannot be a Christian poet: poetry is in some way inimical to Christianity. "An die Madonna" contains the confession:

> *And many a song which to*
> *The Highest, the Father, I once was*
> *Disposed to sing, was lost*
> *To me, devoured by sadness.* [71]

"Der Einzige," with its wish to bring together Christ and the gods of Greece, is more expansive on the nature of this melancholy:

> *And now my soul*
> *Is full of sadness as though*
> *You Heavenly yourselves excitedly cried*
> *That if I serve one I*
> *Must lack the other.* [72]

The reconciliation for which Hölderlin sought has been withheld. He admits to Christ:

> *And yet a shame forbids me*
> *To associate with you*
> *The worldly men.*[73]

The gods of Greece are here presented as profane men among whose number Christ is never to be counted. The poem's final lines read therefore as an objection:

> *The poets, and those no less who*
> *Are spiritual, must be worldly.*[74]

Poetry, as that which fundamentally concerns itself with the beautiful, cannot submit to a failure of the reconciliation of the urbane and the spiritual. Christ can fill Hölderlin as a poet only with sadness. This sadness turns in the second version of "Der Einzige" to rage:

> *For since evil spirit*
> *Has taken possession of happy antiquity, unendingly*
> *Long now one power has prevailed, hostile to song, without resonance,*
> *That perishes in masses, the violence of the mind.*[75]

Antiquity has given way to a monotheism that, in its hostility to the urbane, declares itself the enemy of song. It is intractable and therefore refuses the beautiful. The Christianity that is suggested by these lines is too ascetic to be representative either of the German churches of Hölderlin's day or of the churches as a whole. What this violently recalcitrant Christianity represents is, instead, the ultimate task of poetry as reconciliation. Hölderlin's rage cannot therefore permit itself to terminate in a rejection. As that which is intractable to reconciliation with the urbane, as that which cannot be sung, as that which stands apart from all that is, Christianity here discloses itself as a challenge to the hegemony of the ontic. Poetry can no longer continue in the Greek manner, since with the sounding of this challenge in the Christian revelation the beautiful is only attained through a reconciliation still more inclusive than that undertaken by the Greeks. The ontic can no longer pretend to constitute the domain of the beautiful. The poet who now accomplishes the reconciliation of the beautiful will be the poet of poetry and, as such, this poet will be, according to Heidegger in *Hölderlins Hymnen "Germanien" und "Der Rhein,"* the poet of the Germans.

The reconciliation of Being with beings is the task of German poetry. A true reconciliation differs from a leveling compromise. The beauty of German poetry will not entail a neglect of the national; on the contrary, the beauty of German poetry will think Being as it is not even thought in the Judaic prohibition on images. The poet of the Germans, reconciling Being with beings, will think Being in the transcendence whereby it at once differs from beings and is contaminated with them. The Being of German poetry will be more originary and hence nearer to Dasein precisely because it will not hold itself back and configure itself as a privilege and as the determinate *Heimat* of the elect. Such a *Heimat*, in its absolute difference from the thingly, vitiates this very difference by the distinctness that it shares with the thingly. German poetry will say the Nothing more "clearly" than silence and nonproduction because it will say it in the undecidability of the decision between the work and silence. The poet of the Germans must heed the challenge of the Christian revelation and heed it all the more as he appears to betray it by his engagement with the sensuous—that is his agony and misfortune.

For Hegel, the Christian revelation likewise enacts a rupture within the classical world. Both Hegel and Hölderlin acknowledge the adverse conditions henceforth facing the production of a work of art. Yet whereas Hegel asserts that philosophy alone is able to achieve the reconciliation by which art was once defined, because in the modern age only philosophy can encompass the revealed negativity of Spirit, Hölderlin seeks a poetry that does not neglect the national, because it heeds its challenge to the hegemony of the ontic. Hegel and Hölderlin are thus at odds in their explanations of the decline of Greece. For Hegel, it was rather the Greeks' absolute immersion in the national to the exclusion of the dawning negativity that was responsible for their downfall:

Just as external and actual appearance was essential for the Greek spiritual art-form, so too the absolute spiritual destiny of man was accomplished in the phenomenal world as a real actuality [the state] with the substance and universality of which the individual demanded to be in harmony. This supreme end in Greece was the life of the state, the body of the citizens, and their ethical life and living patriotism. Beyond this interest there was none higher or truer.[76]

In Hegel's account, the exhibition of autonomous subjectivity in the person of Socrates places an intolerable strain on the reconciling powers within the Greek πόλις. The infinite and denationalized negativity of the self-reflective subject opens a fissure in the concrete life of Greek politics and Greek art. As the transcendental, this denationalized subject becomes the deterritorialized territory of the Christian faith as it is formulated in and as Hegel's philosophy. The rupture that Hölderlin and Heidegger explain in terms of the national appears, in Hegel's eyes, as the awakening of Spirit: the encounter with the Nothing becomes the liberation of the subject from all other beings, so that it might finally encounter itself.

Hölderlin does not see that the task in the postclassical age is the reconciliation that would encompass even the universal of absolute subjectivity. The fact that, for Hölderlin, even the Greeks neglected the national indicates that it is toward the specific that art must now turn in order to bring about the reconciliation by which he understands the beautiful. Art has always been too one-sidedly ontic to be beautiful. It has always been too much under the sway of the thing-concepts of classical ontology. Even as mimesis, it has always been too "present" to interrupt the particular's subsumption under the universal. The evil spirit in the hymn "Der Einzige" is the enemy of song, and its unitarity cannot be equated with the universal. Its singleness denotes its jealousy, not its universality. Hölderlin's Christianity, with its Judaic cast, confronts art with its limitations from below, setting against art's universality, not the sublation of the concrete notion, but the recalcitrance of the private.

As the enemy of song, the evil spirit that seized hold of antiquity harbors the possibility of thinking the national. In Book X of the *Confessions*, Saint Augustine invokes "Jerusalem the chaste, our only homeland."[77] More than any other province of the empire, Judaea staged the failure of the cosmopolitanism of the Roman peace. Neither the destruction of the Temple under Titus nor the enforced exile of the Jews under Hadrian sufficed to extinguish Jewish particularism, and even the later ordination of the Jewish people as bankers and intellectuals, as agents of circulation,[78] did not dispel the myth of their secretiveness. In many respects, Judaea was seen to constitute an exorbitant revolt against the commensurable. Christianity, inventing itself as the absolute secret, spread from Judaea to affront the classical world with a pure and internal barbarism. Its secret was simply its rejection of glory. When Jesus rejects the public realm in which the Pharisees performed their good deeds and preaches that in carrying out charitable acts, the left hand should not know what the right hand is doing,[79] he privileges secretiveness over that which stands in the light of presence. The people of the ear was to mark out its difference from the people of the eye. Christianity was an uprising of the concealed with respect also to language. Although the glossolalia of the Gnostics and early Christians occupied the space of language, it yet offered nothing that on account of the universality of its content could be translated. It said the Nothing—not the negativity of the Hegelian ego, but the nothingness of the asignifying. In glossolalia, the harmony of meaning and material, by which Hegel defines classical art, is not disrupted by the preponderant meaning of the Christian Logos. Only within an anachronistically theological interpretation of the early Church is it possible to imagine that the disgust felt by the classical world for Christianity and for Judaism can be explained as a pagan reaction to monotheism. What horrified the classical world was more the secretiveness, the privileging of the private and idiosyncratic (in short, that which was, for the classical world, the idiotic) over the public, the transmittable, the comprehensible and commensurable. Sensitive to this aversion, Saint Paul cautioned in the First Letter to the Corinthians against speaking in tongues, voicing his apprehension that outsiders might hold believers in contempt as mad.[80] Glossolalia is absolute dialect. In focusing his attention on dialect's inability to transmit information, Heidegger proposes an understanding of dialect reminiscent of the early Christian polemic against unconcealment.

Hölderlin's wish to be a Christian poet, expressed in "Der Einzige" and "An die Madonna," is flouted by Christianity's refusal to be reconciled with the light of presence in which the work of art stands. Hölderlin's wish is to be the poet of that which is unsayable within the limits of poetry laid down by the Greeks. Hölderlin's inability to be a national poet is his inability to be a Christian poet. It is the inability of poetry as such, rather than any inability peculiar to Hölderlin, because in both the national and the Christian, at least in Hölderlin's sense, poetry confronts that which is intractable to reification. For Hölderlin, the Fatherland is essentially Christian. It is Hölderlin's absolute ambition as a poet, not any personal *Heimweh*, that determines the national as an object of aspiration. Hölderlin aspires to the Fatherland because he wants more than has ever been wanted. In the lecture course *Heraklitus*, Heidegger draws attention to this aspect of Hölderlin as it is embodied in the name and figure of the eponymous hero of his novel: "Ὑπερίων is the name of the one who goes further than the others, even to that which for 'rational human beings' always goes 'too far.'"[81] For both Hölderlin as a poet and for Heidegger as a thinker, Greece is the point of departure—the Fatherland lies elsewhere as its unfamiliar complement.

Yet in a fragment Hölderlin writes:

About the Highest I will not speak.
But, like the laurel, forbidden fruit
Your country is, above all. To be tasted last
By any man,[82]

The national neglected by the Greeks is here for Hölderlin just as much forbidden fruit as the laurels that the Greeks did not neglect. Heidegger quotes this fragment at the beginning of his lectures *Hölderlins Hymnen "Germanien" und "Der Rhein"* and continues:

The Fatherland, our Fatherland Germania—forbidden to the utmost, withdrawn from the hurry of the everyday and the blare of commotion. The highest and thus the hardest, the last because fundamentally the first—the concealed origin. Thereby we have already said what our beginning with "Germania" does not mean. It is not a question of offering something amenable and useful for daily requirements, thereby securing testimonials for the lecture series so that the pernicious opinion could arise that we are wanting to provide Hölderlin with a cheap timeliness. We do not want to bring Hölderlin into accordance with our time, rather the very opposite: we want to bring ourselves, as well as those to come, under the poet's measure.[83]

Heidegger does not want Hölderlin to appear timely in the winter semester of 1934–35. He does not want Hölderlin's patriotism to appear to anticipate National Socialism. That which makes Hölderlin seem untimely —the prohibition upon the Fatherland—is, for Heidegger, not something that can be held against Hölderlin, since it is Heidegger's age that is out of step. The Fatherland must be prohibited in order to remain the Fatherland: in 1934–35, its time has not yet come. Hölderlin is, for Heidegger, the poet of the no-longer of the Greeks and the not-yet of the Fatherland. He is the poet of the task of the reconciliation of the cosmopolitan with the national, but he is not the poet of the reconciliation itself. For Hölderlin, both the laurels of the public realm and the Fatherland of the secret are forbidden, since he is the poet for whom the necessity of their reconciliation is not to be forgotten through an absorption in the one to the neglect of the other. Hölderlin's poetry, therefore, is not strictly beautiful, even though it records the promise of the greatest beauty. It is neither national nor transnational. Instead, it promises a nationalism more deeply rooted than any chauvinism and a reconciliation more inclusive than any cosmopolitanism.

The impossibility at the heart of Hölderlin's poetry is its position within the cleft between the ontic and the ontological, between Greece and

Judaea. This cleft constitutes the impossibility of the West. It is the "and" in the title of Shestov's *Athens and Jerusalem*, which Shestov himself refused to countenance, preferring a mutually exclusive and global disjunction.[84] (Shestov does not want to know anything of that which Derrida calls the cleft's "hypocrisy.")[85] For Hölderlin, as a poet, there is no choice but to remain within the cleft and to attempt the reconciliation of the thingly and the iconoclastic. If it is ever to be beautiful, poetry has to disorient itself within its Greek positivity, to open *within itself* a distance from the ontic. It must set out for that Hesperia which as the undecidable other of Greece is the Dis-orient, the uncanny orientation of Dasein within the Nothing and the Un-thought of classical ontology. Hesperia, or that which Heidegger names as the Fatherland, is Being. Inasmuch as Greece could thus never have been a Fatherland, even for the Greeks, Klopstock's question "Is Achaea the Teutons' Fatherland?" becomes senseless.[86]

The *Geschlecht* of the Poem

From its cursory employment in *Being and Time*, the word "*Volk*" flares up to a dominance in Heidegger's thinking in the 1930s and early 1940s that was not subsequently sustained. An exception to the apparent ban imposed on "*Volk*"—which is also not an exception—lies in the polysemy of "*Geschlecht*" (species, ethnic group, gender, family, stock, generation, etc.). In the 1952 essay on Georg Trakl, "Language in the Poem," Heidegger addresses the polysemy of "*Geschlecht*" as an occasion for the question of Being. Has the German *Volk* been relieved of its ontological mission? Given that, for Heidegger, the essence of the *Volk* was its mission, the later text cannot be interpreted as either relieving the *Volk* of its mission (as though it were but one of its properties) or replacing it with the *Geschlecht*. That which in 1952 is named *Geschlecht* is better understood as a clarification of that which had previously been named *Volk*. The clarification lies in an emphasis—characteristic of late Heidegger—on the role of difference in the question of Being.

What is important to note is that *Geschlecht* is not simply a cynical substitute for *Volk*. In his essay on Trakl, Heidegger is not transcribing the reflections on Germania and the *Volk* from his lectures on Hölderlin with an eye to a public wary of the National Socialist lexicon. If Heidegger speaks of the West (*das Abendland*) and no longer of Germany, he could hardly expect to evade the charge of chauvinism by a mere expansion of borders. The West for Heidegger in 1952 is no more a determinate territorial entity than the Germania of the lectures on Hölderlin. Having refused to accommodate his understanding of Germania to the times, Heidegger is unlikely to have considered his notion of *Heimat* as baggage to be jettisoned. The change in terms has a philosophical motivation. Among the questions with which he opens his 1946 text on Anaximander, and in which Arendt discerns a new "mood" in response to the so-called Year Zero, Heidegger asks if the West has ever existed. The West, as the land of evening (*das Abendland*), perhaps only first becomes a possibility in the historical darkening of the world. Unlike Germania, *das Abendland* bears in its name the darkness of that which, not pulling back from the night of nihilism, is in a position to think it through to its non-nihilistic essence. The mission of the West, of that which is to be the West, is the mission of that which Heidegger once called the *Volk*.

The West is the land of evening, of lateness and decay: it is the *Heimat* that Trakl calls neither Germany nor Austria. In the essay on Trakl, Heidegger rethinks the originary in terms of lateness and dissolution. One could accordingly argue that the *Volk*, notwithstanding its alignment in Heidegger's thinking with *Mitsein* and transcendence, is too haunted by its unitary and exclusionist character in German nationalism to continue as the agent or, more precisely, the site of the question of Being. Grounded in the reproach that the Cartesian subject is not ecstatic and thus unable to understand Being as other than presence, Heidegger's political engagement in 1933 is the assigning of the task of metaphysics to the Being-with-one-another by which he defines the German people. In 1952, the being that is still more ecstatic than the *Volk*, still more dissolute and hence more auspicious for the question of Being is the riven being of the *Geschlecht*: the *Geschlecht* is a multiplicity.

This polysemy of "*Geschlecht*", according to Heidegger, is not external to the individual significations of the word: "Our language names the human essence shaped from a single blow [*Schlag*] and misshapen [*verschlagen*] in this blow the '*Geschlecht*.' The word signifies the human species [*Menschengeschlecht*] in the sense of humanity, as well as *Geschlechter* in the plural sense of tribes, houses and families, all of these stamped again in the twoness of the *Geschlechter*." [1] A *Geschlecht* can never be integral, because it is, by definition, stamped with a twoness. [2] The people that, for Heidegger in 1952, survives in *Geschlecht* survives only in being given up to division:

With what has this *Geschlecht* been struck, that is, cursed? Curse in Greek is πληγή, our word "*Schlag*" [blow]. The curse of the decaying *Geschlecht* consists therein, that this old *Geschlecht* has been struck apart into the discord of *Geschlechter*. Out of discord each *Geschlecht* strives into the unleashed uproar of the isolated and sheer wildness of wild game. Not twoness as such, but rather the discord is the curse. Out of the uproar of blind wildness, it carries the *Geschlecht* into strife, where it is struck with untrammeled isolation. Thus cleft and shattered, the "decayed *Geschlecht*" can on its own no longer find its proper cast. The proper cast lies only with that *Geschlecht* whose twoness leaves discord behind and wanders ahead into the gentleness of a simple twofold, namely, is strange and thus follows the stranger.[3]

The "decayed *Geschlecht*" does not find its proper cast in being made whole. The *Geschlecht* is cursed, not in being divided, but rather in the aggravation of its division to the point of discord. Falling upon a community as upon the other senses of *Geschlecht*, the proper cast of *Geschlecht* returns it to its essential, yet seemingly paradoxical, solidarity in the loneliness of its members. The *Geschlecht* cannot come to its twofold self *within* the narrow and paranoiacally regulated unity of National Socialism, because such a unity never encompasses *Geschlecht* in its fragmentary whole and thus merely testifies to discord. The *Geschlecht* finds its "proper" cast in the decay and opening up of a unity such as Hitler's *Volk*.

As a letter from 1938 might be taken to suggest, National Socialism prompted in Heidegger an attachment to loneliness: "I believe that an age of loneliness must break over the world if it is once more to draw breath for action that restores to things their essential force."[4] Arguably, the loneliness of which Heidegger is speaking is not the loneliness of the isolation that afflicts the *Geschlecht* in its open discord. In his 1937 lecture course on Nietzsche's doctrine of the Eternal Return, Heidegger writes of loneliness:

In this loneliest loneliness, there is nothing of isolation as separation. On the contrary, it is that isolation which we have to understand as the bringing about of authenticity [*Vereigentlichung*] where human beings, each in his or her self, become peculiar [*eigen*] to themselves. The self, authenticity, is not the "I" but rather that *Da*-Sein in which the relation of the I to the Thou and of the I to the We and the We to the You is grounded.[5]

That which is most proper to the self and that on which we are thrown back in loneliness is the openness and mediation of the site of Dasein. Loneliness is the truth of Being-with-Others, because it first raises the question of who the Others are. The loneliness that appears when the *Geschlecht* is frozen into reactive and antagonistic determinations bears scant resemblance to the loneliness of the relation to the essential. Heidegger speaks of an age of loneliness that is to break over the entire world. Accordingly, he does not situate the loneliness of the relation to the essential in the idiosyncrasy of a numerical minority. The essential is itself the element of loneliness. In its originarity and hence in its difference from the positive, the essential offers nothing against which a being could determine and recompose itself. Once it has set out on the path to this other loneliness and the curativeness of the indeterminacy of the twofold, it is doubtful—as Trakl was well aware—that the *Geschlecht* can remain recognizably human.

But what does it mean in any case to be human? Heidegger's essay on Trakl often recalls his earlier expositions. Yet that which elsewhere appears peremptory and conventional becomes unsettling in the text on Trakl. Heidegger sets himself the task of thinking through Trakl's notion of humanity: "The *Geschlecht* of humanity's 'decayed form' is what the poet calls the 'decaying' *Geschlecht*." [6] Trakl's humanity decays as *Geschlecht*. If it is in the grips of decomposition, if it is not itself, it may then, Heidegger argues, be something else. After having for decades drawn a distinction between the animal and the human, Heidegger in 1952 problematizes the distinction with reference to Trakl's "blue deer":

Who is the blue deer to whom the poet calls out that it recollect the stranger? Is it an animal? To be sure. Is it only an animal? By no means. For it is said to recollect. Its face supposedly looks out for . . . and looks to the stranger. The blue deer is an animal whose animality presumably does not lie in the bestial, but rather in that watchful recollection after which the poet calls. This animality is still distant and scarcely visible. The animality of the animal here in question thus oscillates in the indeterminate. It has not yet been brought into its essence. This animal, namely, the one that thinks, *animal rationale*, humanity, remains, according to an expression of Nietzsche's, not yet firmly established. [7]

Heidegger is not anthropomorphizing Trakl's figures as though only the human were a fit matter for poetry. On the contrary, it is because the human has not yet become recognizable as a distinct entity that it cannot be absolutely distinguished from a blue deer. Heidegger continues:

The proposition does not mean in any way that humanity has not yet been factually "established." It has been only all too definitely. What is meant is that the animality of this animal has not yet been brought "home," into firmness, the ownness of its concealed essence. This determination has been the goal for which Western European metaphysics has been struggling since Plato. Perhaps it struggles in vain. [8]

The animality of the animal that is the human being has not yet been understood. However recognizable the human being is said to be, it has not yet become recognizable *as human*. Whatever is passed off as human, out of impatience and short-sightedness, is simply an imposition: "The blue deer, where and when it essences [*west*], has left the previous essential form of humanity behind. Humanity, as it has been known up to now, decomposes insofar as it loses its essence [*Wesen*], that is, decays [*verwest*]."⁹ The blue deer is the essence of humanity. It emerges with the decay of that which has been understood as "humanity." In decaying, humanity wrests apart artificial configurations of its essence. Decay undermines the rigidity and hence discord through which the *Geschlecht* finds itself cursed. It restores the *Geschlecht* to the gentleness of its double nature.

Decay is not a calamity that befalls the *Geschlecht* from outside, since it is the essence of the *Geschlecht* to decay. The filmmaker Federico Fellini, who likewise did not see decay as a calamity, coined the word "procadence" in the conviction that the negative prefix "de" in "decadence" is misleading. In Trakl's poetry, decay cannot be said to be an unequivocal object of lament. For all the evocations of decay in his work, it is only in the prose poem "Traum und Umnachtung," with its wish that it be spring, that there is anything approaching an aversion. Otherwise, Trakl—unlike, for instance, the great body of satirical literature—forgoes contrasting and condemning decay with images of what might be taken for a prelapsarian humanity. In themselves, the representations of decay in Trakl's poetry offer little by way of eulogy:

> *Decay glows in the green puddle.*
> ("Kleines Konzert," v. 9)

> *Lepers who perhaps decay at night*
> *Read the scattering signs of bird flight.*
> ("Traum des Bösen," vv. 13–14)

> *A herdsman decays on an old stone.*
> ("Im Dorf," v. 2)

> *Soul sang death, the flesh's green decay.*
> ("An einen Frühverstorbenen," v. 11)

These verses do not express an opposition to decay. Given the impassivity with which they are described, the lepers and the herdsman seem not so much to be afflicted by decay as to have decay as their way of Being. These figures are at home in decay. And that is to say, inasmuch as they have *not* congealed into an inalterable form, they are human.

To be human, to be that for whose determination metaphysics struggles in vain, is to be nothing else but decaying and the decadence of finitude. That the blue deer could be human is because it itself hesitates in its essence: "In the poetizing name 'blue deer' Trakl calls that human essence whose countenance, whose countering glance, is seen by the night's blueness in its thinking of the stranger's steps and is thus illumined by the holy. The name 'blue deer' names mortals who recollect the stranger and who would wander with him through the ownness of the human essence."[10]

The blue deer appears in the decay of humanity in response to the promise of the latter's essence. Appearing with the decay of every reification of humanity, the blue deer cannot appear with the factuality of something present-at-hand. The blue deer essentially hesitates, and thus hesitates in its appearance, because it wanders, and it wanders because it dies. The death that Heidegger elsewhere denies the animal[11] is here granted the blue deer. The blue deer dies; it does not merely perish. By means of its essential finitude, it departs in search of that which is proper to the human and hence not present-at-hand. The blue deer, since it is mortal, decays and it is by decaying that it sets out on its quest for the nonpositivity of the human. It embarks for what is most distant without having to move from its place.

The blue deer, because it is never itself, cannot die in the sense of being extinguished. Death changes its nature in Trakl, as Heidegger notes:

In the poem, "Psalm" Trakl says:
> The madman has died.
The next strophe says:
> The stranger is buried.
In the "Siebengesang des Todes," he is called the "white stranger." The last strophe of "Psalm" ends with the line:
> In his grave the white magician plays with his snakes.
The deceased *lives* in his grave. He lives in his chamber, so quietly and lost in thought that he plays with his snakes. They can do nothing against him. They have not been strangled, but their evil has been transformed.[12]

As a figure of decay, the white magician "lives" even in his grave. He lives by dying and not perishing. He continues to "live" by decaying.[13] As it is by decay that the strife of the individuated is mollified, the uproar of the determinate against the determinate yields in the grave to quiet play. For the white magician, his snakes cease to be evil. The curse of the *Geschlecht*, which had brought the snakes into open discord with him, has been lifted. In his decay, the white magician surrenders the ontic ground for his differentiation from the snakes. He dies away from the determinate toward the becoming of decay. He dies toward his snakes.

To be dead here, as Heidegger writes, is not to be no more:

The deceased is the madman. Is this a question of someone who is mentally ill? No. Madness [*Wahnsinn*] here does not mean a thinking [*Sinnen*] that imagines [*wähnt*] nonsense [*Unsinniges*]. "*Wahn*" comes from Old High German *wana* and means: "*ohne*" [without]. The madman thinks, and he thinks even as no one else has yet thought. But he thus remains without the sense [*Sinn*] of others. He is of another sense. "*Sinnan*" signifies originally: to journey, to strive after, to strike out in a direction; the Indo-Germanic root "*sent*" and "*set*" means "way." The one who has departed is the madman, because he is under way in another direction.[14]

The dead and the mad are both engaged in a pursuit of the essence of the human. That is to say, they have both turned away from every determination of humanity. Accordingly, it is among the dead and the mad that *Being and Time* finds its true readers. In their eyes, Dasein is compelled to stand forth from the anthropomorphizations and reifications concealing and debasing it.

Humanity is in decay. Decay is not a property of the human being, let alone a property that would be predated by every other property. On the contrary, decadence is the origin from which humanity falls away. Ceasing to be itself in acquiring its extant, and hence recognizable, attributes, the *Geschlecht* stands under the curse of no longer decaying. What Heidegger writes of decay in Trakl's poetry does not place it in opposition to the origin: "The language sings the song of the departed homecoming, which from the lateness of decay comes to rest in the earliness of the quieter, still un-been beginning."[15] The lateness of decay converges with the earliness of the beginning that continues to "have been" (*gewesen*) because it is not past (*vergangen*) and extinguished as an earlier discrete "now." Trakl's language sings the homecoming of decadence away from its misapprehended, negative nature into its truth as the originary. Decay is not to be overcome for the sake of a return to the origin. Instead, it is to be understood as the originary.

Heidegger accordingly does not ascribe to Trakl a motif of regeneration, as the following lines on the site of his work make clear: "The sitedness of the site [*die Ortschaft des Ortes*] that gathers Trakl's work into itself is the concealed essence of departedness and is called 'Evening Land,' the Occident. This land is older, that is, earlier and therefore more promising than the land conceived as Platonic-Christian, let alone as European."[16] Platonism and Christianity constitute neither the site of Trakl's work nor its promise. For that matter, the Occident is not the site of Trakl's work.

On the contrary, the Occident is the manner in which this work is situated at all. Its occidental site is a being vespertine rather than a geographical location, and it is decadent rather than regenerative. The true *Heimat* of the West, contrary to what the National Socialists believed, is not distinguished by hygiene and racial purity. Precisely because it is decadent, the "Evening Land" is closer to the origin than the land conceived as Platonic-Christian. In its decay, it does not submit to the Platonic-Christian imperative of purification and thus does not set itself apart from the indeterminacy of finitude. Trakl's "Evening Land" would only be identifiable as the distinct geographical entity known as Europe if it submitted to the Platonic-Christian imperative. As the poet of the Occident, Trakl is the poet of the originary. As the poet of the originary promise of decay, he does not subscribe to any Platonic-Christian model of regeneration.[17] That which does not decay, that which in its a-historical immutability informs the Platonic doctrine of Ideas and the Christian doctrine of the soul, has always, in itself, fallen away from originary temporality. The immutability of the Idea and the soul is proof, not so much of their dignity, as of their fallenness, since this immutability is grounded in the derivative understanding of temporality. The soul and the Idea have their roots in the presence of the atomistic "now."

In order to extricate Trakl from the vulgar concept of time, Heidegger opens his text with a violently expropriative reading of a line from the poem "Frühling der Seele" (v. 22):

The soul is strange to the earth.

By means of an examination of the etymology of "*fremd*" (strange), Heidegger here refuses a Christian interpretation of the soul: "But '*fremd*', the Old High German '*fram*', really means: forward to somewhere else, under way toward . . . onward to that which has been kept in store for it."[18] The soul does not set itself apart from the earth. On the contrary, it is a moving-toward-the-earth. It is not present-at-hand either in heaven or on earth. The soul is ecstatic because it is strange (*fremd*), and it therefore cannot be contained in the presence of Christian immortality.[19] Trakl's soul is a being that has transcendence as its Being. It decays within the origin and it is as originary temporality, and hence as Dasein, that it decays.

The origin in Trakl is, for Heidegger, too originary to be metaphysical. It is the essence and homeland seen and thought only by the "madman":

Trakl's poetry sings the song of the soul, which, "strange to the earth," wanders the earth precisely as the quieter homeland of the homecoming *Geschlecht*.

Dreamy romanticism on the periphery of the technico-economic world of modern mass existence? Or—the clear knowledge of the "madman" who sees and thinks differently to the reporters of the topical who exhaust themselves in the recounting of whatever is contemporary, whose calculated future is only ever a prolongation of what is current, a future that is forever without the advent of a destiny that could ever concern humanity at the beginning of its essence?[20]

Trakl's soul is strange to the earth and the origin, but the earth and the origin are, for that reason, not that which is familiar to the reporters of the topical. Heidegger is not attributing to Trakl's soul nostalgia for the lost *Bodenständigkeit* of the familiar. He is not appealing to the origin, to homecoming, and to the homeland in order to substantiate "on the periphery of the technico-economic world" some reactionary cult of the authenticity of the autonomous subject. It is not the petit bourgeois whom he opposes to the leveled existence of the modern world—but then nor is it, as he earlier stresses, the individual who alerts a symptomatology of mental disorders. Heidegger's "madman" is to be thought differently.

In the *Contributions to Philosophy*, Heidegger writes: "In the history of the truth of Being, Dasein is the essential *incident* [*Zwischenfall*], that is, the intervention of that in-between [*Zwischen*] into which humanity must be deranged [*ver-rückt*] if it is ever again to be *itself*."[21] A human being does not so much become mad as become human only in madness. That which now passes for human must hence be torn out of its determinations into the kairological interval that is the madness of Dasein in its essential ecstasy as originary temporality. The mad, following Heidegger in his etymology of "*Wahnsinn*", cannot be said to have embarked on a journey as though it were an activity undertaken by grammatical subjects. The mad *are* the journey in the same exhaustive and essential sense that Dasein is transcendence. Consequently, the origin is the destination of the journey—that toward which the "strange" soul is under way—insofar as it does not denote its conclusion, but rather its consummation as *journey*. The origin is to be understood as ecstatic, and thus as that which is properly human.

In 1952, "madness" thus comes to name the Un-thought of classical ontology, and it is to the "mad" that Heidegger entrusts the question of Being. The essay on Trakl is, accordingly, a further attempt at that critical destruction of the metaphysical tradition undertaken since the 1920s. Where "The Self-Assertion of the German University" appealed to the *Volk*, "Language in the Poem" appeals to the mad and the dead. Precedents, therefore, suggest themselves for that which Heidegger seeks to think with the word "*Wahnsinn*". Nonetheless, the consistency should not be taken for granted. What Heidegger earlier thinks with "transcendence"—the most obvious precursor for his etymology of "*Wahnsinn*"—must be rethought in the light of the later text and its reappraisal of the human. To do so is to ask after the linkages between Dasein, the *Volk,* and the "mad." It is to ask after the nature of the humanity of the being that raises the question of Being.

In the 1929–30 lecture course *The Fundamental Concepts of Metaphysics*, Heidegger offers his most extensive treatment of the difference between the animal and the human. Discussing the essential transcendence of Dasein, he writes:

> For the being-there of Da-sein means *being with others*, precisely in the manner of Dasein, i.e., existing with others. The question concerning whether we human beings can transpose ourselves into other human beings does not ask anything, because it is not a possible question in the first place. It is a meaningless, indeed a nonsensical question because it is fundamentally redundant. . . . Being-with belongs to the essence of man's existence.[22]

Dasein always already transcends. It is not *possible* for human beings to transpose themselves into other human beings, since to attribute transcendence to human beings as a possibility is to transform what is essential into what is optional.

In 1929–30, Heidegger distinguishes between the essential transposition of the human being, the limited transposability of the animal and the nontransposability of the inanimate object:

> In contrast with the stone, the animal in any case does possess the possibility of transposability, but it does not allow the possibility of self-transposition in the sense in which this transpires between one human being and another. The animal both has something and does not have something, i.e., it is deprived of something. We express this by saying that the animal is poor in world and that it is fundamentally deprived of world.[23]

Heidegger stresses that this last proposition is not to be understood as an additional property of the entity that has long been the domain of zoological enquiry:

> Where does the proposition "the animal is poor in world" come from? We can answer once again that it derives from zoology, since this is the science that deals with animals. But precisely because zoology deals with animals this proposition cannot

be a result of zoological investigation: rather, it must be its *presupposition*. For this presupposition ultimately involves an *antecedent determination* of what belongs in general to the *essence of the animal*, that is, a delimitation of the field within which any positive investigation of animals must move.[24]

Admittedly, Heidegger, who thereupon proceeds to talk of earthworms, moles, and beetles, does not appear in *The Fundamental Concepts of Metaphysics* to wish to challenge the traditional delimitations of the zoological.

Twenty years later, however, he calmly announces that a blue deer is human. Why? Because it thinks. At once it seems that he is invoking the arguments of *The Fundamental Concepts of Metaphysics* on the humanity of thinking. There, in §58, Heidegger writes: "Captivation is the condition of possibility for the fact that, in accordance with its essence, the animal *behaves within an environment but never within a world.*"[25] What stands between the animal and a world is its captivation (*Benommenheit*). The nature of this captivation is not to be a captivation with something *as such*. Indeed, in the absence of a grammatical agent for the captivation, "*Benommenheit*" could be more suitably (and more conventionally) translated by "daze"—the captivation that defines itself as an inability to be captivated by something as such. For Heidegger, as for Aquinas, this captivated daze in which the animal lives without relating either to itself or anything outside of itself prevents a world from emerging in the wealth of its articulations:

When we say that the lizard is lying on the rock, we ought to cross out the word "rock" in order to indicate that whatever the lizard is lying on is certainly given *in some way* for the lizard, and yet is not known to the lizard *as* a rock. If we cross out the word we do not simply mean to imply that something else is in question here or is taken as something else. Rather we imply that whatever it is is not accessible to it *as a being.*[26]

For late Heidegger, as is well known, it is the word "Being" that we ought to cross out, in order to indicate that Being as such is not accessible to us. Without access to the Being of beings and thus to what beings are as such, we are not free of the captivation in which the animal lives and perishes.

However, in 1929–30, the question of Being has not yet fully undermined the metaphysical distinction between the animal and the human. The lizard lies on a rock, but it does not lie knowingly on a rock. The rock as such withholds itself. The world refuses itself to the animal in general because it is accessible only to the being that knows. World becomes the prerogative of the human as the being that knows. Heidegger's choice of examples for discussion from the animal kingdom is seemingly dictated by a desire to avert suspicion from the definition of the human as the being that knows. The behavior of bees while feeding furnishes Heidegger with a convenient further example of a being that does not know:

> [T]he bee recognizes that it cannot cope with all the honey present. It breaks off its driven activity because it recognizes the presence of too much honey for it. Yet, it has been observed that if its abdomen is carefully cut away while it is sucking, a bee will simply carry on regardless even while the honey runs out of the bee from behind. This shows conclusively that the bee by no means recognizes the presence of too much honey.[27]

The honey as such does not appear for the bee. Not knowing what it is doing, the bee does not behave within a world.

But what does it mean for world to be tied to the knowability of what is? How can Heidegger's argument in *The Fundamental Concepts of Metaphysics* be brought into agreement with his demotion of epistemology in §13 of *Being and Time*? There he writes: "But a '*commercium*' of the subject with a world does not get *created* for the first time by knowing, nor does it *arise* from some way in which the world acts upon a subject. Knowing is a mode of Dasein founded upon Being-in-the-world. Thus Being-in-the-world, as a basic state, must be Interpreted *beforehand*." [28]

Being-in-the-world is the basis of knowledge and earlier in the same section, Heidegger asserts, "Being-in-the-world, as concern, is *fascinated* [*benommen*] *by* the world with which it is concerned." [29] In *Being and Time*, Dasein knows because it is Being-in-the-world. In *The Fundamental Concepts of Metaphysics*, the bee is not Being-in-the-world because it does not know. There is an asymmetry between the two propositions. In *Being and Time*, Being-in-the-world is the presupposition of knowledge, whereas in *The Fundamental Concepts of Metaphysics* knowledge is the proof of Being-in-the-world. Yet in what way can knowledge be a proof of Being-in-the-world? Beings are knowable because they are cleared in the clearing of beings that is Being-in-the-world. Being-in-the-world is the knowability of what is and Dasein is the being that knows. But Dasein is not the being that knows in the sense that it is a subject that stands over against an object that it submits to scrutiny and about which it draws binding conclusions. Dasein is the being that knows because it is the clearing of beings. The bee is not the being that knows because it is a being that appears in the clearing of beings and is not the clearing itself. In Heidegger's example of the bee, the distinction between the animal and the human is illustrated, but not without ambiguity. The poverty of the bee's world lies in its difference from the knowability of what is, rather than in its nonsensical behavior. In Heidegger's example this is ambiguous. Being-in-the-world appears to be susceptible to verification by a test of expediency. The bee without an abdomen expends energy in the consumption of honey that it cannot retain and thus behaves irrationally: it is not the *animal rationale* and it is not Being-in-the-world. Is this ambiguity, whereby the clearing of beings converges with the being with the most developed sense of the economical, simply a lapse on Heidegger's part?

If it is a lapse, it is one that is rectified in the essay on Trakl. In this later text, Heidegger is much more careful to avoid encouraging readings that would anthropomorphize the clearing of beings. The greater caution alters the cast of the animal in Heidegger's thinking. The question that Derrida raises concerning the tenability of the distinction between the animal and the human in other texts by Heidegger is thus preempted by the essay on Trakl. In "*Geschlecht* II: Heidegger's Hand," Derrida examines the passage on the ape from *What Is Called Thinking?* and addresses his attention to the sentence, "Apes, too, have organs that can grasp, but they do not have hands."[30] Here Heidegger reserves the hand for the human and puts it at a distance from any organic functionalism. Derrida, in response, advances a criticism of the differentiation proclaimed in this sentence and of the logic that informs its counterparts in other texts:

In its very content, this proposition marks the text's essential scene, marks it with a humanism that wanted certainly to be nonmetaphysical—Heidegger underscores this in the following paragraph—but with a humanism that, between a human *Geschlecht* one wants to withdraw from the biologistic determination . . . and an animality one encloses in its organico-biologic programs, inscribes not *some* differences but an absolute oppositional limit.[31]

Heidegger certainly retains the traditional notion of a radical difference between human beings and animals, yet his reasons for doing so are not traditional. For Heidegger, the ape gives itself up to the organic analysis of biology, and as an animal it cannot do otherwise. With the human being, it is another matter. Between the ape and the human being, there are not merely differences in the plural and hence on the level of properties. There is a difference of essence. The humanism that Derrida attributes to Heidegger lies in this incommensurability. Derrida questions whether this absolute oppositional limit—by which the *Geschlecht* would be set rigidly in the discord between the human and the animal—does not collapse of itself. Derrida's question, however, presupposes the vulnerability of Heidegger's thinking to a Hegelian criticism. Is the incommensurability of the ape and the human really the matter of an absolute oppositional limit? Is the human defined as an extant being by the negativity of its opposition to the ape and thus contaminated by the ape in its very essence? For Heidegger, the incommensurability is not a difference between two essences distinct in the same way. The incommensurability is the difference between the clearing of beings, which is thus always already contaminated through its Being-with, and a being that appears in the clearing and allows its enclosure in "organico-biologic programs." And yet the clearing of beings has hands. This, however, is not an objection, since it is the clearing of beings that first "has" anything. Humanism would mark Heidegger's text only if it were denied that the clearing of beings has paws.

Heidegger's distinction between the human and the animal is better understood as an inclusion of the one in the other than as a mutual exclusion. In his 1938–39 lectures on the second of Nietzsche's *Untimely Observations*, Heidegger regrets the possibility of misinterpretation adhering to his discussion of the difference between Dasein and animals in *Being and Time*.[32] In 1927, the Being of animals is to be understood privatively with respect to the Being of Dasein, but "privation" is a poor way of approaching the difference between Being and beings, since it lies in the nature of the viscidity of Being that whatever can be said to differ from Being as such must nevertheless also be acknowledged, in its very difference from Being, to be. An animal is privative in relation to humanity, not in the sense that it is a crippled or stunted human being but in the sense that it falls short, precisely as a determinate being, of the transcendence in which Dasein is swept away from any self-identity. What is at stake for Heidegger is an ontologization (which is to say, an indetermination, a de-anthropo*morph*ization) of humanity rather than an anthropomorphization of Being. Ontologically, the animal that, in 1929–30, is seemingly not thought beyond its comprehension in the prevailing biology relies on humanity in its being an animal as such. A sentence such as the following from the "Letter on 'Humanism'" has therefore to be read for what it does *not* say in the language of humanism: "Because plants and animals are lodged in their respective environments but are never placed freely in the clearing of Being which alone is 'world,' they lack language."[33] Plants and animals are never placed

freely in the clearing of Being because they, unlike Dasein, are not the clearing of Being itself. Plants and animals do not speak, but then it is not one
being among other beings that is here said to speak. The human is not, for
Heidegger, a privileged being. Its difference from other beings as the being
that speaks is the difference of Being from beings. Heidegger thus endows
the "human" with a dignity surpassing that of any earlier humanism. But
Heidegger's apparent humanism is, properly speaking, an anti-humanism,
inasmuch as it does not perpetuate the Christian myth of the human being as a being set apart from, and over, all other beings. This myth, which
endorses the exploitation and manipulation of beings in the service of modern technicism, does not find expression in Heidegger. On the contrary, by
identifying the human with the Being of beings Heidegger does not align
the manipulability of beings with the human, but rather names with the human being the essential resistance of beings to τέχνη. The human becomes
the essential unpresentability of whatever is. It becomes the worlding of the
world in which beings are present but which, as their condition of possibility and thus their truth, is not present itself. And it is not present because
it is the nonpresentability of time. Whereas for Aristotle the human is the
only being that perceives time, for Heidegger the human is time.[34] It is in
the *ecstases* of temporality that the human both announces its incommensurability with the animal and gives itself up to contamination.

In "Language in the Poem," the blue deer is human not simply because it thinks and knows what a bee cannot know. It is human because, in
its harkening to the stranger, it follows him elsewhere and thinks madly,
that is, differently. Since Christian humanism distinguished the human
from the thingly but did not question the distinctness as such of the human, it never reached beyond matters of detail to the "madness" of a thor-
ough critique of reification. It never thought Being as such. A famous sentence from *What Is Called Thinking?* (the series of lectures delivered in the
same period as the composition of "Language in the Poem") reads: "Most
thought-provoking in our thought-provoking time is that we are still not
thinking."[35] The blue deer, which *does* think because it thinks differently
from the thought that is properly a nonthought, accordingly satisfies the
definition of the human being as the thinking animal (Heidegger's less
than honest translation of *animal rationale*). Yet it can be said to satisfy this
definition only by overlooking the fact that the otherness of its thought
calls any definition whatsoever into question. Its thought is less a stable
property of its animality than its madness and decay: the humanity of the

blue deer is its indeterminacy. We who do not yet think are not yet human. Metaphysics prevents us from strictly meeting its definition of humanity as the *animal rationale* because it prevents us from thinking. But in what way are we the human beings who do not yet think? To what degree? Heidegger's response in the text on Trakl is unmistakable: to the degree that we are not under way, that we resist the decomposition essential to the human.[36]

In *The Fundamental Concepts of Metaphysics*, the animal does not grasp beings as they are. And it cannot do so because it is not Being and hence not that which is the knowability of beings. The animal is insufficiently ecstatic and thus insufficiently decadent. The blue deer bears witness to the humanity that thinks itself in the animal. The humanity of the animal is the transcendence that cannot be denied to the Being of any being. To deny the animal knowledge of beings as such is not to deny it transcendence, since inasmuch as the animal *is*, it is transcendent. The constitution of its identity takes into account the world from which the animal is continuously differentiated and toward which it must always be transcending in order for the differentiation to take effect. And if Heidegger's bee is essentially always more than a bee, can it only ever—unthinkingly—be mistaken for a bee? The ecstasy that Heidegger endows with the name of "human" is the Being of beings. The exclusiveness of humanity's title to Being is dictated by the nature of ecstasy itself rather than by a recollection of the Christian hierarchy of terrestrial beings, since a plurality of titles to transcendence would entail the demarcation of regions of Being in defiance of its ecstatic character. Within this ecstasy, beings emerge in the distinctiveness of their individual properties by way of a suppression of their transcendent "humanity." A stone, a twig, a length of thread, as that which is merely present-at-hand, figure among the debris of originary temporality in its disintegration into the atomistic "nows" of reification. Decay is not a secondary effect of the object; rather the object is a secondary effect of decay. Where the blue deer can be said to think, it is because in following the stranger, it transcends more unreservedly than the unthinking consciousness of the epistemological subject. Thought, in the proper sense as the thought of Being, is not a procedure of an extant subject, but the essence of the being-outside-of-itself of originary temporality. The blue deer that truly thinks does not pass beyond itself only as far as an object in whose reflection it then recovers; instead, it thinks so intensely that it decays into the humus of the human, disappearing after the stranger into the origin.

If it is immediately objected that such an interpretation overlooks what is traditional in Heidegger's meditations on humanity, then this *appearance* of conventionality would need to be demonstrated as being more than an appearance. Certainly, the Greek definition of the human being— ζῷον λόγον ἔχον—is retained by Heidegger: "Nor is the capacity to speak merely *one* capability of human beings, on a par with the remaining ones. The capacity to speak distinguishes the human being as a human being. Such a distinguishing mark bears in itself the very design of the human essence." [37]

That which is human speaks. The proposition occupies in Heidegger, however, the status more of a problem than of a definition. What precisely it means to speak is the question that the essay on Trakl and the other essays in the collection *On the Way to Language* attempts to raise. Heidegger repeatedly insists that the essence of language does not disclose itself in its instrumentalization. Language is misunderstood as soon as it is held to be a means of the transmission of information; evidence of comprehension within a discourse does not in itself prove an agent's humanity.

In its efforts to demarcate the animal and the human, *The Fundamental Concepts of Metaphysics* has recourse to a discussion of the nature of language that is considerably more wary, in comparison with its discussion of knowledge, of suggesting any philosophy of consciousness: "The fact that there is an essential distinction between the vocal utterance of the animal (φωνή) and human discourse in the broadest sense is indicated by Aristotle when he says that human discourse is κατὰ συνθήκην, which he interprets as ὅταν γένηται σύμβολον." [38]

Heidegger stresses to his audience in 1929–30 that current theories of the symbol are inadequate for the purpose of understanding Aristotle's sense. What then is the symbol? Heidegger's answer closes the circle: "What Aristotle sees quite obscurely under the title σύμβολον, sees only approximately, and without any explication, in looking at it quite ingeniously, is nothing other than what we today call *transcendence*." [39] The notion of the human that Heidegger defines by transcendence is thus not illuminated by the additional reference to language, since language is likewise defined by transcendence. Dasein speaks: a tautology whose deliberate emptiness displays its distance from positive determinations of humanity and of language. Dasein is whatever speaks, and in the liberated world of decay of Trakl's poetry a blackbird begins to banter with the dead cousin ("Winkel am Wald") and the ocean begins to sing ("Psalm"). Decay is the gift of tongues, and on the near side of reification everything begins to speak. Once language is expounded as transcendence, and not as the comprehensibility of utterances, can it be said that the community it founds, the Being-with-others with which Heidegger equates Dasein, is in any way exclusive? Would it not be a proof of the deficient transcendence of a community, and therefore of its deficient humanity, if it were to distinguish itself from another, from an Other?

In 1934, in the lecture course *Logik als die Frage nach dem Wesen der Sprache*, Heidegger defines the *Volk* by language.[40] Given his earlier definition of language, Heidegger is not substituting the exclusive community of the speakers of a particular language for the exclusive community of the specimens of a particular racial type. The *Volk* of transcendence is a people that cannot extricate itself from other beings. It is incapable of standing over against beings as a subject and it is thus incapable of a more or less humane comportment toward them. Its *humanitas* is shown in the check that it places on the exploitation of beings by withdrawing itself, as the truth of beings, from the domain of τέχνη.

As the *Volk* is defined by transcendence, it cannot come up against another *Volk* from which it would be distinct. There can be only the one *Volk*. But, as Heidegger makes clear in his meditations on the *Geschlecht*, this is very far from amounting to a declaration of the homogeneity of the being that raises the question of Being. The community that assembles in the *ecstases* of originary temporality is the community of the ontological difference. In order for it to be homogeneous, it would first have to surrender to its reification within derivative temporality, whereby it would obtain in the light of presence the properties of its recognizable consistency. Heidegger's community is transcendent only because it is different, only because it is the transcendence that is difference itself. To grasp the *Volk* in its specificity as the *Volk*, rather than as an extant entity among extant entities, can mean nothing other than to grasp it as difference.

In 1952, the question of Being is the question of the *Geschlecht*. Having become the name of the being that raises the question of Being, the *Geschlecht* thinks the question in terms of its own difference. The *Geschlecht* does not think the Being of beings as the Hegelian differentiatedness of beings. Difference is to be thought on its own. Certainly, early Heidegger speaks in the same way of transcendence, rejecting all interpretations that situate it as a relation between the subject and the object.[41] But, as the ambiguity of the example of the bee in *The Fundamental Concepts of Meta-*

physics shows, transcendence is not always sufficiently distinguished from the knowledge that one being has of another being. Transcendence, as the possibility of community, is that which later becomes the difference of the *Geschlecht*. It is the ontological difference, of which Heidegger writes in "The Onto-Theo-Logical Constitution of Metaphysics":

> Thus we think of Being rigorously only when we think of it in its difference with beings, and of beings in their difference with Being. The difference thus comes specifically into view. If we try to form a representational idea of it, we will at once be misled into conceiving of difference as a relation which our representing has added to Being and to beings. Thus the difference is reduced to a distinction, something made up by our understanding (*Verstand*).[42]

The difference between Being and beings—in short, transcendence—is reduced to a distinction belonging to the positivity of the understanding when it is formulated as a distinct being that relates Being and beings as though from outside. In order to avoid such a reification of the ontological difference, it is necessary to think this difference in its immanence to Being and beings. It is necessary to think it in its originarity as the clearing of both Being and beings.

Heidegger's lecture "Language" endeavors to rethink difference in the course of an exegesis of Trakl's poem "Ein Winterabend": "The difference [*Unter-Schied*] is neither distinction nor relation. The difference is in the highest instance the dimension for world and thing."[43] Heidegger here hyphenates the German word for "difference," *Unterschied*, and in thus drawing attention to its elements, *unter* (under) and *Schied* (division) suggests a possibility of understanding difference that is more originary than division and that is hence neither distinction nor relation—difference as the *sublime*, as the passage under the threshold between entities and as the condition of possibility of beings in their multiplicity. This originary difference is not, for Heidegger, the Being that Hegel identifies with the differentiatedness of beings. This originary difference clears Being even in its withdrawal from the recognizability of the differentiatedness of beings. It is the difference of the *Geschlecht* and the basis for its community.

In his reading of Trakl's verse "*Ein* Geschlecht" (*One* Geschlecht) in "Language in the Poem," Heidegger again emphasizes that difference is not the product of negotiations within a binary:

> The "*one*" in "*one* Geschlecht" does not mean "one" instead of "two." The "one" also does not mean the monotony of dull equality. "*One* Geschlecht" does not at

all name any biological fact, neither the condition of being of the one sex [*Eingeschlechtlichkeit*] nor that of being of the same sex [*Gleichgeschlechtlichkeit*]. In the emphatic "*one* Geschlecht," that uniting element conceals itself which unifies out of the spiritual night's gathering blueness.[44]

Heidegger discounts here a series of interpretations of Trakl's verse on the basis solely of their one-sidedness. Oneness, when coupled with the *Geschlecht*, becomes the oneness of multiplicity. Trakl's "*one* Geschlecht" is not so much a unity as that which unifies, although it does not unify in the same way as the Greek One of unconcealment. Trakl's "*one* Geschlecht" conceals itself as the unifying element of the ontological difference. It names the humanity of this difference, as Heidegger writes: "Accordingly, the word '*Geschlecht*' here retains the full manifold meaning already named. It names at once the historical *Geschlecht* of man, humanity in its difference from all other living beings (plants and animals). The word '*Geschlecht*' names then the *Geschlechter*, tribes, clans, families of this human *Geschlecht*. At the same time, the word '*Geschlecht*' always names the twofold of the *Geschlechter*."[45]

The *Geschlecht* that is insinuated to be difference itself cannot be distinguished from other living things, as though it were one living thing among others. It is different from them as the difference from which they break toward their distinct identities as plants and animals. It is the *Geschlecht* informing them as the possibility of their determinacy *and* indeterminacy.

Geschlecht is a word that names difference because it is a poetic word. What it names is originary and, for that reason, can only be named poetically. As Heidegger asserts elsewhere in *On the Way to Language*, the poetic has nothing to do with the secondariness and derivativeness of the ornamental: "Poetry proper is never merely a higher mode (*melos*) of everyday language. It is rather the reverse: everyday language is a forgotten and therefore used-up poem, from which there hardly resounds a call any longer."[46] As everyday language is a used-up poem, it is not by adding senses to the univocality of everyday language that one arrives at poetry. *Geschlecht* is a poetic word in its multiplicity, but this multiplicity is poorly understood as the aggregate of its senses. The multiplicity has to be thought in its originary simplicity. The meaning of the word *Geschlecht* is manifold because it lies in the poetic character of this word not to give itself up to the unequivocality of that which is apprehended in the light of presence. The manifold meaning of the word is a consequence of the originarity that prevents it from ever fully being unconcealed. The poetic word *Geschlecht* thus names the human in its status as an exception to the understanding of Being as presence. In this respect, the *Geschlecht* is a descendent of the German *Volk* of Heidegger's commentaries on Hölderlin. But with the essay on Trakl in 1952, the being that raises the question of Being has shed its overt ties to nationalism and aligned itself with difference.

Heidegger begins "Language in the Poem" with a question about the site of Trakl's poetry and suggests that it is difference itself: "The site gathers unto itself, supremely and in the extreme. That which gathers penetrates and pervades everything. The site, that which gathers, draws into itself, preserves that which it has drawn in, not like an immuring capsule, but rather by illuminating and shining through what has been gathered, and which only thus is released into its own essence."[47] Only difference is able to unify as well as preserve. As the site of Trakl's work, difference is, in a sense, this work itself. And because difference cannot be hypostasized, the work is in some way a non-work: "The poem (*Gedicht*) of a poet remains unspoken. None of the individual texts (*Dichtungen*), not even their totality, says everything. Nonetheless, each text speaks out of the whole of the single poem and at every turn enunciates this poem."[48] Just as there is only the one *Geschlecht* for Heidegger and Trakl, there is for Heidegger only the one poem. And that which allows the poem and the *Geschlecht* to unify hinders them from being present-at-hand.

Exactly why the poem of a poet remains unspoken is not stated. In *Nietzsche*, however, Heidegger explains why the thought (more precisely, the Un-thought) of a thinker remains unsaid. There, in a very un-Hegelian manner, he speaks of the inevitable transgression in commenting upon the Un-thought of another thinker:

> Every thinker oversteps the inner limit of every thinker. But such overstepping is not "knowing it all," since it only consists in holding the thinker in the direct claim of Being, thus remaining within his limitations. This limitation consists in the fact that the thinker can never himself say what is most of all his own. It must remain unsaid, because what is sayable receives its determination from what is not sayable. What is most of all the thinker's own, however, is not his possession, but rather belongs to Being whose transmission thinking receives in its projects.[49]

For Heidegger, the Un-thought of a thinker is not a deficiency for which the thinker can be held to account. Unlike Hegel, for whom the task of thinking is the task of bringing everything to thought, Heidegger concerns himself with the Un-thought for the sake of its *resistance* to presence.

Commentary on the work of a poet is, as it were, a matter of attending to the determining element of the unspoken poem. Commentary takes as its object less the plurality of distinct poems by which the *Geschlecht* has been cursed than the decay that is their "unity" and condition of possibility. The charge of misreading repeatedly leveled at Heidegger's text on Trakl registers, but fails to understand, that it has taken the unspoken poem as its object.[50] The violence of Heidegger's reading, as it bears on the discord of that which is said of the *Geschlecht*, is a corollary of the attempt to think the *Geschlecht* in the un-said gentleness of its simple twofold.

In any case, the question must arise for even the crudest understanding of Trakl's poetry whether fidelity is itself an appropriate criterion in judging discussions of his texts. Fidelity to what? Sense is conspicuously a side-effect in these compositions. On account of the repetition and repositioning of images, Modesto Carone Netto ascribes to Trakl a technique and practice such as that which William Burroughs later employed and propagated under the name of "cut-up."[51] Trakl's poetry has been analyzed as a montage of quotations by Alfred Doppler,[52] as well as by Rudolf D. Schier,[53] who discovers in two verses by Trakl allusions to the Book of Samuel, the Gospel of Saint John, Hölderlin's "Der Winkel von Hahrdt," and Ammer's translation of Rimbaud. Trakl develops an art of quotation quite distinct from that of his contemporary Karl Kraus. The quotation in Trakl is not the object of attack. It is more the symptom of a decomposition. Kraus's personality, which stands over against the quotations and unites them, has no exact counterpart in Trakl. Trakl simply plagiarizes. This defect is, strictly speaking, his great strength. Trakl withstands the temptation to produce a work: the deterritorialization of the individual quoted verses is not thwarted by a reterritorialization on any notion of the poet's "authentic" voice. Trakl's singular poem is elsewhere. The *Geschlecht* is hidden. And it cannot be more thoroughly hidden than on the surface: Richard Detsch contends that Trakl's verse "*Ein* Geschlecht" is itself a quotation of Novalis,[54] whereas Ursula Heckmann believes that Otto Weininger is its inspiration.[55] The singularity of the *Geschlecht* does not isolate the Traklian corpus as its determining principle, since it must for its own part be understood from out of that abyssal absence of such a determining principle which is Trakl's innovation as a montage artist.

Commenting on the notion of singularity in "Language in the Poem," but misapprehending its abyssal character, Derrida justly asserts that Heidegger is unwilling to position Trakl within metaphysics, let alone

Christian theology: "On the contrary, he intends to show that Trakl's *Gedicht* (his poetic work if not his poems) has not only crossed the limit of onto-theology: it allows us to think such a crossing [*franchissement*] which is also an enfranchisement [*affranchissement*]. This enfranchisement, still equivocal in Hölderlin . . . is *univocal* in Trakl."[56] For Heidegger, as Derrida writes, Trakl's *Gedicht* is beyond metaphysics. Trakl's *Gedicht* has crossed the limit of onto-theology and thereby accomplished what "On the Question of Being" declares to be impossible. By means here of an allusion to Heidegger's critique of Jünger's conviction of the violability of the limits of nihilism, Derrida attempts to implicate Heidegger in a self-contradiction. Yet the analysis promptly breaks off before it has become evident that Heidegger understands Trakl's *Gedicht* metaphysically. Only if Trakl's *Gedicht* is understood in terms of an exclusive identity, could it be said to resemble the entities of metaphysics it is claimed to have left behind on this side of the limit of onto-theology. But Trakl's singular poem is not a distinct entity present-at-hand, and although Derrida acknowledges in a parenthesis that Heidegger draws a distinction between Trakl's poem and poems, he does not allow the singular poem's difference from the extantness of the poems to interfere with his criticism. Heidegger does not advance Trakl's missing poem as an alternative and rival to metaphysics. Trakl's missing poem is not to be encountered with metaphysical distinctness on the supposed other side of the limit of onto-theology. The *Gedicht* is more originary than metaphysics because it is decadent. It is too decadent to cross the line and survive intact.

The *Gedicht* is, furthermore, too decadent to bear the discrete and proper name of Georg Trakl. Heidegger reads through the individual poems to Being. Unless "Georg Trakl" is seen as a cipher in "Language in the Poem," unless his poem, following Heidegger on the very first page of the text, is grasped as absent, little more than a mythologization of a poetic corpus may appear. The decadence that emerges within Trakl's poetry does not come to a halt before the proper name. Decay liberates, within the poetry itself as well as the poetry from itself. In an important respect, Trakl reads like the Baroque poets he studied. Generic figures populate his poems—the stranger, the shepherds, the lepers, the lonely, the soldiers—and yet decay works against the consolidation of any given role. In "Ruh und Schweigen" (v. 11–12), Trakl writes:

> *A radiant youth*
> *Appears the sister in autumn and black decay.*

Under the pressure of decay, the cosmological division of labor yields and the sister changes and does not change her sex. She becomes. That she appears a gleaming youth is an "illusion" fomented by decay, whereby decay is both noted and overlooked. The image of the gleaming youth collects itself within decay and steps forth from it consistent and recognizable. Decay as such never appears and it never can appear *as such*. Decay, like Trakl's poem and like Being, is missing.

Trakl's singular poem decays into discrete verses. It falls away from itself in becoming the extant work. Decay is by no means unilateral: the verses decay toward the singular poem and the singular poem decays toward the verses. Or again, the singular poem is decay itself. The composed is a decomposition of decomposition. That Heidegger, in his commentary, wishes to mark such a distinction within decay is explicit in his description of Elis: "Elis is not one who has died and who decays [*verwest*] in the lateness of the lived-out. Elis is the dead who dis-essences [*entwest*] into earliness. This stranger unfolds the human essence forward into the beginning of what has not yet come to be borne."[57] The *Entwesung* of Elis is a decay that is not so much a falling-away as a falling-toward, since it is in and as decay, and the demolition of all previous articulations of humanity, that the human essence comes to light in its originarity. Falling away from this essence, succumbing to a resistance to decay, humanity is estranged from itself. Heidegger comments: "The wanderers who follow the stranger at once see themselves parted 'from loved ones' who, for them, are 'others.' The others—that is the cast [*Schlag*] of the decayed form of humanity."[58] In their first steps after the stranger, the wanderers are still under the curse laid upon the *Geschlecht*. They view themselves as different from other beings rather than as difference itself, rather than as decay. The curse that drives the *Geschlecht* out of the unity of difference into the discord of the opposed effects itself in the decay of decay. The curse, however, does not bring about a reversal of decay, since it conceals rather than heals. But in any case is decay something to be healed?

In a letter to Jean-Michel Palmier, Heidegger insists that decay is to be understood neither existentially nor anthropologically, but ontologically.[59] In *Being and Time*, to whose passages on decay (*Verfallenheit*) Heidegger refers Palmier, there appears the following: "In falling [*als verfallendes*], Dasein *itself* as factical Being-in-the-world, is something *from* which it has already fallen away. And it has not fallen into some entity which it comes upon for the first time in the course of its being, or even one which it has not come upon at all; it has fallen into the *world*, which itself belongs to its Being."[60]

Dasein can never not be decaying as it essentially transcends. At most, it can disguise its worldhood in the opposition of discord. The intimacy of decay, of transcendence and of being-outside-of-itself is never simply cancelled out by discord, since it is the precondition of the latter.

Only within the unity of the *Geschlecht* can dissension arise. This unity, which is the difference of the *Geschlecht*, cannot accordingly be opposed to discord as though the one excluded the other. They are not options facing human communities. It is not a matter of "instantiating," within a specific social body, the differential unity of the *Geschlecht* in the name of an imputedly Heideggerian politics. The feasibility of such an instantiation would depend upon a restriction of the unifying scope of the *Geschlecht*, and thus upon its demotion from difference itself. The unity of the *Geschlecht* is not a Utopia waiting to be realised.[61] From the "realization" of its unity, the *Geschlecht* can only expect impoverishment through the loss of the ages in which it was not realized and in which, as supposedly unrealized, it still gathered itself as its difference from its realization.

Heidegger's voluntaristic tone when he speaks of the *Geschlecht* is ambiguous: "The proper cast lies only with that *Geschlecht* whose twoness leaves discord behind and wanders ahead into the gentleness of a simple twofold, that is, is strange and thus follows the stranger." Heidegger is not here detailing a course of action undertaken by knowing subjects assembled in the *Geschlecht* and by which they differentiate themselves from others. The *Geschlecht* of which he speaks is the ubiquitous, yet everywhere concealed, *Geschlecht* of Being. Being is always *geschlechtlich*, but there is no chosen *Geschlecht*. Every *Geschlecht* has always already been chosen and any comportment on its part toward difference can never appropriate its election, since difference is prior to comportment and overreaches it. The subject that comports itself toward difference, with the gentility it imagines appropriate, merely aligns itself with discord. By its comportment the subject cannot make good the discord in which it is grounded in its opposition to the object and by which the *Geschlecht* is cursed. The unity of the *Geschlecht* is not identical with the reciprocated indulgence of the subjects of liberalism. The last thing that Heidegger could be expected to say is that the curse of the *Geschlecht* is lifted in liberal democracies with their prided tolerance. In any case, the curse cannot be lifted in favor of decay, since the curse is itself also decay—the condition of possibility for that atomization manifest in the discord of the *Geschlecht* lies, for Heidegger, in the decadence of derivative temporality (*die verfallende Zeitigungsart*).

The gentleness of the twofold of the *Geschlecht* is thus too inclusive to be taken for a political model. Derrida, in *Geschlecht* IV, "Heidegger's Ear: Philopolemology," dwells upon the equivocality of the figure of the friend in *Being and Time* and thereby emphasizes the distance between Heidegger's conception of community and a peaceful coexistence:

> [A] larger context . . . seems to indicate that for Heidegger φιλεῖν, on the nonpsychological, nonanthropological, nonethicopolitical plane of the existential analytic and above all of the question of being or φύσις, welcomes within itself, in its very accord, many other modes than that of friendliness, but as well opposition, tension, confrontation, rejection, . . . if not war, at least *Kampf* or πόλεμος. . . . To be opposed to the friend, to turn away from it, to defy it, to not hear it, that is still to hear and keep it, to carry with self, *bei sich tragen*, the voice of the friend.[62]

The friendship that, as Being-with, is definitive of the human being lies outside the gift of the subject. Dasein is essentially and thus inalienably befriended. Even in its seemingly most fundamental isolation, Dasein continues within a community of some kind and of which it stands forever in need, if only so that its isolation might assert itself. Throughout the discord between the isolated individual and the community, there prevails the tenderness of the unitary *Geschlecht* in its transcendence. The Being-with of the *Geschlecht* that is definitive of the human being disappears from view in discord. As a result, Dasein confines itself to its isolation and yet sets itself at variance with solitude. It never beholds itself as fully human and never knows itself as estranged simply from an oxymoronic image of the human. That is to say, in the discord that is the element of its reification the subject fails to perceive its inhumanity. The community from which Dasein can never break is the community of difference. Its specificity is not constituted by exclusion. Hence it cannot limit itself to the concourse of a given species of primates. The age of loneliness, which in 1938 Heidegger believes must fall over the earth, is to scatter the spurious communities that settle in the discord of the *Geschlecht*, disclosing as it were the ecstatic community of the lonely.

Already in the 1934–35 lecture course *Hölderlins Hymnen "Germanien" und "Der Rhein,"* Heidegger writes: "The manner of togetherness of the singular, its world-character, is solitude. It does not separate and expel, but rather bears forth into that originary unity which no community has ever attained."[63] It is for such a nonexclusive community that Heidegger reserves the words "friendship" and "tenderness." And that he should tear these words away from any oppositionality, denying that friendship excludes antagonism, that tenderness is at odds with decay, is not irrelevant to his ambition to think difference as other than a binary and a curse.

But in what sense do the binary and the curse nonetheless remain in place? Heidegger, inquiring into the nature of the language in Trakl's poetry, declares:

> It speaks by answering to that journey on which the stranger moves in advance. The path upon which he has struck out leads away from the old degenerate *Geschlecht*. It offers company on the way to the decline into the preserved earliness of the unborn *Geschlecht*. The language of the poem that has its site in departedness answers to the homecoming of the unborn human *Geschlecht* into the peaceful beginning of its quieter essence.[64]

Does the unborn *Geschlecht* still fall under the sway of discord, inasmuch as it distinguishes itself from its degenerate double? Such a conclusion appears inescapable if the notion of homecoming in the above passage is stripped of its radicality. The home of the *Geschlecht* cannot properly stand over against the homelessness of its degeneration and reification unless it is indeterminate, and as indeterminate its opposition is therefore essentially an inclusion. The path of the stranger leads nowhere, and it is in this nowhere that the *Geschlecht* finds its home. The place of Trakl's poem is, strictly speaking, a no-place. And yet Heidegger writes: "The sitedness of the site that gathers Trakl's work into itself is the concealed essence of departedness, and is called 'Evening Land', the Occident." The West as the land of evening, as the land of decay, is too dissolute, however, to be present-at-hand. Decay is not something that has struck the West. On the contrary, it is its essence. If, in 1912, Trakl wonders whether he should emigrate to Borneo,[65] then there is no necessity that dictates that this should be interpreted as a fantasized flight from the decadence of high capitalism. Decay in Trakl's poetry cannot be reduced to a moral phenomenon and just as Rimbaud, in "L'Impossible," discovers the East in the West, Trakl may have been hoping to come upon the truth of the West in the tropical, and thus more rampant, decomposition of the Indonesian archipelago. When Heidegger ascribes to Trakl a single, yet missing, poem, it is perhaps with an intimation that the decay in Trakl's poems was, for Trakl, himself deficient. The substantiality of the poems is, as it were, an obstacle to the decay that they invoke. Trakl's singular poem is the non-work of the West, and it is by means of the absolute and Utopian decay of its impossibility that it satirically condemns, and in condemning embraces, the partially decomposed figures of the poems themselves. The *Geschlecht*, like the *Volk*, is missing, but only as such can it constitute human community.

Conclusion

Heidegger's conception of the *Volk* cannot be extricated from his engagement with National Socialism. Its importance as a factor in his decision to join the NSDAP was simply too great. And yet its role in determining Heidegger's commitment to Hitler is an insufficient reason for identifying Heidegger's conception of the *Volk* with the National Socialist conception of the Aryan "type" (*Art*). Heidegger's people does not take its definition from biologism. It is, however, through the very radicality with which he rejected biologism that Heidegger is unable to keep his conception of the *Volk* at a distance from the Nazi reification of humanity. Rejecting biologism even to its foundations in the thing-concepts of classical ontology, Heidegger elaborates a conception of the *Volk* that does not rely on the metaphysical understanding of Being as presence.

Heidegger's people is not a being that gives itself up to be apprehended in the light of presence, biologistically or otherwise. It is a being-outside-of-itself. As such, it is essentially corrupt and therefore lacks the means to avoid contamination with the purity of the Aryan "type." But in the fundamental impurity of Heidegger's *Volk*, in the stain of its Nazism, there has also to be discerned a resistance to the regime that extends further, philosophically, than any other resistance. Heidegger's opposition is nonetheless inextricable from acquiescence because it derives from an opposition to the understanding of the distinctness of beings on which Nazism erected its apparatus of terror and in terms of which the enemies of the regime conceived their resistance. The stain on Heidegger's people is a consequence of its undecidability and the challenge it presents to the very possibility of control. Philosophically, Heidegger's conception of *Volk* cannot hold itself back from contact with Nazism: that Heidegger, on the basis of his cruder political sympathies, did not merely not hold himself back is another matter. After the war, the *Volk* does not cease to be corrupt; instead, in the essay on *Geschlecht* this corruption is carried further to include the animal.

For Heidegger, undecidability is the essence of the German *Volk*. It is likewise the essence of Dasein. But is undecidability not annulled through its determination as "German"? And does not the direct association of the *Volk* with Dasein reduce non-German peoples, in a gesture reminiscent of Nazi racism, to beings present-at-hand? What Heidegger means by "German" is, however, at once orthodox and heterodox. The undecidability of Heidegger's *Volk* is the consummation and destruction of the complacent anti-positivism of the tradition of German cultural nationalism. Heidegger's people does not congeal into a stable identity over against the present-at-hand. With Heidegger, the anti-positivism of German cultural nationalism is thought through to a conception of the *Volk* that contests the determination of beings under the metaphysics of presence. German nationalism hence becomes, for Heidegger, inseparable from the question of the Being of Dasein. The *Volk*, through understanding its own difference from the present-at-hand, is able to understand the Being that is proper to Dasein and that has gone unthought since the inception of classical ontology. The *Volk*'s direct association with Dasein is its proximity to an understanding of its Being. Accordingly, the uprising of the German people under Hitler was able to assume in Heidegger's eyes the aspect of a drive to the question of Being. In the prevailing preoccupation with the specificity of the *Volk*, Heidegger was willing to see an engagement with the ontological specificity of human Dasein as such, rather than a hierarchization of races.

In the name of the *Volk* of the question of Being, Heidegger expressed his allegiance to the Hitlerian dictatorship in 1933. And in the name of this conception of the Germans, Heidegger likewise resigned the rectorship of Freiburg University and directed his attention to poetry. Heidegger's people is the people promised first by Hitler and then by Hölderlin. The transition from the state to poetry was not a transition from the biologistically distinct people of National Socialism to the people of Hölderlin's nonpositive nationalism. In 1933, Heidegger's *Volk* is arguably still more of a being-outside-of-itself than the *Volk* of the subsequent lectures on poetry, because it is the people whose impurity encompasses even biologism. In Heidegger's refusal and overdetermined inability to extricate himself from National Socialism, the *Volk* remains in an uncanny play of substitution with the specimens of the Aryan race. Heidegger's people thereby evades the mission of thinking Dasein's difference from the present-at-hand and nonetheless thinks this difference in the impurity proper to it.

Notes

INTRODUCTION

1. See Karl Löwith, *Mein Leben in Deutschland vor und nach 1933*, excerpt translated as "My Last Meeting with Heidegger in Rome, 1936" by Richard Wolin in *The Heidegger Controversy: A Critical Reader*, ed. Richard Wolin (Cambridge, Mass.: MIT Press, 1993), 142.

2. Cf. Johannes Fritsche, *Historical Destiny and National Socialism in Heidegger's "Being and Time"* (Berkeley: University of California Press, 1999), 126: "Even if, however, the section on historicality stood alone and were not preceded by the sections on falling and on conscience and solicitude, one sees easily that Heidegger's concept of historicality is identical to Hitler's and Scheler's ideas of history and thus politically on the Right." Without the mythical past of the pure race or the restoration of objective ethical values, it is not at all easy to see that Heidegger's concept of historicality is *identical* to either Hitler's or Scheler's. However, the more general charge of the reactionary character of Heidegger's concept of historicality is not so quickly answered.

3. Heidegger, "Ansprache am 11. November in Leipzig," in *Reden und andere Zeugnisse eines Lebensweges*, ed. Hermann Heidegger, in *Gesamtausgabe* (Frankfurt a/M: Vittorio Klostermann, 2000), 16: 191. Further references to Heidegger's *Gesamtausgabe* (1975–) use the abbreviation *GA*. Translations are my own unless otherwise indicated.

4. See Erich Jaensch, *Die Wissenschaft und die deutsche völkische Bewegung* (Marburg: N. G. Ewert, 1933).

5. Heidegger, *Being and Time*, trans. John Macquarrie and Edward Robinson (London: SCM Press, 1962), 62. All emphases in the quotations in this book are to be found in the original.

6. Heidegger, *Sein und Zeit*, ed. Friedrich-Wilhelm von Herrmann (1977), in *GA*, 2: 51n.

7. Aristotle, *Metaphysica*, in *The Works of Aristotle*, trans. W. D. Ross (Oxford: Clarendon Press, 1908–52), 8: 998b.

8. Heidegger, *Aristoteles, Metaphysik θ 1–3*, ed. Heinrich Hüni (1981), in *GA*, 33: 47.

9. In the 1951 text "Logos (Heraklit, Fragment 50)" in *Vorträge und Aufsätze*, ed. Friedrich-Wilhelm von Herrmann (2000), in *GA*, 7: 211–34, Heidegger offers a seemingly less oppositional reading of the fragment of Heraclitus better known by the paraphrase "All is One." It is a characteristic of Heidegger's exegeses of foundational philosophical texts that he avoids open polemics and rejections. The reservation that Heidegger utters with regards to the prevalence of the One is thus easily overlooked. The One, for Heidegger, gathers; it is not a fait accompli.

10. Kant, *Critique of Pure Reason*, trans. Norman Kemp Smith (London: Macmillan, 1933), A 598 B 626.

11. Ibid., A 600, B 628.

12. Kierkegaard, *Concluding Unscientific Postscript to Philosophical Fragments*, trans. Howard V. Hong and Edna H. Hong (Princeton, N.J.: Princeton University Press, 1992), 330.

13. Otto Pöggeler, *Martin Heidegger's Path of Thinking*, trans. Daniel Magurshak and Sigmund Barber (Atlantic Highlands, N.J.: Humanities Press International, 1987), 251 n. 32.

14. Heidegger, "Erläuterungen und Grundsätzliches" in *Reden und andere Zeugnisse eines Lebensweges*, in *GA*, 16: 414.

15. Dominique Janicaud, *The Shadow of That Thought*, trans. Michael Gendre (Evanston, Ill.: Northwestern University Press, 1996), 37–41.

16. Heidegger, *Being and Time*, 436. Translation modified.

17. Hans Sluga, *Heidegger's Crisis: Philosophy and Politics in Nazi Germany* (Cambridge, Mass.: Harvard University Press, 1993), 136.

18. Heidegger, *Being and Time*, 428.

19. Ibid., 67.

20. Heidegger, "The Rectorate 1933/34: Facts and Thoughts," in *Martin Heidegger and National Socialism: Questions and Answers*, ed. Günther Neske and Emil Kettering, trans. Lisa Harries (New York: Paragon House, 1990), 19.

21. Heidegger, *Being and Time*, 436.

22. Ibid., 163.

23. Ibid., 155.

24. Ibid., 164.

25. Ibid.

26. Ibid., 165.

27. Georg Lukács, *Die Zerstörung der Vernunft* (Neuwied am Rhein: Luchterhand, 1962), 440.

28. Pierre Bourdieu, *The Political Ontology of Martin Heidegger*, trans. Peter Collier (Stanford: Stanford University Press, 1991), 79.

29. Heidegger, *Being and Time*, 167.

30. Ibid., 168.

31. Heidegger, "Homecoming/To Kindred Ones," in *Elucidations of Hölderlin's Poetry*, trans. Keith Hoeller (New York: Humanity Books, 2000), 48.

32. Heidegger, *Hölderlins Hymnen "Germanien" und "Der Rhein,"* ed. Susanne Ziegler (1980), in *GA*, 39: 56.

33. Heidegger, *Sein und Wahrheit: 1. Die Grundfrage der Philosophie 2. Vom Wesen der Wahrheit*, ed. Hartmut Tietjen (2001), in *GA*, 36–37: 263.

34. Heidegger, *Hölderlins Hymne "Andenken,"* ed. Curd Ochwadt (1982), in *GA*, 52: 131.

35. Heidegger, *Being and Time*, 447.

36. On the people that is born in Romanticism, see Ernst Anrich in his foreword to a wartime edition of Ernst Moritz Arndt, *Germanien und Europa* (Berlin: W. Kohlhammer, 1940), 7: "In the hard struggle to distinguish properly the completely new from both the ideas of 1789 and the powers of absolutism, this minority was not able to come to a full inner victory or to penetrate the nation to such an extent that, even after 1815, the nation could retain the thought in its clarity. What rather took place in the nineteenth century was the reversion and renewed collapse into the ideas of rationalism. Only the far more encompassing and consistent breakthrough of the same idea in the National Socialist revolution has repulsed this."

37. Cf. Marx's letter of May 1843 to Arnold Ruge in *Early Texts*, trans. David McLellan (Oxford: Basil Blackwell, 1971), 74, in which he rebuffs him for quoting the well-known denunciation of the Germans in Hölderlin's *Hyperion* as a description of present conditions: "Your letter, my dear friend, is a good elegy, a choking elegy; but it is definitely not political. No people despairs." Marx's objection is that what in Hölderlin had been politically apposite has, in the space of a few decades, become merely "literary".

38. Ernest Renan, "La Guerre entre la France et l'Allemagne," in *Qu'est-ce qu'une nation?* (Paris: Imprimerie nationale, 1996), 163.

39. Giorgio Agamben, "What Is a People?" in *Means Without End*, trans. Vincenzo Binetti and Cesare Casarino (Minneapolis: University of Minnesota Press, 2000), 35.

40. Heidegger, *Logik als die Frage nach dem Wesen der Sprache*, ed. Günter Seubold (1998), in *GA*, 38: 58.

41. Agamben, *Homo Sacer: Sovereign Power and Bare Life*, trans. Daniel Heller-Roazen (Stanford: Stanford University Press, 1998), 152.

42. Gilles Deleuze and Félix Guattari, *A Thousand Plateaus: Capitalism and Schizophrenia*, trans. Brian Massumi (London: Athlone Press, 1988), 340.

43. See Georg Christoph Lichtenberg, *Aphorisms*, trans. R. J. Hollingdale (Harmondsworth, U.K.: Penguin Books, 1990), 78: "Even if they were of use for nothing else, the poets of antiquity at least enable us here and there to get to know the opinions of the common people. . . . For our folksongs are often full of a mythology known to no one but the fool who made the folksong."

44. Hegel, *The Philosophy of History*, trans. J. Sibree (New York: Dover, 1956), 451–53.

45. Hegel, "The English Reform Bill," in *Political Writings*, trans. T. M. Knox (Oxford: Clarendon Press, 1964), 329.

46. For a discussion of the politicization of Darwin's theories in nineteenth-century Germany, see Daniel Gasman, *The Scientific Origins of National Socialism: Social Darwinism in Ernst Haeckel and the German Monist League* (London: Macdonald, 1971).

47. Fichte, *Addresses to the German Nation*, trans. R. F. Jones and G. H. Turnbull (New York: Harper Torchbooks, 1968), 107.

48. Heidegger, *An Introduction to Metaphysics*, trans. Ralph Manheim (New Haven, Conn.: Yale University Press, 1959), 199.

49. Rainer Marten, "Ein rassistisches Konzept von Humanität," in *Badische Zeitung*, Dec. 19–20, 1987, 14.

50. Silvio Vietta, *Heideggers Kritik am Nationalsozialismus und an der Technik* (Tübingen: Niemeyer, 1989), 91–92.

51. Heidegger, *An Introduction to Metaphysics*, 37–39. Translation modified.

52. See, for instance, Hegel's comments on the decline of philosophy in all nations except Germany in his "Rede zum Antritt des philosophischen Lehramtes an der Universität Berlin," in *Vorlesungsmanuskripte II (1816–1831)*, in *Gesammelte Werke* (Hamburg: Felix Meiner, 1995), 18: 15: "This science has taken its refuge among the *Germans* and lives *alone* still in them; to us the preservation of this *holy light* has been entrusted, and it is our vocation to care for it and to feed it, and to see to it that the *highest* that man can possess, *the self-consciousness of his essence*, is not extinguished and destroyed."

53. Jacques Derrida, *Of Spirit: Heidegger and the Question*, trans. Geoff Bennington and Rachel Bowlby (Chicago: Chicago University Press, 1984), 39–40.

54. Jean-Pierre Faye, *Langages totalitaires* (Paris: Hermann, 1972), 199.

55. Heidegger, "Wege zur Aussprache," in *Aus der Erfahrung des Denkens*, ed. Hermann Heidegger (1983), in *GA*, 13: 17.

56. Hitler, *Mein Kampf*, trans. Ralph Manheim (Boston: Houghton Mifflin, 1943), 56.

57. Nietzsche, *Beyond Good and Evil*, trans. R. J. Hollingdale (Harmondsworth, U.K.: Penguin Books, 1990), 176.

58. Emmanuel Lévinas, "Reflections on the Philosophy of Hitlerism," trans. Séan Hand in *Critical Inquiry* 17 (Autumn 1990): 70.

59. Ibid.

60. See Hitler's remarks to Speer on the justice of the German defeat as quoted in Alan Bullock, *Hitler: A Study in Tyranny* (London: Odhams Press, 1952), 707. Once Germany had been thwarted in its imperialist aspirations, Hitler's reverence for strength—as that which realizes the universal—led him to acknowledge Russia's superiority. Eugenics and German nationalism here part ways. The *Volk*, which had been privileged on the basis of its potential for being bred into the *Herrenvolk* (the restoration of an allegedly pure bloodline was conceived as a means to this end), had not realized itself. For both Hitler and Heidegger, the essence of the

Germans is tied to the future, but for Hitler it was a future in which the present-at-hand was to hold uncontested sway. Hitler argues more like a breeder than a Darwinian when he speaks of the malleability of the Germans, since what is at issue is not Darwin's challenge to the immutability of species but rather the breeder's traditional axiom of the mutability of varieties. And as much as he derides for their unworldliness and bloodless absolutes the idealist and Christian conceptions of humanity, Hitler perpetuates the latter's divide between Man and Nature. He misinterprets the Darwinian doctrine of the survival of the fittest, absolutizing fitness and ignoring that for Darwin it is always a question of an organism's fitness for a specific environment. Fitness takes on a Platonic cast, as can be observed in the regime's attitude to the bearers of physiological abnormalities. The decision of Nature in the struggle for existence was declared to be simply anticipated in the clinical murder of these individuals. But euthanasia is a caricature of the workings of Nature, since the abnormalities are being judged against a necessarily abstract model human being rather than in terms of their effects in the volatile continuum of factors by which Darwin understands environment. Given the volatility of the environment and the multitude of elements composing any organism, it is not possible to deduce from the death of an individual a judgment on the part of Nature with respect to that individual's particular deviation. In National Socialism, the fit human organism, notwithstanding all the strained attempts to furnish a biological explanation for the relative technological superiority of the Germans, is an emanation of the homogenizing procedures of technicism. The practical bloodthirstiness of the regime is a corollary of its ideological anaemia.

61. Ernst Krieck, "Germanischer Mythos und Heideggersche Philosophie," in *Volk im Werden* (1934), included in *Nachlese zu Heidegger*, ed. Guido Schneeberger (Bern, 1962), 225–26.

62. See, e.g., "Qu'est-ce que l'existentialisme?" (1945), 146–47, and "L'Enormité' de Heidegger" (1974), 162, in *De l'existentialisme à Heidegger*, ed. Jean Beaufret (Paris: J. Vrin, 1986).

63. Ulrich Sieg, "Die Verjudung des deutschen Geistes," *Die Zeit* (Hamburg), December 22, 1989, 50. An excerpt from Heidegger's letter to Victor Schoerer, *Ministerialrat* and head of the Baden department of higher education, reads: "it concerns nothing less than the urgent reflection on the choice before which we stand, either to bring once again to our German spiritual life genuine native forces and educators or to deliver it up definitively to the growing Judaization in the broader and narrower sense."

64. Jürgen Habermas, *The Philosophical Discourse of Modernity*, trans. Frederick Lawrence (Cambridge: Polity Press, 1987), 154.

65. Cf. the reading of the *Contributions to Philosophy* offered in Alexander Schwan, "Heideggers *Beiträge zur Philosophie* und die Politik," in *Martin Heidegger: Kunst-Politik-Technik*, ed. Christoph Jamme and Karsten Harries (Munich: Wilhelm Fink, 1992), 185: "Heidegger is consequently now no longer able to associate himself with this folkish science and weltanschauung as in 1933."

66. Heidegger, *Contributions to Philosophy*, trans. Parvis Emad and Kenneth Maly (Bloomington: Indiana University Press, 1999), 103. Translation modified.

67. Cf. the exposition in Richard Polt, "Metaphysical Liberalism in Heidegger's *Beiträge zur Philosophie*," *Political Theory* 25 (October 1997): 665: "Liberalism concerns itself with the maintenance and defense of the 'I'; Nazism concerns itself with the maintenance and defense of the *Volk*, which in this worldview reduces to nothing but a larger 'I'—a willing, representing, power-seeking ego on the scale of an entire race. In both cases, the essence of man is taken for granted and is a form of subjectivity; what is lost is historical openness to Being. However, Heidegger by no means abandons the idea of the *Volk* but makes the essence of the people reside in an elite who are capable of creatively interpreting the truth of Being." Once elitism has been attributed to Heidegger, his critique of subjectivity and the will to power loses its coherence.

68. Heidegger, *Parmenides*, trans. André Schuwer (Bloomington: Indiana University Press, 1992), 137.

69. See, e.g., Robert J. Dostal, "The Public and the People: Heidegger's Illiberal Politics," *Review of Metaphysics* 47 (March 1994): 552: "The over-generalized absurdity of Heidegger's critique is similarly apparent in his attack on leading Nazi intellectuals and on Nazi 'people's science' (*völkische Wissenschaft*) as liberal. Here we see the truth of the claim that Heidegger was unknowing about politics and apolitical."

70. F. M. Barnard, *Herder's Social and Political Thought: From Enlightenment to Nationalism* (Oxford: Clarendon Press, 1965), 166–67.

71. Heidegger, *Logik als die Frage nach dem Wesen der Sprache*, in *GA*, 38: 169.

72. Philippe Lacoue-Labarthe, *Heidegger, Art, and Politics: The Fiction of the Political*, trans. Chris Turner (London: Basil Blackwell, 1990), 95.

73. For a report on this colloquium, see Jean-Paul Aron, *Les Modernes* (Paris: Gallimard, 1984), 122.

74. Deleuze and Guattari, *What is Philosophy?* trans. Hugh Tomlinson and Graham Burchill (London: Verso, 1994), 109.

75. Ibid., 108.

76. Ibid., 109.

77. Reported in Heinrich Wigand Petzet, *Encounters and Dialogues with Martin Heidegger, 1929–1976*, trans. Parvis Emad and Kenneth Maly (Chicago: University of Chicago Press, 1993), 37.

78. Deleuze and Guattari, *What is Philosophy?* 109.

79. Ibid., 108.

80. Deleuze, *Cinema 2: The Time-Image*, trans. Hugh Tomlinson and Robert Galeta (Minneapolis: University of Minnesota Press, 1989), 220.

81. Heidegger, "Die gegenwärtige Lage und die künftige Aufgabe der deutschen Philosophie," in *Reden und andere Zeugnisse eines Lebensweges*, in *GA*, 16: 333.

82. Heidegger, "Hölderlin's Earth and Heaven," in *Elucidations of Hölderlin's Poetry*, trans. Hoeller, 200–201.

83. Heidegger, "Die deutsche Universität," in *Reden und andere Zeugnisse eines Lebensweges*, in *GA*, 16: 302.

84. Hobbes, *Leviathan*, ed. Richard Tuck (Cambridge: Cambridge University Press, 1991), 114.

85. Hobbes, *De Cive*, ed. Howard Warrender (Oxford: Clarendon Press, 1983), 151.

86. Heidegger, "Zum Semesterbeginn (3. November 1933)," in *Reden und andere Zeugnisse eines Lebensweges*, in *GA*, 16: 184.

87. Hegel, *The History of Philosophy*, trans. E. S. Haldane (London: Routledge & Kegan Paul, 1955), 1: 60.

88. Heidegger, *What Is Philosophy?* trans. William Kluback and Jean T. Wilde (London: Vision Press, 1956), 31.

89. Heidegger, "Only a God Can Save Us," trans. Maria P. Alter and John D. Caputo in *Heidegger Controversy*, ed Wolin, 104. See also Otto Pöggeler, *Die Frage nach der Kunst: Von Hegel zu Heidegger* (Munich: Alber, 1984), 30, where Pöggeler records a remark by Heidegger from 1974 lamenting the destructiveness of democracy.

90. Kant, *Toward Perpetual Peace* in *Practical Philosophy*, trans. Mary J. Gregor (Cambridge: Cambridge University Press, 1996), 324.

CHAPTER I

1. Heidegger, *Being and Time*, 438.

2. Heidegger, *Die Kategorien- und Bedeutungslehre des Duns Scotus*, in *Frühe Schriften*, ed. Friedrich-Wilhelm von Herrmann (1978), in *GA*, 1: 411.

3. Heidegger, "The Idea of Philosophy and the Problem of Worldview," in *Towards the Definition of Philosophy*, trans. Ted Sadler (London: Athlone Press, 2000), 81.

4. Hans A. Fischer-Barnicol, "Spiegelungen-Vermittlungen," in *Erinnerungen an Martin Heidegger*, ed. Günther Neske (Pfullingen: Günther Neske, 1977), 100: "I remembered that Heidegger had once described Hegel as his 'great adversary.'"

5. Heidegger, *Sein und Wahrheit: 1. Die Grundfrage der Philosophie 2. Vom Wesen der Wahrheit*, in *GA*, 36–37: 14.

6. Carl Schmitt, *Staat, Bewegung, Volk* (Hamburg: Hanseatische Verlagsanstalt, 1933), 32.

7. Hegel, *Phenomenology of Spirit*, trans. A. V. Miller (Oxford: Oxford University Press, 1977), 18–19.

8. Heidegger, "Die Negativität: Eine Auseinandersetzung mit Hegel aus dem Ansatz in der Negativität (1938/39, 1941)," in *Hegel*, ed. Ingrid Schüßler (1993), in *GA*, 68: 24.

9. Hegel, *Philosophy of Nature: Being Part Two of the Encyclopaedia of the Philosophical Sciences*, trans. A. V. Miller (Oxford: Oxford University Press, 1970), 444.

10. Ibid., 441.

11. Ibid.

12. Ibid., 36.

13. Ibid., 28.

14. Ibid., 34.

15. Heidegger, *Being and Time*, 482.

16. Ibid., 483.

17. Denise Souche-Dagues, "The Dialogue Between Heidegger and Hegel," in *Heidegger: Critical Assessments*, ed. Christopher Macann (London: Routledge, 1992), 2: 249.

18. Ibid.

19. Heidegger, *Being and Time*, 485.

20. Cf. Jere Paul Surber, "Heidegger's Critique of Hegel's Notion of Time," *Philosophy and Phenomenological Research* 39 (1978–79): 358–77. Surber attempts to weaken Heidegger's critique of Hegel's understanding of time by drawing attention to the one-sidedness of any claim about a particular moment in Hegel's system. Yet it is the philosophical basis of the very notion of totality that is at stake in Heidegger's retrieval of the ecstatic character of transcendence.

21. Heidegger, *The Concept of Time*, trans. William McNeill (Oxford: Blackwell, 1992), 21.

22. Hegel, *Philosophy of Nature: Being Part Two of the Encyclopaedia of the Philosophical Sciences*, 35.

23. Heidegger, *Hegel's Phenomenology of Spirit*, trans. Parvis Emad and Kenneth Maly (Bloomington: Indiana University Press, 1994), 38–39.

24. Ibid., 100.

25. Heidegger, *Being and Time*, 56.

26. Heidegger, *Contributions to Philosophy*, 188. Translation modified. Heidegger's *Was ist Metaphysik* (1929) is translated under the title "What Is Metaphysics?" in Heidegger, *Basic Writings*, ed. David Farrell Krell (San Francisco: Harper, 1993).

27. Hegel, *Philosophy of Right*, trans. T. M. Knox (Oxford: Oxford University Press, 1952), 10.

28. Heidegger, *Hölderlins Hymnen "Germanien" und "Der Rhein,"* in *GA*, 39: 72–73.

29. Heidegger, *Being and Time*, 298.

30. Ibid., 306–7.

31. Ibid., 281.

32. Ibid., 279.

33. Ibid., 287.

34. Ibid., 288.

35. Ibid., 309.

36. Ibid., 310.

37. Ibid.

38. Heidegger, "The Call to the Labor Service," trans. William S. Lewis, in *Heidegger Controversy*, ed. Wolin, 55.

39. Hegel, "Rede zum Antritt des philosophischen Lehramtes an der Universität Berlin," in *Vorlesungsmanuskripte II (1816–1831)*, in *Gesammelte Werke*, 18: 18: "The taciturn essence of the universe does not have in itself any power that could offer resistance to the daring of knowledge; it must open itself up before it, and lay its wealth and its depths before its eyes and deliver itself up to be enjoyed." This eroticization of knowledge will be complemented and unsettled in Kafka by an eroticization of the condition of being known. See the last of the "Reflections on Sin, Suffering, Hope, and the True Way," in Franz Kafka, *Wedding Preparations in the Country*, trans. Ernst Kaiser and Eithne Wilkins (London: Secker & Warburg, 1954), 53: "There is no need to leave the house. Stay at your table and listen. Don't even listen, just wait. Don't even wait, be completely quiet and alone. The world will offer itself to you to be unmasked, it can't do otherwise, in raptures it will writhe before you."

40. Hegel, *Philosophy of Right*, trans. Knox, 134.

41. Jacques Taminiaux, "Finitude and the Absolute: Remarks on Hegel and Heidegger," in *Heidegger: The Man and the Thinker*, ed. Thomas Sheehan (Chicago: Precedent, 1981), 187–208.

42. Hegel, *System of Ethical Life and First Philosophy of Spirit*, trans. H. S. Harris and T. M. Knox (Albany: State University of New York Press, 1979), 144.

43. Heidegger, "On the Question of Being," trans. William McNeill, in *Pathmarks*, ed. McNeill (Cambridge: Cambridge University Press, 1998), 311.

44. Michel Foucault, "A Preface to Transgression," in *Language, Counter-Memory, Practice*, trans. Donald F. Bouchard and Sherry Simon (Ithaca, N.Y.: Cornell University Press, 1977), 35–36.

45. Hegel, *Philosophy of Right*, trans. Knox, 155.

46. Hitler, *Mein Kampf*, 393.

47. Ernst Cassirer, *The Myth of the State* (New Haven, Conn.: Yale University Press, 1974), 293.

48. Hegel, *Phenomenology of Spirit*, 117.

49. See Montaigne, "That to Philosophize Is to Learn to Die," in *The Complete Works of Montaigne*, trans. Donald M. Frame (London: Hamish Hamilton, 1958), 60: "Premeditation of death is premeditation of freedom. He who has learned how to die has unlearned how to be a slave. Knowing how to die frees us from all subjection and constraint. There is nothing evil in life for the man who has thoroughly grasped the fact that to be deprived of life is not an evil."

50. Hegel, *Phenomenology of Spirit*, 119.

51. Heidegger, "Overcoming Metaphysics," trans. Joan Stambaugh, in *Heidegger Controversy*, ed. Wolin, 69.

52. Heidegger, "Letter from Heidegger to Marcuse of January 20, 1948," trans. Richard Wolin, in *Heidegger Controversy*, ed. Wolin, 162.

53. Cf. Karl Jaspers, *Notizen zu Martin Heidegger*, ed. Hans Saner (Munich: R. Piper, 1978), 79. Jaspers decries the irresponsible affirmation of Marxism that he sees in the "Letter on 'Humanism.'"

54. Heidegger, "Letter on 'Humanism,'" trans. Frank A. Capuzzi, in *Pathmarks*, ed. McNeill, 258–59.

55. Ibid., 259.

56. Marx, *Critique of Hegel's 'Philosophy of Right,'* trans. Annette Jolin and Joseph O'Malley (Cambridge: Cambridge University Press, 1970), 14–15.

57. Marx and Engels, *The German Ideology*, trans. S. Ryazanskaya (London: Lawrence & Wishart, 1965), 168.

58. See E. Oldemeyer, "Eher auf Husserl als auf Lukács zielend," *Frankfurter Allgemeine Zeitung*, March 3, 1988, 9.

59. Lucien Goldmann, *Lukács and Heidegger: Towards a New Philosophy*, trans. William Q. Boelhower (London: Routledge & Kegan Paul, 1977), 13 et passim.

60. Kostas Axelos, *Einführung in ein künftiges Denken: Über Marx und Heidegger* (Tübingen: Max Niemeyer, 1966), 17.

61. Georg Lukács, *History and Class Consciousness*, trans. Rodney Livingstone (London: Merlin Press, 1971), xxxvi.

62. Ibid., xx.

63. Ibid., xxiii–iv.

64. Ibid., xxii–iii.

65. Ibid., xxiv.

66. Ibid., xxiii.

67. Althusser, *For Marx*, trans. Ben Brewster (London: Penguin Books, 1969), 222n.

68. Heidegger, *Sein und Wahrheit: 1. Die Grundfrage der Philosophie 2. Vom Wesen der Wahrheit*, in *GA*, 36–37: 151.

69. Heidegger, *Contributions to Philosophy*, 224. Translation modified.

CHAPTER 2

1. José Ortega y Gasset, *The Revolt of the Masses* (London: Unwin, 1961), 10.

2. Christopher Fynsk, "But Suppose We Were to Take the Rectorial Address Seriously . . . Gérard Granel's *De l'université*," *Graduate Faculty Philosophy Journal* 14–15 (1991): 342–43.

3. It is hard, and arguably reprehensible, to imagine what the Nazi symbol once suggested. Consider Marie von Thurn und Taxis's description of Rilke's living quarters in Muzot in her 1932 *Erinnerungen an Rainer Maria Rilke* (Frankfurt a/M: Insel, 1966), 112: "Beside it the meager bedroom and the little house chapel—above the narrow Gothic door, strange and mysterious, the swastika. Everything seems to have been made for the poet."

4. Joseph Goebbels, *Goebbels spricht: Reden aus Kampf und Sieg* (Oldenburg: Gerhard Stalling, 1933), 75.

5. Heidegger, "The Rectorate 1933/34: Facts and Thoughts," in *Martin Heidegger and National Socialism: Questions and Answers*, ed. Günther Neske and Emil Kettering, trans. Lisa Harries (New York: Paragon House, 1990), 22.

6. Ibid., 23.

7. Heidegger, "Only a God Can Save Us," in *Heidegger Controversy*, ed. Wolin, 95.

8. Heidegger, "Telegramm an den Reichskanzler," in *Reden und andere Zeugnisse eines Lebensweges*, in *GA*, 16: 105.

9. Heidegger, "The Self-Assertion of the German University," trans. William S. Lewis in *Heidegger Controversy*, ed. Wolin, 31. Translation modified.

10. William McNeill, *The Glance of the Eye: Heidegger, Aristotle, and the Ends of Theory* (Albany: State University of New York Press, 1999), 140.

11. Heidegger, "Nur ein Gott kann uns noch retten," in *Reden und andere Zeugnisse eines Lebensweges*, in *GA*, 16: 657. This is one of the sentences that, without Heidegger's knowledge, were deleted by the editors of *Der Spiegel* from the first published version of the interview. See the relevant editorial notes in the *Gesamtausgabe*.

12. See, e.g., Ernst Krieck's rectorial address, *Die Erneuerung der Universität* (Frankfurt a/M: H. Bechhold, 1933), 11: "Once the barriers between the various sciences have been broken through, from within every specialist question the view would open on the great ideological [*weltanschaulich*] interconnection of sense, whereby the organic union, the living exchange between all individual disciplines would be produced."

13. Heidegger, "Letter on 'Humanism,'" in *Pathmarks*, ed. McNeill, 261.

14. Heidegger, "Self-Assertion of the German University," in *Heidegger Controversy*, ed. Wolin, 38.

15. Ibid., 35.

16. Rüdiger Safranski, *Martin Heidegger: Between Good and Evil*, trans. Ewald Osers (Cambridge, Mass.: Harvard University Press, 1998), ascribes to the rectorial address a central metaphor of struggle, which he believes can be narrowed to the metaphor of "a shock-troop engagement" (p. 243). But argument by analogy is, by nature, poor criticism.

17. Heidegger, *Sein und Wahrheit: 1. Die Grundfrage der Philosphie 2. Vom Wesen der Wahrheit*, in *GA*, 36–37: 90–91.

18. Ibid., 91–92.

19. Heidegger, "Self-Assertion of the German University," in *Heidegger Controversy*, ed. Wolin, 30.

20. Heidegger, *Einleitung in die Philosophie*, ed. Otto Saame and Ina Saame-Speidel (1996), in *GA*, 27: 7–8.

21. Heidegger, *Sein und Wahrheit: 1. Die Grundfrage der Philosphie 2. Vom Wesen der Wahrheit*, in *GA*, 36–37: 255.

22. Heidegger, "Erläuterungen und Grundsätzliches," in *Reden und andere Zeugnisse eines Lebensweges*, in *GA*, 16: 410–11.

23. Heidegger, "Only a God Can Save Us," in *Heidegger Controversy*, ed. Wolin, 95. Translation modified.

24. Heidegger, "Self-Assertion of the German University," in *Heidegger Controversy*, ed. Wolin, 37.

25. Heidegger, *What Is a Thing?* trans. W. B. Barton Jr. and Vera Deutsch (Chicago: Regnery, 1967), 150.

26. See, e.g., Ludwig Bieberbach, *Die völkische Verwurzelung der Wissenschaft (Typen mathematischen Schaffens)* (Heidelberg: Kommissionsverlag der Weiß'-schen Universitätsbuchhandlung, 1940). For Bieberbach, in what amounts to a vulgarization of Pierre Duhem's work on the differences between French and British physics, the theories of various modern mathematicians can be seen to betray the race of the exponent and simultaneously their profundity or artificiality.

27. Heidegger, *Logik als die Frage nach dem Wesen der Sprache*, in *GA*, 38: 122.

28. Heidegger's letter of resignation to the minister in Karlsruhe is dated April 14, 1934, and is reproduced in *Reden und andere Zeugnisse eines Lebensweges*, in *GA*, 16: 272. The date of this letter contradicts *Der Spiegel*'s claim, which Heidegger gladly takes up, that he resigned in February 1934. See Heidegger, "Only a God Can Save Us," in *Heidegger Controversy*, ed. Wolin, 100.

29. Heidegger, "Erläuterungen und Grundsätzliches," in *Reden und andere Zeugnisse eines Lebensweges*, in *GA*, 16: 414.

30. Heidegger, "As When on a Holiday . . . ," in *Elucidations of Hölderlin's Poetry*, trans. Hoeller, 86.

31. Ibid., 83.

32. Ibid., 93. Translation modified.

33. Ibid. Translation modified.

34. For all his evocations fo the pre-Socratics, Heidegger is often closer to late antiquity, specifically to the inversions of Gnosticism. Hans Jonas, in an appendix to *The Gnostic Religion* (Boston: Beacon Press, 1963), discusses what he considers to be the Gnostic elements in Heidegger's thought. But he does not treat the antinomianism that is a characteristic of early and middle Heidegger and that comes to its fullest expression in the strategy of failure in the rectorial address.

35. Compare the lecture "The Thing" from 1950, with its meditation on the void of the intact jug, with the rag-and-bone man's fascination for broken equipment in *Being and Time*.

36. Clemens August Hoberg, *Das Dasein des Menschen: Die Grundfrage der Heideggerschen Philosophie* (Zeulenroda: Bernhard Sporn, 1937), 8.

37. Ibid., 90.

38. Ibid.

39. Heidegger, *Introduction to Metaphysics*, 103.

40. Acknowledging Heidegger's reservations about preclassical Greece, Reiner Schürmann, *Heidegger on Being and Acting: From Principles to Anarchy*, trans. Christine-Marie Gros (Bloomington: Indiana University Press, 1990), curiously sees therein his distance from the German Romantics. In what way were the Romantics intent on "reviving experiences inspired by pre-classical Greece" (p. 218)? Schürmann does not elaborate. Indeed the most obvious example of a work in-

spired by preclassical Greece, Kleist's *Penthesilea*, invokes the heroic age in order to subject its notion of glory to the Romantic figure of the secret.

41. Falsehood and glory were by no means considered mutually exclusive in pre-Socratic Greece, as Jacob Burckhardt is at pains to stress throughout his *Greeks and Greek Civilization*, trans. Sheila Stern (London: Fontana, 1998).

42. Aristotle, *Politics*, trans. H. Rackham (London: William Heinemann, 1932), 1253.

43. Deleuze and Guattari, *Thousand Plateaus*, 230.

44. Ibid., 214–15.

45. Hannah Arendt, *The Life of the Mind*, vol. 2: *Willing* (New York: Harcourt Brace Jovanovich, 1978), 188–89.

46. Heidegger, *Vom Wesen der Wahrheit: Zu Platons Höhlengleichnis und Theätet*, ed. Hermann Mörchen (1988) in *GA*, 34: 143.

47. Heidegger, *Hölderlin's Hymn "The Ister,"* trans. William McNeill and Julia Davis (Bloomington: Indiana University Press, 1996), 72.

48. Pöggeler, *Martin Heidegger's Path of Thinking*, trans. Magurshak and Barber, 249 n. 20.

49. Heidegger, *Sein und Wahrheit: 1. Die Grundfrage der Philosphie 2. Vom Wesen der Wahrheit*, in *GA*, 36–37: 231.

50. Heidegger, "On the Essence of Truth," trans. John Sallis, in *Pathmarks*, ed. McNeill, 140.

51. Ibid., 141.

52. Ibid., 142.

53. Ibid., 143–44.

54. Ibid., 145–46.

55. Ibid., 147–48.

56. Heidegger, *Sein und Wahrheit: 1. Die Grundfrage der Philosophie 2. Vom Wesen der Wahrheit*, in *GA*, 36–37: 225.

57. Philippe Lacoue-Labarthe, "Transcendence Ends in Politics," in *Typography: Mimesis, Philosophy, Politics*, ed. Christopher Fynsk (Cambridge, Mass.: Harvard University Press, 1989), 287.

58. Heidegger, "Self-Assertion of the German University," in *Heidegger Controversy*, ed. Wolin, 38–39. Translation modified.

CHAPTER 3

1. The first of the five quotations from Hölderlin that Heidegger discusses in the lecture "Hölderlin and the Essence of Poetry," in *Elucidations of Hölderlin's Poetry*, trans. Hoeller, 51.

2. Heidegger, "Only a God Can Save Us," in *Heidegger Controversy*, ed. Wolin, 101.

3. Heidegger, "Letter to the Rector of Freiburg University, November 4, 1945," trans. Richard Wolin, in *Heidegger Controversy*, ed. Wolin, 65.

4. Heidegger, *Hölderlins Hymne "Andenken,"* in *GA*, 52: 78.

5. Heidegger, *Schelling: Vom Wesen der menschlichen Freiheit (1809)*, ed. Ingrid Schüßler (1988), in *GA*, 42: 40.

6. Heidegger, *Hölderlin's Hymn "The Ister,"* trans. McNeill and Davis, 54–55.

7. Heidegger, *Hölderlins Hymne "Andenken,"* in *GA*, 52: 134.

8. Heidegger, *Hölderlins Hymnen "Germanien" und "Der Rhein,"* in *GA*, 39: 17.

9. Heidegger, *Nietzsche: Europäischer Nihilismus*, ed. Petra Jaeger (1986), in *GA*, 48: 333.

10. Heidegger, "Der Anfang des Abendländischen Denkens: Heraklit," in *Heraklit*, ed. Manfred S. Frings (1979), in *GA*, 55: 83.

11. Heidegger, *Introduction to Metaphysics*, 203. Translation modified.

12. Nietzsche, *The Will to Power*, trans. Walter Kaufmann and R. J. Hollingdale (New York: Vintage Books, 1968), 17.

13. Heidegger, *Heraklit*, in *GA*, 55: 123.

14. Ibid., 180–81.

15. Heidegger, "Overcoming Metaphysics," trans. Joan Stambaugh, in *Heidegger Controversy*, ed. Wolin, 82–83. Translation modified.

16. Heidegger, *What Is Called Thinking?* trans. J. Glenn Gray (New York: Harper & Row, 1968), 66.

17. Heidegger, "Overcoming Metaphysics," in *Heidegger Controversy*, ed. Wolin, 84–85.

18. Heidegger, *Hölderlins Hymnen "Germanien" und "Der Rhein,"* in *GA*, 39: 220.

19. Heidegger, *Nietzsche*, trans. David Farrell Krell (San Francisco: Harper & Row, 1979), 1: 74.

20. Ibid., 159.

21. Ibid., 160.

22. Heidegger, "The Origin of the Work of Art," trans. Albert Hofstadter, in *Basic Writings*, ed. Krell, 170.

23. Ibid., 161.

24. Ibid.

25. Ibid., 159.

26. Heidegger, *Being and Time*, 99.

27. Ibid., 97.

28. Ibid., 102–3.

29. Heidegger, *Die Metaphysik des deutschen Idealismus*, ed. Günter Seubold (1991), in *GA*, 49: 44.

30. Heidegger, *Being and Time*, 100.

31. Ibid., 105.

32. Heidegger, "Origin of the Work of Art," in *Basic Writings*, ed. Krell, 162.

33. Cf. Derrida, *The Truth in Painting*, trans. Geoff Bennington and Ian McLeod (Chicago: Chicago University Press, 1987), 318 et seq. Derrida argues that Heidegger cannot without contradiction claim to see a pair of peasant's shoes

when he "confirms fully that his project was to go beyond the picture as representation" (p. 321).

34. Plato, *The Republic*, in *The Dialogues of Plato*, trans. B. Jowett (Oxford: Clarendon Press, 1953), 2: 597a–b.

35. Heidegger, *Nietzsche*, trans. Krell, 1: 185.

36. Philippe Lacoue-Labarthe, "The Caesura of the Speculative," in *Typography*, ed. Fynsk, 231, discusses this agreement as it relates to Heidegger's enquiry into the essence of truth in his readings of Hölderlin: "It is true that Heidegger constantly sought in Hölderlin the possibility of backing up from the assumption in the speculative mode of *adaequatio* and of 'exiting' *from within* the onto-theologic. This is why the 'logic' of ἀλήθεια can also be inscribed as the 'logic' of *Ent-fernung* [*é-loignement* or '(dis)distancing']. But who knows whether this 'logic' itself (including, too, what ceaselessly carries it off in its most demanding moments) is not also penetrated throughout by (if not subject to) mimetology?" The implication of this logic within mimetology is not pursued by Lacoue-Labarthe to its ground within Heidegger's own thinking.

37. Heidegger, *Nietzsche*, trans. Krell, 1: 186.

38. Heidegger, *The Principle of Reason*, trans. Reginald Lilly (Bloomington: Indiana University Press, 1991), 34.

39. Cf. Claude Lévi-Strauss, *The Savage Mind* (London: George Weidenfeld & Nicolson, 1966), 30–31n.: "Non-representational painting does not, as it thinks, create works which are as real as, if not more real than, the objects of the physical world, but rather realistic imitations of non-existent models."

40. Quoting the passage from *The Principle of Reason* in his essay "Im Horizont der Zeit: Heideggers Werkbegriff und die Kunst der Moderne," in *Kunst und Technik: Gedächtnisschrift zum 100. Geburtstag von Martin Heidegger*, ed. Walter Biemel and Friedrich-Wilhelm von Herrmann (Frankfurt a/M: Klostermann, 1989), Gottfried Boehm discusses the paintings of Mondrian and Tobey and disputes whether Heidegger does not mistake the nature of their art (pp. 279–84). The apparent conservatism of Heidegger's position derives from his adherence to Plato's definition of art. Boehm's genuine obscurantism is manifest in his assumption of the self-evidence of his definition of art for which Mondrian and Tobey are presented as illustrations and the de facto delimitations.

41. For an objection, which is itself a review of the objections, to Heidegger's readings of Plato's meditations on the essence of truth, see Robert J. Dostal, "Beyond Being: Heidegger's Plato," in *Martin Heidegger: Critical Assessments*, ed. Christopher Macann (London: Routledge, 1992), 2: 61–89. However much the distortions and oversights in Heidegger's readings of both Plato and Nietzsche count against them as strict exegeses of philosophical texts, the problem of presence that they help to delineate, and that elucidates the conception of the political shared by National Socialism and its military opponents, retains its status.

42. Heidegger, "Plato's Doctrine of Truth," trans. Thomas Sheehan, in *Pathmarks*, ed. McNeill, 164.

43. Ibid., 173.

44. Heidegger, *Plato's Sophist*, trans. Richard Rojcewicz and André Schuwer (Bloomington: Indiana University Press, 1997), 440.

45. Heidegger, "Plato's Doctrine of Truth," in *Pathmarks*, ed. McNeill, 177.

46. Ibid., 179.

47. Ibid., 174.

48. Cf. John Sallis, *Echoes: After Heidegger* (Bloomington: Indiana University Press, 1990), 33n. Sallis proposes mimesis as a definition of that which in *Kant and the Problem of Metaphysics* is discussed as "repetition." Mimesis would thus be the repetition that discloses the Un-thought of that which is repeated (Heidegger's thinking of mimesis is to be traced to his own hermeneutic practice).

49. Heidegger, "Origin of the Work of Art," in *Basic Writings*, ed. Krell, 204–5. Translation modified.

50. Krzysztof Ziarek, *The Historicity of Experience: Modernity, the Avant-Garde, and the Event* (Evanston, Ill.: Northwestern University Press, 2001), 35.

51. Plato, *The Symposium*, trans. W. Hamilton (Harmondsworth, U.K.: Penguin Books, 1951), 205c.

52. Heidegger, "Origin of the Work of Art," in *Basic Writings*, ed. Krell, 184.

53. Heidegger, *Metaphysik und Nihilismus*, ed. Hans-Joachim Friedrich (1999), in *GA*, 67: 108.

54. Heidegger, "Origin of the Work of Art," in *Basic Writings*, ed. Krell, 197.

55. Heidegger, "Hölderlin and the Essence of Poetry," in *Elucidations of Hölderlin's Poetry*, trans. Hoeller, 55–56.

56. Heidegger, "Letter on 'Humanism,'" in *Pathmarks*, ed. McNeill, 243.

57. Heidegger, "Hölderlin and the Essence of Poetry," in *Elucidations of Hölderlin's Poetry*, trans. Hoeller, 60.

58. Heidegger, *Hölderlins Hymnen "Germanien" und "Der Rhein,"* in *GA*, 39: 33.

59. Heidegger, *Basic Concepts*, trans. Gary E. Aylesworth (Bloomington: Indiana University Press, 1993), 32.

60. Ibid., 34.

61. See Wilhelm von Schramm, "Schöpferische Kritik des Krieges," in *Krieg und Krieger*, ed. Ernst Jünger (Berlin: Junker & Dünnhaupt, 1930), 31–49.

62. For an account of the similarly non-nostalgic, yet protechnological conservatism that was exploited by the Nazis in reconciling modernization with German nationalism, see Jeffrey Herf, *Reactionary Modernism: Technology, Culture, and Politics in Weimar and the Third Reich* (Cambridge: Cambridge University Press, 1984).

63. Heidegger, "Abendgespräch in einem Kriegsgefangenenlager in Rußland zwischen einem Jüngeren und einem Älteren," in *Feldweg-Gespräche (1944/45)*, ed. Ingrid Schüßler (1995), in *GA*, 77: 232–33.

64. Ibid., 234.

65. Cf. Deleuze and Guattari, *Kafka: Toward a Minor Literature*, trans. Dana

Polan (Minneapolis: University of Minnesota Press, 1986), 98n, where they discern in Hölderlin an art of waiting as a defense against contiguity.

66. See Hannah Arendt's treatment of the distinction between οἶκος and πόλις in *The Human Condition* (Chicago: University of Chicago Press, 1958), 28–37.

67. Heidegger, *Introduction to Metaphysics*, 152–53. Translation modified.

68. Max Kommerell, *Der Dichter als Führer in der deutschen Klassik* (Frankfurt a/M: Klostermann, 1942), 474.

69. Heidegger, *Besinnung*, ed. Friedrich-Wilhelm von Herrmann (1997), in *GA*, 66: 37.

70. Ibid., 190–91.

71. Hölderlin, "The Significance of Tragedies," in *Essays and Letters on Theory*, trans. Thomas Pfau (Albany: State University of New York Press, 1988), 89.

72. Hölderlin, "Remarks on 'Oedipus,'" in *Essays and Letters on Theory*, trans. Pfau, 101–2.

73. Heidegger, *Vom Wesen der Wahrheit: Zu Platons Höhlengleichnis und Theätet*, ed. Hermann Mörchen (1988), in *GA*, 34: 64.

74. See the recollection in the foreword to the first edition of his *Frühe Schriften* in *Frühe Schriften*, ed. Friedrich-Wilhelm von Herrmann, in *GA*, 1 (1978): 56.

75. Walter Benjamin, "Two Poems by Friedrich Hölderlin," in *Selected Writings*, ed. Marcus Bullock and Michael W. Jennings (Cambridge, Mass.: Harvard University Press, 1996), 1: 34.

76. Hölderlin, *Poems and Fragments*, trans. Michael Hamburger (London: Routledge & Kegan Paul, 1966), 407.

77. Heidegger, *Hölderlins Hymnen "Germanien" und "Der Rhein,"* in *GA*, 39: 100.

78. The coherence between Heidegger's account of the revelation of world in the experience of broken, missing, and inappropriate equipment and his definition of the world-historical mission of the Germans in the encounter with τέχνη is obscured by Hubert L. Dreyfus in his identification of world with cultural practices. What could other peoples be expected to gain from an insight into the unarticulated "know-how" of being German? That world, for Heidegger, is not cosmopolitan does not at all imply that the differentiality of world resolves into different worlds, each standing apart from the others. World is not cosmopolitan, because it can only truly be world as the Being that in its transcendence is still *higher* than the Aristotelian One and its presence. Cf. Hubert L. Dreyfus, "Heidegger on the Connection Between Nihilism, Art, Technology, and Politics," in *The Cambridge Companion to Heidegger*, ed. Charles Guignon (Cambridge: Cambridge University Press, 1993), 295: "It would make no sense for us, who are active, independent, and aggressive—constantly striving to cultivate and satisfy our desires—to relate to things the way the Japanese do; or for the Japanese (before their understanding of being was interfered with by ours) to invent and prefer Styrofoam teacups." Is

not the fact of interference proof that the Japanese understanding of being was always already open to the questionableness of its "own" unity? Heidegger explicitly discusses the questionableness of the unity of the worlds of various peoples when he elaborates Hölderlin's account of the constitutive and vertiginous interrelations between Greece and Germany. Even if, chronologically, Heidegger figures in intellectual histories between Oswald Spengler and Thomas S. Kuhn, his thinking is poorly expounded so long as its radical difference from talk of the souls of cultures and paradigms is underplayed.

79. Heidegger, *Hölderlins Hymne "Andenken,"* in *GA*, 52: 74.

80. Ibid., 75.

81. Ibid., 113.

82. Ibid., 66.

83. Kafka, "Josephine the Singer, or the Mouse Folk," trans. Willa and Edwin Muir in *The Complete Stories*, ed. Nahum N. Glatzer (New York: Schocken Books, 1972), 370.

84. Ibid., 367–68.

85. Heidegger, *Hölderlins Hymnen "Germanien" und "Der Rhein,"* in *GA*, 39: 290.

CHAPTER 4

1. Hegel, *Early Theological Writings*, trans. T. M. Knox (Gloucester: Peter Smith, 1970), 149.

2. Taking up Paul Ricoeur's questions to Heidegger at Cerisy on the Hebraic tradition, Marlène Zarader writes in *La Dette impensée: Heidegger et l'héritage hébraïque* (Paris: Seuil, 1990), 213–14: "What, therefore, seems to me objectionable in the Heideggerian text is not that the Hebraic component is passed over in silence (one could indeed admit that this silence is legitimate), but rather that it *returns* without ever being identified, that it returns in a text that does everything to render the identification impossible." Zarader, who here takes Heidegger to task for omitting to identify the return, elsewhere theorizes the impossibility of identification that is intrinsic to this return.

3. Heidegger, *Sein und Wahrheit: 1. Die Grundfrage der Philosophie 2. Vom Wesen der Wahrheit*, in *GA*, 36–37: 89.

4. Jean-François Lyotard, *Heidegger et "les juifs"* (Paris: Éditions Galilée, 1988), trans. Andreas Michel and Mark S. Roberts as *Heidegger and "the jews"* (Minneapolis: University of Minnesota Press, 1990), 29. And see Victor Farías, *Heidegger et le nazisme* (Paris: Verdier, 1987).

5. Cf. Friedrich Franz von Unruh, *Friedrich Hölderlin* (Stuttgart: Georg Truckenmüller, 1942), 6: "The longing, which—peculiarly enough—for a millennium beheld the 'Holy Land' in the exotic, finds its way home." Unruh sees solely an opposition to Judaea in Hölderlin's presentation of Germany as the Holy Land. Whether through its substitution for the Holy Land, Germany can, indeed, break with Judaea is never doubted.

6. Heidegger, *Hölderlins Hymne "Andenken,"* in *GA*, 52, 134–35.

7. Heidegger, *Grundfragen der Philosophie*, ed. Friedrich-Wilhelm von Herrmann (1984), in *GA*, 45: 5.

8. Franz Rosenzweig, *The Star of Redemption*, trans. William W. Hallo (New York: Holt, Rinehart & Winston, 1971), 300. Originally published as *Der Stern der Erlösung* (Frankfurt a/M: J. Kauffmann, 1921).

9. Alfred Rosenberg, *Der Mythus des 20. Jahrhunderts* (Munich: Hoheneichen, 1934), 426.

10. Heidegger, *Hölderlin's Hymn "The Ister,"* trans. McNeill and Davis, 79–80.

11. Ibid., 80–81.

12. Ibid., 82.

13. Ibid.

14. Heidegger, *Parmenides*, trans. Schuwer, 90.

15. Hölderlin, *Sämtliche Werke*, ed. Friedrich Beissner (Stuttgart: W. Kohlhammer, 1946–), 2, 1: 228.

16. Heidegger, *Hölderlins Hymnen "Germanien" und "Der Rhein,"* in *GA*, 39: 121.

17. Cf. David Farrell Krell, *Daimon Life: Heidegger and Life-philosophy* (Bloomington: Indiana University Press, c1992), 179: "Heidegger's nationalism . . . will escape unscathed the rigors to which Heidegger almost everywhere else subjects his heritage."

18. Heidegger, *Being and Time*, 143–44.

19. Cf. Hubert L. Dreyfus, *Being-in-the-world* (Cambridge, Mass.: MIT Press, 1991), 137. Dreyfus mistakes the nature of Heidegger's correction, believing that Heidegger merely shifts the focus from the body to the accessibility of equipment.

20. Kant, "What Is Orientation in Thinking?" in *Political Writings*, trans. H. B. Nisbet (Cambridge: Cambridge University Press, 1991), 238.

21. Hegel, *The History of Philosophy*, trans. E. S. Haldane and Frances H. Simson (London: Routledge & Kegan Paul, 1955), 3: 216.

22. Kant, *Critique of Pure Reason*, A 26 B 42.

23. Heidegger, *History of the Concept of Time*, trans. Theodore Kisiel (Bloomington: Indiana University Press, 1992), 230.

24. Kant, *Logic*, trans. Robert S. Hartman and Wolfgang Schwarz (Indianapolis: Bobbs-Merrill, 1974), 29.

25. Heidegger, *Contributions to Philosophy*, 49.

26. Kant, *Critique of Pure Reason*, B 39–40.

27. Ibid., A 174 B215.

28. For an exposition of his concept of *Lebensraum*, see Hitler's speech of February 15, 1942 in *"Es spricht der Führer": 7 exemplarische Hitler-Reden*, eds. Hildegard von Kotze and Helmut Krausnick (Gütersloh: Signert Mohn, 1966), 305–28.

29. Heidegger, *Sein und Wahrheit: 1. Die Grundfrage der Philosophie 2. Vom Wesen der Wahrheit*, in *GA*, 36–37: 210.

30. Hölderlin, "Selected Letters. No. 236. To Casimir Ulrich Böhlendorff," in *Essays and Letters on Theory*, trans. Pfau, 149–50.

31. Heidegger, *Hölderlin's Hymn "The Ister,"* trans. McNeill and Davis, 136.

32. Heidegger, *Hölderlins Hymnen "Germanien" und "Der Rhein,"* in *GA*, 39: 220.

33. Hölderlin, "The Perspective from Which We Have to Look at Antiquity," in *Essays and Letters on Theory*, trans. Pfau, 39.

34. Hölderlin, "Selected Letters. No. 240. To Casimir Ulrich Böhlendorff," in *Essays and Letters on Theory*, trans. Pfau, 152.

35. Wilhelm Michel, *Hölderlins Abendländische Wendung* (Weimar: Feuer, 1922), 7.

36. In "Das abendländische Gespräch," in *Zu Hölderlin: Griechenlandreisen*, ed. Curd Ochwadt (2000), in *GA*, 75: 79, Heidegger cautions against reading place in Hölderlin's poetry geographically.

37. Heidegger, "Hölderlin and the Essence of Poetry," in *Elucidations of Hölderlin's Poetry*, trans. Hoeller, 64.

38. Heidegger, *Hölderlins Hymnen "Germanien" und "Der Rhein,"* in *GA*, 39: 214.

39. Heidegger, *Logik als die Frage nach dem Wesen der Sprache*, in *GA*, 38: 70.

40. Ibid., 83.

41. Freud, "The 'Uncanny,' " in *The Standard Edition of the Complete Psychological Works of Sigmund Freud*, ed. James Strachey (London: Hogarth Press and Institute of Psycho-Analysis, 1953–75), 17: 220–21.

42. Ibid., 226.

43. Ibid., 245.

44. Heidegger, *Being and Time*, 233. Translation modified.

45. Ibid., 230.

46. Ibid., 234.

47. Ibid., 231.

48. Ibid., 234.

49. Ibid., 231.

50. Heidegger, "Der Ursprung des Kunstwerkes," in *Holzwege*, ed. Friedrich-Wilhelm von Herrmann (1977), in *GA*, 5: 41.

51. In his reading of the Jewish influence in Heidegger's notion of *Heimat*, John D. Caputo ignores the essential unpresentability of the Fatherland as it is experienced in anxiety and does not allow the prohibition of images and the comparable task of thinking Being's difference from beings to ground critiques of the territorialism and racism of Nazi Germany and the modern state of Israel. See Caputo, "People of God, People of Being: The Theological Presuppositions of Heidegger's Path of Thought," in *Appropriating Heidegger*, ed. James E. Faulconer and Mark A. Wrathall (Cambridge: Cambridge University Press, 2000), 99: "We need to break with the deeply hierarchical logic of original and derivative, with the myth of the originary language, the originary people, the original land, by means

of which Heidegger reproduces the myth of God's chosen people, of God's promised land, which is no less a problem for religion and the root of its violence. We
need to break with the logic that allows the myth to flourish that certain human
beings speak the language that being or God would speak, had they vocal chords
and lungs and writing instruments, the murderous twin myths of the people of
God and of the people of being, myths which license murder in the name of God
or in the name of the question of being."

52. Luce Irigaray, *The Forgetting of Air in Martin Heidegger*, trans. Mary Beth
Mader (London: Athlone Press, 1999), 166.

53. "Of the reduction to nothingness that he put in place between the other
and himself so as to return to an other that is already produced by him. That is
already ensnared in his world," Irigaray writes of Heidegger and alterity, with un-
avowed irony (ibid., 98) This is the same irony that a few years later appears in
Lyotard's thinking of "the jews" as the ". . ." of primal repression. Irigaray, unlike
Heidegger, knows the name of the Other and thereby exposes herself to the irony
of "crossing the line" without truly leaving classical ontology.

54. Heidegger, "Homecoming/To Kindred Ones," in *Elucidations of Hölderlin's Poetry*, trans. Hoeller, 42.

55. Heidegger, *Being and Time*, 234.

56. Cf. Emil Kettering, *Nähe: Das Denken Martin Heideggers* (Pfullingen:
Neske, 1987), 201: "Not-being-at-home is not simply the fortuitously given starting point that is to be left behind as quickly as possible and that for itself is without foundation. Instead, the experience of not-being-at-home is constitutive for
becoming-at-home. Only the conscious appropriation of not-being-at-home renders becoming-at-home possible." Kettering is led astray by the occasional Hegelian reminiscence in Heidegger's exposition to a valorisation of consciousness. Dasein does not become at home through becoming conscious that it is not at home.
On the contrary, it becomes (always already) at home through the consternation
of that which, as its being at home in the ontic, is named "consciousness."

57. Heidegger, "Sprache und Heimat," in *Aus der Erfahrung des Denkens*, in
GA, 13: 156–57.

58. Ibid., 155.

59. Theodor Adorno, "Parataxis," in *Notes to Literature*, trans. Shierry Weber
Nicholsen (New York: Columbia University Press, 1992), 117.

60. Ibid., 117.

61. Nietzsche, "Antwort," in *Werke: Kritische Ausgabe*, ed. Giorgio Colli and
Mazzino Montinari (Berlin: Walter de Gruyter, 1967–), 7, 3: 38.

62. Heidegger, *1. Nietzsches Metaphysik 2. Einleitung in die Philosophie: Dichten
und Denken*, ed. Petra Jaeger (1990), in *GA*, 50: 124.

63. Martin Heidegger and Erhart Kästner, *Briefwechsel*, ed. Heinrich W. Petzet (Frankfurt a/M: Insel, 1986), 59.

64. Hölderlin's assessment of the transnationality of Greek art recalls Goethe's
remarks to Eckermann on January 31, 1827, but, needless to say, omits Goethe's en-

dorsement of world literature. See Eckermann, *Conversations with Goethe*, trans. John Oxenford (London: J. M. Dent & Sons, 1930), 165–66.

65. When in her "Heidegger's Philosophy of Art," in *Heidegger: The Man and the Thinker*, ed. Thomas Sheehan (Chicago: Precedent, 1981), Sandra Lee Bartky treats the notion of "earth" in "The Origin of the Work of Art," she interprets it as the material medium: "Here that pervasive obscurity which is so prominent a feature of Heidegger's style . . . tends to disguise the vacuousness of what is expressed" (p. 264). But the vacuousness here attributed to the notion of the material medium of the work of art is the vacuousness of that which is merely imagined to be self-evident. The non-Greek who is born for art takes to the material medium whose strict formlessness is its invisibility, its concealment in that which Heidegger names "the earth." The formlessness of the material medium is the Nothing: to give form to the material medium, to found a realm of art is to work against the Nothing, to neglect the concealment of the national and to think truth as presence—in short, it is to be Greek. Heidegger's opposition of "earth" and "world" in "The Origin of the Work of Art," contrary to Bartky, has to be understood in relation to the dilemma of the exposition of the ontological difference. World, as the presencing of Being in that which is present is to be "corrected" in its slide toward presence by earth, as the absence of Being from beings, which in its turn has to be "corrected" in its simple inversion of presence.

66. Hegel, *Aesthetics*, trans. T. M. Knox (Oxford: Clarendon Press, 1975), 290–91.

67. Hölderlin, "On the Operations of the Poetic Spirit," in *Essays and Letters on Theory*, trans. Pfau, 80.

68. Hölderlin, "Remarks on 'Oedipus'," in ibid., 107.

69. Hölderlin, *Hyperion, or The Hermit in Greece*, trans. Willard R. Trask, in Hölderlin, *"Hyperion" and Selected Poems*, ed. Eric L. Santner (New York: Continuum, 1990), 67.

70. Heidegger, *Hölderlins Hymne "Andenken,"* in *GA*, 52: 141.

71. Hölderlin, *Poems and Fragments*, trans. Hamburger, 519.

72. Ibid., 449.

73. Ibid., 451.

74. Ibid., 453.

75. Ibid., 459.

76. Hegel, *Aesthetics*, 509–10.

77. Saint Augustine, *Confessions*, trans. R. S. Pine-Coffin (Harmondsworth, U.K.: Penguin Books, 1961), 243.

78. See Max Horkheimer and Theodor W. Adorno, *Dialectics of Enlightenment*, trans. John Cumming (London: Verso, 1979), 172.

79. Matt. 6: 3.

80. 1 Cor. 14: 23.

81. Heidegger, *Heraklit*, in *GA*, 55: 31.

82. Hölderlin, *Poems and Fragments*, 537.

83. Heidegger, *Hölderlins Hymnen "Germanien" und "Der Rhein,"* in *GA*, 39: 4.

84. Lev Shestov, *Athens and Jerusalem*, trans. Bernard Martin (Athens: Ohio University Press, 1966).

85. Jacques Derrida, "Violence and Metaphysics: An Essay on the Thought of Emmanuel Lévinas," in *Writing and Difference*, trans. Alan Bass (London: Routledge & Kegan Paul, 1978), 153.

86. Klopstock, "Der Hügel und der Hain," in *Klopstocks Werke*, ed. R. Hamel (Berlin: W. Spemann, n.d.), 3: 139.

CHAPTER 5

1. Heidegger, "Die Sprache im Gedicht: Eine Erörterung von Georg Trakls Gedicht," in *Unterwegs zur Sprache*, ed. Friedrich-Wilhelm von Herrmann (1985), in *GA*, 12: 45–46. In translating "*Geschlecht*," Peter D. Hertz's English translation, "Language in the Poem," in *On the Way to Language* (New York: Harper & Row, 1971) offers at each turn, with inescapable arbitrariness, only one of its senses. Hertz translates the last instance of the word *Geschlecht* in the quoted passage as "sex." Certainly "sex" is one of the senses of *Geschlecht* and among those not yet listed the predominant one, but is duality enough to identify "sex" and thus justify the translation? Heidegger's increasing linguistic purism after *Being and Time* denies him the Latinate *Sex* for denoting "sex" to the exclusion of all the other senses of *Geschlecht*. Robert Minder, in "Heidegger und Hebel oder die Sprache von Messkirch," in *"Hölderlin unter den Deutschen" und andere Aufsätze zur deutschen Literatur* (Frankfurt a/M: Suhrkamp, 1968), 86–153, discerns xenophobia in Heidegger's linguistic purism.

2. That this twoness of the *Geschlecht* is to be interpreted as the difference between the human male and female of metaphysical biology is the reductive presupposition of David Farrell Krell's essay "Schlag der Liebe, Schlag des Todes: On a Theme in Heidegger and Trakl," in *Radical Phenomenology: Essays in Honor of Martin Heidegger*, ed. John Sallis (Atlantic Highlands, N.J.: Humanities Press, 1978), 238–58. Heidegger's text leaves open the question whether twoness determines the *Geschlecht* as "sex" or submits this signification itself to another folding.

3. Heidegger, "Die Sprache im Gedicht," in *Unterwegs zur Sprache*, in *GA*, 12: 46.

4. Martin Heidegger and Elisabeth Blochmann, *Briefwechsel, 1918–1969*, ed. Joachim W. Storck (Marbach am Neckar: Deutsche Schillergesellschaft, 1989), 91.

5. Heidegger, *Nietzsches metaphysische Grundstellung im abendländischen Denken: Die ewige Wiederkehr des Gleichen*, ed. Marion Heinz (1986), in *GA*, 44: 23.

6. Heidegger, "Die Sprache im Gedicht" in *Unterwegs zur Sprache*, in *GA*, 12: 46.

7. Ibid., 41.

8. Ibid.

9. Ibid., 42.

10. Ibid.

11. See the central discussion in §§47–9 in *Being and Time.*

12. Heidegger, "Die Sprache im Gedicht," in *Unterwegs zur Sprache*, in *GA*, 12: 48–49.

13. Cf. Jean-Daniel Krebs, "Georg Trakl: Les Poèmes du non-retour," *Germanica* 1 (1987): 32–48. Krebs brings out a motif of homecoming to the grave in Trakl's poetry. But it must be asked whether death in Trakl instantiates a notion of stasis or whether pilgrimage arrives at the accelerated decomposition of death as the homeland of nonpositive humanity.

14. Heidegger, "Die Sprache im Gedicht," in *Unterwegs zur Sprache*, in *GA*, 12: 49.

15. Ibid., 70.

16. Ibid., 73.

17. Egon Vietta, in "Georg Trakl in Heideggers Sicht," *Die Pforte* 5 (1953), dismisses any reading of "the beyond" in Trakl in terms of Christian eschatology. See ibid., 355: "The beyond of this poem becomes all the more *unheimlich*, particularly since everywhere it is evident that it is the poem of a journey: a journey—to the Occident."

18. Heidegger, "Die Sprache im Gedicht," in *Unterwegs zur Sprache*, in *GA*, 12: 37.

19. Cf. Peter Schünemann, *Georg Trakl* (Munich: C. H. Beck, 1988), 53: "Behind the experience of Christ on Golgotha, frequently presented in the lyrics of Trakl's final years, there appears a primordial image in which the fear of being abandoned by God is extinguished—the deeper fear alone remains: the soul, it too, is in the end mortal."

20. Heidegger, "Die Sprache im Gedicht," in *Unterwegs zur Sprache*, in *GA*, 12: 76.

21. Heidegger, *Beiträge zur Philosophie: Vom Ereignis*, ed. Friedrich-Wilhelm von Herrmann (Frankfurt a/M: Klostermann, 1989), in *GA*, 65: 317

22. Heidegger, *The Fundamental Concepts of Metaphysics*, trans. William McNeill and Nicholas Walker (Bloomington: Indiana University Press, 1995), 205–6.

23. Ibid., 211.

24. Ibid., 186.

25. Ibid., 239.

26. Ibid., 198.

27. Ibid., 242.

28. Heidegger, *Being and Time*, 90.

29. Ibid., 88.

30. Heidegger, *What Is Called Thinking?* trans. Gray, 16.

31. Jacques Derrida, "*Geschlecht* II: Heidegger's Hand," in *Deconstruction and Philosophy*, ed. John Sallis (Chicago: University of Chicago Press, 1987), 173–74.

32. Heidegger, *Zur Auslegung von Nietzsches II. Unzeitgemässer Betrachtung*, ed. Hans-Joachim Friedrich (2003), in *GA*, 46: 243–44.

33. Heidegger, "Letter on 'Humanism,'" in *Pathmarks*, ed. McNeill, 248.

34. Cf. Heidegger, *Die Grundbegriffe der antiken Philosophie*, ed. Franz-Karl Blust (1993), in *GA*, 22: 311, where he discusses Aristotle's *De anima* and the human being's imputedly exclusive perception of time on the basis of a supposed ability to resist its instincts.

35. Heidegger, *What Is Called Thinking?* trans. Gray, 6.

36. Although Descartes refuses the definition of humanity as *animal rationale* because it is a definition proceeding by genus and specific difference, this refusal does not prevent the reification of the human in Cartesian thought. Humanity congeals in its new abstraction.

37. Heidegger, "The Way to Language," trans. David Farrell Krell, in *Basic Writings*, ed. Krell, 397.

38. Heidegger, *Fundamental Concepts of Metaphysics*, 307.

39. Ibid., 308.

40. Heidegger, *Logik als die Frage nach dem Wesen der Sprache*, in *GA*, 38: 169.

41. Cf. Heidegger's own emphatic correction of readings of *Being and Time* in *The Metaphysical Foundations of Logic*, trans. Michael Heim (Bloomington: Indiana University Press, 1984), 168: "Transcendence, being-in-the-world, is never to be equated and identified with intentionality." Transcendence is to be understood, Heidegger stresses, as the transcendence toward Being of beings.

42. Heidegger, "The Onto-Theo-Logical Constitution of Metaphysics," in *Identity and Difference*, trans. Joan Stambaugh (New York: Harper & Row, 1969), 62.

43. Heidegger, "Die Sprache," in *Unterwegs zur Sprache*, in *GA*, 12: 23.

44. Heidegger, "Die Sprache im Gedicht," in *Unterwegs zur Sprache*, in *GA*, 12: 74.

45. Ibid., 74–75.

46. Heidegger, "Language," in *Poetry, Language, Thought*, trans. Albert Hofstadter (New York: Harper & Row, 1971), 208.

47. Heidegger, "Die Sprache im Gedicht," in *Unterwegs zur Sprache*, in *GA*, 12: 33.

48. Ibid.

49. Heidegger, "Recollection in Metaphysics," in *The End of Philosophy*, trans. Joan Stambaugh (New York: Harper & Row, 1973), 77–78.

50. An early example is W. H. Rey, "Heidegger–Trakl: Einstimmiges Zwiegespräch," in *Deutsche Vierteljahrsschrift für Literaturwissenschaft und Geistesgeschichte* 34 (1956): 89–136.

51. Modesto Carone Netto, *Metáfora e montagem* (São Paulo: Perspectiva, 1974), 154–55.

52. Alfred Doppler, "Bemerkungen zur poetischen Verfahrensweise Georg

Trakls," in *Sprache und Bekenntnis*, ed. Wolfgang Frühwald and Günter Niggl (Berlin: Duncker & Humblot, 1971), 355.

53. Rudolf D. Schier, "'Afra': Towards an Interpretation of Trakl," *Germanic Review* 41 (1966): 270n.

54. Richard Detsch, "Unity and Androgyny in Trakl's Works and the Writings of Other Late Nineteenth and Early Twentieth Century Authors," in *The Dark Flutes of Fall: Critical Essays on Georg Trakl*, ed. Eric Williams (Columbia, S.C.: Camden House, 1991), 115.

55. Ursula Heckmann, *Das verfluchte Geschlecht: Motive der Philosophie Otto Weiningers im Werk Georg Trakls* (Frankfurt a/M: Peter Lang, 1992), 206.

56. Derrida, *Of Spirit*, 86.

57. Heidegger, "Die Sprache im Gedicht," in *Unterwegs zur Sprache*, in *GA*, 12, 51.

58. Ibid., 45.

59. Heidegger, letter of May 9, 1972, to Jean-Michel Palmier, translated as a frontispiece in Jean-Michel Palmier, *Situation de Georg Trakl* (Paris: Pierre Belfond, 1987), 10.

60. Heidegger, *Being and Time*, 220.

61. Cf. the definition of "communism" in terms of *Mitsein* and the consequent reassessment of the betrayal of the various communist regimes proposed in Jean-Luc Nancy, *The Inoperative Community*, ed. Peter Connor (Minneapolis: University of Minnesota Press, 1991), 1–15.

62. Jacques Derrida, "Heidegger's Ear: Philopolemology," trans. John P. Leavey Jr., in *Reading Heidegger: Commemorations*, ed. John Sallis (Bloomington: Indiana University Press, 1993), 176.

63. Heidegger, *Hölderlins Hymnen "Germanien" und "Der Rhein,"* in *GA*, 39: 227–28.

64. Heidegger, "Die Sprache im Gedicht," in *Unterwegs zur Sprache*, in *GA*, 12: 70.

65. See letter of April 24, 1912, to Erhard Buschbeck, in Georg Trakl, *Nachlass und Biographie*, ed. Wolfgang Schneditz (Salzburg: Otto Müller, 1949), 28.

Index

Cultural Memory in the Present

Martin Seel, *Aesthetics of Appearing*

Nanette Salomon, *Shifting Priorities: Gender and Genre in Seventeenth-Century Dutch Painting*

Jacob Taubes, *The Political Theology of Paul*

Jean-Luc Marion, *The Crossing of the Visible*

Eric Michaud, *The Cult of Art in Nazi Germany*

Anne Freadman, *The Machinery of Talk: Charles Peirce and the Sign Hypothesis*

Stanley Cavell, *Emerson's Transcendental Etudes*

Stuart McLean, *The Event and its Terrors: Ireland, Famine, Modernity*

Beate Rössler, ed., *Privacies: Philosophical Evaluations*

Bernard Faure, *Double Exposure: Cutting Across Buddhist and Western Discourses*

Alessia Ricciardi, *The Ends Of Mourning: Psychoanalysis, Literature, Film*

Alain Badiou, *Saint Paul: The Foundation of Universalism*

Gil Anidjar, *The Jew, the Arab: A History of the Enemy*

Jonathan Culler and Kevin Lamb, eds., *Just Being Difficult? Academic Writing in the Public Arena*

Jean-Luc Nancy, *A Finite Thinking*, edited by Simon Sparks

Theodor W. Adorno, *Can One Live after Auschwitz? A Philosophical Reader*, edited by Rolf Tiedemann

Patricia Pisters, *The Matrix of Visual Culture: Working with Deleuze in Film Theory*

Andreas Huyssen, *Present Pasts: Urban Palimpsests and the Politics of Memory*

Talal Asad, *Formations of the Secular: Christianity, Islam, Modernity*

Dorothea von Mücke, *The Rise of the Fantastic Tale*

Marc Redfield, *The Politics of Aesthetics: Nationalism, Gender, Romanticism*

Emmanuel Levinas, *On Escape*

Dan Zahavi, *Husserl's Phenomenology*

Rodolphe Gasché, *The Idea of Form: Rethinking Kant's Aesthetics*

Michael Naas, *Taking on the Tradition: Jacques Derrida and the Legacies of Deconstruction*

Herlinde Pauer-Studer, ed., *Constructions of Practical Reason: Interviews on Moral and Political Philosophy*

Jean-Luc Marion, *Being Given That: Toward a Phenomenology of Givenness*

Theodor W. Adorno and Max Horkheimer, *Dialectic of Enlightenment*

Ian Balfour, *The Rhetoric of Romantic Prophecy*

Martin Stokhof, *World and Life as One: Ethics and Ontology in Wittgenstein's Early Thought*

Gianni Vattimo, *Nietzsche: An Introduction*

Jacques Derrida, *Negotiations: Interventions and Interviews, 1971–1998*, ed. Elizabeth Rottenberg

Brett Levinson, *The Ends of Literature: The Latin American "Boom" in the Neoliberal Marketplace*

Timothy J. Reiss, *Against Autonomy: Cultural Instruments, Mutualities, and the Fictive Imagination*

Hent de Vries and Samuel Weber, eds., *Religion and Media*

Niklas Luhmann, *Theories of Distinction: Re-Describing the Descriptions of Modernity*, ed. and introd. William Rasch

Johannes Fabian, *Anthropology with an Attitude: Critical Essays*

Michel Henry, *I am the Truth: Toward a Philosophy of Christianity*

Gil Anidjar, *"Our Place in Al-Andalus": Kabbalah, Philosophy, Literature in Arab-Jewish Letters*

Hélène Cixous and Jacques Derrida, *Veils*

F. R. Ankersmit, *Historical Representation*

F. R. Ankersmit, *Political Representation*

Elissa Marder, *Dead Time: Temporal Disorders in the Wake of Modernity (Baudelaire and Flaubert)*

Reinhart Koselleck, *The Practice of Conceptual History: Timing History, Spacing Concepts*

Niklas Luhmann, *The Reality of the Mass Media*

Hubert Damisch, *A Childhood Memory by Piero della Francesca*

Niklas Luhmann, *Love as Passion: The Codification of Intimacy*

Mieke Bal, ed., *The Practice of Cultural Analysis:*
Exposing Interdisciplinary Interpretation

Jacques Derrida and Gianni Vattimo, eds., *Religion*